COOKING À LA HEART

COOKING À LA HEART

**Delicious Heart Healthy
Recipes to Reduce Risk of
Heart Disease and Stroke**

Written by:
Linda Hachfeld, M.P.H., R.D.
Betsy Eykyn, M.S.

THIRD EDITION

APPLETREE
PRESS, INC.

Mankato, Minnesota

Published by Appletree Press, Inc.
151 Good Counsel Drive   Suite 125   Mankato, Minnesota 56001
Phone: (507) 345-4848

Book Design by Harlan Bloomer, M.F.A.
Revised Design by Kimberly Cossairt
Illustrations by Barry Travis, Larry Eppard, Mike Winchester, Kate Thomssen, and Sue Davies

Acknowledgement: Copyright © 1988 by
Mankato Heart Health Program Foundation, Inc.

First Edition, first through fourth printings: 37,500 copies
Second Edition, first through eighth printings: 65,500 copies
Third Edition, first printing: 2,000 copies
Total in print: 105,000 copies

Library of Congress Cataloging-in-Publication Data

Hachfeld, Linda Jane, 1952-
    Cooking À La Heart.
    Delicious Heart Healthy Recipes to Reduce the Risk
    of Heart Disease and Stroke.

Bibliography: p. [433]-438
Includes Index.
1. Low-fat diet—Recipes   2. Low-cholesterol diet—Recipes
3. Salt-free diet—Recipes   4. Cookery, Minnesota.   5. Nutrition   6. Health.
I. Eykyn, Betsy.   II. Appletree Press, Inc.   III. Mankato Heart Health Program Foundation
IV. Title.

RM 237.H33 1992   641.53   91-7680
ISBN 10: 1-891011-09-X
ISBN 13: 978-1-8910110-9-2

🌲 Printed on paper from a well-managed forest.

Printed in the United States of America

COOKING À LA HEART is recommended by experts...

"This is a terrific book! It has everything you want from a cookbook for your patients, including nutrient analysis, fiber content and good background information."
Nadine Braunstein, R.D., Boston, Massachusetts

"This may become the 'bible' for heart healthy eating. It has lots of practical advice with a wide array of community tested recipes."
Jane Andrews, R.D., Rochester, New York

"Eating good food does make a difference to health and quality of life! This book teaches preventive nutrition—not just for heart disease. I highly recommend it!"
Kathy King, R.D., Lake Dallas, Texas

"**Cooking À La Heart** offers a practical, hands-on guide to healthy eating. Up-to-date nutrition information and a wide variety of recipes with nutrient breakdown will surely help the reader translate scientific information into day-to-day menus for the family."
Liz Weiss, M.S., R.D., Former Producer
CNN Nutrition News Atlanta, Georgia

"If you're determined to make more than a half-hearted attempt this year to be kind to your health, this should be your first resolution: Get a copy of **Cooking À La Heart**."
Eleanor Ostman, Former Food & Nutrition Editor
St. Paul Pioneer Press Dispatch St. Paul, Minnesota

"**Cooking À La Heart** is a wonderful investment for heart-healthy eating and cooking. The first chapter is terrific! It explains healthy dietary recommendations and shows how to make substitutes for rich foods without compromising flavor. This book is very complete!"
Angela Allen, Health Editor
The Columbian Newspaper Van Couver, Washington

Reviewers and Readers highly recommend COOKING À LA HEART...

"The recipes are simple and inventive, proof that eating healthily does not have to mean giving up favorite foods... the cookbook begins with a primer that is one of the best sources of nutritional information we've run across... Practical & functional at a very fair price."
Harrowsmith Magazine

"**Cooking À La Heart** presents unified dietary guidelines that are clearly explained in an eye-catching format. The recipes are carefully written with complete directions and many interesting serving ideas. The broad range of enticing recipes will appeal to a variety of clients. It is visually attractive and presents scientifically accurate material in an enthusiastic, positive manner that motivates and supports heart healthy food selection and preparation behaviors.
Journal of Nutrition Education

"Last fall I received your book, **Cooking À La Heart**, for my birthday. I fell in love with it. Not only does it have wonderful recipes, but it is also very informative. I've learned so much from your book."
Pat Sahli, Colorado Springs, Colorado

"Your book is just what I needed after my bypass surgery! It is a wonderful resource book for healthy eating."
Jenelda Moore, Valdez, Alaska

"My husband and I are both on a low-cholesterol diet and sometimes it's difficult to know just what I can substitute in my regular recipes. Your book is so very helpful."
Mrs. Darlene Richmond, Bear Lake, Michigan

ACKNOWLEDGEMENTS

We are grateful to the following for the time and the effort they have devoted to this project:

Cookbook Steering Committee:

Linda Hachfeld, M.P.H., R.D.
Principal Author and
   Cookbook Coordinator

Betsy Eykyn, M.S.
Contributing Author and
   Recipe Editor

Nadine Sugden, B.A.
Taste-testing Coordinator and
   Editor

Shirley Durfee, B.S.
Associate Editor

Marion Lutes, B.S.
Assistant Editor

Harlan Bloomer, M.F.A.
Book Design

Richard Swanson, M.S.
Mankato Heart Health
   Program Director

Joyce Nettleton, D. Sc., R.D.
Special Advisor

Special Support:

Ogden Confer, Sr.
George Peterson
Jane Confer
Dorothy Radichel
Barry Travis

Tim Desley
Herb Mocol
Jane Brody
Henry Blackburn, M.D.
Joanne DeVore, R.D.

Reviewers:

Henry Blackburn, M.D.
Rebecca Mullis, Ph.D., R.D.
Mary Winston, Ed.D., R.D.

Liz Weiss, M.S., R.D.
Kathy King, R.D.
Joyce Nettleton, D.Sc., R.D.

Heart Health Advisory Board Members:

Jerry Crest
Mayor David Dehen, D.C.
John Eustermann, M.D.
Virgil "Hap" Halligan
Vera Kvamme, R.N.
Mary Lofy
Fred Lutz, Jr.
William Manahan, M.D.
Rich Meyer
Betty Nelson
C.R. Nelson

Margaret Preska, Ph.D.
Joe Richter
Jim Schindle
Roger Schoeb
Rolf Storvick, M.D.
John Votca
Rev. Stephanie Frey
Mary Hall
Richard Helgesen, Ph.D.
Jared How
Starr Kirklin

Mike Kluck
John Linder
Delwin Ohrt, M.D.
R.J. Rehwaldt, Ph.D.
Steward Siebens
Paul Stevens
Don Stordahl
Ken Snyder
Brett Taylor, Jr.
Tommy Thompson
Rev. Jack Weston

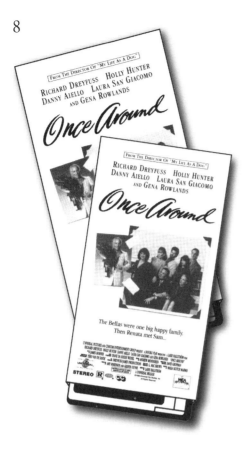

We at Appletree Press are very pleased and flattered that **Cooking À La Heart** was **the** book selected in the romantic comedy, *Once Around*, originally released in 1991. Available for rental on DVD and VHS, this funny and touching story shows the plight of how heart disease affects everyone in a family. We think you will enjoy this critically acclaimed tale of life, love and chance. And, oh, yes, watch for your favorite cookbook in its starring role!

"You have to see this picture."
　　Gene Siskel
　　Siskel & Ebert

"Funny, flavorful and touching!"
　　David Sheehan,
　　KNBC-TV

"Out of the blue comes a remarkable fresh comedy! It's thrilling to see a film so honest and humane. Don't let it slip away."
　　Lawrence Frascella,
　　US Magazine

TABLE OF CONTENTS

PREFACE

In the quarter century during which I have been writing about medicine and health, it has become increasingly clear that we live—and that we die—as we eat. Our twenty-first century habits—particularly our current penchant for high-fat, high-sugar and high-calorie foods along with inadequate physical exercise—dramatically increase our chances of developing heart disease, cancer, obesity, high blood pressure, diabetes, osteoporosis and other ailments that unnecessarily tarnish the Golden Years of so many millions of Americans.

Through reasonable modifications in how we choose, prepare and serve our foods we can go a long way towards reducing the toll of premature and preventable illness and increase our chances for a long, happy, healthy life.

Eating healthfully is neither difficult nor boring. Nor is it a life of deprivation and self denial. Rather, as diners who follow the guidelines, recipes and menu plans of **Cooking À La Heart** are destined to discover, healthful eating is a stimulating trip into new and familiar taste sensations that can help to keep you enjoying good food for many more years than you otherwise might.

Jane Brody
Personal Health Columnist
The New York Times

DEDICATION

Mankato, Minnesota, set in a wooded river valley, is a typical midwestern small city. What makes it unique are the people whose wide interests were focused in 1980 on their personal wellness by the Minnesota Heart Health Program. Mankato task forces pioneered numerous activities to develop an educational process to determine if a community could change its habits and customs to reduce the risk of cardiovascular disease.

Mankato's citizens have given a resounding "yes!" to this question.

Today, when we glance out the windows of the Program's office, located on the main intersection of town, we can see joggers and others walking briskly on the sidewalks. These same people, in the winter, enjoy walking in the nearby enclosed shopping mall or running on indoor tracks at the state university, up on the hill, or at the YMCA. Many also record their time spent in physical activity for their businesses' part in the "Shape-Up Challenge".

A restaurant in the same downtown mall is one of thirteen in town with hearts on the menu highlighting selections which meet the low-fat, low-sodium criteria of "Dining à la Heart". This program began with restaurateurs and local citizens sitting around a table brainstorming ways to help diners make healthy choices and feel good about them.

Grocery stores all over town have labels on their food shelves and in the meat and dairy cases designating foods which are low in sodium and fat and qualify for "Shopping Smart".

Down the street from the office a billboard proclaims "Check your blood pressure", offering free Blood Pressure Council measurements. Another, farther out, asks "Do you know your cholesterol level?".

Changes in school lunches went along with the "Hearty Heart" curriculum on diet and exercise; the children "Jog and Log" for 10 minutes a day in class; and they compete with their favorite recipes in the "Heart's Delight" recipe contest.

"Quit and Win" campaigns have helped to clean the air by motivating smokers to put out their cigarettes.

Early results from the study indicate that Mankatoans truly have benefitted from the variety of changes they've made and there is interest in continuing to move ahead into even healthier life-styles. In answer to the numerous requests from those who sincerely want to know how to prepare meals at home which are heart healthy, we have written this book.

We dedicate "**Cooking À La Heart**" to all those who have so enthusiastically supported the Mankato Heart Health Program.

Nadine Sugden
Contributing Editor

INTRODUCTION

A long Minnesota tradition, exploring the causes of heart attack and stroke, has resulted in the finding that there are sick (and well) populations just as there are sick (and well) individuals! This central idea led to the Mankato Heart Health Program and one of its many exciting community outcomes, **Cooking À La Heart**.

We and our colleagues overseas found people (e.g., Eastern Finland), having far more heart attacks than we, and others (e.g., the Greek islands and southern Japan) with almost none at all. We also demonstrated that the most consistent and powerful influence on the community-wide risk of heart attacks is the average blood cholesterol level. Where it is high, there are many heart attacks. Where it is low, there are virtually none. Where it goes up or down over time, so, after a few years, do the deaths from heart attack.

These findings in populations, combined with clinical and laboratory research, indicated to us some years ago that blood cholesterol level is the central factor in a community's risk of cardiovascular disease. Mass elevated cholesterol level is, in turn, most strongly influenced by the habitual eating customs of a community. Living then in a country where heart attack risk overall is relatively high, your and my individual risk depends importantly on other factors, especially our heredity, but also smoking habits and blood pressure.

Studies in Minnesota also established clearly that we can substantially modify our blood cholesterol level, that of our family and even whole communities. The cholesterol-lowering eating pattern is easy, palatable, attractive and economic. Preventive experiments indicate that heart attack risk is reduced in groups by about 2% for every 1% average cholesterol-lowering. Moreover, in Minnesota over the past 20 years more healthy eating and exercise patterns, decreasing smoking and control of high blood pressure have contributed to the recent 30% fall in coronary death rates.

But the background for **Cooking À La Heart** goes even farther back in time, to when all people on earth were either hunters or gatherers. Today we remain fundamentally adapted to that eating and lifestyle because it is only about 500 generations since agriculture and civilization began. It has been only 10 generations since the Industrial Revolution began and only a couple of generations since automation and automotion and affluence have affected most of us.

Few would choose to return to hunter-gatherer times, or even to the lifestyle of heart attack-free Mediterranean and Asian farmers. The more we understand those earlier lifestyles, the better we can adapt our ways to modern abundant eating and sedentary living.

As best we can piece it together, the hunter-gatherer lifestyle, to which our bodies adapted through the centuries, was characterized by regular physical activity to secure food and subsistence, up to 30 hours a week. This alternated with rest and socialization, in a harmonious cycle. It is likely that our major foods were plants, rich in starches, fiber, vegetable protein, minerals and vitamins. These plant foods were the staples that allowed humankind to survive and thrive throughout the ages. Hunting for more concentrated food was an early and major adaptation. Humans have sought out and eaten meat opportunistically, probably for all time. But "the opportunity" did not arrive all that often.

In addition, the diet to which we are metabolically adapted contained far more potassium than sodium, in legumes, fruits and vegetables, just the opposite of now. The heavy use of salt started only "recently" in history, with trade and the need to preserve food. Our body requirements for salt are quite low, as colleagues have found in South American Indians who work effectively near the equator with no added salt intake.

Most modern ethnic cuisines derive from the peasant dishes and traditional eating patterns of agriculturalists and pasturalists over the last 10,000 years. By trial and error, word of mouth, and example, healthy eating patterns were passed down, varied, attractive, and healthful, among Mediterranean, Middle Eastern and Asian cultures. They evolved with appropriate combinations of vegetable protein, such as beans and rice, tortillas and beans and the delightful combinations in couscous and other classic staples. This healthful eating pattern is punctuated, on occasion by small servings of meat and fowl, varying amounts of fishes and seafoods, and dominated by lots of legumes, starches, fruits and vegetables.

But all of a sudden, in a very few generations, industrial society produced the opportunity and economic capacity to eat more and fatter, sweeter and saltier foods, and new "staples" of Western countries. We have added easily accessible and concentrated calories of sucrose and alcohol. The crowning blow was the disappearance of physical activity in our occupations, along with the automobile and "enforced" sedentation of mass television. On top of that came the mass addiction to American-style cigarettes.

There is a paradox in all this. Efficient American farms and agribusiness have eliminated deficiency disease for most of our society. This, along with better sanitation and medical care, has resulted in many more of us surviving to older ages. But the down side is the arrival of the insidious, mass, middle-age diseases related to modern lifestyles, i.e., fatty artery disease, heart attack, stroke, obesity, diabetes, chronic lung disease from smoking, and the increased rates of cancer related to smoking and to fatty eating patterns.

The Minnesota Heart Health Program brings good news. Heart attack rates are coming down. People are finding that healthier lifestyles open new and attractive benefits. The food industry and agriculture are moving rapidly to offer us more healthy choices. In **Cooking À La Heart**, the innovative volunteers of the Mankato Heart Health Program have found an American way to make our eating pattern more healthy, while at the same time, attractive and convenient. In **Cooking À La Heart** you will find that something good happened in a Minnesota town, and you can apply it to your family's healthier lifestyle.

Henry Blackburn, M.D.
Principal Investigator,
Minnesota Heart Health Program

A WORD ABOUT THE
MANKATO HEART HEALTH PROGRAM

In 1980, the Minnesota Heart Health Program, a pioneering effort in heart disease prevention, was begun by the Division of Epidemiology, School of Public Health at the University of Minnesota and funded by the National Heart, Lung and Blood Institute. This research and demonstration project is based on the premise that a community, by working to change habits and customs that had led to a high rate of heart attack and stroke, can reduce its risk of cardiovascular disease and improve its quality of life.

The Mankato Heart Health Program was the first of three field sites in the Minnesota Program that focused on the whole community with emphasis on those still healthy. Over the life of the project, a Mankato-University partnership has tested educational strategies and evaluated community-wide changes in:

- eating patterns, which contribute to high blood cholesterol, high blood pressure and being overweight;

- smoking habits;

- physical activity and fitness;

- incidence and severity of heart disease.

Messages to encourage more healthy choices were started during public screening followed by mass media communication promoting programs for education of adults, youth and family and health professionals.

A Community Advisory Board was formed to insure community input, promote general awareness and give acceptance and understanding of the program.

Interest in continuing the many successful programs following termination of the research project led the Board to form the Mankato Heart Health Program Foundation, Inc., and to incorporate some of its activities into existing agencies and organizations. The nonprofit Foundation has supported the ongoing efforts in health promotion and launched new initiatives of its own, of which **Cooking À La Heart** is a major example. Its attractive format and contents were developed, tested and written by Mankato volunteers and published locally. Proceeds from book sales return to the community through health promotion programs.

Read, eat and enjoy!

1

Cooking À La Heart
DIETARY RECOMMENDATIONS

*Our health is
in our hands.*

A heart healthy lifestyle is an *all healthy* lifestyle! Not only can the recommendations found in this book help your heart stay fit, they can also help you live longer and enjoy those added years in good health. Cardiovascular disease (CVD) deaths have declined in the last 25 years, yet it remains America's No. 1 killer, affecting an estimated one in three adults[1].

Our goal in writing this chapter is to provide you with meaningful and useful information in understanding that what and how much we eat affects not only how we feel today but whether we can stay healthy for tomorrow.

In **Cooking À La Heart**, we have brought together the nutritional recommendations of the nine leading agencies which study the connections between lifestyle and health. Our guidelines and recipes are consistent with the recommendations of the following agencies:

*Principles of
heart-healthy
living from
the experts.*

- The United States Department of Health and Human Services (HHS)
- The United States Department of Agriculture (USDA)
- The American Heart Association (AHA)
- The Centers for Disease Control (CDC)
- The American Dietetic Association (ADA)
- The Heart, Lung, and Blood Institute (NHLBI)
- The Institute of Medicine (IOM)
- The Heart, Lung, and Blood Institute (NHLBI)
- The National Cholesterol Education Program (NCEP)

1. Eat a Variety of Foods.

*We need over
50 nutrients
to stay
healthy.*

Good nutrition is the result of long-term eating patterns. Nutritionists recognize that we need over 50 different nutrients to stay healthy. These include fats, proteins, carbohydrates, vitamins, minerals and water, all of which are found in foods in varying amounts. No single food or food group supplies all the essential nutrients in the amounts we need. When planning, shopping, and preparing meals for yourself and others, use the following guide for a varied and nutritious diet.

Table 1: USDA Food Guide at 2000 Calories

Food Group:	Daily Servings:	Serving Examples:
Breads, Cereals and other Grain products	6 (ounce) equivalents (include half as whole-grain products)	1/2 cup rice, pasta, cooked cereal; 1 slice bread; 1 cup of ready-to-eat breakfast cereal = 1 ounce equivalent
Fruits	2 cups	A piece of whole fruit such as an apple, orange, kiwi; 1/2 cup dried fruit; 1 cup 100% fruit juice = 1 cup fruit
Vegetables	2 1/2 cups	1 cup cooked or raw vegetable or vegetable juice; 2 cups raw leafy greens = 1 cup vegetables
Legumes, Fish, Poultry, Lean Meat, Nuts, Seeds and Eggs	5 1/2 ounce-equivalents	1/4 cup cooked dry beans, tofu; 1 tablespoon peanut butter; 1 egg; 1/2 ounce seeds or nuts = 1 ounce-equivalent
Low-fat Dairy	3 servings	1 cup low-fat milk, yogurt; 1 1/2 ounces low-fat or natural cheese; 2 ounces low-fat processed cheese = 1 serving
Oils	6 teaspoons	1 tablespoon low-fat mayonnaise, 2 tablespoons light salad dressing or 1 teaspoon of vegetable oil = 1 teaspoon equivalent
Discretionary Calorie Allowance	265 calories	Use for added sugar, jam, or small dessert

Source: US Dept of Health and Human Services and USDA. Dietary Guidelines for Americans, 2005. Home and Garden Bulletin No. 232. Washington, D.C.: U.S. Gov't Printing Office, 2005. Also available online at www.healthierus.gov/dietaryguidelines

The DASH Diet (Table 2) is a proven healthy eating plan that can reduce your risk of heart disease. DASH (which stands for Dietary Approaches to Stop Hypertension) is a heart-healthy diet that limits saturated fat, cholesterol and sodium. It requires no special foods, accommodates varied types of cuisines and special dietary needs (ie, diabetes, gluten free, anticarcinogenic).

DASH focuses on an increased intake of foods rich in nutrients (such as potassium, calcium, magnesium, soluble fiber) that can lower LDL cholesterol, prevent or lower blood pressure, and promotes weight loss. DASH relies on eating more fruits, vegetables, whole grains, legumes, and includes nuts and seeds.

Table 2: DASH Diet at 2000 Calories a Day

Food Group	Daily Servings	Serving Sizes
Grains*	6 - 8	1 slice bread, 1 oz dry cereal, 1/2 cup cooked rice, pasta or cereal
Vegetables	4 - 5	1 cup raw leafy vegetables, 1/2 cup cut-up raw or cooked vegetables 1/2 cup vegetable juice
Fruits	4 - 5	1 medium fruit, ¼ cup dried fruit 1/2 cup fresh, frozen, or canned fruit 1/2 cup fruit juice
Dairy	2 - 3	1 cup low-fat or fat-free milk or yogurt 1 1/2 oz low-fat or fat-free cheese
Lean meats, poultry, and fish	6 or less	1 oz cooked meats, poultry, or fish 1 egg
Nuts, seeds, and legumes	4 – 5 per week	1/3 cup (1 1/2 oz) nuts, 2 Tbsp nut butter 2 Tbsp or 1/2 oz seeds 1/2 cup cooked legumes (dry beans & peas)
Fats and oils	2 - 3	1 tsp soft margarine, 1 tsp vegetable oil, 1 Tbsp mayonnaise, 2 Tbsp salad dressing
Sweets and added sugar	5 or less per week	1 Tbsp sugar, 1 Tbsp jelly or jam, 1/2 cup sorbet, gelatin, 1 cup lemonade

Whole grains are recommended for most grain servings as a good source of fiber and nutrients

Source: US Dept of Health and Human Services, NIH Publication No. 06-4082, Available online at www health.gov/dietaryguidelines/dga2005/document/html/appendixA.htm, accessed September 4, 2006

2. Maintain Healthy Weight.

Excess body weight raises the risk of four major lifestyle-related diseases: heart disease, high blood pressure, diabetes and cancer. Based on the Surgeon General's report, approximately 61% of adults, 13% of children aged 6 to 11 years, and 14% of adolescents aged 12 to 19 years are overweight or obese. Obesity is associated with elevated triglycerides (blood fat) and decreased heart-protecting HDL cholesterol. High blood pressure is twice as common in adults who are obese than in those who are at a healthy weight. A weight gain of 11 to 18 pounds increases a person's risk of developing type 2 diabetes to twice that of individuals who have not gained weight. Being overweight and obesity are associated with an increased risk for some types of cancer including endometrial (cancer of the lining of the uterus), colon, gall bladder, prostate, kidney, and postmenopausal breast cancer. And, excess body fat can lead to premature death. An estimated 300,000 deaths per year may be attributable to obesity.

To determine a healthy body weight, use Table 32 on page 431 (*see APPENDIX: Body Mass Index (BMI) Calculator*). Notice that you have a "range" of healthy weights" based on your height. A ***BMI* of *19-24.9 is a healthy weight***; less than 19 is considered to be underweight; 25-29 is overweight; and a BMI greater than 30 is considered obese. The BMI Calculator is not an "end-all", it's just a tool, and it has a few shortcomings. First, it's a chart for adults only (growth curve charts are used for children) and it is important to realize that not everyone who is in the elevated risk category is truly at higher risk of heart disease.

The BMI chart reflects generalized risk for a large number of people, not for each individual. For example, a smoker or sedentary person who is at a healthy weight might have a higher risk for heart disease than someone who is overweight but physically fit. And if you are athletic or muscular, the BMI may not be your best tool to determine weight status.

Body weight is not always an accurate measure of excess body fat. Answering "yes" to any of the following questions indicates you are carrying excess body fat:

Excess body weight is hazardous to our health.

Check your Body Mass Index

Are you carrying excess body fat?

- Is your waist measurement close to or larger than your chest measurement?
- Is a fold of skin pinched from the back of your upper arm more than an inch thick?
- Does your middle interfere with the sight of your toes?
- Do you see ridges or bulges where there shouldn't be any when you are undressed?

Research shows that the site of fat accumulation influences the risk of coronary heart disease. People who carry their extra body fat around their middle—nicknamed "apples" are more likely to suffer a heart attack and have a tenfold greater risk of stroke than those whose body fat collects on their hips and thighs—called "pears".

Why is a thick waist risky?

Belly fat is visceral fat—an active fat, which continually pumps artery-clogging fatty acids into your blood stream. In addition, visceral fat releases appetite-regulating hormones and starts a chain of biochemical events that leads to insulin resistance (precursor to type 2 diabetes). While hip, thigh, and butt fat are relatively benign, belly fat ratchets up the odds for blood clots, high blood pressure, diabetes, and elevated blood lipids.

Determine if you are at risk by measuring your waist with a tape measure. To measure your waist correctly, stand and place a tape measure snugly around your middle, just above your hipbones. Measure your waist just after you breathe out. Generally, men with waists over 40 inches and women with waists over 35 inches are at higher risk of diabetes, problems with cholesterol and triglycerides, high blood pressure and heart disease.

Physical Inactivity is a major risk factor for heart disease.

Most adults spend 19 - 22 hours a day being "un-active". We're on the job behind a desk for 7-9 hours, behind the wheel of a car for 1-2 hours, eating takes 2-3 hours, watching television or on the home computer for 3 hours, and asleep for 7-8 hours a day! That's a lot of sitting. In 2002, 25 percent of adult Americans did not participate in any leisure-time physical activity and in 2003, 38 percent of students in grades 9 to 12 viewed television 3 or more hours a day.[2] According to the CDC, 60 percent of Americans are not meeting the recommended levels of physical activity.

To reduce the risk of heart disease, adults need only do about 30 minutes of moderate activity on most, and preferably all, days of the week. This level of activity can also lower your chances of

Move more

having a stroke, colon cancer, high blood pressure, and diabetes[2]. If you're also trying to manage your weight and prevent gradual, unhealthy weight gain, try to get 60 minutes of moderate to vigorous-intensity activity on most days of the week.

Those who are trying to keep weight off should aim a bit higher: 60 – 90 minutes of moderate-intensity activity daily, without taking in extra calories. Our bodies were designed for exercise. Even if you are not overweight your body needs regular physical exercise. Get in motion by incorporating different types of activity as defined in the table below.

Table 3: Types of Physical Activity

Type of Activity	What It Does	Examples of Activity
Aerobic:	Uses large muscle groups and causes your body to use more oxygen, which benefits the heart.	*Moderate:* hiking, dancing, bicycling, walking at 3.5 mph, light gardening/yard work *Vigorous:* running/jogging, swimming, aerobics, walking at 4.5 mph, heavy yard work, bicycling at more than 10 mph, basketball
Resistance or Strength Training	Firms, strengthens, and tones muscles; improves bone strength, balance, and coordination.	Pushups, lunges, bicep curls using dumbbells, stability ball leg curls
Flexibility Exercises	Stretch and lengthen muscles, improves joint flexibility, keeps muscles limber	Stretching moves while standing pushing with hands upward or against a wall; sitting on the floor doing leg stretches
OTHER MOVES **Pilates**	Strengthens body's torso strengthen and tone muscles, increase flexibility	Series of mat exercises or special exercise machines available at some health clubs
Tai chi	Gentle calming practice can help to improve flexibility and balance, gradually builds muscle strength	Ancient Chinese practice based on shifting body weight through series of slow movements that flow into one graceful gesture
Yoga	Regular yoga practice may help to minimize weight gain as we age. Improves flexibility, balance	System of physical postures, stretching and breathing techniques. Styles range from slow and gentle to athletic and muscle strength and relaxation vigorous

Source: U.S. Dept of Health and Human Services, *Your Guide to Physical Activity and Your Heart*, NIH Publication No. 06-5714; June, 2006

Benefits of regular exercise

You may not feel much differently when you first begin to exercise, but there's a good chance that in six months you will:

- Have improved your physical appearance.
- Look and feel more alert.
- Feel more energetic, agile and in control of your body.
- Be better able to cope with stress, tension, and depression.
- Have reduced your percentage of body fat. (The recommended percentage of body fat is 15-18% for men and 20-25% for women.)
- Have a better regulated appetite.
- Have stronger bones, thus, reducing the risk of osteoporosis.
- Have improved circulation.
- Have a better blood pressure reading.
- Have an improved blood chemistry.
- Have a more efficient heart capable of accomplishing the same amount of work with less effort.

These benefits can be achieved with exercise that is:

Brisk	raising heart and breathing rates
Sustained	done at least in 10 minute intervals without interruption, three or more times a day
Regular	repeated at least five times a week

Avoid Calorie Creep

The USDA estimates that Americans now consume 148 more calories per day than 20 years ago. That doesn't sound like much, but it works out to an extra 15 pounds every year! How much food should you eat in a day? Most women need approximately 1,800 calories a day for good health and men need 2,400. That usually works out to 400 to 500 calories for breakfast, 400 to 600 for lunch, 600 to 800 for dinner and two snacks of roughly 200 calories each. Use Table 33 on page 432 (*see APPENDIX: Estimated Calorie Needs*) to determine how many calories to aim for based on your age, gender and activity level.

Applying the "10-Calorie Rule"

A gradual but guaranteed way to lose excess body fat is to decrease the number of calories you now consume and increase the number of calories you burn. We recommend following the 10-Calorie Rule which allows you 10 calories a day for each *current* pound of body weight. Weight loss will be a safe 1 to 2 pounds a week, and if you stick with this formula, those extra pounds will *stay* lost.

Avoid weight cycling or the "yo-yo" effect, which results from repeated weight loss followed by weight gain. The lose-regain syndrome is most apt to occur with fad diets that promote rapid weight loss. Dieters lose weight only to gain it all back when they return to their former eating patterns. Indeed, they may even gain back more weight than they lost.

Evidence suggests that the cycle dieter loses weight primarily from lean muscle mass, while the weight re-gained is usually in the form of fat. Losing weight by reducing calories becomes increasingly difficult for repeat dieters. Our researchers found that dieters on a second cycle of dieting took twice as long to lose the same amount of weight they lost on the first cycle, and they gained it back three times as fast!

When losing weight, make a serious commitment to maintain that loss. Look carefully at your overall eating pattern to see where you can cut unwanted calories. Here are some places to start.

Calorie-Cutting Tips:

Downsize your Portions

- Calories do count. Most of us underestimate the size of our portions and calories (by at least 25 percent). Use a food and activity journal (See *HealthCheques™* self-monitoring tools on page 445) to record what you eat and drink; oftentimes, just writing it down stops mindless eating.
- Practice intuitive eating. Take your time to eat, wait 20-minutes before going back for seconds, turn off the TV during meals, and halfway through your meal, put your fork down and consider your level of hunger and fullness.

Listen to your body

- Going back for seconds? If hunger persists, have a second helping of lower calorie food. Select steamed vegetables, a green salad or fresh fruit.
- If you overindulge at one meal, cut back on what you eat the rest of the day. Don't punish yourself by repeating the performance, get back on schedule. One lapse is only that—it does not mean defeat.

Manage your calories

- Never eat directly out of the bag, box or carton. Put a single serving in a bowl or on a plate and put the package away.
- Go single-serve. Instead of buying a half-gallon of your favorite ice cream, buy a single serving at your favorite eatery.
- Use a salad plate (9-10") instead of a dinner plate (12-14"); less real estate means smaller servings. Make half your plate fruit and vegetables.
- Include low-fat and nonfat dairy products; don't eliminate this valuable food group.
- Limit alcohol consumption; alcohol undermines discretion and determination to eat wisely.
- Limit total meat consumption to no more than 6 ounces a day; select the leanest cuts and remove all visible fat (*see MEAT Section*)

Eating out tips

- When eating out, order a salad and share an entrée with a companion. Or order an appetizer as your main dish and a salad, soup or steamed vegetable as your side dish.
- At home, bake, broil, roast, grill, steam or microwave foods without adding fat. Avoid all frying; skim the fat from broths and soups.
- Season with spices and herbs in place of high-fat spreads or fat-laden sauces (*see SEASONING section*)

Go to the party

- If you're bringing food to a party, make it low-calorie. Then, you'll always have a wise choice available to you. If you're hosting an event, plan a nutritionally balanced menu. (*see CHAPTER 2-Meal Planning*)
- Watch what you drink. Currently, Americans consume 21 percent of calories from beverages alone. Water with lemon is always a refreshing thirst-quencher.

Keep track of your progress

- Don't neglect daily exercise. No matter how busy you are, make exercise a part of your daily routine.
- Recognize what you achieve...a new habit, eating more fruits and vegetables, saying "no" to empty calories. Reward yourself with music, a trip, a massage. You're a success!

3. Choose a Diet Low in Fat, Saturated Fat and Cholesterol.

A diet high in fat raises blood cholesterol levels.

A diet high in fat, especially saturated fat, trans fat and cholesterol causes elevated total and LDL cholesterol levels (*see page 33 for Desirable Blood Fat Levels*). High blood cholesterol levels are a major risk for heart attacks and stroke and can be reduced by making wise dietary choices. NCEP prevention studies show that for every *1 percent reduction in total or LDL cholesterol, you can reduce your risk of developing heart disease by approximately 2 percent*[4,5]. This doesn't sound like much, but it's significant. For example, if you reduce your LDL cholesterol level from 150 mg/dL to 110 mg/dL, (a 26% reduction) you would cut your risk of heart disease by more than half!

Healthful dietary fat targets, as a percentage of caloric intake, have been established by the American Heart Association (AHA), the National Cholesterol Education Program (NCEP), the Department of Health & Human Services (HHS), the US Dept of Agriculture (USDA) and the Institute of Medicine (IOM). Refer to Table 31 (*see APPENDIX: Daily Dietary Fat Recommendations to Reduce Risk of CVD*) for a comparison of their recommendations for total fat, saturated fat, trans fat and cholesterol.

How much fat should we eat?

Use Table 4 to find your recommended range for total fat, saturated fat, trans fat and cholesterol. Your goal is to eat within the recommended ranges.

Table 4: Recommended Daily Fat, Saturated Fat, Trans Fat & Cholesterol Intake

Total Calories	Fat 20 - 35% (grams)	Saturated Fat 7 - 10% (grams)	Trans Fat <1% (grams)	Dietary Cholesterol (milligrams)
1200	27 – 46	9 – 13	0 - 1	<300
1500	33 - 58	12 – 17	0 - 1	<300
1800	40 – 70	14 - 20	0 - 2	<300
2000	44 – 77	16 - 22	0 - 2	<300
2200	49 – 85	17 - 24	0 - 2	<300
2500	56 – 97	19 - 28	0 - 2	<300
2800	62 - 108	22 - 31	0 - 3	<300

Based on the 2005 Dietary Guidelines for Americans, the American Heart Association 2006 Diet & Lifestyle Recommendations, and the 2002 National Cholesterol Education Program Third Report.

How To Reduce The Fat In Your Diet

Ounce for ounce, fat has more than twice as many calories as carbohydrates or protein.

Awareness of the number of calories and grams of fat in foods will help you reduce the percentage of fat in your diet. Fat contains 9 calories per gram or 45 calories for every teaspoon while protein and carbohydrates contain only 4 calories per gram or 16 calories a teaspoon. In many cases, a simple substitution of a lower fat version of the same product, such as extra-lean hamburger for regular or a change in preparation method such as broiled instead of deep fried, makes a substantial reduction in the number of calories and amount of fat. Switching to low-fat dairy products reduces both the amount of total fat and saturated fat in your diet.

Looking for low fat products is now much easier with the Nutrition Facts panel on all or most packaged foods. Use this panel to compare the fat content of similar foods and to choose lower fat versions. Some foods make strong claims about the amount of fat in their products. The chart below identifies what the claims mean, if you see them on the label (see Chart on page 291 for "extra-lean" and "lean" claims on meat packages).

Use the Nutrition Facts Panel

Much of the fat we eat is "hidden" or invisible (*see Table 5: Fat Equivalents*). You must count both visible and invisible fat. Remember, the total amount of fat is important for calorie control; therefore, you have some latitude to allow for your personal taste. For example, if you prefer to drink 2% milk rather than skim you can moderate your fat intake by omitting 1 teaspoon of fat elsewhere in your day's meals. You can exchange the fat in a cup of whole milk for the sour cream on your baked potato, or the margarine on your bread.

Fat Claims on Food Labels

Fat Claim:	What it Means:
Fat-free	Less than 0.5 grams of fat per serving.
Low saturated fat	1 gram or less per serving and 15% or less of calories from saturated fat
Low-fat	3 grams or less per serving
Reduced fat	At least 25 percent less fat than the regular version
Light in fat	Half the fat compared to the regular version

Table 5: Fat Equivalents

Food Item:	Fat Equivalent:
1 cup whole milk	= 1 cup skim milk + 2 teaspoons fat
1 cup 2% milk	= 1 cup skim milk + 1 teaspoon fat
8 ounces plain low-fat yogurt	= 1 cup skim milk + 1 teaspoon fat
1.5 ounces natural cheese	= 1 cup skim milk + 3 teaspoons fat
2 ounces processed American cheese	= 1 cup skim milk + 4 teaspoons fat
1/2 cup ice cream	= 1/3 cup skim milk + 2 teaspoons fat + 3 teaspoons sugar
2 ounces beef/pork bologna	= 1 ounce lean meat + 4 teaspoons fat
2 ounces light bologna	= 1 ounce lean meat + 1 teaspoon fat
3 ounces extra-lean hamburger	= 1 ounce lean meat + 2 teaspoons fat
3 ounce regular hamburger	= 1 ounce lean meat + 4 teaspoons fat

Fats in food vary.

Fats and oils are part of a healthful diet, but the type of fat makes a difference to heart health, and the total amount of fat consumed is also important. High intake of saturated fat, *trans* fats, and cholesterol increases the risk of unhealthy blood lipid levels *(see page 33 for desirable blood lipid levels)*, which in turn, may increase the risk of coronary heart disease.

There are three major categories of fat in the diet: saturated (including trans), monounsaturated (MUFA) and polyunsaturated fat. Saturated fat (fats that are naturally solid at room temperature, such as butter and hydrogenated shortening) is considered "bad" fat because it raises LDL cholesterol and promotes atherosclerosis. Food sources of saturated fat include hydrogenated vegetable oil, animal fat, coconut oil, and cocoa butter. Just a note, the one food that contributes the most saturated fat in our diet today is cheese.

Limit your intake of saturated fats.

Read the Nutrition Facts panel on food packages to determine the amount of saturated and trans fat in a serving. The American Heart Association recommends no more than 7% of our total daily calories come from saturated fat.

Trans fats are worse for your heart than saturated fat because they raise LDL cholesterol levels *and* lower HDL cholesterol, which together increases the risk for heart disease, stroke, and high blood pressure. Some researchers also suspect that *trans* fats further threaten your heart by increasing inflammation and making cells resistant to insulin.

Trans fats
are harmful.

Trans fats are produced when liquid vegetable oil is heated and transformed into a solid form called "partially hydrogenated." Common food sources of *trans* fat are fast-foods (such as French fries, onion rings, fried chicken nuggets and fish fillets); commercially prepared foods (such as chips, crackers, cookies, doughnuts, Danish); and partially hydrogenated oils found in our kitchens as vegetable shortening and stick margarines.

To determine if a food has *trans* fat, read the ingredient label and look for "partially hydrogenated" in the list. Products with less than 0.5 gram per serving are allowed to list *trans* fat content as zero. The American Heart Association advises Americans to limit their *trans* fat intake to less than 1% of total daily calories, or about 2 grams per day.

Polyunsaturated
fats are liquid
at room
temperature.

Unsaturated fats include polyunsaturated and monounsaturated fats. Polyunsaturated fats, provided by plants and seafood are liquid at room temperature. Corn, safflower, sunflower and soybean oils are examples of polyunsaturated fats. Monounsaturated fats are also liquid at room temperature.

Olive and canola oil, avocados, nuts and fish are rich in monounsaturated fats. Studies indicate that monounsaturated fats when used in place of saturated, *trans*, and polyunsaturated fats, lower LDL cholesterol, slightly increase HDL cholesterol and reduce triglycerides. But, watch your portions—all fats are calorie-dense, so a little goes a long way. To meet the total fat recommendation of 20–35 percent of calories, most dietary fats should come from sources of omega 3-rich polyunsaturated and monounsaturated fatty acids.

Choose
monounsaturated
fats.

Fats vary in degree of saturation because of their differing fatty-acid composition. No fat is 100 percent saturated or unsaturated. The relative fat composition of margarines and other fats are expressed as a P:S ratio. This ratio compares the amount of polyunsaturated fat (P) to the amount of saturated fat (S). Unfortunately, the P:S ratio understates the relative amount of total unsaturated fats. Monounsaturated fats were not included and their beneficial effects on blood cholesterol levels overlooked. Table 6 gives a corrected ratio of poly and monounsaturated fats to saturated fats. Choose a fat with a high unsaturated to saturated ratio whenever possible.

Table 6: Unsaturated : Saturated Ratio of Selected Fats

| | TYPE OF FAT | | | UNSATURATED:SATURATED |
	Polyunsaturated	Monounsaturated	Saturated	Ratio
Canola	32	62	6	15.7:1
Safflower	75	12	9	9.6:1
Sunflower	66	20	10	8.6:1
Corn	59	24	13	6.4:1
Soybean	59	23	14	5.9:1
Olive	9	72	14	5.8:1
Liquid Margarine	45	35	16	5:1
Peanut	32	46	17	4.6:1
Sesame Seed	40	40	18	4.4:1
Mayonnaise	60	20	20	4:1
Partially Hydrogenated Margarine	19	58	23	3:1
Hydrogenated Shortening	25	50	25	3:1
Cottonseed	52	18	26	2.7:1
Chicken Fat	26	45	29	2.5:1
Lard	8	50	42	1.4:1
Beef Fat	4	48	48	1:1
Butter	trace	40	60	0.7:1
Palm Kernel	2	10	80	0.2:1
Coconut	2	6	87	0.1:1

Source: US Dept. of Agriculture, Agriculture Research Service, 2006. USDA Nutrient Database for Standard Reference, Release 20 (2007). Available online at www.nal.usda.gov/fnic/foodcomp.
Note: Other substances, such as water and vitamins, make up the total composition (100%).

A Word About Omega-3 Fatty Acids

Fish provides a protective benefit against heart disease.

Omega-3 fatty acids benefit the hearts of healthy people, and those at high risk of, or already have cardiovascular disease. Several epidemiologic and clinical trials have shown that Omega-3 fatty acids reduce cardiovascular incidence. People at risk for coronary heart disease can benefit from consuming Omega-3 fatty acids from both plants and marine (fish) sources.

Alpha-linolenic acid (ALA) is an essential Omega-3 fat. The word "essential" means that we must eat ALA in our diets because our bodies cannot make it, just like Vitamin C and calcium. Foods rich in ALA include flax (flax oil), canola oil, English walnuts, walnut oil, soybean oil and wheat germ. The Institutes of Medicine, which establishes nutrient requirements, says that people should get 1.1 to 1.6 grams a day of ALA. That's about what the typical American adult currently consumes. This amount can be found in a tablespoon of canola oil, a tablespoon and a half of soybean oil, or 6 walnut halves.

Omega-3 fatty acids are healthy fats.

Two well-studied Omega-3 fats are eicosapentaenoic acid (EPA) and docosahexaenoic acid (DHA), which are found mainly in cold-water fatty fish like salmon, tuna, herring, brook trout, mackerel and sardines. White fish like haddock, cod, flounder, sole and orange roughy, along with fried fish fillets made from white fish have very small amounts of EPA and DHA. It was the Greenland Eskimos who first revealed the benefit of eating fish to decrease heart disease. In a recent study, people who ate enough fish to get 5.5 grams of Omega-3 fatty acids in a month—just one 3-ounce serving of salmon weekly—had only half the risk of sudden cardiac arrest as people who ate no Omega-3s.

Omega-3 fats keep the body's cell membranes flexible and elastic to help cells work properly, block the actions of some compounds that cause inflammation, raise HDL cholesterol levels, lower triglycerides levels, and guard against dangerous heart arrhythmias.

Dietary Recommendations for Omega-3 Fatty Acids

Eat fish twice a week.

The ideal amount needed isn't clear. The American Heart Association recommends that healthy adults eat fish (particularly fatty fish) at least two times a week and include oils and foods rich in ALA. For those adults with coronary heart disease, it

Omega-3 fatty acids from food is preferable.

is recommended that they consume about 1 gram of EPA and DHA a day, preferably from fatty fish. For those adults who need to lower their triglycerides *(see Desirable Lipid Levels on page 33)*, the American Heart Association recommends 2 to 4 grams of EPA and DHA per day provided as capsules under a physician's care. But, the American Heart Association makes it very clear—increasing Omega-3 fatty acid intake through foods is preferable; please refer to Table 7 for the Omega-3 fatty acid content of various fish and to Table 23 *(see FISH & SEAFOOD section)* for the Omega-3, mercury content and environmental impact of eating commonly purchased fish.

Table 7: Total Fat, Omega-3 Fatty Acid and Calorie Content of Fish

(As found in 3.5 ounces raw fillet)

Fish:	Fat Content: *(g)*	Omega-3 fatty acids: *(mg)*	Calories:
Atlantic Mackerel	13.9	2600 mg	175
Albacore Tuna	7.2	2100 mg	170
Sockeye Salmon	8.6	2300 mg	160
Pacific Herring	13.9	1800 mg	160
Sardines	6.8	1200 mg	135
Rainbow Trout	3.4	1100 mg	130
Smelt	2.6	800 mg	100
Brook Trout	2.7	600 mg	110
Pollock	1.0	500 mg	80
Tuna, unspecified	2.7	500 mg	110
Atlantic Cod	<1.0	300 mg	75
Ocean Perch	2.8	200 mg	105
Northern Pike	<1.0	100 mg	85
Crustaceans:			
Crab, Alaska King	<1.0	300 mg	86
Shrimp, unspecified	1.1	300 mg	91
Lobster, Northern	<1.0	200 mg	113
Mollusks:			
Oysters, Pacific	2.3	600 mg	90
Scallops, Atlantic	<1.0	200 mg	80
Clams, hardshell	<1.0	trace	80

Source: US Dept. of Agriculture, Agriculture Research Service, 2006. USDA Nutrient Database for Standard Reference, Release 20 (2007). Available online at www.nal.usda.gov/fnic/foodcomp.

Blood Cholesterol

Important heart-health numbers to know.

It is important to distinguish between cholesterol in the blood and cholesterol in food. The chart below gives the desirable levels of blood lipids & blood pressure for healthy adults (general population), adults with diabetes, and adults with coronary heart disease as determined by the National Cholesterol Education Program.

Table 8: Desirable Blood Fats & Blood Pressure Levels

Blood Lipids & Blood Pressure	General Population	Diabetes	Coronary Heart Disease
Cholesterol	<200 mg/dL	<200 mg/dL	<180 mg/dL
LDL (bad)	<100 mg/dL	<100 mg/dL	<70-100 mg/dL
HDL (good)	>40 mg/dL (men) >50 mg/dL (women)	>45 mg/dL (men) >55 mg/dL (women)	>55 mg/dL
Triglycerides	<150 mg/dL	<150 mg/dL	<150 mg/dL
Blood Pressure	<120/80 mmHg	<130/80 mmHg	<120/80 mmHg

Source: National Heart, Lung & Blood Institute. *Your Guide to a Healthy Heart*; NIH Publication #06-5269; December 2005.

It's important to reduce total blood cholesterol.

The amount of cholesterol circulating in our blood is a major factor determining our vulnerability to heart disease. Since cholesterol is not soluble in water, it cannot travel through blood unaided. Instead, it is carried in envelopes known as lipoproteins.

High Density Lipoproteins (HDL) act as "vacuum cleaners" by removing LDL cholesterol from the artery walls and taking it to the liver for excretion. It is known as the "good" cholesterol and the higher the HDL value, the better for your health. HDLs are so potent that every one-point increase in HDL levels reduces heart attack risk by 3 to 4 percent. A low HDL value is now considered a stand-alone risk factor for heart disease, especially for women.

It's even more important to lower your LDL cholesterol.

Low Density Lipoproteins (LDL) and Very Low Density Lipoproteins (VLDL) are the main carriers of cholesterol. They form the foundation for heart-threatening plaques by embedding cholesterol in artery walls, which in turn, narrow coronary arteries. Artery-clogging LDL cholesterol is referred to as "bad" cholesterol. The lower the LDL value, the better for your health. For every one-point drop in LDL levels, heart risk falls by 2 percent.

To decrease triglycerides

Triglycerides aren't a form of cholesterol. They are bits of fat in the bloodstream that are made from excess calories eaten from any source—carbohydrates, fat or protein. Recent studies suggest that triglycerides alone can predict heart attack risk, since they encourage atherosclerosis, especially in women.

To decrease Triglycerides:

- stop smoking
- reduce all alcohol consumption
- reduce excess body weight
- replace saturated fats with monounsaturated fats
- increase omega-3 fats; eat fatty fish
- eat fewer refined carbohydrates, more whole grains

To enhance HDL cholesterol

To increase HDL cholesterol:

- Move! 30-60 minutes physical activity most everyday
- reduce excess body weight
- stop smoking
- avoid trans fat, increase omega-3 fats

To decrease LDL cholesterol

To decrease LDL cholesterol:

- eat less saturated and *trans* fat
- replace with monounsaturated fats
- reduce excess body weight
- eat foods high in fiber, especially soluble fiber
- increase physical activity level

Dietary cholesterol occurs *only* in foods of animal origin. Organ meats, egg yolk, lobster, and shrimp are high in cholesterol. High-fat dairy products, red meats, poultry and fish also contain cholesterol. Vegetables, fruits, grains and all vegetable oils are cholesterol-free. Table 9 gives the cholesterol content of selected foods. Please refer to Table 24 (*see POULTRY section*) and Table 25 (*see MEAT section*) for cholesterol content of various poultry and several red meat cuts.

Total daily intake of dietary cholesterol should not exceed 300 milligrams.

Table 9: Cholesterol Content of Selected Foods

(3-ounce portions)

Food Item:	Cholesterol: *(mg)*
Beef Liver	330
Egg, 1 large	213
Shrimp, mixed species	130
Beef, avg of all cuts, lean	73
Pork chop, center cut, lean	70
Lobster, northern	65
Chicken, white meat, no skin	65
Butter, 1 tablespoon	30
Milk, 1%; 1 cup	15

Source: The Food Processor SQL Nutrition Analysis Program, Version 9.9 (ESHA Research); Salem, OR.

4. Choose a Diet With Plenty of Vegetables, Fruits and Unrefined Whole Grains.

Aim for a daily fiber intake of 25 – 35 grams. By increasing fiber in our diet we can reduce the risk of chronic diseases, including stroke, high blood pressure, type 2 diabetes and cancers in certain sites (mouth, pharynx, larynx, lung, esophagus, stomach and colon-rectum). In one study, women who consumed the most servings of whole grains had more than a 30 percent decrease in risk of death from heart disease than the women who ate less than one serving per day.

Increasing fiber intake can help reduce risk of heart disease.

The benefit of whole grains applies to men, too. In the Physician's Health Study, researchers concluded that higher whole-grain cereal consumption compared to refined grains was found to significantly reduce the risk of dying from heart disease and from all other causes. The men lived longer and were healthier when they included whole grains.

According to the USDA, most of us barely get one whole-grain serving per day, and only 7 percent of Americans eat three a day. Be sure half of your grain servings in a day are whole grain.

When we talk about fiber, we are referring to the part of whole grains, vegetables, legumes, fruits and nuts that resists digestion in the gastrointestinal tract. Because fiber is not digested and absorbed, it is excreted from the body. Fiber helps move food

Be a label detective; first ingredient, "whole wheat" or "whole grain."

through the intestines and out of the body, thus reducing the time that potentially damaging substances are in contact with intestinal surfaces. Fiber also delays stomach emptying which helps you retain a feeling of fullness longer. Fiber binds with bile acids, forcing excess cholesterol to convert to bile acids and eliminates them from the body. Different types of fiber act differently in our bodies. Fiber is categorized as either water "insoluble" or "water soluble." Wheat and corn bran, fruits, vegetables and nuts are high in insoluble fiber. They promote bowel regularity and may help reduce the risk of colon cancer.

Soluble fiber is important because it reduces total and LDL cholesterol levels. Oat and barley products, fruits such as apples, pears and oranges, and beans and legumes contain soluble fiber. Studies performed at Northwestern University Medical School indicate that an increase in soluble fiber from oat products lowered serum cholesterol by 15 to 20 percent and LDL cholesterol from 12 to 24 percent. See Table 10 for more information about the role of insoluble and soluble fibers.

Table 10: Fiber at a Glance

Types of Fiber:	Major Food Sources:	Mechanisms of Action:	Effects on Health:
Insoluble Fibers	Wheat bran Cereals Vegetables Nuts Popcorn Brown Rice	Increases Bulk: • Speeds stool through bowel (laxative effect). • Exerts less pressure on bowel walls.	Possibly Prevents: • Appendicitis • Constipation • Diverticulosis (itis) • Varicose Veins
		• Makes it less likely for cancer-causing toxins to come into prolonged contact with bowel or be absorbed.	• Possibly reduces risk of colon cancer. • Improves nutrition.
		• High intake interferes with absorption of minerals.	• Potential for mineral depletion, particularly in the elderly and very young.
Soluble Fibers	Barley Legumes Oats Fruit (apples, citrus, bananas, berries, pears, peaches, nectarines, plums) Vegetables (broccoli, brussel sprouts, carrots) Soy	• Delays stomach emptying, which slows release of sugar into the bloodstream.	• Aids weight loss (feel full longer). • Stabilizes blood sugar in diabetics.
		• Gummy substances bind with bile acids, forcing excess cholesterol to convert to bile acids.	• Lowers high blood cholesterol. • Lowers LDL cholesterol
		• Improves absorption of minerals (except calcium).	• Improves nutrition.

Caution!
Increase fiber
gradually.

While the heart experts recommend a daily consumption of 25-35 grams of mixed dietary fiber, most of us average only about 11 grams a day. Along with this recommendation comes the advice that increasing dietary fiber intake should be done gradually. Digestive discomfort (bloating and gas) may occur when fiber intake is increased too suddenly. Give yourself six to eight weeks to methodically increase your fiber intake to allow the body time to adjust. Drink at least a quart of fluids daily to avoid constipation.

Cereal brans are the most concentrated sources of dietary fiber. Whole-grain cereals and breads, fruits, vegetables and legumes are other good sources. Meat, milk and oil products do not contain fiber.

Increase your intake by including fiber from all sources. Foods that are good sources of fiber are typically low in fat, cholesterol and calories. Table 11 gives the dietary fiber content in average serving sizes of selected foods.

Table 11: Fiber Content of Foods

Food Item:	Serving Size:	Dietary Fiber: *(grams)*
Bread & Cereals:		
Whole Wheat Bread	1 slice	2 g
White Bread	1 slice	0 g
Bran Muffin	1 2-ounce muffin	3 g
Bagel, Cinnamon Raisin	1 2-ounce bagel	1 g
Raisin Bread	1 slice	1 g
All-Bran® Cereal, original	1/2 cup	10 g
Cheerios-type Cereal	1 cup	3 g
Kashi®, GoLean®	3/4 cup	10 g
Grape Nuts® Cereal, original	1/2 cup	5 g
Raisin Bran-type Cereal	1 cup	8 g
Shredded Wheat Cereal, original	2 biscuits	6 g
Oatmeal-regular, quick, cooked	1 cup	4 g
Rice Krispies® Cereal	1 1/4 cups	0 g
Legumes:		
Kidney Beans, cooked	1/2 cup	7 g
Navy Beans, cooked	1/2 cup	6 g
Lentils, cooked	1/2 cup	8 g
Baked Beans, w/pork, can	1/2 cup	7 g

continued on next page

Table 11: Fiber Content of Foods, (continued)

Food Item:	Serving Size:	Dietary Fiber: *(grams)*
Pasta & Rice:		
Macaroni, cooked	1 cup	2 g
Rice, brown	1/2 cup	2 g
Rice, white	1/2 cup	1 g
Spaghetti, whole wheat	1 cup	4 g
Spaghetti, regular	1 cup	2 g
Nuts:		
Almonds	23 nuts	3 g
Peanuts, dry roasted	39 nuts	2 g
Filberts/Hazelnuts	20 nuts	3 g
Fruits:		
Apple (with peel)	1 medium	4 g
Apple (w/o peel)	1 medium	1 g
Banana	1 medium	3 g
Cantaloupe	1 cup	1 g
Grapefruit	1/2 medium	1 g
Orange	1 medium	3 g
Pear (with peel)	1 medium	4 g
Pear (w/o peel)	1 medium	2 g
Prunes (dried plums)	3 medium	2 g
Raspberries	1 cup	8 g
Strawberries	1 cup	4 g
Juices:		
Apple	1 cup	0 g
Grape	1 cup	0 g
Orange	1 cup	0 g
Vegetables:		
Broccoli, cooked	1/2 cup	2 g
Brussel Sprouts	1/2 cup	2 g
Corn, plain, cooked	1/2 cup	2 g
Peas, cooked	1/2 cup	4 g
Potato (with skin)	1 medium	3 g
Potato (w/o skin)	1 medium	2 g

Source: Stephenson, J. and Bader, D., *HealthCheques™: Carbohydrate, Fat & Calorie Guide,* Mankato, Minn: Appletree Press, 2009

5. Use Sugars Only in Moderation.

Sugar provides no nutritional benefit to our diet.

Besides the obvious adverse effect on weight, tooth decay is another major problem related to eating too much sugar. Tooth decay is more than a matter of how much sugar you eat; both the form of and the frequency with which you eat it are significant. Sticky or chewy sugary foods stay on the teeth longer and cause more problems than other sweets. Sugary foods eaten between meals are more likely to cause tooth decay than those eaten at mealtime.

The average person consumes 128 pounds of sugar a year or 3/4 cup a day! Sugar provides only simple carbohydrates which do not have the nutritional benefits of complex carbohydrates and fiber and provides nutritionally-empty calories. A diet high in sugar also tends to be a diet high in fat (pastries, frozen desserts, candies, cookies, and cakes). Strive to reduce your daily sugar intake by at least half.

Contrary to popular belief, honey does not provide useful amounts of vitamins or minerals.

Since sugar is our most popular food additive, most everything on the grocery shelf contains sugar. You may not recognize sugar even if you read ingredient labels because sugar is known by several different names. Look for: maltose, dextrose, sucrose, fructose, lactose, invert sugar, brown sugar, turbinado, raw sugar, confectioners sugar, honey, corn sweeteners, corn syrup, and molasses. Molasses is the only sugar that has *some* redeeming nutritional value. The darker the molasses, the higher the amount of calcium, iron, potassium and B vitamins content. Blackstrap molasses contains the highest amount of vitamins and minerals.

The table below identifies the amount of sugar in some of the foods we eat.

Table 12: Sugar Equivalents

Food Item:	Fat Equivalent:
1 teaspoon jam or jelly	= 1 teaspoon sugar, syrup or molasses
1 ounce chocolate candy bar	= 2 teaspoons fat + 5 teaspoons sugar
1/2 cup frozen sweetened fruit	= 1/2 cup unsweetened fruit + 6 teaspoons sugar
1/2 cup fruit, canned in heavy syrup	= 1/2 cup unsweetened fruit + 4 teaspoons sugar
1/2 cup fruit, canned in light syrup	= 1/2 cup unsweetened fruit + 2 teaspoons sugar
8 ounces low-fat vanilla yogurt	= 8 ounces low-fat milk + 4 teaspoons sugar
8 ounces low-fat fruit yogurt	= 8 ounces low-fat milk + 7 teaspoons sugar
1/2 cup ice cream	= 1/2 cup skim milk + 2 teaspoons fat + 3 teaspoons sugar

continued on next page

Table 12: Sugar Equivalents, (continued)

Food Item:	Fat Equivalent:
1/2 cup ice milk	= 1/2 cup skim milk + 1 teaspoon fat + 3 teaspoons sugar
1/2 cup lowfat frozen yogurt	= 1/3 cup skim milk + 4 teaspoons sugar
2 oatmeal cookies	= 1 slice bread + 1 teaspoon fat + 1 teaspoon sugar
1/6 of a 9-inch apple pie	= 2 slices bread + 1/3 med apple + 3 teaspoons fat + 6 teaspoons sugar

Source: The Food Processor SQL Nutrition Analysis Program, Version 9.9 (ESHA Research); Salem, OR.

Artificial Sweeteners

Use artificial sweeteners sparingly.

Artificial sweeteners are a calorie-free alternative to sugar. FDA has approved acesulfame K (Sunnett), aspartame (NutraSweet, Equal), neotame, saccharin (Sweet 'N Low) and sucralose (Splenda). All are intensely sweet and are generally 160-220 times sweeter than sugar. Although some contain calories, you need so very little, that the calories are negligible. Controversy surrounds their use because of proven safety. Animal studies abound, but studies are lacking in long-term use in humans.

In **Cooking À La Heart**, we've used them sparingly. The 2005 Dietary Guidelines state clearly our need to reduce refined carbohydrate intake. Artificial sweeteners impart a desired sweet taste without the "empty" calories. We believe it's an individual decision to use them or not. Surely, people with diabetes and those seeking to reduce their excess body weight find their life more pleasurable by having a wider food selection available because of artificial sweeteners.

Artificial (non-caloric) sweeteners are popular because people are trying to avoid calories. Interestingly enough, no study has ever shown that the use of artificial sweeteners helps people lose weight and keep it off.

Use no more than 1/4 cup of sweetener to one cup of flour.

Instead of using artificial sweeteners, we encourage simply reducing the amount of sugar in traditional recipes. The sugar in many recipes can be reduced by 1/3 to 1/2 without affecting the taste or texture of the product. A helpful guideline for baked goods is to use no more than 1/4 cup of sweetener (sugar, honey, molasses, etc.) to one cup of flour.

Curb your sweet tooth.

We suggest the following tips to curb your sweet tooth:

- Don't keep soft drinks, candy, cookies and cakes on hand. Instead, have a plentiful supply of teas, decaffeinated coffees, fresh fruits, vegetables and popcorn.
- Serve a variety of fruits for desserts *(see FRUIT DESSERT section)*. Fresh fruits and fruits frozen without sugar are available year 'round in all parts of the country.
- To add flavor without adding calories, use sweet spices such as cinnamon, nutmeg, allspice, and ginger. Vanilla, almond and chocolate extracts also add a touch of sweetness.

Tips to reduce sugar intake.

- Use juices such as orange juice or apple juice concentrate in place of sugar. Making your own sweets allows you to reduce the amount of sugar, fat and sodium. In most recipes the quality of your product will not be affected if you reduce the sugar to one-half the original amounts.
- Don't buy either diet or regular soft drinks. Both perpetuate our desire to have sweet foods and beverages. Try drinking water with ice or lemon, or the many bottled waters flavored without added sweeteners or sugar.
- Buy fresh fruit or fruit packed in water or natural juices.

Avoid rewarding children with food, especially sweets. Use your ingenuity to devise enjoyable alternatives which could include extra time or special attention from you.

6. Use Salt and Sodium Only in Moderation.

One out of every three persons has high blood pressure.

About one in three people has elevated blood pressure (hypertension). Because hypertension often produces no symptoms, blood pressure should be checked regularly. High blood pressure greatly increases the risk of heart attack, stroke and kidney disease.

You are more likely to develop high blood pressure if you have:

- a family history of the disease
- excess body weight
- high alcohol consumption
- an inactive lifestyle
- a high fat diet
- high sodium intake

Studies show weight loss reduces high blood pressure.

Many studies show positive results when people with high blood pressure reduce their body weight, increase their physical activity, reduce alcohol consumption and restrict their sodium intake. Approximately one-third of people with high blood pressure are sodium-sensitive and would benefit from a reduction in sodium intake. Unfortunately, it's very hard to tell if a person is truly sodium-sensitive; so, as a general rule, sodium restriction is recommended for *all* people with high blood pressure. Some research suggests that increases in dietary calcium and potassium may also help to lower high blood pressure. Studies of various populations show that those with low-fat and low-sodium diets seldom develop high blood pressure. Your food choices can make a difference!

The difference between salt and sodium.

Sodium and salt are often confused. Salt contains 40 percent sodium and 60 percent chloride. Sodium occurs naturally in foods in small amounts. Most is added to foods in processing, mainly as salt. An estimated 75 percent of our sodium intake comes from processed foods such as packaged dinners, cheese, canned soups and vegetables, packaged and prepared desserts, processed and cured meats and fast foods. Natural salt content of foods accounts for 10 percent of total intake while our discretionary salt use provides another 10-15 percent. We currently eat anywhere from 2,300-10,000 milligrams of sodium a day.

The National Research Council of the National Academy of Sciences suggests that a "safe and adequate" range of daily sodium intake is between 1100-3300 milligrams. This is equivalent to the amount of sodium in 1 to 1 1/2 teaspoons of salt.

Sodium is needed to regulate water balance and maintain proper fluid volume in and around our body's cells. Sodium acts like a sponge to hold water. When too much sodium is present, excess water may be retained and this can lead to high blood pressure.

Look for sodium on the label.

It is essential to read the Nutrition Facts Panel on a food product when regulating your sodium intake. Two out of every three teaspoons of salt in the average diet comes from packaged food. Once there, it cannot be removed.

The Food and Drug Administration (FDA) have established guidelines for foods that make claims about sodium. Food labels can help you choose items lower in sodium.

Sodium Claims on Food Labels

Sodium Claim:	What it Means:
Sodium free or Salt free	Less than 5 mg of sodium per serving.
Very Low sodium	35 mg or less of sodium per serving
Low sodium	140 mg or less of sodium per serving
Low-sodium meal	140 mg or less of sodium per 3 1/2 oz (100 g)
Reduced or Less sodium	At least 25 percent less sodium than the regular version
Light in sodium	50 percent less sodium than the regular version
Unsalted or No Salt Added or without added salt	No salt is added to the product during processing (*this is not a sodium-free food*)

If you use processed foods, look for the products that have reduced salt or no salt added to them. Several food manufacturers are responding to consumer demand for less sodium and have made entire product lines available to meet this demand. There are many sodium-reduced canned vegetables, tomato products, canned fish, crackers, breads, soups and cereals.

We suggest the following tips to reduce sodium in your diet:

Tips to reduce sodium

- Give yourself time to adjust to less salt. Salt is an acquired taste that often takes several weeks to modify.

- Use salt-free seasonings for cooking. *See the SEASONINGS Section* for herb blends that will enhance the flavor of foods without adding salt and fat. Remember, flavored salts such as onion salt or celery salt are still salt and contain 2000 milligrams of sodium in each teaspoon.

- Replace high-sodium ingredients in recipes with low-sodium products. For example, substitute low-sodium soy sauce for regular and low-sodium tomato products for high-sodium sauces, juices or canned tomato solids.

- Buy and use cookbooks that are geared to a healthier lifestyle. There are several good low-fat and low-sodium cookbooks available today which replace the "standards" which call for much more fat, salt and sugar than is necessary or desirable.

• Buy unsalted snacks. There is a variety, including nuts, crackers, pretzels and corn chips available without added salt. Freshly popped popcorn, too, is a good snack if prepared and served without adding fat or salt. Our Appetizer Section has several tasty low-sodium recipes.

• When dining out, order your food unsalted and dressings on the side. This will allow you to control the amounts of both salt and fat.

The following chart and tables will help you identify sodium amounts and sources.

Salt To Sodium Conversions

1/8 teaspoon salt = 300 milligrams sodium
1/4 teaspoon salt = 600 milligrams sodium
1/2 teaspoon salt = 1,150 milligrams sodium
3/4 teaspoon salt = 1,700 milligrams sodium
1 teaspoon salt = 2,300 milligrams sodium

Table 13: Sodium-Containing Ingredients and Their Uses in Foods:

Baking soda	leavening agent and alkalizer
Baking powder	leavening agent
Brine	preservative
Disodium phosphate	emulsifier, stabilizer, buffer, used in quick cooking cereals and processed cheese
Monosodium glutamate (MSG)	flavor enhancer
Sodium acetate	pH control
Sodium aluminum sulfate	leavening
Sodium benzoate	preservative (used in condiments)
Sodium calcium alginate	thickener and smooth texture
Sodium caseinate	thickener and binder
Sodium citrate	pH control and buffer, used to control acidity in fruit drinks and soft drinks
Sodium diacetate	preservative
Sodium erythrobate	preservative
Sodium hydroxide	pH control, buffer
Sodium nitrite	preservative
Sodium nitrate	preservative
Sodium proprionate	preservative, mold inhibitor
Sodium phosphate	emulsifier, stabilizer, buffer
Sodium saccharin	artificial sweetener
Sodium sorbate	preservative
Sodium stearyl fumarate	bleaching agent, dough conditioner, maturing agent
Sodium sulfite	preservative for dried fruits, bleaching agent for some fresh fruits

Table 14: Sodium Content of Selected Foods

Food Item:	Serving Size:	Sodium *(mg)*
Fruits & Vegetables:		
Fresh Green Beans	1/2 cup cooked	5 mg
Canned Green Beans	1/2 cup cooked	250 mg
Canned Baked Beans	1/2 cup	340 mg
Any Fresh or Canned Fruit	1 piece	0-5 mg
Canned V-8® Juice Cocktail	1 cup	620 mg
Low-Sodium V-8® Vegetable Juice	1 cup	140 mg
Prepared Main Courses:		
Swanson® Turkey Dinner	1 meal	1,630 mg
Healthy Choice® Frozen Cheese Pizza	6 ounces	600 mg
LaChoy® canned chop suey, beef	1 cup	924 mg
Kraft® macaroni & cheese (prepared from mix)	1 cup	610 mg
Hunt's® Manwich Sloppy Joe Sauce as prepared served on hamburger roll	6.6 ounces	1,008 mg
Campbell's® New England Clam Chowder	1 cup	1,002 mg
Starkist® Tuna in spring water	1/4 cup	250 mg
Bread & Cereals:		
Pepperidge Farm® Whole Wheat Bread	1 slice	149 mg
Cheerios®, original	1 cup	280 mg
Kashi® Heart to Heart™	3/4 cup	90 mg
Shredded Wheat	2 biscuits	0 mg
Oatmeal, cooked (no-salt-added)	3/4 cup	1 mg
Cream of Rice, cooked (no-salt-added)	3/4 cup	1 mg
Cheese & Processed Meats:		
Cheddar Cheese	1 ounce	180 mg
Cottage Cheese, low-fat, 1% fat	1/2 cup	459 mg
Cream Cheese, fat free	2 Tbsp.	200 mg
Mozzarella, part-skim	1 ounce	180 mg
Swiss Cheese, natural	1 ounce	50 mg
American Process Cheese	1 ounce	405 mg
Parmesan, grated	1 Tbsp.	128 mg
Crab, canned	1/2 cup	225 mg
Bacon	2 slices	202 mg
Ham, cured, lean	3 ounces	1,129 mg
Frankfurter, Beef, Pork, Turkey	1 frank	458 mg

continued on next page

Table 14: Sodium Content of Selected Foods, (continued)

Food Item:	Serving Size:	Sodium: *(mg)*
Chips, Crackers & Snacks:		
Fritos® Corn Chips	32 chips	170 mg
Popcorn, microwave, butter	3 cups	180 mg
Pretzels, thin twists, large	9 twists	560 mg
Saltines	5 crackers	220 mg
Nabisco® Low Salt Wheat Thins®	16 crackers	80 mg
Olives, green w/pimento	5 medium olives	350 mg
Pickles, dill	1 medium	220 mg
Bouillon Cube, chicken	1 cube	1,100 mg
Fast Foods:		
Burger King® Chicken Specialty, w/mayo	1 sandwich	1,270 mg
Burger King® Double Whopper®, w/mayo	1 sandwich	950 mg
Dairy Queen® Hog Dog	1 sandwich	880 mg
Dairy Queen® Peanut Buster® parfait	1 parfait	400 mg
Domino® Pepperoni Pizza, thin crust	1/4 pizza	1,108 mg
Hardee's® Big Roast Beef™	1 sandwich	1,140 mg
Hardee's® Hot Ham 'N' Cheese™	1 sandwich	1,390 mg
Hardee's® Bacon, w/egg & cheese	1 sandwich	1,420 mg
KFC® (2 pieces chicken, mashed potatoes, gravy, coleslaw, roll, wing & side breast)	1 dinner	1,954 mg
Long John Silver's® Fish & Fries	3 fish & 3 ounces fries	2,429 mg
McDonald's® Hamburger	1 sandwich	506 mg
McDonald's® Big Mac	1 sandwich	1,070 mg
McDonald's® Chicken McNuggets	6 pieces	680 mg
Taco Bell's® Bean Burrito	1 burrito	1,200 mg
Taco Bell's® Taco, hard, regular	1 taco	350 mg
Taco Bell's® Taco Salad, w/salsa & shell	1 salad	1,670 mg
Subway® Chipotle Southwest Turkey Bacon	1 (6 inch) sandwich	1,260 mg
Subway® Classic Salad, Tuna	1 salad	880 mg
Wendy's® Chili	Small	870 mg
Wendy's® Mandarin Chicken™ Salad, w/o almonds & noodles	1 salad	650 mg
Wendy's® Broccoli & Cheese Baked Potato	1 potato	510 mg

Source: Stephenson, J. and Bader, D., *HealthCheques™: Carbohydrate, Fat & Calorie Guide*, Mankato, Minn: Appletree Press, 2007.

Your drinking water can also be a source of sodium.

While the food sources of sodium are generally recognized, the contribution of sodium from drinking water may be overlooked. Drinking water may account for up to 10% of an individual's daily sodium consumption. The American Heart Association recommends a limit of 20 mg of sodium per liter of water as a standard for persons suffering from heart or kidney ailments and require a low-sodium diet. The Environmental Protection Agency (EPA) does not regulate the maximum level of sodium in water, though it also considers the optimal level of sodium in drinking water to be 20 milligrams of sodium a liter or less. Drinking water can contribute a significant amount of sodium if your water is softened. The amount of sodium added by a water softener can be as high as 100 mg a liter. Check with your local Department of Public Health to find out about your water supply.

7. If You Drink Alcoholic Beverages, Do So in Moderation.

Beneficial effects of moderate drinking.

Studies show that moderate drinking (one drink for women, two drinks for men) of alcoholic beverages lowers heart-disease risk. Alcohol protects your heart by increasing HDL cholesterol levels. Studies show that one or two alcoholic drinks a day may raise HDL cholesterol by an average of 4 mg/dL.

Compared to teetotalers, moderate drinkers tend to have greater HDL levels and lower heart-disease rates. The flavonoids (phytochemicals, quercetin) found in red wine (from the grape skin) also protect LDL cholesterol from oxidation, thus, preventing damage to artery walls and dangerous blood clots from forming.

This makes one almost want to take up drinking but alcohol consumption is not without risk. When taken in excess of energy need, it is converted to body fat and stored. When consumed in moderate amounts, it can stimulate the appetite, thus causing weight gain. When alcohol contributes a substantial portion of the calories in a person's diet, its effects are harmful.

Alcohol consumption is not without risk!

Chronic consumption of alcoholic beverages in large amounts damages the heart and cardiovascular system. Heavy drinkers (4 to 5 drinks a day) have a greater risk of hypertension, increasing the risk of stroke and kidney failure and increasing the likelihood of liver damage. Heavy consumption of alcohol significantly increases the risk of cancers of the mouth, throat, esophagus and liver. Cancer risk is especially high for heavy drinkers who smoke.

For women, the increased risk of cancer (particularly breast cancer) with drinking must be weighed against the potential benefit of lowering heart-disease risk. And young women who drink heavily risk giving birth to children with birth defects. Fetal Alcohol Syndrome (FAS) symptoms include a varying degree of mental deficiency, facial abnormalities and defects of the heart, lungs, joints and sex organs. Pregnant women are advised not to drink alcohol before or during pregnancy.

Do not begin drinking on the basis of health.

The American Heart Association and the National Cancer Institute recommend discriminate use of alcohol, in moderate amounts not to exceed 1 ½ ounces of ethanol a day. To stay within those guidelines, daily intake should not exceed one drink a day for women and two drinks a day for men.

What's a Drink?

· 1 1/2 ounces of hard liquor, 80 proof
· 5 ounces of wine
· 12 ounces of beer
· 16 ounces of 3.2 beer

To Conclude

Staying healthy is about choices, moderation, and balance. The food and physical activity choices we make every day affects our health. The more we know, the better choices we can make. There is no "one" superfood or exercise that can give us everything we need to stay healthy. Variety is important, as is finding the time to try new behaviors that support and sustain a healthy lifestyle. Healthy habits take effort and time to become routine. Here is a "Top 10" Websites List to help you stay focused.

Excellent resources for healthy eating & exercise information

1. DASH Diet. Contact the Health Information Center at (301) 592-8573 or http://emall.nhlbihin.net to purchase a copy of the NIH Publication No. 06-4082 (cost, with shipping is $6.60). This publication provides a week's worth of DASH menus (ranging from 1600 to 3100 calories a day) in sodium levels of 2,300 mg or 1,500 mg of sodium per day.

2. National Heart, Lung and Blood Institute
   www.nhlbi.nih.gov
3. Dietary Guidelines.
   www.healthierus.gov/dietaryguidelines.
4. American Heart Association. www.americanheart.org
5. MyPyramid www.mypyramid.gov
6. America on the Move www.americaonthemove.org
7. Shape Up America! www.shapeup.org
8. 5 A Day The Color Way www.5aday.com
9. Whole Grains Council www.wholegrainscouncil.org
10. The Heart Truth: A National Awareness Campaign On
    Women and Heart Disease
    www.nhlbi.nih.gov/health/hearttruth

References

1) Rosamond, W., Flegal, Kl, Friday, G., et al. Heart disease and stroke statistics-2007 update: A report from the American Heart Association Statistics Committee and Stroke Statistics Subcommittee. *Circulation* 115: e69-e171, 2007.

2) Behavioral Risk Factor Surveillance System, Surveillance for Certain Health Behaviors Among Selected Local Areas-United States, Behavioral Risk Factor Surveillance System, 2002, Morbidity and Mortality Weekly Report (MMWR), 53, No SS-05. http://www.cdc.gov/brfss/.

3) U.S. Dept of Health and Human Services, *Your Guide to Physical Activity and Your Heart*, NIH Publication No. 06-5714. June, 2006.

4) Tall, Alan, Protease variants, LDL, and coronary heart disease, *New England Journal of Medicine* 354 (2006): 1310-1312.

5) National Cholesterol Education Program (NCEP) Expert panel on Detection, Evaluation, and Treatment of High Blood Cholesterol in Adults (Adult Treatment Panel III). *Third Report of the National Cholesterol Education Program* (NCEP) Expert Panel on Detection, Evaluation, and Treatment of High Blood Cholesterol in Adults (Adult Treatment Panel III) final report. Circulation 106: 3143-3421, 2002.

2

COOKING À LA HEART

*Reshaping
eating
patterns*

Understanding the guidelines for a healthier heart is one thing, but implementing them can be quite another. Changing our eating habits requires motivation and commitment over time. We suggest starting with small, manageable changes and gradually, you will reach an eating pattern that will fit you for life.

Begin by taking inventory of the kinds and amounts of food you presently eat. In order to make changes, you must know what needs to be changed. By identifying your present eating habits, you will be able to spot areas in which you can make more healthful choices. A *food diary* can reveal habits that keep you from your best health such as meal skipping, unplanned snacking or dining on quick, high-calorie foods and drinks, constant nibbling through meal preparation or uncontrolled snacking during leisure time.

Identify only one or two problems that you'd like to work on. *Be realistic* in your expectations and set attainable goals. For example, it may take three months before the family accepts the change from 2% milk to skim milk. *Choose the area of least resistance.* Reducing fat and sodium in recipes, replacing ice cream with ice milk or offering fruit instead of high-calorie chips, cookies and candies are possible places to start.

Be flexible. Experiment. Try different brands and make compromises with your family to allow for individual tastes. Remember, *it takes time* to make changes which are accepted and adopted as a regular part of the family's lifestyle. Mark Twain said that a habit cannot simply be tossed out the window. It should be escorted like an old friend, down the stairs, one step at a time and out the door.

*Develop an archive
of rich-tasting,
heart-healthy
recipes for your
family.*

You will find numerous suggestions in this chapter to help you get started. The *Shopping à la Heart Section* guides you in grocery selection. The *Recipe Modification Guidelines Table* highlights changes you can make in traditional recipes. *The Meal Planning Section* provides sample menus and shows you how to plan your own tasty, wholesome meals using **Cooking À La Heart** recipes and explains the nutrient analyses.

Help at the Grocery Store

Today at the supermarket, almost every packaged food offers nutrition information about their product on the Nutrition Facts panel. You'll find nutrient values for calories, total fat, saturated fat, trans fat, cholesterol, sodium, other select minerals (potassium, calcium) carbohydrates, (broken into fiber and sugars), protein and vitamins A, and C. In addition, the American Heart Association has a food certification program called, Heart-Check (featured by a red heart with a white check mark along with their name). Following are some tips about these two helpful programs.

- Be mindful of the serving size and number of servings in the package. The serving stated is actually a "portion", not necessarily the amount recommended. This label states a serving is a cup, if you ate two cups, you'd have consumed twice the calories, fat, saturated fat, trans fat, and sodium. Serving sizes always matter.

- Look at the %Daily Value (DV) column, these percentages tell you how one serving contributes to a 2,000 calorie diet. If the %DV is *5% or less*, it is *Low* in that nutrient; if the %DV is *20% or more*, that nutrient is *High*. Heart-healthy foods would have a low %DV for total fat, saturated fat, trans fat, cholesterol and sodium; and a high %DV for fiber, Vitamin A, Vitamin C and calcium. You can compare the %DV between two similar products to determine which would be a healthier choice.

- One program that specifically identifies heart-healthy foods on the label (for healthy people over age 2) is the American Heart Association Food Certification Program. It clearly identifies heart-healthy choices on the grocery shelf with its bold and visible heart-check mark. To be certified, a product must meet certain nutrition criteria for total fat, saturated fat, trans fat, cholesterol and sodium. These criteria are applied to standard serving sizes as defined by FDA for each particular food type. Please visit heartcheckmark.org for more information.

Nutrition Facts

Serving Size 1 cup (228g)
Servings Per Container 2

Amount Per Serving

Calories 250	Calories from Fat 110

	% Daily Value*
Total Fat 12g	18%
Saturated Fat 3g	15%
Trans Fat 1.5g	
Cholesterol 30mg	10%
Sodium 470mg	20%
Total Carbohydrate 31g	10%
Dietary Fiber 0g	0%
Sugars 5g	
Protein 5g	

Vitamin A	4%
Vitamin C	2%
Calcium	20%
Iron	4%

* Percent Daily Values are based on a 2,000 calorie diet. Your Daily Values may be higher or lower depending on your calorie needs:

	Calories:	2,000	2,500
Total Fat	Less than	65g	80g
Sat Fat	Less than	20g	25g
Cholesterol	Less than	300mg	300mg
Sodium	Less than	2,400mg	2,400mg
Total Carbohydrate		300g	375g
Dietary Fiber		25g	30g

Shopping à la Heart

Heart-healthy choices can be found in almost every grocery aisle.

Produce

All fresh fruits and vegetables fit! Serve a fruit at every meal, a vegetable or two for lunch and dinner and use both fruits and vegetables for snacks.

Canned Goods

Select sodium-reduced vegetables, soups and canned meats. Select only water-packed fish and water- or juice-packed fruits.

Cereals

Select whole-grain cereals. Choose cereals with 5 g of fiber or more per serving and a low %DV value for sugar and sodium.

Frozen Foods

Read the Nutrition Facts panel. Choose plain, frozen (steamfresh) vegetables and fruits with no-sugar-added. Choose frozen dinners (meals) that contain 18 g or less fat, no trans fat, low %DV for saturated fat and no more than 800 mg of sodium per serving.

Dairy

Buy skim or 1% milk. Purchase part-skim, low-fat, reduced-fat cheese, cottage cheese and yogurt. Purchase fresh eggs or use frozen egg substitute made from egg whites if you have a high cholesterol level.

Refrigerated Case

Choose 100% fruit juices instead of fruit drinks. Select whole-grain pocket breads, wraps, English muffins and bagels. Avoid high-fat, processed meats like sausage, bologna, salami and hot dogs. Use the Nutrition Facts panel to choose lower sodium versions.

Fish, Poultry & Meat

Select fish rich in omega-3 fats and try to fit fish twice a week into your meal plan. Select lean poultry, pork, and beef selecting "loin" cuts such as sirloin steak, pork tenderloin, extra-lean ground beef, and "round" cuts of lean red meat. Remove the skin from poultry before eating.

Dry Goods

Select whole grains such as brown and wild rice, whole-wheat pasta, barley and legumes. Use recipes to increase your consumption of dry beans and whole grains (see *GRAINS, PASTA & LEGUMES and SALAD Sections*).

Bakery

Purchase whole grain breads and buns, check the label for the first ingredient to state "whole grain". Avoid trans fat-containing doughnuts and pastries. Make your own heart-healthy baked goods from **Cooking Á La Heart** (*see BREADS and DESSERTS Sections*).

Spices   All spices fit. Select blends without added salt or sodium. Choose 'powders' over 'flavored salts'. Try new spices, and make your own blends featured in the *SEASONING Section*.

Beverages & Snacks   Choose sugar-free and sodium-free bottled waters. Select sodium-reduced crackers made from whole grains, choose microwave popcorn with low %DV values for fat, saturated fat and contain no trans fat. Enjoy a variety of unsalted nuts.

Fats, Oils, Margarines & Spreads   Choose heart-healthy monounsaturated fats such as canola, flaxseed, hazelnut, olive and high-oleic safflower and sunflower oils. Use other vegetable oils sparingly. Do not buy shortenings or "partially hydrogenated" oils. Avoid all fat that's solid at room temperature. Buy tub margarines and spreads that list 'liquid' oil as the first ingredient. Go one step further and purchase those brands that contain omega-3 fats and flax and are labeled 'light'. Choose fat-free or light mayonnaise or a canola oil-based mayonnaise and fat-free salad dressings. Use both the ingredient label and the Nutrition Facts panel to choose heart-healthy products.

Table 15: Recipe Modification Guidelines

When your recipe calls for:	Use these Heart-Healthy Alternatives:
1 whole egg	2 egg whites or 1/4 cup egg substitute or 1 egg white and 1 teaspoon oil *
1 cup butter or shortening	1 cup soft margarine * or 2/3 cup oil
1/2 cup butter or shortening	1/2 cup soft margarine or 1/3 cup oil
1 cup light cream	1 cup evaporated skim milk or 3 Tablespoons oil and skim milk to equal 1 cup
1 cup heavy cream	1 cup evaporated skim milk or 2/3 cup skim milk and 1/3 cup oil
1 cup heavy cream (soups)	1 cup unsweetened condensed milk
1 cup sour cream	1 cup plain low-fat yogurt, 1 cup fat-free sour cream, or MOCK SOUR CREAM, *(see APPETIZER & DIPS Section)*
1 ounce (a square) baking chocolate	3 tablespoons powdered cocoa and 1 tablespoon oil
Chocolate chips	Raisins or dried fruit for half or all the chips.
Cream Cheese	Use "light" or fat-free cream cheese or MOCK CREAM CHEESE, *(see APPETIZER & DIPS Section)*

continued on next page

Table 15: Recipe Modification Guidelines (continued)

When your recipe calls for:	Use these Heart-Healthy Alternatives:
2 strips bacon	1 ounce lean Canadian bacon or 1 ounce reduced-sodium lean ham
Regular ground beef	Extra-lean ground beef or 1/2 pound extra-lean ground beef plus 14-oz. can cooked lentils or beans
Deep-fried meats, poultry & fish	Broiled, baked, braised or grilled lean meats, poultry and fish
Fat for sautéing or broiling	Use 1/2 the amount of fat or sauté in stock, wine, or water; invest in good quality nonstick cookware and cook with little or no added fat.
Cheddar, colby & American cheese	Choose a cheese with 5g or less fat per ounce
1 can Condensed cream soup	Condensed Cream Soup Mix or Medium White Sauce, *(see SOUP Section)*
Cream of celery soup	Medium White Sauce + 1/4 cup chopped celery
Cream of chicken soup	Medium White Sauce + 2 sodium-reduced chicken bouillon cubes
Cream of mushroom soup	Medium White Sauce + 1 cup chopped fresh mushrooms
1 cup all-purpose white flour	3/4 cup all-purpose white flour + 1/4 cup bran or 1/2 cup all-purpose white flour + 1/2 cup whole-wheat flour or 1 cup whole-wheat flour minus 2 Tablespoons, decreasing the oil by 1 Tablespoon and increasing the liquid by 1-2 Tablespoons
Sugar	Reduce amount. Reduction can be up to 1/2 of the original amount. Use no more than 1/4 cup of sweetener to each cup of flour.
Salt	Reduce amount or leave out. You may increase other spices and herbs.
Tomato juice	Use no-salt-added tomato juice or dilute one 6-ounce can of no-salt-added tomato paste with 3 cans water.
Tomato paste	Use no-salt-added tomato paste.
Tomato sauce	Use no-salt-added tomato sauce or one 6-ounce can no-salt-added tomato paste with 1 can water.

* margarine refers to any spread made with "liquid" canola or olive oil.

Successful Meal Planning

*Meal
Planning*

Keep menus simple by making fewer dishes and serving adequate portions. Make double or triple amounts of main dishes and baked goods and freeze for later use. Planning menus for a week in advance allows you to organize your meal preparation time most efficiently. Most importantly, everyone can share meal planning, cooking and clean-up tasks within the household. Shared responsibility provides children with valuable learning experiences.

Menu planning becomes more rewarding as you discover the many ways to achieve a healthful good-tasting diet. In this section, we provide several menu combinations adaptable to your family's needs and tastes. You will find family menus for a week, suggestions for summer and winter entertaining, picnic fare and special occasions.

*Where to
Begin*

No one should expect every meal to be perfectly balanced; strive to balance your diet over the course of a week. Try to include on a daily basis a minimum of:

- 6 servings of whole-grain bread, cereal, pasta or rice;

- 8-9 servings of fruits and vegetables, including good Vitamin A, Vitamin C and Vitamin E-source foods. Eat the rainbow—from blueberries to carrots and tomatoes to pineapple, have as many different-colored fruits and veggies as possible each day to get the widest variety of nutrients;

- 2 servings (a total of 5 1/2 ounce-equivalents) of a high-protein food (combination of complementary vegetable proteins, fish, poultry or lean red meats);

- 3 servings of calcium-rich dairy foods such as low-fat milk, cottage cheese or yogurt

*Advantages
of Meal
Planning*

Planning meals in advance saves time, money and reduces hassle. With a week's plan in hand you'll:

- save shopping time
- avoid impulse buying
- make better use of leftovers
- have an answer to the perennial question: "What's for dinner?"

Start by planning a day's menu. For each meal select a "theme" or type of main dish and build around it.

THEMED MENU IDEAS

SALAD MEAL

Large Bowl of Mixed Greens

Suggested Accompaniments:
- slivered lean meats
- low-fat cottage cheese, low-fat cheese
- onions and other raw vegetables
- tomatoes and sprouts
- homemade croutons and salad dressings
- nuts and seeds
- breads, muffins, quick bread
- soup

CASSEROLE MEAL

Any Baked Main Dish

Suggested Accompaniments:
- soup
- vegetables
- salads
- breads
- fruit

VEGETABLE MEAL

Vegetable Main Dish such as:
- ♥ Cauliflower Walnut Casserole
- ♥ Curried Rice Stuffed Tomato
- ♥ Tofu Italiano

Suggested Accompaniments:
- breads, muffins, rolls
- soups
- fruits
- salads

LEGUME OR GRAIN MEAL

Legume or Grain Dish such as:
- ♥ Savory Black Beans
- ♥ Rice with Pine Nuts
- ♥ Barley Pilaf

Suggested Accompaniments:
- bits of meat and lots of vegetables, stir-fried, curried or steamed
- nuts and seeds
- breads
- salad

SOUP MEAL

A Hearty Soup such as
- ♥ Cream of Morel Soup
- ♥ Creole-Style Lentil Stew
- ♥ Curried Squash-Apple Bisque

Suggested Accompaniments:
- raw vegetable platter with dips
- homemade breads, dinner rolls,
- muffins
- fruits
- baked low-fat dessert

BREAD MEAL

Loaves of Freshly-Made Bread served on boards, pocketbread, muffins

Suggested Accompaniments:
- low fat cheeses
- sandwich filling such as:
  - ♥ Veggie-Cheese Pockets
  - ♥ Grilled Zucchini-Parmesan
  - ♥ Tofu Salad
- leafy greens
- tomatoes, sprouts, onions and other raw vegetables
- hot or cold drinks, nogs

continued on page 60

A Week's Worth of Family Fare *(Menu selections are recipes in Cooking À La Heart).*

	Sunday	Monday	Tuesday
Breakfast	**Brunch** Hot Citrus Fruit Compote Apple Cinnamon Pancakes w/ Spicy Yogurt Topping	Citrus Juice or Orange Oat Bran Cereal Blueberry Muffin w/ Tub Margarine Skim Milk	Energy Breakfast Nog Whole-Grain Cold Cereal Whole Wheat Toast w/ Tub Margarine Skim Milk
Lunch	Vegetable Quiche Cranberry Coffee Cake Fruit Preserves Tub Margarine Beverage	Italian Pasta Salad Sour Milk Rolls w/ Tub Margarine Fresh Fruit Pecan Meringues Beverage	Fish Salad Verde Hearty Wheat Buns w/ Tub Margarine Berries 'n Cannoli Cream Beverage
Supper	Cucumber & Tomato Salad Sole Rolls on a bed of Green Rice Asparagus Oriental Carrot Cake (freeze leftover cake) Beverage	Antipasto (Spinach- Stuffed Cherry Tomatoes, Stuffed Celery and Marinated Vegetables) Tofu Italiano Tossed Mixed Greens w/ Dilled Vinaigrette Dressing Hearty Wheat Buns Apples w/ Caramel Sauce Beverage	Chicken Almond Stir-Fry on Bed of Brown Rice Orange Cauliflower Salad w/ Surprise Dressing Whole Wheat French Bread Sparkling Fruit Beverage
Snacks	Berry Milk Shake Pretzels Air-Popped Popcorn	Bread Sticks Grapes Skim Milk	Fruit Chewy Oatmeal Cookie

A Week's Worth of Family Fare, (continued)

Wednesday	Thursday	Friday	Saturday
Fresh/Frozen Peaches or Banana Soft Boiled Egg Scrapple Reduced-Calorie Syrup Hot Cocoa	Cantaloupe Hot or Cold Cereal Pecan Oat Muffin w/ Tub Margarine Skim Milk	Citrus Juice Wellness Granola Toasted English Muffin Fruit Preserves Skim Milk	Apple Juice Whole-Wheat Waffles w/Fruit Topping Cottage Cheese and Peaches w/ Cinnamon Beverage
Health Salad w/ Surprise Dressing Cranberry Bread Vanilla Pudding w/ Sliced Strawberries Beverage	Baked Beans Grilled Zucchini Parmesan Fresh Apple Beverage	Gazpacho Hot Chicken Pockets Rice Pudding Beverage	Turkey Vegetable Soup Date Sandwich Spread on Whole-Grain Bread Fresh Pear Beverage
Grilled Herbed Burgers Potato Salad Vinaigrette Coleslaw Broccoli-Corn Salad Watermelon Beverage	Baked Salmon Steaks w/ Lemon Steamed New Potatoes Citrus Spinach Salad w/ Mazatlan Dressing Raspberry Chiffon Pie w/ Nut Crust Beverage	Veggie-Nut Pizza on Yeast Crust Apple Spinach Salad Ice Milk w/ Honey Fudge Sauce Beverage	Garden-Green Salad Pork Chop w/ Garlic Sauce on Caraway Rice Carrots Eléganté Four-Grain Bread Cranberry Steamed Pudding Beverage
Mulled Cider Whole-Wheat Soft Pretzel	Skim Milk Carrot Cake (leftover)	Sparkling Water Banana	Orange-Yogurt Popsicles Popcorn

Summer Buffet

Raspberry Punch
Assorted Raw Vegetables
Herbed Cheese Dip
Salmon Yogurt Dip
Spinach Crêpe Wheels
Julian's Fish Appetizer
Wild Rice Chicken Salad
Baked Garlic Tomatoes
Honey Whole-Wheat Bread
Fruit Pizza
Beverage

Picnic Menu

Marinated Vegetables
Curry Glazed Chicken on the Grill
Tabouleh Salad
Confetti Apple Slaw
Rhubarb Cake
Bread Sticks
Beverage

Summer Porch Lunch

Chilled Pea Soup
Thai Style Fried Fish
Rice
Strawberry Rhubarb Gelatin Salad
Blueberry Muffin

Lunch for Bridge Club

Fish Florentine
Sour Milk Rolls w/Preserves
Pear & Grapefruit Toss w/Mint
Chocolate Mousse

Soup & Salad for Saturday Lunch

Potato and Leek Soup
Citrus Beet Salad

Winter Buffet

Mulled Cider
Vegetable Platter
Baked Eggplant Dip
Salsa
Cocktail Meatballs
Savory Stuffed Mushrooms
Chicken Waikiki
Rice and Pine Nuts
Sweet Potatoes and Apples
24-Hour Layered Salad
Old-Fashioned Potato Rye Bread
New Zealand Pavlova
Beverage

Casseroles for Potluck Suppers

Wild Rice Chicken Casserole
Crockpot Stroganoff
Cabbage Casserole
Busy Day Pork Stew

Super Bowl Sunday Supper

Salsa
Homemade Tortilla Chips
Black Bean Chili
Rice
Green Salad w/Creamy Salad Dressing
Corn Zephyrs
Butterscotch Pudding
Applesauce Spice Cookies

Salads to Go
24-Hour Layered Salad
Italian Salad

Trim the Tree
Wassail
Spicy Popcorn to Eat
Plain Popcorn to String
Fresh Fruit to Dip in
  Banana Yogurt Dressing
Lentil Soup
Confetti Appleslaw
Date Bars

Sunday Night Supper
Mulligatawny Soup
Cauliflower Salad
Rolls
Dessert

Initiation for the Beginner "I Can't Believe it's Heart-Healthy"
Marinated Flank Steak, Grilled
Potato Salad Vinaigrette
Ratatouille
Coleslaw
Baked Glazed Pears
  or
Peach Yogurt Pie

Sweet Endings Buffet
Fruit & Cheese Platter
Pear & Grapefruit Toss w/ Mint
Spicy Pumpkin Bars
New Zealand Pavlova
Caramel Sauce over Sliced Apples
Hot Tea

Recipes are controlled for:
- *calories*
- *fat*
- *sodium*
- *no trans fat*

A Word About The Recipes in Cooking Á La Heart

The recipes in **Cooking Á La Heart** are made with ingredients known to benefit heart health. The recipes use a minimal number of processed foods, feature mostly fresh, whole foods, call for unrefined carbohydrates and use a minimal amount of added sugar.

The recipes are calorie, fat, and sodium controlled, have no added saturated fat (other than what is found naturally in dairy and meat products) and contain no trans fats. In addition, the recipes are sensitive to the type of fat, encouraging the use of monounsaturated fats, such as canola or olive oil. If a recipe calls for "extra-light" olive oil, it's because of the taste (a very light to no olive flavor), not because extra-light has fewer calories, which it does not). Tub or "soft" margarines were used because they contain "liquid" fats that contain no saturated or trans fats. "Light" tub margarines are made with a high percentage of water, and should not be used in baking, which will produce an undesirable-tasting and appearing product. The authors have

Nutrient Analysis

followed the American Heart Association's Diet Goals and Recommendations for Reducing Risk of CVD (*see APPENDIX Tables 29 and 30*).

The nutrition-analysis software program, The Food Processor SQL Nutrition Analysis Program, Versions 9.9 and 10 (2006 –2007) from ESHA Research based in Salem, Oregon was used to analyze each recipe. As an adjunct to this program, the USDA Nutrient Database for Standard Reference, Release 20 (2007) was used for Meats, Poultry and Fish.

Each recipe includes nutrition information based on a single serving and provides values for calories, protein, carbohydrate, fat, cholesterol, sodium, and dietary fiber,(when one gram or more was present). When 10 percent or more of the RDI (Recommended Dietary Intake) for calcium is present in a single serving, calcium values are provided and when an ingredient containing omega-3 fats is used in the recipe, the omega-3 fats value is provided. These values can be found at the bottom of the page for each recipe.

If an ingredient is listed as (optional, or as a garnish) in the recipe, its nutrient value is NOT calculated in the nutrient profile. When ingredient choices appear (such as frozen egg substitute or eggs), the first ingredient listed is analyzed.

Exchange Lists

Food exchanges have been calculated for all recipes in **Cooking Á La Heart** and can be found at the bottom of the page for a single serving. The Exchange System is a method of grouping together foods that have about the same amount of calories, carbohydrate, fat and protein. This allows one to 'exchange' one food in the group for another. The American Diabetic Association AND the American Dietetic Association developed the Exchange System over 50 years ago, initially for the management of diabetes.

Today, it continues to be used for this purpose and is also used for weight management and as a wonderful guide to healthy eating. It's important to be mindful of what one eats. Eating wisely and well is advised for all of us, not just for people with diabetes. For more information on the Exchange List for Diabetes, please visit these online sites, www.diabetes.org (for the American Diabetic Association) and www.eatright.org (for the American Dietetic Association).

Carbohydrate (Carb) Choices

Also provided at the bottom of the page with the nutrient analysis for single servings, is a value called, Carb Choices. When managing diabetes, weight loss, or metabolic syndrome, it is important to know the amount of carbohydrate content of the foods one eats. To control both blood sugar (glucose) levels and discourage insulin resistance, budgeting one's carbohydrates intake is important. The recipes in **Cooking Á La Heart** provide both the total amount of carbohydrate (found in the Analysis per Serving); and the Carb Choices (immediately under the Exchanges). The carbohydrate choices are based on the following equation:

The ranges in the chart below were used to determine the equivalent carbohydrate servings or carb choices in the recipes.

One carb choice =
15 g carb,
as found in:
- 1 starch, OR
- 1 fruit, OR
- 1 milk

Carbohydrate Conversion Chart	
Carbohydrate (grams)	Carb Choices
0 – 5	0
6 – 10	1/2
11 – 20	1
21 – 25	1 1/2
26 – 35	2
36 – 40	2 1/2
41 – 50	3

The Fiber bonus: If a food (or recipe) contains 5 grams or more dietary fiber per serving, subtract half that number from the total carbohydrate grams. For example, a 23-gram carbohydrate portion with 6 grams of fiber would count as 20 grams of carbohydrate (23 – 3 = 20 grams). This would make it equivalent to 1 carbohydrate serving/choice instead of 1 1/2.

As A
Reminder...

Keep in mind a teaspoon of fat is equivalent to 5 grams of fat and a teaspoon of salt contains 2300 milligrams of sodium. To make the nutrition information meaningful, let's assume an active woman consumes 1800 calories daily. Of those calories, she should consume a maximum of 540 calories as fat. At 9 calories a gram, the 540 calories translates to 60 grams of fat or 12 teaspoons daily. An active man who consumes 2400 calories daily, should consume no more than 720 calories or 80 grams of fat or 16 teaspoons daily.

The following guidelines are provided to assist you in determining how the recipes can fit into your daily meal plan.

Fat:	Limit to 25-35% of total calories, mostly from monounsaturated sources.
Saturated Fat:	Less than 7% of total daily calories.
Cholesterol:	Aim to eat less than 300 milligrams per day; 200 milligrams per day if you have heart disease.
Sodium:	Aim to eat less than 2300 milligrams of sodium per day.
Fiber:	Strive to consume between 25-35 grams per day.
Calcium:	Women should consume between 1000-1300 milligrams per day; postmenopausal women, 1200 milligrams per day; and children and men, 800-1200 milligrams per day.

Abbreviations Key

(Abbreviations found in this book include the following:

Carb = carbohydrate
g = grams
mg = milligrams
min = minutes
mini = miniature
pkg = package

Appetizers, Dips & Beverages

One cannot think well, love well, or sleep well if one has not dined well.

Virginia Woolf

COLD APPETIZERS

Julian's Fish Appetizer 75
Marinated Vegetables 72
Shrimp Apple Slices 80
Spinach Crêpe Wheels 79
Stuffed Snow Peas. 69
Vegetable Platter 69

COLD BEVERAGES

Berry Milk Shake 90
Christmas Cranberry Float 86
Citrus Refresher 89
Energy Nog 88
Orange Milk Shake. 79
Raspberry Punch 88

DIPS

Baked Eggplant Dip 86
Garbanzo Spread 84
Herbed Cheese Dip. 82
Hummus Bi Tahini. 83
Mock Cream Cheese. 82
Mock Sour Cream 81
Variations:
    Creamy Dip 81
    Dill Dip 81
    Horseradish Dip. 81
    Mustard Dip. 81
Salmon Yogurt Dip. 84
Spinach Dip 85

HOT APPETIZERS

Chicken Appetizers. 73
Cocktail Meat Balls 77
Pizza Bites 78
Savory Stuffed Mushrooms. 70
Spicy Fish Bites. 74
Steak Sticks. 76
Tomatoes Stuffed with Spinach. . . . 71

HOT BEVERAGES

Instant Cocoa Mix 90
Mulled Cider 87
Wassail 87

HOT OR COLD BEVERAGES

Fruit Warmer 85
Tomato Juice Cocktail 89

APPETIZERS & DIPS

Appetizers can whet or curb your appetite

Often known as canapés or hors d'oeuvres, appetizers can either whet your appetite for the next course or they can help fill you, thus curbing your appetite and preventing you from overeating.

Appetizers need not be calorie laden or greasy; they can be crunchy, dipped, spread, speared, filled or picked up and eaten with fingers and still make a worthwhile nutritional contribution.

Our appetizers are imaginative and festive while low in fat, cholesterol, sodium and calories. We have handpicked this section of appetizers to offer you a variety of flavors and textures. Whatever your tastes, you can present an attractive and nutritious array of appetizers sure to please your guests.

Appetizer Tips

- Add garnishes to make hor d'oeuvres visually appealing. Fresh vegetables, cut decoratively, make beautiful edible garnishes. Hollowed-out bell peppers, large mushrooms or cucumbers make wonderful dip containers.

- When serving more than one appetizer, select a variety of colors, shapes, tastes and textures.

- For appetizers preceding dinner, allow two or three large appetizers or four to six bite-sized appetizers a person.

- Avoid repetition; don't serve steak sticks with a beef meal or stuffed tomatoes with a tomato-based entrée.

- For a party that doesn't include dinner, prepare a variety of hors d'oeuvres. For 8 to 12 people, serve four types of hors d'oeuvres; for 14 to 18 people, five to six types, allowing three to four pieces for each person.

- Appetizers are well worth the effort. Many of our selections can be made several days ahead and stored in either the freezer or refrigerator. An hour or so before serving time, arrange, cover and leave at room temperature. Remember to use small serving plates to help your guests control food portions.

BEVERAGES

Don't ignore calories beverages can provide

There are as many ways to serve beverages as there are recipes. Beverages can be tasty eye-openers in the morning, an interesting accompaniment to a meal, a soothing snack for children or simple refreshments to be enjoyed by themselves.

Because beverages are so easy to sip or drink, we tend to ignore their calories and can consume large numbers of calories in very small quantities. Check some of your favorite beverages in the chart below. Keep in mind, calories are not the only standard by which to judge. Beverages can be valuable sources of vitamins and minerals but often drinks such as sodas, fruit drinks, ades, punches and shakes are high in calories and are hidden sources of fat and sodium while making little or no other nutritional contribution.

Table 16: Calorie, Fat and Sodium Comparison of Select Beverages

Beverage:	Calories:	Fat: (grams)	Sodium: (mg)
Coffee, brewed, 12 fl. oz.	7	trace	7
Caffé Latte, w/ whole milk, 12 fl. oz.	210	11	170
Caffé Latte, w/ nonfat milk, 12 fl. oz.	120	0	170
Tea, brewed, 12 fl. oz.	3	trace	11
Chai Tea, w/ whole milk, 12 fl. oz	210	6	85
Chai Tea, w/ nonfat milk, 12 fl. oz.	170	0	95
Fruit Juice:			
Orange, 8 fl. oz.	114	0	26
Tomato, 8 fl. oz.	50	0	860
Fruit Drink or Ade, 12 fl. oz.	187	0	39
Soda, carbonated, 12 fl. oz.	150	0	75
Soda, carbonated, diet, 12 fl. oz.	0	0	52
Milk:			
Whole (3.5%), 8 fl. oz.	150	8	120
2%, 8 fl. oz.	130	5	125
1%, 8 fl. oz.	110	2	130
Skim, 8 fl. oz.	90	0	130
Denny's® Milkshake, 8 fl. oz.	373	17	181
Cooking À La Heart Berry Milkshake, 8 fl. oz.	183	1	85
Hot Cocoa, whole milk, 8 fl. oz.	213	8	156
Cooking À La Heart Hot Cocoa, 8 fl. oz.	99	1	94

Source: The Food Processor SQL Nutrition Analysis Program, Version 9.9 (ESHA Research); Salem, OR.

VEGETABLE PLATTER

Colorful, tasty and nutritious — the vegetable platter is the center of attraction on any table.

Asparagus spears, steamed
Beet slices or cubes, cooked
Broccoli florets
Cauliflower florets
Carrot wheels or strips
Celery sticks
Cherry tomatoes
Cucumber slices or spears
Green beans, whole and
   steamed
Green onions
Green or sweet red bell pepper
   strips or rings
Mushrooms, whole or sliced
Pea pods, raw or steamed

Wash and cut vegetables into bite-sized portions.

Steam vegetables such as asparagus or green beans until crisp-tender. Plunge into cold water. Drain.

Chill all vegetables. Arrange on platter and serve with a tasty, heart-healthy dip.

STUFFED SNOW PEAS

Makes 30 appetizers; 10 servings

30 **fresh snow peas**
1/4 **cup light cream cheese**
1/8 **teaspoon dill weed**
 2 **green onions, with some tops,**
    finely chopped

Blanch peas for 10 seconds. Dip in cold water and drain. Mix cream cheese, dill weed and green onion.

Open pea along one edge and stuff with about 1/2 teaspoon of cheese mixture.

Nutrient Analysis: 3 pea pods
Exchanges: free
Carbohydrate Choices: 0

Calories: 19   Protein: 1g   Carbohydrates: 1g
Fat: 1g   Cholesterol: 3mg   Sodium: 31mg

SAVORY STUFFED MUSHROOMS

Makes 12 appetizers; 6 servings

12 large, 2" diameter
    mushrooms
2 tablespoons finely chopped
    onion
2 tablespoons finely chopped
    celery or green pepper
2 tablespoons tub margarine
1 cup fine, soft whole wheat
    bread crumbs
1 teaspoon lemon juice
1 tablespoon sherry
1/4 teaspoon garlic powder
1/8 teaspoon pepper
1/4 teaspoon dried basil, crushed
1 teaspoon parsley flakes
1/2 cup grated part-skim
    mozzarella or 1/4 cup
    Parmesan cheese

Wipe mushrooms with damp cloth and remove stems. Chop stems finely.

Sauté mushroom stems, onion and celery or green pepper in margarine in a small skillet.

Combine bread crumbs, lemon juice, sherry, garlic powder, pepper, basil, parsley and mozzarella or Parmesan in a bowl. Add sautéed mixture and mix well.

Stuff mushrooms caps and place on nonstick-sprayed baking sheet. Bake 15 minutes, then broil until nicely browned. Serve warm.

Oven: 350° Broil
Time: 15 minutes, 2 to 3 minutes

Nutrient Analysis: 2 mushrooms
Exchanges: 1 vegetable, 1 fat
Carbohydrate Choices: 1/2

Calories: 92   Protein: 4g   Carbohydrates: 7g
Fat: 6g   Cholesterol: 5mg   Sodium: 143mg
Dietary Fiber: 1g   Calcium: 73mg

TOMATOES STUFFED WITH SPINACH

Filling will stuff 6 medium tomatoes to serve as a luncheon entrée or vegetable side dish; increase baking time about 10 minutes.

Makes about 2 cups; stuffing for 36 cherry tomatoes or mushrooms; 12 servings

1/2 cup sodium-reduced, defatted chicken broth
1 (10-ounce) package frozen chopped spinach
1 small onion, finely chopped
3 tablespoons light mayonnaise
36 cherry tomatoes or large mushrooms

Place broth and frozen spinach block in a small saucepan. Cover and heat on low for 5 minutes, turning block after 2 minutes. When spinach is JUST thawed, stir in chopped onion and mayonnaise. Simmer uncovered, stirring frequently until liquid and mixture is consistency of creamed spinach.

Stuff cherry tomatoes or large mushroom caps and bake. Serve hot or cold.

Oven: 350°
Time: 10 to 15 minutes

Nutrient Analysis: 3 stuffed cherry tomatoes or 3 stuffed large mushrooms

Exchanges: 1 vegetable	*Calories: 38 Protein: 1 g*	*Carbohydrates: 6 g*
Carbohydrate Choices: 1/2	*Fat: 2 g Cholesterol: 1 mg*	*Sodium: 163 mg*
	Dietary Fiber: 1 g	

MARINATED VEGETABLES

Makes 8 cups; 16 servings

1 (8-ounce) can button
    mushrooms, drained
1 green pepper, cut in strips
1 carrot, sliced in rounds
1 head cauliflower, broken into
    florets
1 (16-ounce) can or 2 (10-ounce)
    packages frozen artichoke
    hearts, cut into fourths
12 small white onions or 6 to 8
    green onions with 1" of their
    tops
1 1/2 cups wine vinegar
1 teaspoon sugar
1/2 teaspoon pepper
2 teaspoons dried oregano,
    crushed
2 teaspoons dried tarragon,
    crushed
1/2 cup vegetable oil
1/2 cup olive oil
    Cherry tomatoes (optional)
    Chopped fresh parsley
    (optional)

Combine mushrooms, green pepper, carrot, cauliflower, artichokes and onions in a large bowl.

Heat vinegar in a saucepan and stir in sugar, salt, pepper, oregano and tarragon. Cool slightly and add oils. Mix well.

Pour dressing over vegetables, stir, cover and refrigerate for 24 hours before serving. Stir occasionally while vegetables are marinating.

To serve, drain and arrange in a lettuce-lined bowl. Garnish with cherry tomatoes and sprinkle with parsley. Provide cocktail forks or toothpicks for spearing vegetables.

Nutrient Analysis: 1/2 *cup*
Exchanges: 1 vegetable, 1/2 *fat*
Carbohydrate Choices: 1

Calories: 53   Protein: 2g   Carbohydrates: 7g
Fat: 3g   Cholesterol: 0mg   Sodium: 102mg
Dietary Fiber: 2g

CHICKEN APPETIZERS

Makes 50 appetizers; 25 servings

3   whole chicken breasts, boned
     and skinned
3/4 cup melted tub margarine
1/4 teaspoon garlic powder
1/4 teaspoon dry mustard
1/2 teaspoon dried basil, crushed
3/4 cup fine dry bread crumbs
1/2 cup grated Parmesan cheese
1/2 cup chopped fresh parsley

Cut chicken into bite-sized pieces.

Combine margarine, garlic powder, mustard and basil in a large bowl. Add chicken pieces to margarine mixture and stir.

In a separate bowl, mix bread crumbs, Parmesan and parsley. Remove chicken from margarine and add to crumb mixture. Toss until chicken pieces are well coated with crumbs.

Spread on baking sheet or broiler pan and bake, turning once. Serve with ORIENTAL SWEET-SOUR SAUCE, *(page 167)*.

Oven: 400°
Time: 12 to 15 minutes

Nutrient Analysis: 2 appetizers
Exchanges: 1 very lean meat, 1 fat   Calories: 93   Protein: 6g   Carbohydrates: 2g
Carbohydrate Choices: 0   Fat: 6g   Cholesterol: 13 mg   Sodium: 116 mg

SPICY FISH BITES

Quick and easy to prepare in your microwave.

Makes 16 appetizers; 8 servings

1/3	cup plain low-fat yogurt
1/2	teaspoon grated lime peel
2	tablespoons fresh lime juice
1/2	teaspoon ground cumin
1/4	teaspoon ground coriander
1/4	teaspoon paprika
1/8	teaspoon pepper
1	pound frozen cod or other white fish
4	lime wedges (optional)

Mix together the yogurt, lime peel, lime juice, cumin, coriander, paprika and pepper. Cut fish into 16 appetizer-sized cubes and add to marinade.

Chill fish in marinade 2 to 3 hours. Microwave on high 5 to 7 minutes or until fish is flaky. Let stand 3 minutes.

Serve sprinkled with paprika and garnished with lime wedges.

Nutrient Analysis: 2 appetizers
Exchanges: 1 very lean meat
Carbohydrate Choices: 0

Calories: 54   Protein: 11 g   Carbohydrates: 1 g
Fat: 1 g   Cholesterol: 25 mg   Sodium: 38 mg
Omega-3: 0.11 g

JULIAN'S FISH APPETIZER

Or serve as a summer entrée for four accompanied by a crisp green salad and crunchy French bread.

Makes 16 appetizers; 8 servings

1	pound white fish fillets (walleye, roughy or cod)
1/2	cup water
1/4	cup lemon juice or 1/3 cup dry white wine
1	tablespoon grated onion

SAUCE:

1/4	teaspoon prepared mustard
4	tablespoons light mayonnaise
3	drops Tabasco sauce
1/2	teaspoon sodium-reduced Worcestershire sauce
1/2	tablespoon lemon juice

Paprika (optional)
Fresh parsley sprigs (optional)

Heat the poaching liquid of water, lemon juice or wine and onion in electric skillet to 280° (stove top skillet, medium-high heat until bubbling). Place whole fillets in liquid and poach gently for 5 to 8 minutes. Remove fish and place in a flat glass casserole dish. Cool poaching liquid and pour over fish. Refrigerate until ready to serve.

For sauce: Mix together mustard, mayonnaise, Tabasco, Worcestershire and lemon juice.

Remove fish from poaching liquid and cut into 16 appetizer-sized pieces. Top with sauce, sprinkle with paprika and garnish with parsley. Serve chilled.

Nutrient Analysis: 2 appetizers
Exchanges: 1 lean meat
Carbohydrate Choices: 0

Calories: 75   Protein: 10 g   Carbohydrates: 2 g
Fat: 3 g   Cholesterol: 27 mg   Sodium: 97 mg
Omega-3: 0.11 g

STEAK STICKS

A versatile marinade. Chicken or pheasant—boned, cubed, marinated and grilled on wooden skewers and served with a variety of spicy mustards—is also outstanding.

Makes 10 skewers; 10 servings

1	garlic clove, minced
1/2	medium onion, minced
2	teaspoons sugar
1/4	cup sodium-reduced soy sauce
1/4	cup dry wine
1	teaspoon grated fresh ginger
3/4	pound lean round steak, 1/2" to 3/4" thick
10	wooden skewers

Soak wooden skewers in water for half an hour to keep them from catching fire on the grill.

Combine garlic, onion, sugar, soy sauce, wine and ginger in a medium bowl.

Cut steak into thin slices and place in marinade. Marinate for at least 2 hours, stirring occasionally. Thread steak strips ribbon fashion on 6" wooden skewers.

Broil or grill, turning once, to desired degree of doneness. Serve hot.

Nutrient Analysis: 1 skewer

Exchanges: 1 very lean meat	Calories: 50	Protein: 8g	Carbohydrates: 3g
Carbohydrate Choices: 0	Fat: 1g	Cholesterol: 15mg	Sodium: 115mg

COCKTAIL MEAT BALLS

The secret to these zesty meat balls is the allspice. After meat balls are baked, they can be frozen until ready to use. Serve in YOGURT SAUCE (below) or your own particular favorite. ORIENTAL SWEET-SOUR and SALSA are popular variations.

Makes 60 meat balls; 20 servings

1	pound extra-lean ground beef, double grind if possible
1/3	cup dry bread crumbs
1/4	cup ground onion
1/3	cup skim milk
1	egg white, beaten
1/4	teaspoon salt
1/4	teaspoon ground allspice
1/8	teaspoon pepper

YOGURT SAUCE:

3	teaspoons low-sodium, beef-flavored bouillon granules
1 1/2	cups water
1	tablespoon cornstarch
1/2	cup plain low-fat yogurt

Mix beef, bread crumbs, onion, milk, egg white, salt, allspice and pepper in a medium bowl. Shape into tiny balls and place on jelly roll pan or baking sheets with sides. Bake until brown.

For sauce: Shortly before serving, dissolve bouillon granules in water. Mix cornstarch with one tablespoon yogurt and stir into remaining yogurt. Add yogurt to bouillon. Add meat balls and heat gently. (The yogurt mixture may look curdled at first, but it will become creamy as it simmers.)

Serve in a chafing dish with the YOGURT SAUCE to keep meat balls warm and moist.

Oven: 400°
Time: 12 to 15 minutes

Nutrient Analysis: 3 meat balls

Exchanges: 1 very lean meat   *Calories: 43   Protein: 5g   Carbohydrates: 3g*
Carbohydrate Choices: 0   *Fat: 1g   Cholesterol: 12mg   Sodium: 103mg*

PIZZA BITES

Makes 32 appetizers; 16 servings

8	medium tomatoes; peeled, seeded and chopped
1	cup chopped onion
2-4	tablespoons chopped green chiles
1/4	cup chopped green bell pepper
1	teaspoon ground cumin
1	teaspoon dried oregano, crushed
1	teaspoon dried basil, crushed
	Dash cayenne pepper
8	slices firm-textured bread
2	cups shredded part-skim farmer cheese

Combine tomatoes, onion, chiles and bell pepper in a medium saucepan. Cook over medium heat, stirring occasionally, until tomatoes are tender. Drain juice and stir in cumin, oregano, basil and cayenne pepper.

Remove crusts from bread and toast slices. Arrange toasted slices on large baking sheet. Divide the tomato mixture among the bread slices. Top with shredded cheese.

Place under broiler and broil until the cheese melts, 1 to 2 minutes. Cut diagonally into quarters to serve.

Nutrient Analysis: 2 appetizers
Exchanges: 2 vegetable, 1/2 fat
Carbohydrate Choices: 1

Calories: 83   Protein: 5g   Carbohydrates: 11g
Fat: 3g   Cholesterol: 6mg   Sodium: 141mg
Dietary Fiber: 1g   Calcium: 116mg

SPINACH CRÊPE WHEELS

Makes 72 appetizers; 24 servings

CRÊPES:

   3 eggs
1 1/2 cups skim milk
   1 cup all-purpose flour
  1/2 teaspoon freshly ground pepper
  1/3 cup chopped cooked spinach
        (1/2 pound fresh spinach or
        1/2 package frozen spinach)
   1 cup finely chopped green
        onions
   1 tablespoon olive oil

FILLING:

   2 (8-ounce) containers fat-free
        cream cheese at room
        temperature
   1 teaspoon freshly ground pepper
  1/2 cup finely chopped fresh basil
        or 2 tablespoons dried basil
   1 tablespoon vodka
   2 teaspoons grated lemon rind
   4 garlic cloves, minced
1 1/2 ounces dehydrated sun-dried
        tomatoes, finely chopped
  1/2 cup pine nuts, toasted

Combine the eggs, milk, flour and pepper in a blender or food processor. Process until well blended, about 1 1/2 minutes. Pour into a large bowl and whisk in the spinach and green onions.

Warm a 10" skillet over moderate heat and brush lightly with oil. Pour about 1/4 cup batter into hot pan, tilting to coat evenly. Cook until lightly browned (about 2 minutes). Flip the crêpe and cook until brown spots begin to appear on the second side, 15 to 20 seconds longer. Remove the crêpe from the pan and let cool. Repeat with remaining batter and oil to make 12 crêpes. Crêpes can be made ahead and refrigerated for 3 days or frozen for 2 weeks. Return to room temperature before filling.

For filling: Stir together the cream cheese, pepper, basil, vodka, lemon rind and garlic in a medium bowl.

Lay the crêpes, spotted side up, on a flat surface and spread each with about 2 tablespoons of the cheese mixture. Sprinkle each crêpe with 1 to 1 1/2 teaspoons each sun-dried tomatoes and pine nuts.

Roll crêpes tightly and wrap in plastic wrap. Refrigerate for at least 1 hour. (Can be prepared up to one day in advance and refrigerated until ready to slice.)

Trim the ends of each crêpe roll. Cut on the diagonal into 6 slices. Serve at room temperature.

Nutrient Analysis: 3 appetizers
Exchanges: 1 lean meat, 1/2 starch
Carbohydrate Choices: 1/2

Calories: 100   Protein: 6g   Carbohydrates: 9g
Fat: 4g   Cholesterol: 30mg   Sodium: 156mg
Dietary Fiber: 2g

SHRIMP APPLE SLICES

Makes 48 appetizers; 16 servings

2-3   red Delicious apples
2 1/2 tablespoons lemon juice
2   tablespoons minced red onion
1   tablespoon minced fresh parsley
1   tablespoon minced fresh dill or
          1 teaspoon dried dill weed
4   teaspoons prepared white
          horseradish, drained
1/8   teaspoon freshly ground pepper
2   tablespoons light mayonnaise
48   tiny frozen shrimp, thawed
      Sprigs of fresh dill (optional)

Core and mince half of 1 apple; toss with 1/2 tablespoon lemon juice. Core and cut enough of the remaining apple to make 48 1/4" slices. Toss with remaining 2 tablespoons lemon juice.

Combine the minced apple, onion, parsley, dill, horseradish, pepper and mayonnaise, in a medium bowl.

Pat apple slices dry and top with 1 teaspoon of apple-onion mixture and a shrimp. Garnish with small sprigs of fresh dill.

Nutrient Analysis: 3 appetizers
Exchanges: 1/2 fruit
Carbohydrate Choices: 0

Calories: 39   Protein: 3g   Carbohydrates: 5g
Fat: 1g   Cholesterol: 23mg   Sodium: 42mg
Dietary Fiber: 1g

MOCK SOUR CREAM

This can be substituted for sour cream in dips, spreads and dressings. For heated foods such as stroganoff, plain low-fat yogurt is the recommended substitute.

Makes 2 cups; 16 servings

2   cups low-fat cottage cheese
2   tablespoons lemon juice
1/4   cup skim milk

Process cottage cheese and lemon juice in food processor or blender until creamy.

Add skim milk to desired consistency.

To transform the "sour cream" into tasty dips, add the following ingredients and mix well.

VARIATIONS:

HORSERADISH DIP

1   tablespoon prepared horseradish

DILL DIP

2   tablespoons fresh dill or 2 teaspoons dried dill weed
2   tablespoons chopped green onion

CREAMY DIP FOR VEGETABLES

1/4   cup chopped fresh parsley
2   tablespoons chopped green onion
1   tablespoon light mayonnaise
1   teaspoon sodium-reduced Worcestershire sauce

MUSTARD DIP

1/2   teaspoon Dijon mustard
3   drops Tabasco sauce
1/2   small onion
2   tablespoons chopped fresh parsley
1   tablespoon minced chives
1-2   tablespoons skim milk, if necessary

Nutrient Analysis: 2 tablespoons	Mock Sour Cream	Horseradish	Dill	Creamy	Mustard
Exchanges:	all variations: 1/2 very lean meat				
Carbohydrate Choices:	0	0	0	0	0
Calories:	27	23	23	31	25
Protein:	4g	4g	4g	4g	4g
Carbohydrates:	2g	1g	1g	2g	2g
Fat:	1g	0g	0g	1g	0g
Cholesterol:	2 mg	1 mg	1 mg	1 mg	1 mg
Sodium:	127 mg	120 mg	118 mg	126 mg	122 mg

MOCK CREAM CHEESE

Slightly softer than regular cream cheese, MOCK CREAM CHEESE makes an excellent base for dips and spreads. The addition of a tablespoon or two of powdered sugar to each cup of cream cheese transforms it into a yummy dessert topping.

Makes 2 cups; 16 servings

1/2 (15-ounce) carton ricotta cheese
1/2 (14-ounce) carton dry curd
     cottage cheese
1/4 cup plain low-fat yogurt

Place ricotta and cottage cheese in blender or food processor bowl. Cover and blend or process at medium speed until smooth. The secret of success is blending long enough so that the ricotta loses its grainy texture.

Blend in yogurt. Cover and chill overnight to set.

Nutrient Analysis: 2 tablespoons
Exchanges: 1/2 very lean meat
Carbohydrate Choices: 0

Calories: 30   Protein: 4g   Carbohydrates: 2g
Fat: 1g   Cholesterol: 7mg   Sodium: 30mg

HERBED CHEESE DIP

Makes 3 cups; 24 servings

2 cups small curd, low-fat
    cottage cheese
1 cup light mayonnaise
1/2 cup grated onion
1/2 teaspoon garlic powder
1 teaspoon dry mustard
1/2 teaspoon celery seed
1/4 teaspoon pepper
1/4 teaspoon Tabasco sauce
1/2 teaspoon sodium-reduced
    Worcestershire sauce

Thoroughly blend cottage cheese, mayonnaise, onion, garlic powder, mustard, celery seed, pepper, Tabasco and Worcestershire.

Refrigerate for at least an hour (overnight is better) before serving.

Serve with a medley of raw vegetables, such as carrots, celery, mushrooms, green pepper, broccoli, cauliflower and cherry tomatoes. Or try lightly blanched green beans or snow peas.

Nutrient Analysis: 2 tablespoons
Exchanges: 1 fat
Carbohydrate Choices: 0

Calories: 48   Protein: 2g   Carbohydrates: 2g
Fat: 4g   Cholesterol: 4mg   Sodium: 160mg

HUMMUS BI TAHINI

A traditional recipe from the Middle East. Chickpeas are also known as garbanzo beans; tahini is a sesame-seed paste available in most food stores.

Makes 1 1/4 cups; 10 servings

1/4	cup sesame seed, toasted
1	tablespoon lemon juice
1	garlic clove, halved
1	cup chickpeas (garbanzo beans), cooked and drained
3	tablespoons plain low-fat yogurt
1/2	teaspoon ground cumin
1/4	cup fresh chopped parsley
1/8	cup sliced ripe olives (optional)
	Whole wheat pita bread

Combine sesame seed, lemon juice and garlic in a food processor or blender. Process or blend until well mixed.

Add chickpeas, yogurt and cumin. Process until smooth. Stir in parsley.

Place dip in a small bowl and garnish with sliced olives if desired. Serve with pita bread cut in triangles.

Nutrient Analysis: 2 tablespoons　　　　Calories: 51　　Protein: 3g　　Carbohydrates: 5g
Exchanges: 1 lean meat　　　　　　　　　Fat: 2g　　Cholesterol: 0mg　　Sodium: 92mg
Carbohydrate Choices: 0　　　　　　　　Dietary Fiber: 1g

GARBANZO SPREAD

Flavors will be enhanced by preparing 24 hours in advance.

Makes 3 cups; 24 servings

1/2	onion, chopped
2	tablespoons olive oil
1/2	bunch parsley, finely chopped
1	teaspoon dried basil, crushed
1/2	teaspoon dried oregano, crushed
1/4	teaspoon ground cumin
1	garlic clove, minced or 1/4 teaspoon garlic powder
	Juice of 1 lemon
3	cups cooked garbanzo beans (chickpeas), mashed
2/3	cup sesame seeds, ground (optional)
	Parsley for garnish (optional)

Sauté onion in oil until soft. Add parsley, basil, oregano, cumin and garlic, cooking just long enough to soften parsley. Thoroughly mix onion-herb mixture with lemon juice, garbanzo beans and sesame seeds.

Pack into a bowl and chill overnight. Unmold onto serving plate and garnish with parsley. Serve with crackers or celery sticks.

Nutrient Analysis: 2 tablespoons
Exchanges: 1 lean meat
Carbohydrate Choices: 0

Calories: 60   Protein: 3 g   Carbohydrates: 5 g
Fat: 3 g   Cholesterol: 0 mg   Sodium: 93 mg
Dietary Fiber: 2 g

SALMON YOGURT DIP

Makes 1 1/2 cups; 12 servings

1	(15-ounce) can salmon*, drained
1/4	cup finely chopped onions
1/2	teaspoon prepared mustard
1	teaspoon sodium-reduced Worcestershire sauce
8	ounces plain low-fat yogurt

Blend salmon, onions, mustard and Worcestershire in a blender on low speed. Stir in yogurt. Do not overblend or dip may become watery. Serve chilled.

* Substitute a can of clams or shrimp for the salmon for a tasty variation.

Nutrient Analysis: 2 tablespoons
Exchanges: 1 1/2 lean meat
Carbohydrate Choices: 0

Calories: 65   Protein: 9 g   Carbohydrates: 2 g
Fat: 2 g   Cholesterol: 15 mg   Sodium: 45 mg
Calcium: 122 mg   Omega-3: 0.43 g

SPINACH DIP

Everybody's favorite dip served in a "bread bowl".

Makes 3 cups; 12 servings

1 (10-ounce) package frozen
    chopped spinach
1/4 cup finely chopped onion
1/4 cup chopped green pepper
1/4 teaspoon garlic powder
1 cup plain low-fat yogurt
1 cup small curd cottage cheese or
    8-ounce package light cream
    cheese
1 (8-ounce) can sliced water
    chestnuts, drained
1 round loaf of bread, uncut

Thaw and drain spinach well. Combine spinach, onion, green pepper, garlic powder, yogurt, cottage cheese or cream cheese and water chestnuts. Mix well and chill.

Slice off top of bread and scoop out center. Cut bread from center into cubes. Fill center of bread with dip and surround with bread cubes and unsalted crackers.

Nutrient Analysis: 4 tablespoons (dip)
Exchanges: 1 vegetable
Carbohydrate Choices: 1/2

Calories: 44   Protein: 4g   Carbohydrates: 6g
Fat: 1g   Cholesterol: 2mg   Sodium: 126mg
Dietary Fiber: 2g

FRUIT WARMER

It makes a good cooler, too!

Makes 4 cups; 4 servings

2 cups unsweetened orange juice
1 cup low-calorie cranberry juice
    cocktail
1 cup unsweetened pineapple
    juice
1 tablespoon lemon juice
1 cup water
    Fresh mint leaves (optional)

Combine all fruit juices and water in a saucepan. Heat over medium heat until mixture comes to a boil. Reduce heat and simmer 3 to 5 minutes. Serve hot garnished with mint leaves.

Nutrient Analysis: 1 cup
Exchanges: 1 1/2 fruit
Carbohydrate Choices: 1 1/2

Calories: 104   Protein: 0g   Carbohydrates: 25g
Fat: 0g   Cholesterol: 0mg   Sodium: 15mg

BAKED EGGPLANT DIP

Eggplant dip or "Poor Man's Caviar" can be made ahead of serving time. It will keep several days in the refrigerator. Tahini (sesame seed) paste is available in most food stores.

Makes 2 cups; 16 servings

1	large eggplant
1/2	garlic clove, minced
1/4	cup tahini paste
1/4	cup lemon juice
1/2	tablespoon olive oil
1/8	teaspoon salt
1/4	teaspoon white pepper
1	tablespoon finely chopped parsley (optional)

Wash and dry eggplant. Leave on skin and stem. Pierce with fork several times. Place on baking sheet and bake at 350° for 1 hour. Cool slightly. Under cold running water, remove skin and stem. Drain well.

Mash eggplant with a fork. Add garlic, tahini paste, lemon juice, olive oil, salt and pepper. Mix until well blended.

Place in serving bowl and garnish with chopped parsley.

Nutrient Analysis: 2 tablespoons
Exchanges: 1/2 fat
Carbohydrate Choices: 0

Calories: 35	*Protein: 1g*	*Carbohydrates: 3g*
Fat: 2g	*Cholesterol: 0mg*	*Sodium: 21mg*
Dietary Fiber: 1g		

CHRISTMAS CRANBERRY FLOAT

To trim calories, substitute club soda for ginger ale.

Makes 10 cups; 10 servings

6	cups low-calorie cranberry juice cocktail, chilled
1	quart diet ginger ale or club soda, chilled
1	pint lemon, pineapple, orange or lime sherbet

Combine cranberry juice and ginger ale in a 4-quart pitcher or punch bowl. Just before serving, add sherbet and ice as desired. For a festive touch, float scoops of sherbet on top. Serve immediately.

Nutrient Analysis: 1 cup with sherbet
Exchanges: 1 carbohydrate
Carbohydrate Choices: 1

Calories: 68	*Protein: 0g*	*Carbohydrates: 16g*
Fat: 1g	*Cholesterol: 2mg*	*Sodium: 42mg*

MULLED CIDER

Mulled—heated and spiced—drinks are a great warm up!

Makes 9 cups; 9 servings

6 cups apple cider
2 2/3 cups water
3 tablespoons lemon juice
2 cinnamon sticks
1/2 teaspoon whole cloves
1/2 teaspoon whole allspice
Orange or lemon slices for
garnish (optional);
Cinnamon sticks for stirrers
(optional)

Simmer cider, water, lemon juice and spices together in a large saucepan for 10 to 15 minutes. Strain and serve hot, garnished with a fruit slice and a cinnamon stick.

WASSAIL

Wassail is a beverage used to toast health and good will! Traditionally, it was made with wine or ale spiced with apple and sugar.

Makes 9 cups; 9 servings

2 3/4 cups pineapple juice

Substitute pineapple juice for the water in MULLED CIDER recipe.

Nutrient Analysis: 1 cup	Mulled Cider	Wassail
Exchanges:	1 1/4 fruit	2 fruit
Carbohydrate Choices:	1	2
Calories:	81	124
Protein:	0g	0g
Carbohydrates:	20g	31g
Fat:	0g	0g
Cholesterol:	0mg	0mg
Sodium:	17mg	17mg

ENERGY NOG

Energy packed with vitamins and minerals.

Makes 3 cups; 3 servings

1   cup plain low-fat yogurt
2/3 cup orange juice
1/2 cup cooked pitted dried plums,
      drained
1   tablespoon wheat germ
8   ice cubes
    Nutmeg

Combine yogurt, orange juice, dried plums and wheat germ in a blender. Blend until smooth.

Add ice cubes and blend again until smooth. Pour into glasses and sprinkle with nutmeg. Serve immediately.

Nutrient Analysis: 1 cup
Exchanges: 1 skim milk, 1 fruit
Carbohydrate Choices: 2

Calories: 161   Protein: 6g   Carbohydrates: 32g
Fat: 1g   Cholesterol: 5mg   Sodium: 73mg
Dietary Fiber: 2g   Calcium: 134mg

RASPBERRY PUNCH

Deliciously refreshing! The word "punch" comes from the East Indian word "puny" meaning five, so-called for its five ingredients: spirit, citrus juice, spices, tea and water. Introduced into England from Spain, it was also called "contradiction" because it used spirit to make it strong, water to make it weak, lemon to make it sour and sugar to make it sweet.

Makes 3 quarts; 12 servings

20 ounces frozen IQF,
      unsweetened raspberries or
      strawberriess
2   cups unsweetened orange juice
1   (6-ounce) can frozen lemonade
4   cans water
    Ice
1   quart club soda

Thaw raspberries or strawberries and mash with a fork or potato masher. Mix berries with orange juice, lemonade and water.

Just before serving, pour fruit mixture over ice and add club soda.

Nutrient Analysis: 1 cup
Exchanges: 1 fruit
Carbohydrate Choices: 1

Calories: 71   Protein: 0g   Carbohydrates: 18g
Fat: 0g   Cholesterol: 0mg   Sodium: 22mg
Dietary Fiber: 2g   Calcium: 88mg

CITRUS REFRESHER

Makes 4 quarts; 16 servings

4 cups fresh orange juice
4 cups unsweetened pineapple
    juice
2 cups low-calorie cranberry juice
    cocktail
2 oranges, sliced and cut into
    quarters
1 lemon, sliced and cut into
    halves
1 lime, sliced
2 cups crushed ice
2 cups club soda

Combine orange, pineapple and cranberry juice. Prepare oranges, lemon and lime; add to juice. Chill. Just before serving, add ice and club soda.

Nutrient Analysis: 1 cup   *Calories: 81*   *Protein: 0g*   *Carbohydrates: 20g*
Exchanges: 1 1/4 fruit   *Fat: 0g*   *Cholesterol: 0mg*   *Sodium: 8mg*
Carbohydrate Choices: 1   *Dietary Fiber: 1g*

TOMATO JUICE COCKTAIL

Makes 6 cups; 6 servings

1 (46-ounce) can low-sodium
    tomato juice
2 teaspoons wine vinegar
1/4 teaspoon sugar
1 bay leaf
1/4 teaspoon parsley flakes, crushed
1/4 teaspoon dried basil, crushed
1/4 teaspoon dried chervil, crushed
1/2 teaspoon sodium-reduced
    Worcestershire sauce

Combine tomato juice, vinegar, sugar, bay leaf, parsley, basil, chervil and Worcestershire in a large saucepan. Bring to a boil. Reduce heat, simmer 10 minutes. Serve hot or cold.

Nutrient Analysis: 1 cup   *Calories: 38*   *Protein: 2g*   *Carbohydrates: 9g*
Exchanges: 2 vegetable   *Fat: 0g*   *Cholesterol: 0mg*   *Sodium: 22mg*
Carbohydrate Choices: 1/2   *Dietary Fiber: 2g*

INSTANT COCOA MIX

For cocoa-mocha... add hot coffee instead of water to cocoa mix.

Makes 16 cups; 16 servings

4   cups nonfat dry milk powder
1   cup confectioner's sugar
3/4 cup unsweetened cocoa powder

Mix together milk powder, sugar and cocoa. Place 1/3 cup cocoa mix in a cup and stir in a small amount of warm water to make paste. Fill cup with boiling water. Stir and serve.

Store cocoa mix in airtight container.

Nutrient Analysis: 1/3 cup mix in water
Exchanges: 1 skim milk
Carbohydrate Choices: 1

Calories: 99   Protein: 7g   Carbohydrates: 18g
Fat: 1g   Cholesterol: 3mg   Sodium: 94mg
Dietary Fiber: 1g   Calcium: 215mg

BERRY MILKSHAKE

Makes 4 cups; 4 servings

1   cup frozen IQF, unsweetened
    strawberries
1   cup frozen IQF , unsweetened
    raspberries
1   cup cold skim milk
1   cup plain low-fat yogurt
4   teaspoons powdered egg white,*
    or equivalent of 2 egg whites
1/4 cup honey
1/2 teaspoon vanilla
    Strawberries or raspberries for
    garnish, (optional)

* We suggest using a commercial pasteurized egg product to avoid the possibility of a foodborne illness from eating raw egg products.

Place strawberries, raspberries and 1/2 cup milk in blender. Blend on high speed 1 minute or until smooth. Add remaining milk, yogurt, powdered egg white, honey and vanilla. Blend until frothy.

Serve immediately in tall, chilled glasses. Garnish with berries.

Nutrient Analysis: 1 cup
Exchanges: 1 skim milk, 1 1/2 fruit
Carbohydrate Choices: 2 1/2

Calories: 188   Protein: 9g   Carbohydrates: 39g
Fat: 1g   Cholesterol: 5mg   Sodium: 85mg
Dietary Fiber: 3g   Calcium: 273mg

BREADS

Here is bread, which strengthens man's heart, and therefore called the staff of life.

Matthew Henry

BREADS

Breads can help us increase our daily fiber intake

Recent research indicates that we need to increase our intake of complex carbohydrates and fiber. This section is especially valuable in helping you attain this goal. Choosing whole-grain recipes for making breads, muffins, coffee cakes, waffles and pancakes is a big step toward boosting complex carbohydrates and dietary fiber. A diet high in all types of fiber may reduce the risk of colon-rectal cancers and may also provide a cardiovascular bonus by reducing serum cholesterol levels.

Whole-grain breads and cereals are also recommended in reducing diets. The popular notion that breads are fattening and should be eliminated from a reducing diet has been disproven. In one research study (American J. Clin. Nutr. 32:1703, 1979) overweight college-age men on a restricted calorie diet consumed 12 slices of high-fiber bread each day. These men lost 19 pounds in 8 weeks. A control group ate the same diet except white enriched bread was substituted for the high-fiber bread, and lost only 14 pounds in the same time period. This study is the bearer of good news for two reasons. First, both groups lost weight while eating 12 slices of bread a day. Second, those who ate high-fiber bread also reduced their calorie intake. So, the bottom line is— don't omit bread if concerned about weight control.

The availability of new hybrid and high-protein flours has made it almost possible for man to "live by bread alone." As long as we use whole grains and include nuts or seeds and bits of fruit along with egg white and low-fat milk, breads truly are the "staff of life." Whole-grain breads can provide ample protein, complex carbohydrates, many vitamins and minerals and liberal amounts of fiber while adding little fat or sodium.

Breads provide protein and little fat or cholesterol

To substitute whole wheat flour for white flour, follow these guidelines. For each cup of all-purpose flour, use one of the following:
- 1 cup whole wheat flour minus 2 tablespoons
- 1/2 cup white flour + 1/2 cup whole wheat flour
- 3/4 cup white flour + 1/4 cup wheat germ and/or bran

These flour combinations are equivalent to 1 cup wheat flour:
- 1/2 cup rye flour + 1/3 cup potato flour
- 1/3 cup rye flour + 5/8 cup rice flour
- 1 cup soy flour + 3/4 cup potato flour
- 5/8 cup rice flour + 1/3 cup potato flour
- 1/2 cup cornstarch + 1/2 cup rye flour
- 1/2 cup cornstarch + 1/2 cup potato flour

Flour substitutes for 1 cup measure

Various flours in the following quantities can be substituted for 1 cup of wheat flour:

- 1 cup corn flour
- 3/4 cup coarse cornmeal
- 3/4 cup cornstarch
- 1 cup barley
- 7/8 cup buckwheat
- 1/2 cup ground nuts or seeds
- 5/8 cup potato flour
- 3/4 cup potato starch
- 7/8 cup rice flour
- 1 1/4 cups rye flour
- 3/4 cup soybean flour or other bean flour
- 1 cup tapioca flour
- 1 cup millet
- 1 1/3 cups ground rolled oats
- 1 1/8 cups oat flour

Flour substitutes for 1 tablespoon measure

To replace 1 tablespoon wheat flour as a thickener for sauces, gravies and puddings, use one of the following:

- 1/2 tablespoon agar
- 1/2 tablespoon arrowroot
- 1 tablespoon bean flour
- 1/2 tablespoon cornstarch
- 1/2 tablespoon guar gum
- 1/2 tablespoon plain gelatin
- 1/2 tablespoon potato starch
- 1 tablespoon rice flour (brown, white, sweet rice)
- 2 tablespoons uncooked rice
- 1 1/2 tablespoons tapioca flour
- 2 teaspoons quick-cooking tapioca
- 1 teaspoon Xanthan gum

PECAN OAT MUFFINS

A moist, delicately flavored muffin; that's also sugar-free!

Makes 18 muffins; 18 servings

3/4	cup finely chopped pecans
1	cup rolled oats
1	cup all-purpose flour
1/2	cup whole wheat flour
1/2	teaspoon baking soda
1/2	teaspoon baking powder
3	tablespoons tub margarine
3	tablespoons honey
1	cup sour skim milk* or buttermilk
1	egg
1/4	teaspoon vanilla

* To sour milk, place 1 tablespoon lemon juice or mild vinegar in a 1 cup measure. Add skim milk to make 1 cup.

Mix and dry-roast pecans and oats by stirring in heavy skillet over low heat for about 10 minutes or toast on a baking sheet in a 200° oven for 10 minutes.

Sift together flours, soda and baking powder. Stir in dry-roasted pecans and oats. Make a well in center of dry ingredients.

Melt margarine and honey together. Beat honey mixture into sour milk or buttermilk, add the egg and vanilla until well blended. Pour into well made in the dry ingredients and mix only until moistened.

Fill nonstick-sprayed or paper-lined muffin tins two-thirds full. Bake. Remove muffins from tins and cool on wire rack. Serve warm or at room temperature.

Oven: 350°
Time: 20 to 25 minutes

Nutrient Analysis: 1 muffin   Calories: 122   Protein: 3 g   Carbohydrates: 15 g
Exchanges: 1 starch, 1 fat   Fat: 6 g   Cholesterol: 12 mg   Sodium: 74 mg
Carbohydrate Choices: 1   Dietary Fiber: 1 g

BANANA BRAN MUFFINS

An excellent source of fiber with no added sugar.

Makes 24 muffins; 24 servings

2	cups whole wheat flour
1 3/4	cups unprocessed bran
1	tablespoon baking soda
1 3/4	cups sour skim milk* or buttermilk
1	cup mashed ripe bananas
1	egg
3/4	cup apple juice concentrate
1/4	cup tub margarine, melted
2	egg whites
1/4	cup chopped dates
1/4	cup chopped nuts

To sour milk, place 2 tablespoons lemon juice or mild vinegar in a 2 cup measure. Add milk to make 1 3/4 cups.

Combine flour, bran and baking soda.

Mix together sour skim milk or buttermilk, bananas, egg, apple juice concentrate and melted margarine. Stir into dry ingredients.

Beat egg whites until stiff. Fold beaten egg whites, dates, and nuts into mixture. Fill nonstick-sprayed or paper lined muffin tins two-thirds full. Bake. Remove muffins from tins and cool on wire rack. Serve warm or at room temperature.

Oven: 375°
Time: 15 to 20 minutes

Nutrient Analysis: 1 muffin
Exchanges: 1 starch, 1/2 fat
Carbohydrate Choices: 1

Calories: 106   Protein: 3g   Carbohydrates: 17g
Fat: 3g   Cholesterol: 9mg   Sodium: 193mg
Dietary Fiber: 3g

BLUEBERRY MUFFINS

Makes 12 muffins; 12 servings

1 cup all-purpose flour
1 cup whole wheat flour
1/2 cup plus 1/2 tablespoon sugar
1 tablespoon baking powder
1/2 teaspoon cinnamon
1 1/2 to 2 cups fresh or unthawed frozen blueberries
1/4 cup tub margarine, melted
1/2 cup skim milk
1 egg
1 egg white
1/2 teaspoon vanilla

Combine flours, 1/2 cup sugar, baking powder and cinnamon in a medium mixing bowl.

In a separate bowl, toss blueberries with 1 tablespoon of the flour mixture and set aside.

After margarine has cooled slightly, stir in milk, egg, egg white and vanilla. Add mixture to dry ingredients and stir until well-moistened. Stir in berries.

Spoon batter into nonstick-sprayed muffin tins. Sprinkle tops with remaining 1/2 tablespoon sugar. Bake until golden. Let muffins stand for 5 minutes before removing from tins. Serve warm or at room temperature.

Oven: 400°
Time: 20 minutes

Nutrient Analysis: 1 muffin
Exchanges: 1 1/2 starch, 1 fat
Carbohydrate Choices: 2

Calories: 159   Protein: 4g   Carbohydrates: 27g
Fat: 4g   Cholesterol: 18mg   Sodium: 150mg
Dietary Fiber: 2g

CARROT BRAN MUFFINS

Makes 12 muffins; 12 servings

1	cup 40% bran flakes
3/4	cup skim milk
2	cups finely shredded carrots
1	cup whole wheat flour
1	teaspoon baking powder
1/2	teaspoon baking soda
1/4 to 1/2	teaspoon cinnamon
2	tablespoons brown sugar
2	tablespoons extra-light olive oil
1	tablespoon lemon juice
1	egg, slightly beaten

Combine bran flakes, milk, and carrots; let stand 5 minutes.

Combine flour, baking powder, soda and cinnamon.

Stir sugar, oil, lemon juice and egg into carrot mixture. Add liquid mixture to flour mixture stirring until moistened.

Fill nonstick-sprayed or paper-lined muffin tins half full. Bake. Remove from tins and cool on wire rack. Serve warm or at room temperature.

Oven: 400°
Time: 20 to 25 minutes

Nutrient Analysis: 1 muffin
Exchanges: 1 starch, 1/2 fat
Carbohydrate Choices: 1

Calories: 95   Protein: 3g   Carbohydrates: 15g
Fat: 3g   Cholesterol: 18mg   Sodium: 145mg
Dietary Fiber: 2g

VEGETABLE CORNMEAL MUFFINS

Using stone-ground cornmeal, makes a tastier muffin.

Makes 12 muffins; 12 servings

1	cup all-purpose flour
1/2	cup cornmeal
1	tablespoon sugar
1	tablespoon baking powder
3/4	teaspoon Italian seasoning
1/8	teaspoon garlic powder
2	eggs, beaten
1	tablespoon extra-light olive oil
1/3	cup skim milk
1/2	cup frozen whole kernel corn
1/3	cup chopped green pepper
1/4	cup finely chopped onion

Combine flour, cornmeal, sugar, baking powder, Italian seasoning and garlic powder.

Mix beaten eggs, oil and milk; stir into dry ingredients. Stir in corn, green pepper and onion.

Bake in nonstick-sprayed or paper-lined muffin tins. Remove from tins and serve hot.

Oven: 400°
Time: 20 to 25 minutes

Nutrient Analysis: 1 muffin
Exchanges: 1 starch
Carbohydrate Choices: 1

Calories: 93   Protein: 3g   Carbohydrates: 16g
Fat: 2g   Cholesterol: 36mg   Sodium: 129mg
Dietary Fiber: 1g

ROLLED BISCUITS

This very light, flaky biscuit was a Grand Prize Winner in the Heart's Delight Recipe Contest.

Makes 18 biscuits; 18 servings

1 1/2	cups all-purpose flour
1/2	cup whole wheat flour
1	tablespoon baking powder
1/3	cup vegetable oil
1/2	cup skim milk
1/4	cup buttermilk

Sift together flours and baking powder. Add oil and blend with a fork until mixture looks like coarse crumbs. Add skim milk and buttermilk and stir.

Knead gently on a floured board 6 to 8 times. Roll out to 1/2" thick. Cut biscuits in 2" rounds. Bake biscuits on ungreased baking sheet. Serve hot with honey.

Oven: 450°
Time: 10 to 12 minutes

Nutrient Analysis: 1 biscuit
Exchanges: 1/2 starch, 1 fat
Carbohydrate Choices: 1/2

Calories: 84   Protein: 2g   Carbohydrates: 10g
Fat: 4g   Cholesterol: 0mg   Sodium: 74mg
Dietary Fiber: 1g

APPLE CINNAMON PANCAKES

Top pancakes with our tasty, low-calorie FRUIT TOPPING, (see page 391) instead of the overly-sweet commercial syrups.

Makes 16 pancakes; 8 servings

1	cup all-purpose flour
1/2	cup whole wheat flour
2	tablespoons sugar
1	tablespoon baking powder
1	teaspoon cinnamon
3	egg whites, beaten
3/4	cup skim milk
2	tablespoons tub margarine, melted
1	cup unsweetened applesauce

Mix together flours, sugar, baking powder and cinnamon.

Combine the beaten egg whites, milk, margarine and applesauce and stir into the flour mixture just until moistened.

Pour batter from pitcher or large spoon onto hot griddle. When pancakes are puffed and full of bubbles, turn and brown other side.

Griddle: 350°

Nutrient Analysis: 2 pancakes
Exchanges: 1 1/2 starch, 1/2 fat
Carbohydrate Choices: 1 1/2

Calories: 142   Protein: 5 g   Carbohydrates: 25 g
Fat: 3 g   Cholesterol: 1 mg   Sodium: 209 mg
Dietary Fiber: 2 g   Calcium: 118 g

WHOLE WHEAT WAFFLES

Tender and light and thoroughly delicious! Top waffles with FRUIT TOPPING (see page 391).

Makes 10 waffles; 10 servings

1 1/2	cups whole wheat flour
1/4	cup all-purpose flour
2	teaspoons baking powder
2	eggs, separated
1 1/2	cups skim milk
3	tablespoons extra-light olive oil
2	tablespoons honey

Heat waffle iron while making batter. Stir together flours and baking powder.

Beat egg yolks until they are lemon colored. Add milk, oil and honey. Blend well and stir into the dry ingredients.

Beat egg whites until stiff, and fold into batter. Pour batter onto lightly oiled, hot waffle iron. Bake until steaming stops. Lift waffle from iron with a fork.

Nutrient Analysis: 1 waffle
Exchanges: 1 1/2 starch, 1 fat
Carbohydrate Choices: 1 1/2

Calories: 152   Protein: 6 g   Carbohydrates: 21 g
Fat: 6 g   Cholesterol: 43 mg   Sodium: 115 mg
Dietary Fiber: 2 g   Calcium: 97 g

CORN BREAD

Makes 8 x 8" pan; 16 servings

2   egg whites
1/4 cup plain low-fat yogurt
3/4 cup skim milk
3   tablespoons honey
1   cup yellow cornmeal
1/4 cup all-purpose flour
3/4 cup whole wheat flour
2   teaspoons baking powder
1/2 teaspoon baking soda
3   tablespoons melted tub
       margarine
1   cup shredded carrots (optional)

Beat together egg whites, yogurt, milk and honey.

Mix together cornmeal, flours, baking powder and soda in a separate bowl.

Combine liquid ingredients, dry ingredients, melted margarine and carrots (if desired). Stir just enough to blend. Over-stirring will make bread tough. Spread into a nonstick-sprayed 8 x 8" pan. Bake. Serve hot.

Oven: 425°
Time: 20 minutes

MEXICORN BREAD VARIATION

1   teaspoon SEASONING BLEND
       #7, *(page 379)*
1   cup whole kernel corn, frozen or
       sodium-reduced canned
1   tablespoon chopped pimiento
1   tablespoon finely diced sweet or
       hot green pepper

Follow the basic recipe for CORN BREAD, decreasing the honey to 1 tablespoon and omitting the carrots. Add the ingredients in this recipe to the dry ingredients in the above method. Stir just enough to blend. Continue following the directions, oven temperature and baking time as above.

Nutrient Analysis: 1 serving	*Corn Bread*	*Mexicorn Bread*
Exchanges:	*1 starch, 1/2 fat*	*1 starch, 1/2 fat*
Carbohydrate Choices:	*1*	*1*
Calories:	*95*	*108*
Protein:	*3g*	*3g*
Carbohydrates:	*17g*	*19g*
Fat:	*3g*	*3g*
Cholesterol:	*0mg*	*0mg*
Sodium:	*124mg*	*146mg*
Dietary Fiber:	*1g*	*2g*

CORN ZEPHYRS

A very light corn puff that's also sugar free!

Makes 16 corn puffs; 8 servings

1   cup stone-ground white
     cornmeal
1   cup cold water
1/2   teaspoon salt
3   cups boiling water
1   tablespoon tub margarine
4   egg whites

Mix cornmeal, cold water and salt. Add slowly to boiling water, whisking constantly. Cook over low heat, stirring frequently, for 30 minutes. Remove from heat and lightly oil top with margarine. Let cool.

Whip egg whites until stiff and fold into cooled cornmeal mixture. Spoon onto nonstick-sprayed baking sheet. Bake. Remove immediately from baking pan. Serve hot.

Oven: 350°
Time: 25 to 30 minutes

Nutrient Analysis: 2 corn puffs
Exchanges: 1 starch
Carbohydrate Choices: 1

Calories: 81   Protein: 3g   Carbohydrates: 12g
Fat: 2g   Cholesterol: 0mg   Sodium: 185mg
Dietary Fiber: 2g

SCRAPPLE

There are many varieties of scrapple but our favorite has the addition of cooked pork stripped from neck bones. Scrapple freezes well. Slice when cold and freeze in individual portions.

Makes 9 x 5" pan; 12 servings

1-2   **pounds pork neck bones**
1/2   **large onion, sliced**
2   **celery ribs with leaves**
4-5   **whole peppercorns**
  Water to cover
1   **cup cornmeal**
1   **cup cold water**
1/2   **teaspoon salt**
1/2   **teaspoon freshly grated nutmeg**
4   **cups boiling liquid (reserved neck bone liquid plus water)**

Cover neck bones with water in a saucepan. Add onion, celery and peppercorns and bring to a boil. Reduce heat and simmer until meat falls from bones (about 2 hours). Strain and refrigerate reserved liquid until fat congeals on top. Remove fat and discard. Pick meat from bones and chop finely.

Mix cornmeal, cold water, salt and nutmeg. Add gradually, stirring constantly, to 4 cups of boiling liquid (reserved meat liquid plus water). Continue stirring and cook over low heat until thickened (about 15 minutes). Cool to lukewarm, add pork and turn into a loaf pan that has been rinsed in cold water. Cover with a sheet of wax paper and chill well.

Slice cold mush into 1/2" slices and sauté on both sides very slowly (30 to 45 minutes) in 1 to 2 tablespoons margarine. If you try to rush it, the slices will fall apart. Serve with warm syrup.

Nutrient Analysis: 1 slice
Exchanges: 1/2 starch
Carbohydrate Choices: 1/2

Calories: 61   Protein: 3g   Carbohydrates: 10g
Fat: 1g   Cholesterol: 5mg   Sodium: 111mg
Dietary Fiber: 1g

APPLESAUCE NUT BREAD

Very dense and moist. This flavorful loaf is white in color rather than the golden or brown of many of the other quick bread loaves.

Makes 9 x 5" loaf pan; 20 servings

1/2	cup granulated sugar
1	cup unsweetened applesauce
1/3	cup canola oil
4	egg whites or egg substitute equal to 2 eggs
3	tablespoons skim milk
2	cups sifted all-purpose flour
1	teaspoon baking powder
1/2	teaspoon cinnamon
1/2	teaspoon nutmeg
3/4	cup chopped pecans

TOPPING:

1/4	cup brown sugar
1/2	teaspoon cinnamon
1/4	cup chopped pecans

Combine sugar, applesauce, oil, egg whites and milk in a large mixing bowl. Mix together thoroughly. Set aside.

Sift together the flour, baking powder, cinnamon and nutmeg. Beat dry ingredients into the applesauce mixture until well-combined. Stir in the pecans.

Pour the batter into a nonstick-sprayed 9 x 5" loaf pan.

For topping: Combine the brown sugar, cinnamon and pecans. Sprinkle evenly over the batter and bake. Cap loosely with foil after the first 30 minutes of baking. When done (a toothpick inserted near the center should come out clean and dry), remove the bread from the pan and cool on a rack.

Oven: 350°
Time: 60 minutes

Nutrient Analysis: 1 slice
Exchanges: 1 starch, 1 1/2 fat
Carbohydrate Choices: 1

Calories: 154   Protein: 3g   Carbohydrates: 19g
Fat: 8g   Cholesterol: 0mg   Sodium: 34mg
Dietary Fiber: 1g

CRANBERRY BREAD

1 cup all-purpose flour
1 cup whole wheat flour
1/2 cup brown sugar
1 1/2 teaspoons baking powder
1/2 teaspoon baking soda
1/4 teaspoon cinnamon
1/4 teaspoon ground cloves
    Grated rind of 1 orange
3/4 cup orange juice
2 egg whites or egg substitute
    equal to 1 egg
1/4 cup tub margarine, melted
1 cup firm, fresh cranberries
1/2 cup chopped nuts (walnuts, pecans)

Makes 9 x 5" loaf pan; 20 servings

Sift together flours, sugar, baking powder, baking soda, cinnamon and cloves. Set aside.

Lightly beat together orange rind, orange juice, egg whites and melted margarine. Stir the liquid ingredients into the dry ingredients.

Coarsely chop the cranberries and add them along with the chopped nuts to the batter. Mix well.

Pour into a nonstick-sprayed loaf pan. Bake until a toothpick inserted near the center comes out clean and dry. Cool on wire rack and remove from pan. Wrap tightly to store.

Oven: 350°
Time: 60 minutes

Nutrient Analysis: 1 slice
Exchanges: 1 starch, 1 fat
Carbohydrate Choices: 1

Calories: 113   Protein: 2g   Carbohydrates: 17g
Fat: 4g   Cholesterol: 0mg   Sodium: 89mg
Dietary Fiber: 1g   Omega-3: 0.27g

MOLASSES BROWN BREAD

An old-fashioned brown bread with plump raisins. A bonus—no sugar added!

Makes 9 x 5" loaf pan; 16 servings

1/2	cup whole wheat flour
1/2	cup all-purpose flour
1	teaspoon baking soda
1/2	teaspoon cinnamon
1	egg
1	cup 100% bran cereal
1/2	cup seedless raisins
2	tablespoons extra-light olive oil
1/3	cup molasses
3/4	cup very hot water

Sift together flours, soda and cinnamon. Set aside.

Beat egg in a large mixing bowl until foamy. Mix in cereal, raisins, oil, molasses and water. Add dry ingredients stirring only until combined.

Spread evenly in a nonstick-sprayed loaf pan. Bake until toothpick inserted near center comes out clean and dry. Remove from pan or tins; slice and serve hot.

Oven: 350°
Time: 45 minutes

Nutrient Analysis: 1 slice   Calories: 92   Protein: 2g   Carbohydrates: 18g
Exchanges: 1 starch   Fat: 2g   Cholesterol: 13mg   Sodium: 114mg
Carbohydrate Choices: 1   Dietary Fiber: 2g

LEMON BREAD

Light, tasty and moist!

Makes 9 x 5" loaf pan; 20 servings

1	cup all-purpose flour
1/2	cup whole wheat flour
2	teaspoons baking powder
2	tablespoons tub margarine
3/4	cup granulated sugar
1	egg
1	egg white
1/2	cup skim milk
	Grated rind of 1 lemon
1/2	cup chopped nuts

GLAZE:

	Juice of one lemon
1	tablespoon confectioners' sugar

Sift together flours and baking powder.

Cream together margarine and sugar. Stir in egg, egg white, milk and lemon rind.

Mix thoroughly with dry ingredients. Stir in chopped nuts.

Pour into nonstick-sprayed loaf pan and let stand for 20 minutes. Bake until toothpick inserted near center comes out clean and dry.

For glaze: Blend together lemon juice and confectioners' sugar. Brush or drizzle hot loaf with lemon juice and powdered sugar glaze. Cool on wire rack and remove from pan.

Oven: 350°
Time: 45-50 minutes (Check after 40 minutes. Don't over bake.)

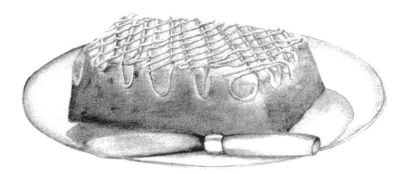

Nutrient Analysis: 1 slice
Exchanges: 1 starch, 1/2 fat
Carbohydrate Choices: 1

Calories: 100   Protein: 2g   Carbohydratess: 16 g
Fat: 3g   Cholesterol: 11 mg   Sodium: 59 mg
Dietary Fiber: 1g   Omega-3: 0.27g

ORANGE BREAD

**Makes two 8 1/2 x 4 1/2" loaf pans;
36 servings (18 slices a loaf)**

1 1/2   cups whole wheat flour
1 1/2   cups all-purpose flour
  3/4   cup sugar
  1-2   tablespoons grated orange peel
   2   teaspoons baking powder
  3/4   cup orange juice
  1/2   cup skim milk
  1/2   cup canola oil
   2   egg whites or 1 egg, slightly
       beaten
  1/2   cup chopped nuts (optional)

TOPPING:
   1   tablespoon sugar
  1/2   teaspoon cinnamon

Mix flours, sugar, orange peel and baking powder.

Stir together juice, milk, oil and egg. Add to dry ingredients and stir. Stir in nuts.

Pour into two 8 1/2 x 4 1/2" nonstick-sprayed loaf pans. Sprinkle with sugar and cinnamon mixture. Bake until a toothpick inserted towards the middle comes out clean and dry.

Oven: 350°
Time: 50 minutes

Nutrient Analysis: 1 slice
Exchanges: 1 starch, 1/2 fat
Carbohydrate Choices: 1

Calories: 96   Protein: 2g   Carbohydrates: 13g
Fat: 4g   Cholesterol: 0mg   Sodium: 28mg
Dietary Fiber: 1g

PUMPKIN BREAD

Pureed squash can be substituted for the pumpkin.

**Makes two 9 x 5" loaf pans; 40 servings
(20 slices a loaf)**

2	cups canned or cooked, pureed pumpkin
2	cups sugar
1	cup canola oil
2/3	cup water
2	eggs
2	egg whites
2	cups whole wheat flour
1 1/2	cups all-purpose flour
2	teaspoons baking soda
1 1/2	teaspoons nutmeg
1/2	teaspoon ginger
1 1/2	teaspoons cinnamon

Blend pumpkin, sugar, oil, water, eggs and egg whites in a large bowl.

Add flours, soda, nutmeg, ginger and cinnamon. Blend at low speed until moistened, then beat 1 minute at medium speed.

Pour batter into two nonstick-sprayed and floured (bottom only) loaf pans. Bake until toothpick inserted near center comes out clean. Cool 5 minutes and remove from pan. Cool completely on wire rack.

Oven: 350°
Time: 60 to 75 minutes

Nutrient Analysis: 1 slice
Exchanges: 1 starch, 1 fat
Carbohydrate Choices: 1

Calories: 135   Protein: 2g   Carbohydrates: 19g
Fat: 6g   Cholesterol: 11mg   Sodium: 69mg
Dietary Fiber: 1g

CRANBERRY COFFEE CAKE

Makes 8 x 8" baking pan; 16 servings

1 1/2 cups all-purpose flour
1/2 cup whole wheat flour
1 tablespoon baking powder
1/2 cup sugar
5 tablespoons tub margarine
2 egg whites
1/2 cup skim milk
1 cup fresh cranberries, chopped
    coarsely

TOPPING:

1/4 cup flour
1/4 cup sugar
2 tablespoons tub margarine

Combine flours, baking powder, and sugar. Cut in margarine with a pastry blender until mixture looks like coarse crumbs.

Combine egg whites with milk and stir into dry mixture. Mix well.

Spread batter in a nonstick-sprayed 8 x 8" pan. Sprinkle cranberries over top.

Combine flour and sugar for topping. Cut in margarine with pastry blender until crumbly. Sprinkle over cranberries. Bake. Serve warm.

Oven: 375°
Time: 35 to 40 minutes

Nutrient Analysis: 1 serving   Calories: 148   Protein: 3g   Carbohydrates: 24g
Exchanges: 1 1/2 starch, 1 fat   Fat: 5g   Cholesterol: 0mg   Sodium: 129mg
Carbohydrate Choices: 1 1/2   Dietary Fiber: 1g

YOGURT COFFEE CAKE

The good taste of sour-cream coffee cake without the fat.

Makes 1 angel food or Bundt cake pan; 32 servings

1/2 cup tub margarine
1/4 cup canola oil
1 teaspoon vanilla
1/2 cup plus 2 tablespoons sugar
1 egg
2 egg whites
1 cup plain low-fat yogurt
2 cups flour
1 teaspoon baking soda
1 teaspoon baking powder

Blend together margarine and oil. Add vanilla and sugar and beat well. Mix in egg and egg whites one at a time. Blend in yogurt.

Sift flour, soda and baking powder together. Add to egg mixture and beat well.

Place half of mixture in bottom of a nonstick-sprayed angel food or Bundt cake pan.

continued on next page

YOGURT COFFEE CAKE, (continued)

NUT FILLING:

- 1/2 cup chopped nuts
- 2 tablespoons sugar
- 1 teaspoon cinnamon

Sprinkle with nut mixture. Pour remaining batter over nut mixture. Bake until a toothpick inserted near center comes out clean and dry. Cool and remove from pan.

Oven: 350°
Time: 45 to 50 minutes

Nutrient Analysis: 1 slice
Exchanges: 1 starch, 1 fat
Carbohydrate Choices: 1

Calories: 104	*Protein: 2g*	*Carbohydrates: 11g*
Fat: 6g	*Cholesterol: 7mg*	*Sodium: 86mg*

CASSEROLE BREAD

Lots of flavor with the texture of homemade bread. Delicious!

Makes 1 1/2 quart casserole; 16 servings

- 1 1/2 cups whole wheat flour
- 1 cup all-purpose flour
- 1/2 cup quick-cooking rolled oats
- 1/3 cup brown sugar, packed
- 1 tablespoon finely grated orange peel
- 2 teaspoons baking powder
- 1/2 teaspoon baking soda
- 1 3/4 cups sour skim milk* or buttermilk
- 1 egg white
- 2 tablespoons sunflower seeds
- 1 tablespoon wheat germ
- 1 tablespoon honey

*To make sour milk, place 2 tablespoons lemon juice or vinegar in a 2 cup measure. Add skim milk to measure 1 3/4 cups.

Combine flours, oats, sugar, orange peel, baking powder and baking soda in a large bowl until well blended. Add milk and egg white. Stir just until ingredients are moistened. Stir in the sunflower seeds.

Sprinkle a nonstick-sprayed 1 1/2 quart casserole lightly with wheat germ. Pour batter into casserole. Bake. If necessary, cover loaf with foil during the last 15 minutes of baking to prevent over-browning.

Cool in casserole for 15 minutes; turn out on wire rack. Brush top of loaf with honey and sprinkle with additional sunflower seeds if desired. Serve warm or cool.

Oven: 350°
Time: 50 to 60 minutes

Nutrient Analysis: 1 slice
Exchanges: 1 1/2 starch
Carbohydrate Choices: 1 1/2

Calories: 120	*Protein: 5g*	*Carbohydrates: 24g*
Fat: 1g	*Cholesterol: 1mg*	*Sodium: 109mg*
Dietary Fiber: 2g		

APPLE MUFFIN CAKE

Bake in an 8-cup charlotte pan to create a giant muffin. It could also be baked in an 8-cup soufflé dish or a 9" tube pan.

Makes one 8-cup charlotte pan or soufflé dish; 16 servings

2	cups all-purpose flour
1	tablespoon baking powder
1/2	teaspoon baking soda
1 1/4	teaspoons cinnamon
1/2	teaspoon allspice
1/4	teaspoon cloves
1	cup sugar
1/4	cup tub margarine
1	cup low-fat vanilla-flavored yogurt
1	egg
1	egg white
1	cup finely diced, peeled apple
1	tablespoon fine dry bread crumbs

Combine flour, baking powder, baking soda, cinnamon, allspice, cloves and sugar. Blend well.

Melt margarine and remove from heat. Stir in yogurt and beat in egg and egg white.

Beat the margarine mixture into the dry ingredients and blend until batter is smooth and satiny. Stir in apple.

Sprinkle a nonstick-sprayed 8-cup charlotte pan or soufflé dish with bread crumbs, tapping out excess. Scrape batter into pan and smooth it level. Bake until a tooth pick inserted near the center comes out clean and dry. Serve warm or at room temperature.

Oven: 350°
Time: 45 to 60 minutes
    (check at 45 if using tube pan)

Nutrient Analysis: 1 slice
Exchanges: 2 starch
Carbohydrate Choices: 2

Calories: 151   Protein: 3g   Carbohydrates: 28g
Fat: 3g   Cholesterol: 14mg   Sodium: 157mg
Dietary Fiber: 1g

UNLEAVENED BREAD

A pleasant change from dinner rolls.

**Makes two round loaves; 12 servings
(6 slices a loaf)**

1 1/2	cups whole wheat flour
1/2	cup all-purpose flour
1	teaspoon baking soda
1/4	teaspoon salt
1/4	cup canola oil
3/4	cup water
1/4	cup honey

Sift together flours, soda and salt. Add oil, water and honey. Mix thoroughly.

Knead well on floured board. Roll the dough flat, about 1/2" thick. Shape into two round loaves, score top and place on nonstick-sprayed baking sheet. Bake. Serve warm or cold.

Oven: 350°
Time: 20 to 25 minutes

Nutrient Analysis: 1 slice
Exchanges: 1 1/2 starch, 1 fat
Carbohydrate Choices: 1 1/2

Calories: 140   Protein: 3 g   Carbohydrates: 22 g
Fat: 5 g   Cholesterol: 0 mg   Sodium: 154 mg
Dietary Fiber: 2 g

OLD-FASHIONED POTATO RYE BREAD

The day spent making this old-fashioned bread is well rewarded—four delicious loaves of bread and they freeze well. To bake bread in stages: Sponge may be refrigerated overnight after adding molasses, sugar, margarine and seeds. Dough may be refrigerated overnight (well-wrapped) after loaves are formed. Final rising time will increase to about three hours.

Makes four 8 x 4" loaves; 64 servings (16 slices a loaf)

2	medium potatoes
1	quart potato water
1 1/2	cups sugar, divided
2	packages active dry yeast
8	cups all-purpose flour
1/2	cup molasses
1/2	cup margarine
1	teaspoon salt
2	tablespoons caraway seed, crushed
1	teaspoon anise seed, crushed
1	teaspoon fennel seed, crushed
4	cups rye flour

Peel and boil two medium-sized potatoes in water. Mash the potatoes and add enough water to make one quart. Cool to lukewarm.

Dissolve the yeast with 1/2 cup of the sugar in the potato water. Let stand for 10 minutes. Add 4 cups of the all-purpose flour. Let this sponge rise in a warm place for 30 minutes.

Mix the molasses, the remaining cup of sugar, margarine, salt, caraway, anise and fennel together. Add to the sponge. Stir in the remaining 4 cups all-purpose flour and all the rye flour. Knead well. (This is a firm dough and it will take at least 10 minutes of kneading by hand.)

Let rise until double (about 3 hours). Punch down and let rise until double again (about 2 hours).

Form into 4 balls and let them rest for 15 minutes. Shape into loaves. Let rise in nonstick-sprayed pans until double (about 1 1/2 hours). Bake. Immediately remove bread from pans and cool on wire racks or across top edges of bread pans.

Oven: 350°
Time: 50 to 60 minutes

Nutrient Analysis: 1 slice
Exchanges: 1 1/2 starch
Carbohydrate Choices: 1 1/2

Calories: 118   Protein: 3g   Carbohydrates: 24g
Fat: 1g   Cholesterol: 0mg   Sodium: 50mg
Dietary Fiber: 1g

FOUR GRAIN BREAD

Makes one 9 x 5" loaf; 16 servings

1	cup whole wheat flour
1/2	cup rye flour
1/2	cup rolled oats
1/4	cup cornmeal
3	tablespoons molasses
1	tablespoon canola oil
1/2	teaspoon salt
1	cup boiling water
1	package active dry yeast
1/4	cup warm water (105-115°)
1 to 1 1/4	cups all-purpose flour

Blend whole wheat flour, rye flour, oats, cornmeal, molasses, oil, salt and boiling water in a large mixing bowl. Set aside.

Sprinkle yeast over warm water in cup measure. Stir to dissolve. Stir into grain mixture. Gradually stir in all-purpose flour, adding just enough to make a stiff dough.

Turn dough out onto floured surface and knead until smooth and elastic. Lightly oil large bowl and place dough in bowl turning once to coat with oil. Cover with damp cloth and let rise in warm place until double (45 to 90 minutes).

Punch down and shape into loaf. Place in non-stick sprayed pan, cover, and let rise again until double (45 to 75 minutes). Bake. Remove from pan and cool on wire rack or across edges of bread pan.

Oven: 375°
Time: 30 to 35 minutes

Nutrient Analysis: 1 slice
Exchanges: 1 starch
Carbohydrate Choices: 1

Calories: 107   Protein: 3g   Carbohydrates: 20g
Fat: 1g   Cholesterol: 0mg   Sodium: 74mg
Dietary Fiber: 2g

HONEY WHOLE WHEAT BREAD

Some of our readers claim this to be the best bread they've ever tasted.

Makes three 8 x 4" loaves; 48 servings (16 slices a loaf)

4   cups whole wheat flour
       (or 3 cups whole wheat
       flour and 1 cup cracked
       wheat)
1/2   teaspoon salt
2   packages active dry yeast
3   cups skim milk
1/2   cup honey
2   tablespoons canola oil
1   egg
4 1/2 to 5 cups all-purpose flour

Combine 3 cups of the whole wheat flour, salt, and yeast in a large bowl.

Combine milk, honey and oil in a saucepan over low heat. Heat until warm. Pour over flour mixture and blend well. Add egg and beat well. Add the remaining cup of whole wheat flour. Add the all-purpose flour, 1 cup at a time, until mixture forms a stiff dough.

Turn dough out onto floured surface and knead until smooth and elastic (about 7 minutes). Lightly oil a large bowl and place dough in bowl turning once to coat with oil. Cover with damp cloth and let rise in warm place until double (45 to 60 minutes).

Punch down, divide into thirds and shape into loaves. Place in three nonstick-sprayed 8 x 4" loaf pans, cover and let rise again until double (30 to 45 minutes.)

Place loaves in COLD oven and set at 400°. Bake 10 minutes. Reduce oven temperature to 375° and bake 30 more minutes or until golden. Remove loaves from pans and cool on wire rack or across edges of bread pans.

Oven: COLD set at 400° for 10 minutes;
375° for 30 minutes

Nutrient Analysis: 1 slice
Exchanges: 1 starch
Carbohydrate Choices: 1

Calories: 102   Protein: 4g   Carbohydrates: 20g
Fat: 1g   Cholesterol: 6mg   Sodium: 34mg
Dietary Fiber: 2g

OATMEAL BREAD

Raisins or cut-up dates make a tasty addition to this bread.

Makes two 9 x 5" loaves; 32 servings

2	packages active dry yeast
1	cup warm water
1/4	cup dark molasses
1/2	teaspoon salt
5 1/2 to 6	cups all-purpose flour, divided
1 1/4	cups scalded skim milk, cooled to lukewarm
1/4	cup honey
1	egg
2	tablespoons softened margarine
1	cup quick-cooking rolled oats
1	cup raisins or coarsely cut up dates

Combine yeast, warm water, molasses, salt and 1/2 cup flour in a large bowl. Beat until smooth and let stand in a warm place for 15 minutes.

Add milk, honey, egg, 2 cups flour, margarine and oats. Beat 2 minutes with electric mixer.

Gradually add 3 to 3 1/2 cups flour and raisins or dates if desired. Form into smooth ball, cover with bowl and let stand 10 minutes.

Knead dough for 5 minutes and shape into 2 balls. Cover with bowl and let rest for 10 minutes. Shape into 2 loaves and place in nonstick-sprayed loaf pans. Cover with damp cloth and let rise in warm place until double (45 to 60 minutes). Bake.

Oven: 375°
Time: 35-40 minutes

Nutrient Analysis: 1 serving
Exchanges: 1 1/2 starch
Carbohydrate Choices: 1 1/2

Calories: 122   Protein: 3g   Carbohydrates: 25g
Fat: 1g   Cholesterol: 7mg   Sodium: 52mg
Dietary Fiber: 1g

FRENCH BREAD

This bread is extra good and crusty if baked on an ungreased, shiny pan (foil) with a pan of hot water on the oven shelf below it.

Makes two French loaves; 20 servings (10 slices a loaf)

1	package active dry yeast
2	cups lukewarm water, divided
1 1/2	teaspoons salt
4	cups all-purpose flour
1	tablespoon sugar

Dissolve yeast in 1 cup of the water.

Mix salt, flour and sugar in a large bowl. Stir in yeast mixture and just enough of the second cup of water to hold dough together. Cover. Let rise until double.

Punch down and knead until smooth and elastic. Divide in half and shape into two long, thin loaves. Place on ungreased, foil-covered baking sheet. Slash loaves diagonally at 2" intervals. Bake.

Oven: 375°
Time: 45 minutes

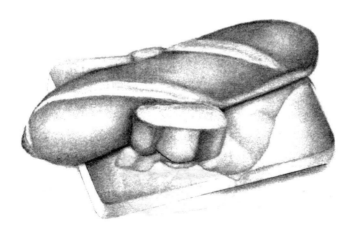

Nutrient Analysis: 1 slice
Exchanges: 1 starch
Carbohydrate Choices: 1

Calories: 83　Protein: 3g　Carbohydrates: 19g
Fat: 0g　Cholesterol: 0mg　Sodium: 175mg
Dietary Fiber: 1g

WHOLE WHEAT FRENCH BREAD

**Makes three French loaves; 48 servings
(16 slices a loaf)**

1	package active dry yeast
1	tablespoon honey
3	cups lukewarm water
5	cups all-purpose flour, divided
1	tablespoon canola oil
2 1/2	teaspoons salt
2	cups wheat germ
2	cups whole wheat flour
1/8	cup cornmeal

Dissolve yeast and honey in water. Mix in 3 cups of the all-purpose flour, 1 cup at a time. Stir batter 100 times. Cover and set in warm place for 30 minutes.

Stir in oil and salt. Add wheat germ and whole wheat flour, 1 cup at a time. Dough should be stiff enough to turn out, but still sticky. Turn onto floured surface and knead 10 minutes, adding as much of the remaining 2 cups of all-purpose flour as necessary to make dough smooth and elastic. Shape into ball.

Lightly oil a large bowl and place dough in bowl turning once to coat with oil. Cover with damp cloth and let rise in warm place until double (45 to 60 minutes). Punch down and let double again.

Turn dough onto floured board (it will be soft). Divide into thirds and shape into 14 x 2" loaves. Place on nonstick-sprayed baking sheet sprinkled lightly with cornmeal. Slash loaves diagonally at 3" intervals. Cover and let rise 30 minutes. Place pan of boiling water on bottom shelf of preheated oven. Bake loaves on middle shelf.

Oven: 400°
Time: 40 to 45 minutes

Nutrient Analysis: 1 slice
Exchanges: 1 starch
Carbohydrate Choices: 1

Calories: 83   Protein: 4g   Carbohydrates: 16g
Fat: 1g   Cholesterol: 0mg   Sodium: 121mg
Dietary Fiber: 2g

BREAD STICKS

Bread sticks can be made ahead of time and frozen. Reheat just before serving.

Makes 36 dinner sticks; 54 cocktail sticks

2	packages active dry yeast
2 1/4	cups warm water
3	cups all-purpose flour
3	cups whole wheat flour

COATING:

1	egg white, beaten
1/3 to 1/2	cup sesame or poppy seeds

Sprinkle yeast over water, dissolve and let stand for 5 minutes.

Mix flours together. Measure 4 1/2 cups of mixed flour into a large bowl. Gradually pour in yeast mixture and mix well with a spoon and then with hands. Add flour as needed from remaining 1 1/2 cups to form stiff dough. Place dough on floured board. Knead 3 to 5 minutes.

Lightly oil a large bowl and place dough in bowl turning once to coat with oil. Cover with damp cloth and let rise in warm place until double (about 2 hours). Punch down. Place on unfloured board and knead lightly. Divide into 36 (54 for cocktail sticks) equal parts and shape into balls. Let dough rest 15 minutes.

Stretch each ball into a 1/2 x 2 1/2" stick. Place on nonstick-sprayed baking sheets. Brush sticks with egg white and sprinkle with sesame or poppy seeds. Bake.

Oven: 425°
Time: 10 minutes

Nutrient Analysis:	1 dinner stick	1 cocktail stick
Exchanges:	1 starch	1/2 starch
Carbohydrate Choices:	1	1/2
Calories:	80	53
Protein:	3g	2g
Carbohydrates:	16g	10g
Fat:	1g	0g
Cholesterol:	0mg	0mg
Sodium:	3mg	2mg
Dietary Fiber:	2g	1g

SOFT PRETZELS

Children love to help make these!

Makes 16 pretzels; 16 servings

1   loaf frozen 100% whole wheat
    bread dough
1/2 cup poppy or sesame seeds

Cover dough and thaw overnight in refrigerator or for several hours at room temperature until soft enough to shape.

On a floured surface, cut dough the long way into 8 strips. Cover and let rise 10 minutes.

Roll each strip on floured surface until 1/2" thick and 18-20" long. Cut each strip in half and twist into pretzel shape. Place on a nonstick-sprayed baking sheet. Brush with lukewarm water. Sprinkle with poppy or sesame seeds.

Let rise, uncovered, for 15 to 20 minutes. Place a shallow pan of hot water on bottom shelf of preheated oven. Bake pretzels on middle shelf.

Oven: 425°
Time: 10 to 15 minutes

Nutrient Analysis: 1 pretzel
Exchanges: 1 starch
Carbohydrate Choices: 1

Calories: 80   Protein: 4g   Carbohydrates: 15g
Fat: 1g   Cholesterol: 0mg   Sodium: 140mg
Dietary Fiber: 2g

SOUR MILK ROLLS

Makes 24 rolls; 24 servings

3 cups whole wheat flour, divided
2 packages active dry yeast
3 tablespoons sugar
1/2 teaspoon salt
1/2 teaspoon baking soda
1 1/4 cups sour skim milk* or
     buttermilk
1/2 cup water
2 tablespoons canola oil
1 to 1 1/2 cups all-purpose flour

To sour milk, place 1 tablespoon lemon juice or vinegar in a 2 cup measure. Add skim milk to measure 1 1/4 cups.

Combine 1 1/2 cups of the whole wheat flour, yeast, sugar, salt and baking soda in a large mixing bowl.

Combine sour milk, water and oil in a saucepan and heat until warm (120 to 130°). Add to flour mixture and beat with electric mixer for 3 minutes at medium speed. Stir in remaining 1 1/2 cups whole wheat flour plus enough all-purpose flour (1 to 1 1/2 cups) to make a soft dough.

Knead on floured board for 5 minutes or until dough is smooth and elastic. Lightly oil large bowl and place dough in bowl turning once to coat with oil. Cover with damp cloth and let rise in warm place until double (30 to 45 minutes). Punch down, divide into 24 pieces. Shape into balls and place on nonstick-sprayed baking sheet. Cover. Let rise in warm place until almost double, (20 to 30 minutes). Bake.

Oven: 400°
Time: 15 to 20 minutes

Nutrient Analysis: 1 roll
Exchanges: 1 starch
Carbohydrate Choices: 1

Calories: 104   Protein: 4g   Carbohydrates: 19g
Fat: 1g   Cholesterol: 0mg   Sodium: 81mg
Dietary Fiber: 2g

HEARTY WHEAT BUNS

Makes 36 (3"- diameter) buns; 36 servings

1 1/4   **cups lukewarm water**
1/4   **cup soft margarine**
3   **tablespoons brown sugar**
1/2   **teaspoon salt**
1/3   **cup honey**
3/4   **cup skim milk, scalded**
1/2   **cup wheat germ**
2   **packages active dry yeast**
1/3   **cup warm water**
1   **teaspoon baking powder**
3   **cups whole wheat flour**
3   **cups all-purpose flour**

Combine 1 1/4 cups water, margarine, sugar, salt and honey in a large bowl. Pour scalded milk over wheat germ and cool to lukewarm. Add milk mixture to ingredients in large bowl. Mix.

Dissolve yeast in 1/3 cup warm water and let stand 5 minutes. Add to liquid ingredients and beat well with a wooden spoon.

Mix baking powder and whole wheat flour. Alternately add whole wheat and all-purpose flour (about 1 cup at a time) until dough is stiff enough to handle. Turn out dough onto floured surface and knead until smooth and elastic (about 10 minutes).

Lightly oil a large bowl and place dough in bowl turning once to coat with oil. Cover with damp cloth and let rise in warm place until double. Punch down and shape into 36 buns. Place on nonstick-sprayed baking sheet, cover and let rise again until almost double. Bake until nicely browned.

Oven: 350°
Time: 10 to 15 minutes

Nutrient Analysis: 1 bun
Exchanges: 1 starch
Carbohydrate Choices: 1

Calories: 105   Protein: 3g   Carbohydrates: 20g
Fat: 2g   Cholesterol: 0mg   Sodium: 58mg
Dietary Fiber: 2g

HERB SEASONED CROUTONS

This savory salad topping is equally as good as a garnish for soup or as a base for poultry stuffing. Choose your favorite herbs for variation.

Makes 4 cups; 16 servings

10	slices whole wheat bread
1/4	cup canola oil
1/4	cup grated Parmesan cheese
1/2	teaspoon dried herbs (majoram, basil, thyme), crushed

Brush both sides of bread with oil. Sprinkle with cheese and crushed herbs. Cut into 1/2" cubes.

Bake on 15 x 10" jelly roll pan, stirring occasionally. Store in airtight container.

Oven: 300°
Time: 30 minutes or until dry.

Nutrient Analysis: 1/4 cup
Exchanges: 1/2 starch, 1 fat
Carbohydrate Choices: 1/2

Calories: 80   Protein: 2g   Carbohydrates: 8g
Fat: 5g   Cholesterol: 1mg   Sodium: 116mg
Dietary Fiber: 1g

SALADS

♥

*Salad refreshes without weakening
and comforts without irritating
and I have a habit of saying that it
makes us younger.*

Jean Brillat-Savarin

SALADS

FRUIT SALADS

MAIN DISH SALADS

Chicken:

Fish:

Grain / Pasta / Legume:

SALADS

Have a salad at least once a day.

Thanks to modern agriculture, a variety of fresh fruits and vegetables are available year 'round making salad variation limitless.

The keys to making successful salads are fresh ingredients and a willingness to experiment. Salads, whether served as a main dish or as an accompaniment, are foods for health-conscious people. Dark greens used in preparing salads are high in vitamins A and C, fiber, calcium and iron and are low in calories, sodium and fat. However, if iceberg lettuce is the only green you use, you are selecting the one weakling in a family of nutritional champions. Any other lettuce or leafy green vegetable would be a better choice. Here are the "green" facts:

Table 17: Raw Greens Comparison (3.5 Ounces)

Type:	Calories:	Vitamin A: Value (IU)	Vitamin C: (mg)	Fiber: (g)	Calcium: (mg)	Iron: (mg)	Comments
Iceberg or crisphead lettuce	13	330	4	.5	19	.5	The most popular kind of lettuce, but the least nutritious.
Butterhead, Bibb, or Boston lettuce	13	970	8	.5	35	2.0	Sweet and delicate taste.
Romaine or Cos lettuce	16	2600	24	.7	68	1.4	Strong taste, used in Caesar salads.
Loose-leaf lettuce	18	1900	18	.7	68	1.4	Sweet and delicate taste.
Arugula or roquette	23	7400	91	.9	309	1.2	Strong and peppery; spices up a salad.
Chicory or curly endive; radicchio	23	400	24	.8	100	.9	Slightly bitter. Mix with milder greens.
Escarole	17	2050	7	.9	52	.8	An endive with broad leaves.

continued on next page

Table 17: Raw Greens Comparison for 3.5 Ounces, (continued)

Type:	Calories:	Vitamin A: (IU)	Vitamin C: (mg)	Fiber: (g)	Calcium: (mg)	Iron: (mg)	Comments:
Spinach	22	6700	28	.9	100	2.7	Eat raw or cooked. High in folacin and potassium. It's iron is poorly absorbed by the body.
Watercress	11	4700	43	.7	120	.2	Pungent. In cabbage family. Add to salads or sandwiches.
Dandelion greens	45	14000	35	1.6	187	3.1	Pungent. Very nutritious. Use young leaves in salads; sauté tough leaves.
Turnip greens	27	7600	60	.8	190	1.1	Strong flavor. More nutritious than the root vegetable. Eat raw or cooked.
Swiss chard	19	3300	30	.8	51	1.8	Mild flavor. Steam or sauté.
Kale	50	8900	120	1.5	135	1.7	Mild, cabbage-like taste. Cook or use in salads. Highly nutritious.
Collards	19	3300	23	.6	117	.6	Strong flavor. In cabbage family; related to kale. Steam or sauté.

Source: Food Processor SQL Nutrition Analysis Program, ESHA Research; © 2006-07; Salem OR.

CHICKEN SALAD HAWAIIAN

Makes 6 cups; 8 servings

1 1/2   pounds (4 cups) diced cooked
       chicken
  1   cup drained, unsweetened
       pineapple chunks
  1   (8-ounce) can water chestnuts,
       drained and thinly sliced
  2   green onions, thinly sliced
2/3   cup chopped celery
  1   cup HAWAIIAN DRESSING,
       (page 162)
1/3   cup unsalted slivered almonds,
       toasted
  4   cups salad greens

Combine chicken, pineapple, water chestnuts, green onions and celery in a mixing bowl. Pour HAWAIIAN DRESSING over chicken mixture and toss lightly.

Chill in refrigerator, covered, at least 1 hour before serving. Serve salad, sprinkled with toasted almonds, on crisp greens.

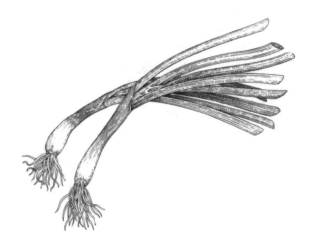

Nutrient Analysis: 3/4 cup
Exchanges: 3 very lean meat, 2 vegetable, 1 fat
Carbohydrate Choices: 1

Calories: 200   Protein: 22g   Carbohydrates: 17g
Fat: 5g   Cholesterol: 52mg   Sodium: 212mg
Dietary Fiber: 4g

LAYERED CHICKEN SALAD

Prepare several hours to one day ahead of serving time so flavors blend. Squares cut from a pan make it easy to serve.

Makes 13 x 9" pan; 8 servings

1	(11-ounce) can mandarin orange segments
3/4	cup light mayonnaise
3/4	cup low-fat plain yogurt
2	teaspoons curry powder
1/4	teaspoon ground coriander (optional)
2	tablespoons syrup from orange segments
4	cups fresh spinach, washed and drained
1	(10-ounce) package frozen peas
1 1/2	cups diced, cooked chicken or 1 (9-ounce) package frozen diced chicken breast
1	(8-ounce) can sliced water chestnuts, drained
1/2	cup chopped red onion
1	medium cucumber, halved lengthwise and sliced

Drain oranges, reserving 2 tablespoons of the syrup and a few orange segments.

Blend together mayonnaise, yogurt, curry powder, coriander and reserved syrup. Set aside.

Tear spinach into bite-sized pieces and place in a 13 x 9" pan. Layer peas, chicken, water chestnuts, onion and cucumber over spinach.

Spread mayonnaise mixture over salad and garnish with reserved orange segments. Cover and refrigerate several hours or overnight. Cut in squares to serve.

Nutrient Analysis: 1 serving
Exchanges: 1 lean meat, 1 starch, 1 1/2 vegetable
Carbohydrate Choices: 1

Calories: 142   Protein: 13 g   Carbohydrates: 20 g
Fat: 3 g   Cholesterol: 24 mg   Sodium: 275 mg
Dietary Fiber: 6 g

WILD RICE CHICKEN SALAD #1

A vinaigrette-based salad with vegetables, beans and nuts.

2	cups cooked wild rice
1	cup (10-ounce can) diced cooked chicken
1	cup chopped celery
1/4	cup unsalted nuts
1	cup chopped onions
1	cup cooked garbanzo beans (chickpeas)
1	cup sliced fresh mushrooms
1	cup fresh broccoli pieces, blanched
3/4	cup HERBED VINAIGRETTE DRESSING, *(page 159)*
8	lettuce leaves
8	tomato wedges (optional)

Makes 8 cups; 8 servings

Toss together rice, chicken, celery, nuts, onion, chickpeas, mushrooms, broccoli and dressing in a large bowl.

Refrigerate several hours to allow flavors to blend. Serve on lettuce leaves and garnish with tomato wedges.

Nutrient Analysis: 1 cup
Exchanges: 1 lean meat, 1 starch,
1 vegetable, 2 fat
Carbohydrate Choices: 1 1/2

Calories: 245   Protein: 10g   Carbohydrates: 21g
Fat: 14g   Cholesterol: 12mg   Sodium: 50mg
Dietary Fiber: 4g   Omega-3: 0.49g

WILD RICE CHICKEN SALAD #2

A mayonnaise-based salad with vegetables, grapes, and nuts added.

2/3 cup light mayonnaise
1/3 cup skim milk
 2 tablespoons lemon juice
 3 cups (1 1/4 pounds) diced cooked chicken
 3 cups cooked wild rice
1/2 cup finely chopped green pepper
1/2 cup finely sliced green onion
 1 (8-ounce) can sliced water chestnuts, drained
1/2 teaspoon white pepper
1/2 pound seedless green grapes; halved (about 1 1/2 cups)
1/2 cup unsalted cashews
 4 cups salad greens

Makes 8 cups; 8 servings

Blend mayonnaise, milk and lemon juice in a small bowl. Set aside.

Combine chicken, rice, green pepper, onion, water chestnuts, and pepper in a medium bowl. Fold in mayonnaise mixture. Cover and refrigerate 2 to 3 hours.

Just before serving, fold in grapes and cashews. Arrange on salad greens on individual salad plates. Garnish with grape clusters, if so desired.

Nutrient Analysis: 1 cup
Exchanges: 2 very lean meat, 1 starch,
1 fruit, 1 vegetable, 1 fat
Carbohydrate Choices: 2 1/2

Calories: 276   Protein: 20 g   Carbohydrates: 38 g
Fat: 6 g   Cholesterol: 39 mg   Sodium: 225 mg
Dietary Fiber: 5 g

STRAWBERRY RHUBARB GELATIN SALAD

Makes 13 x 9" pan; 12 servings

 3 cups diced rhubarb
1/2 cup water
 2 (0.3-ounce) packages sugar-free strawberry-flavored gelatin
 No-calorie sweetener to equal 1/2 to 3/4 cup sugar
 1 (20-ounce) can unsweetened crushed pineapple

Cook rhubarb in water in a large saucepan, until tender.

Add gelatin and stir until dissolved. Stir in sweetener to taste. Add pineapple and stir. Pour into 13 x 9" pan and refrigerate until set.

Nutrient Analysis: 1 serving
Exchanges: 1 fruit
Carbohydrate Choices: 1

Calories: 53   Protein: 1 g   Carbohydrates: 16 g
Fat: 0 g   Cholesterol: 0 mg   Sodium: 45 mg
Dietary Fiber: 1 g

CHICKEN LENTIL SALAD

Makes 4 cups; 4 servings

  2/3 cup lentils, dry
1 1/2 cups water
  1/4 to 1/2 cup light mayonnaise
    2 tablespoons chopped green
         onion
  1/4 teaspoon Tabasco sauce
    1 cup (10-ounce can) diced
         cooked chicken
  1/2 cup diced celery
  1/2 cup diced cucumber
  1/4 cup diced green pepper
    1 (2-ounce) jar chopped pimiento
    2 cups salad greens
         Chopped parsley for garnish
         (optional)

Thoroughly rinse dry lentils in cold water, removing any damaged pieces and foreign material. Drain. Place lentils in a heavy saucepan, add water. Bring to a boil, reduce heat and simmer, covered, for about 20 minutes. Do not overcook; lentils should be tender, with skins intact. Drain immediately and refrigerate until cool.

Stir together mayonnaise, green onion and Tabasco in a small bowl.

Toss lentils, chicken, celery, cucumber, green pepper, and pimiento with dressing, in a medium bowl. Cover and refrigerate for an hour or more to allow flavors to blend.

Just before serving, arrange on crisp greens and garnish with chopped parsley.

Nutrient Analysis: 1 cup
Exchanges: 2 very lean meat, 1 starch, 2 vegetable
Carbohydrate Choices: 2

Calories: 207   Protein: 22 g   Carbohydrates: 27 g
Fat: 3 g   Cholesterol: 31 mg   Sodium: 221 mg
Dietary Fiber: 13 g

CHICKEN WALDORF BLOSSOMS

Pretty red "blossoms" filled with crunchy chicken salad.

Makes 3 cups; 4 servings

1 1/2 cups diced cooked chicken
      or 1 (9-ounce) package
      frozen diced chicken breast
  1 small apple, chopped
1/2 cup chopped celery
1/3 cup light mayonnaise
     Dash pepper
  4 tomatoes
  4 lettuce leaves
1/4 cup chopped walnuts

Combine chicken, apple, celery, mayonnaise and pepper. Cover and chill to blend flavors.

Cut each tomato into 6 sections almost to stem end and place on a lettuce leaf. Fill each tomato with 1/2 cup chicken mixture. Sprinkle each with a tablespoon of walnuts.

Nutrient Analysis: 3/4 cup
Exchanges: 2 1/2 very lean meat, 1/3 fruit,
        2 vegetable, 1 fat
Carbohydrate Choices: 1

Calories: 206   Protein: 20g   Carbohydrates: 17g
Fat: 7g   Cholesterol: 46mg   Sodium: 226mg
Dietary Fiber: 3g   Omega-3: 0.72g

IMAGINATION VEGETABLE SALAD

Use your imagination to personalize this salad. Consider using other vegetables to replace those listed: such as, broccoli, cauliflower, cherry tomatoes, button mushrooms, snow peas, red cabbage, artichoke hearts, and/or zucchini.

Makes 7 1/2 cups; 10 servings

  4 carrots
  4 stalks celery
  1 large green pepper
  1 large sweet red pepper
  2 cucumbers
1/2 red onion
1 1/4 cups IMAGINATION
      VINAIGRETTE DRESSING,
      (page 160)

Scrape carrots and cut on diagonal into 1/4" pieces. Slice celery into 1" long matchsticks. Cut green pepper into 1/2" squares. Slice red pepper into strips. Score cucumbers and slice thinly. Chop onion or slice onion thinly and separate into rings.

Add your own "imagination" vegetables. Toss with dressing. Cover and chill for 1 to 2 hours or longer. Just before serving, toss again.

Nutrient Analysis: 3/4 cup
Exchanges: 2 vegetable, 1 fat
Carbohydrate Choices: 1

Calories: 87   Protein: 2g   Carbohydrates: 11g
Fat: 4g   Cholesterol: 0mg   Sodium: 45mg
Dietary Fiber: 3g

CRUNCHY TUNA SALAD

Makes 3 cups; 4 servings

1/4   cup bulgur
1/2   cup hot water
1/2   cup plain low-fat yogurt
  2   tablespoons chopped fresh mint
      or 2 teaspoons dried mint,
      crushed
  1   tablespoon lemon juice
  1   tablespoon Dijon mustard
  2   tablespoons thinly sliced green
      onion
  1   (6 1/2 or 7-ounce) can water-
      packed tuna, drained
  1   medium tomato, seeded and
      diced
  1   cup diced zucchini or cucumber
  4   lettuce leaves

Combine bulgur and water in a medium bowl. Let stand 30 minutes. Drain well. Stir yogurt, mint, lemon juice, mustard and green onion into bulgur.

Add tuna, tomato and zucchini or cucumber. Stir gently to break up tuna and coat with yogurt mixture.

To serve, line small plates with lettuce leaves and top with tuna mixture.

Nutrient Analysis: 3/4 cup
Exchanges: 1 1/2 very lean meat, 1/2 starch,
1/2 vegetable, 1 fat
Carbohydrate Choices: 1

Calories: 120   Protein: 15g   Carbohydrates: 13g
Fat: 1g   Cholesterol: 15mg   Sodium: 215mg
Dietary Fiber: 3g   Omega-3: 0.15g

WINTER FRUIT SALAD

Makes 6 cups; 12 servings

  1   large orange, peeled and
      sectioned
  1   medium pear, cubed
  2   bananas, sliced
  1   cup red or purple grapes
1/2   cup diced, dried plums
1/2   cup walnuts, toasted
  1   cup SPICY YOGURT FOR
      FRUIT, *(page 163)*

Combine orange, pear, banana, grapes, dried plums and walnuts in a medium bowl.

Just before serving, add dressing to fruit and toss well.

Nutrient Analysis: 1/2 cup
Exchanges: 1 fruit, 1 fat
Carbohydrate Choices: 1

Calories: 102   Protein: 2g   Carbohydrates: 17g
Fat: 4g   Cholesterol: 1mg   Sodium: 10mg
Dietary Fiber: 2g   Omega-3: 0.47g

FISH SALAD VERDE

Makes 6 (4-ounce) servings

1   pound fresh spinach, torn into
    bite-sized pieces
1 1/2   pounds any white fish fillets
1/2   cup white wine or lemon juice
1   tablespoon Dijon mustard
1/4   cup olive oil
1   teaspoon grated lime rind
1/4   cup lime juice
1/2   teaspoon dried tarragon,
    crushed
1/2 to 1 teaspoon sugar
    Dash pepper
1/4   cup plain low-fat yogurt
2   medium tomatoes, cut into
    wedges

Wash spinach thoroughly and pat dry. Finely chop enough spinach to measure 1/4 cup; set aside. Refrigerate remaining spinach leaves.

Place wine or lemon juice in a large skillet. Add water to a depth of 1" and bring to a boil. Place fillets in water; cover and reduce heat to simmer. Poach fish 5 to 10 minutes until translucent white. Remove from poaching liquid and cool.

Place mustard in medium bowl and gradually beat in oil with wire whisk. Add lime peel and juice, chopped spinach, tarragon, sugar and pepper and whisk thoroughly. Stir in yogurt and set aside.

To serve, arrange spinach leaves on large platter. Break fish into pieces and place on top of spinach. Surround with tomato wedges. Spoon dressing over all.

Nutrient Analysis: 4 ounces
Exchanges: 3 lean meat, 1 vegetable, 2 fat
Carbohydrate Choices: 1/2

Calories: 290   Protein: 25 g   Carbohydrates: 8 g
Fat: 17 g   Cholesterol: 69 mg   Sodium: 156 mg
Dietary Fiber: 3 g   Calcium: 132 mg   Omega-3: 1.79 g

SEASHORE SALAD OR SPREAD

Serve as a salad or as an appetizer, spread on crackers.

Makes 6 cups; 6 servings

1/2　cup ripe olives, halved
1 1/2　cups chopped celery
　4　green onions, sliced
　1　medium green pepper, chopped
　1　(8-ounce) can sliced water
　　　chestnuts, drained
　2　(8-ounce) bags frozen Pacific
　　　fish and crab meat blend, drained
1 1/2　cups CREAMY SALAD
　　　DRESSING, *(page 161)*

Combine olives, celery, onions, green pepper, water chestnuts and seafood.

Just before serving, toss with dressing. Serve on a bed of lettuce greens.

Nutrient Analysis: 1 cup
Exchanges: 2 lean meat, 2 vegetable
Carbohydrate Choices: 1

Calories: 150 Protein: 17g Carbohydrates: 14g
Fat: 4g   Cholesterol: 49mg   Sodium: 330mg
Dietary Fiber: 4g Calcium: 142mg Omega-3: 0.20g

SALAD NIÇOISE

*Salade Niçoise—a combination of cooked and raw vegetables, fish and a rich-tasting
Provencal dressing—is a luncheon favorite from the Mediterranean.*

Makes 4 servings

1/2　pound green beans, trimmed
　　　(about 2 cups)
　4　small new potatoes
　4　cups romaine lettuce, torn into
　　　bite-sized pieces
　2　tomatoes, quartered
　1　small red onion, sliced
1/2　green pepper, cut into strips
　2　(3-ounce) cans sardines or 1
　　　(7-ounce) can tuna or salmon,
　　　drained and rinsed
　1　small bunch radishes, sliced
　　　(optional)

Blanch or steam green beans until crisp tender. Drain and chill. In small saucepan, cook potatoes until tender (about 15 minutes). Drain and cool; slice 1/4" thick and refrigerate.

Combine beans, potatoes, lettuce, tomatoes, onion and green pepper in a salad bowl. Arrange sardines, tuna or salmon neatly over the top. Dress lightly with HERBED VINAIGRETTE DRESSING and garnish with radishes.

Nutrient Analysis: 1 serving
Exchanges: 2 lean meat, 1 starch, 2 vegetable
Carbohydrate Choices: 1

Calories: 205   Protein: 15g   Carbohydrates: 26g
Fat: 6g   Cholesterol: 35mg   Sodium: 407mg
Dietary Fiber: 6g Calcium: 108mg Omega-3: 1g

HOT SALMON RICE SALAD

Makes 1 1/2-quart casserole; 6 servings

 1 (16-ounce) can salmon
 2 cups cooked brown rice
 1 cup thinly sliced celery
 1/2 cup chopped fresh parsley
 1/4 cup sliced ripe olives
 1/2 cup light mayonnaise
 1/2 cup plain low-fat yogurt
 1 tablespoon lemon juice
   Pepper to taste
 1/3 cup sliced almonds
 2 tablespoons grated Parmesan
   cheese
   Paprika

Drain salmon liquid into mixing bowl. Flake salmon and add rice, celery, parsley and olives. Mix well.

Combine mayonnaise, yogurt and lemon juice. Add to salmon mixture and toss lightly. Season to taste with pepper.

Spoon mixture into a nonstick-sprayed casserole. Sprinkle with almonds, cheese and paprika. Bake until heated through and golden brown.

Oven: 350°
Time: 30 minutes

Nutrient Analysis: 1 cup
Exchanges: 3 lean meat, 1 starch, 1 vegetable
Carbohydrate Choices: 1 1/2

Calories: 255   Protein: 20 g   Carbohydrates: 22 g
Fat: 10 g   Cholesterol: 46 mg   Sodium: 333 mg
Dietary Fiber: 3 g Calcium: 252 mg Omega-3: 1.31 g

HOT SEAFOOD SALAD

Makes 1 1/2-quart casserole; 6 servings

 1 medium green pepper, minced
 1 medium onion, minced
 1 cup finely chopped celery
 6 ounces frozen crab meat or 3
   seafood sticks
 8 ounces frozen cooked shrimp
 1 teaspoon sodium-reduced
   Worcestershire sauce
 1/2 cup light mayonnaise
 1/2 cup whole wheat bread crumbs

Combine green pepper, onion, celery, crab meat, shrimp, Worcestershire and mayonnaise.

Place in nonstick-sprayed casserole and top with bread crumbs. Bake uncovered.

Oven: 350°
Time: 35 minutes

Nutrient Analysis: 1 cup
Exchanges: 2 lean meat, 1 starch
Carbohydrate Choices: 1

Calories: 137   Protein: 15 g   Carbohydrates: 14 g
Fat: 4 g   Cholesterol: 82 mg   Sodium: 389 mg
Dietary Fiber: 2 g   Omega-3: 0.28 g

ITALIAN PASTA SALAD

Makes 10 cups; 10 servings

1 (1-pound) box whole wheat
    rotini or shell pasta
1 cup sliced carrots
2 medium zucchini, sliced
1 (6-ounce) jar marinated
    artichoke hearts
1/4 cup sliced ripe olives
4 ounces part-skim mozzarella
    cheese, cubed
1/4 cup Parmesan cheese

DRESSING:

Reserved marinade from
    artichoke hearts
1/4 cup olive oil
2 tablespoons white wine vinegar
1 1/2 teaspoons dry mustard
1 teaspoon dried oregano, crushed
1 teaspoon dried basil, crushed
2 garlic cloves, minced

Cook pasta until al dente, about 10 minutes.
Drain and rinse in cold water.

Steam carrot slices 15 minutes, add zucchini
and steam 5 to 10 more minutes until just crisp-
tender. Drain and rinse in cold water.

Drain artichokes, reserving marinade. Quarter.

Place pasta, zucchini, carrots, artichokes, olives,
mozzarella and Parmesan in a bowl.

For dressing: Combine reserved marinade, olive
oil, vinegar, mustard, oregano, basil and garlic.
Add to pasta-vegetable mixture and mix well.

Chill several hours or overnight.

Nutrient Analysis: 1 cup
Exchanges: 1/2 lean meat, 2 starch,
1 vegetable, 1 fat
Carbohydrate Choices: 2 1/2

Calories: 270   Protein: 11 g   Carbohydrates: 38 g
Fat: 10 g   Cholesterol: 8 mg   Sodium: 169 mg
Dietary Fiber: 5 g   Calcium: 132 mg

LENTIL CONFETTI SALAD

Makes 3 cups; 6 servings

2/3	cup lentils, dry
1 1/2	cups water
1	cup cooked brown rice
1/2	cup IMAGINATION VINAIGRETTE DRESSING, *(page 160)*
1/2	cup seeded, diced tomato
1/4	cup chopped green pepper
3	tablespoons chopped onion
2	tablespoons chopped celery
1/4	cup chopped fresh parsley
1/2	teaspoon dried oregano, crushed Freshly ground pepper
5	lettuce leaves

Thoroughly rinse dry lentils in cold water, removing any damaged pieces and foreign material. Drain. Place lentils in a heavy saucepan; add water. Bring to a boil, reduce heat and simmer, covered, for about 20 minutes. Do not overcook; lentils should be tender, with skins intact. Drain immediately.

Combine lentils with cooked rice and pour dressing over mixture. Refrigerate until chilled.

Add tomatoes, green pepper, onion, celery, parsley, oregano and pepper. Mix well. Serve on lettuce leaves.

Nutrient Analysis: 1/2 cup
Exchanges: 1 starch, 1 vegetable, 1 fat
Carbohydrate Choices: 1 1/2

Calories: 154   Protein: 7g   Carbohydrates: 24g
Fat: 4g   Cholesterol: 0mg   Sodium: 13mg
Dietary Fiber: 8g

TABBOULEH SALAD

Add diced cooked chicken or seafood to tabbouleh for a tasty main dish salad.

Makes 6 cups; 12 servings

1	cup bulgur
2	cups hot water
3/4	cup chopped fresh parsley
1/4	cup chopped fresh mint or 2 teaspoons dried mint, crushed
1/4	cup chopped green onion
1	teaspoon dried oregano, crushed
6	tablespoons lemon juice
6	tablespoons olive oil

Soak bulgur in hot water for 15 to 30 minutes. Drain off any excess water.

Combine bulgur, parsley, mint, onion and oregano in a large bowl. Add lemon juice, olive oil, salt, pepper and additional spices if desired. Mix well. Refrigerate for 2 to 4 hours.

continued on next page

TABBOULEH SALAD, (continued)

1/4 teaspoon salt
Freshly ground pepper to taste
1/2 cup peeled, chopped cucumber
2 tomatoes, peeled, seeded and chopped
2 cups romaine lettuce leaves
Plain low-fat yogurt (optional)

For a more spicy mix add:
1/8 teaspoon ground allspice
1/8 teaspoon nutmeg
1/8 teaspoon ground cloves
1 teaspoon cinnamon
5 drops Tabasco sauce

Just before serving, stir in chopped cucumber and tomatoes. Serve on romaine leaves and garnish with a dollop of yogurt if desired.

Nutrient Analysis: 1/2 cup
Exchanges: 1 starch, 1 fat
Carbohydrate Choices: 1

Calories: 117   Protein: 2g   Carbohydrates: 12g
Fat: 7g   Cholesterol: 0mg   Sodium: 53mg
Dietary Fiber: 3g

DILLED BEAN SALAD

Makes 3 cups; 6 servings

1 (16-ounce) can small white beans (navy), drained
1 large carrot, shredded
1 green onion, finely sliced
2 tablespoons fresh lime juice
1 tablespoon vegetable oil
2 teaspoons chopped fresh dill or 1 teaspoon dried dill weed
1/2 teaspoon sugar
1/8 teaspoon freshly ground pepper
6 lettuce leaves, preferably red-tipped

Combine beans, carrot, green onion, lime juice, oil, dill, sugar and pepper in a medium bowl. Cover and refrigerate until well chilled.

Line 6 salad plates with lettuce leaves; spoon bean salad on top.

Nutrient Analysis: 1/2 cup
Exchanges: 1 starch, 1/2 fat
Carbohydrate Choices: 1

Calories: 118   Protein: 6g   Carbohydratess: 18g
Fat: 3g   Cholesterol: 0mg   Sodium: 347mg
Dietary Fiber: 5g

WONDERFUL MISCELLANEOUS SALAD

A real crowd pleaser!

Makes 12 cups; 24 servings

2 cups chopped fresh broccoli
2 ribs celery, chopped
4 green onions, sliced
1 green pepper, chopped
1/2 cup green beans, or peas, or carrots or zucchini, raw and sliced
1/2 cup raisins
2 cups cooked brown rice
1 1/4 cups cooked or canned garbanzo beans (chickpeas) or kidney beans
1/4 cup slivered almonds
1/2 cup unsalted sunflower seeds
1 1/2 cups grated Parmesan or Romano cheese
1 1/4 cups IMAGINATION VINAIGRETTE DRESSING, *(page 160)*

CREAMY DRESSING:

1/2 cup light mayonnaise
1 cup plain low-fat yogurt
2 teaspoons curry powder
1/2 teaspoon ground turmeric
1/2 teaspoon chili powder
1/2 teaspoon ground ginger
1/2 teaspoon paprika

Mix broccoli, celery, onions, green pepper, green beans or peas, or carrots or zucchini, raisins, rice, garbanzo beans, almonds, sunflower seeds, and grated cheese in a large bowl.

Add vinaigrette dressing and toss.

For dressing: Combine mayonnaise, yogurt, curry powder, turmeric, chili powder, ginger and paprika in a small bowl. Blend well. Add to salad and toss again. Cover and chill salad thoroughly.

Toss salad again just before serving.

Nutrient Analysis: 1/2 cup
Exchanges: 1 starch, 1 fat
Carbohydrate Choices: 1

Calories: 135   Protein: 5g   Carbohydrates: 13g
Fat: 7g   Cholesterol: 6mg   Sodium: 189mg
Dietary Fiber: 2g   Calcium: 106mg

APPLE SPINACH SALAD

Makes 4 cups; 4 servings

4 cups spinach leaves
1 1/2 tablespoons vegetable oil
2 tablespoons cider vinegar
1/8 teaspoon salt
Pinch sugar
1 medium tart apple, diced
1/4 cup chopped red onion
1/4 cup dried currants or chopped raisins

Wash spinach thoroughly. Pat dry. Tear spinach into bite-sized pieces; set aside in salad bowl.

In a small bowl, mix oil, vinegar, salt and sugar. Add apple, onion and currants to dressing and toss to coat. Cover and let stand at least 10 minutes.

Add dressing to salad bowl and toss with spinach.

Nutrient Analysis: 1 cup
Exchanges: 1 fruit, 1 fat
Carbohydrate Choices: 1

Calories: 106   Protein: 1g   Carbohydrates: 16g
Fat: 5g   Cholesterol: 0mg   Sodium: 112mg
Dietary Fiber: 3g

CITRUS SPINACH SALAD

Spinach and citrus fruit are a tasty combination and a healthful one. Citrus aids the absorption of iron from the iron-rich spinach.

Makes 6 cups; 6 servings

1/3 cup MAZATLAN LIME DRESSING, *(page 157)*
5 cups fresh spinach
1 1/2 cups sliced fresh mushrooms
2 oranges, peeled and sectioned or 1 (11-ounce) can mandarin oranges, drained
1/2 large red onion, sliced and separated into rings
1/2 (8-ounce) can sliced water chestnuts, drained

Make salad dressing and refrigerate until ready to serve.

Combine spinach, mushrooms, orange sections, onion and water chestnuts in a large bowl. Just before serving, toss with dressing

Nutrient Analysis: 1 cup
Exchanges: 1/2 fruit, 1 vegetable, 1 fat
Carbohydrate Choices: 1

Calories: 100   Protein: 2g   Carbohydrates: 14g
Fat: 5g   Cholesterol: 0mg   Sodium: 36mg
Dietary Fiber: 3g

ORANGE CAULIFLOWER SALAD

Makes 6 cups; 6 servings

2   cups fresh spinach
2   oranges, peeled and sectioned
       or 1 (11-ounce) can mandarin
       oranges, drained
2   cups uncooked cauliflower florets
1/4 cup chopped green pepper
3/4 cup SURPRISE DRESSING,
       (page 156)

Wash and dry spinach. Toss spinach, oranges, cauliflower, green pepper and dressing in a large salad bowl.

Nutrient Analysis: 1 cup
Exchanges: 1 fruit, 1/2 vegetable
Carbohydrate Choices: 1

Calories: 68   Protein: 2g   Carbohydrates: 16g
Fat: 0g   Cholesterol: 0mg   Sodium: 38mg
Dietary Fiber: 2g

24-HOUR LAYERED SALAD

This make-ahead salad can be made with a variety of vegetables. It is a good recipe for using up small amounts of vegetables on hand.

Makes 13 x 9" pan; 12 servings

1   head lettuce, shredded
1   large onion, sliced and separated
       into rings
1   cup diced celery
1   (8-ounce) can sliced water
       chestnuts, drained
4   hard-cooked egg whites, chopped
2   cups frozen peas, uncooked
1   cup plain low-fat yogurt
1/2 cup light mayonnaise
2   teaspoons sugar
6   ounces part-skim mozzarella
       cheese, shredded (about 1 1/2 cups)

In a 13 x 19" pan, layer vegetables in the order given: lettuce, onion rings, celery, water chestnuts, egg whites and peas.

Mix together yogurt and mayonnaise. Spread over layered vegetables and sprinkle with sugar. Top with shredded cheese.

Refrigerate overnight. Cut in squares to serve.

Nutrient Analysis: 1 serving
Exchanges: 1/2 very lean meat, 1/2 starch,
*   1 vegetable, 1 fat*
Carbohydrate Choices: 1

Calories: 135   Protein: 8g   Carbohydrates: 13g
Fat: 6g   Cholesterol: 13mg   Sodium: 224mg
Dietary Fiber: 4g   Calcium: 151mg

GREEN SALAD

Makes 6 cups; 6 servings

1   small head romaine lettuce
1   small head red leaf lettuce or
      curly endive
6   green onions with tops, thinly
      sliced
6   large fresh mushrooms, thinly
      sliced
1/4   cup walnuts, coarsely chopped
1   small bunch fresh parsley, finely
      chopped
3/4   cup SURPRISE DRESSING,
      (page 156)

Wash and dry lettuce. Tear into bite-sized pieces and place in large salad bowl.

Add onion, mushrooms, walnuts and parsley. Just before serving, toss with dressing.

Nutrient Analysis: 1 cup
Exchanges: 1/2 starch, 1 vegetable, 1/2 fat
Carbohydrate Choices: 1

Calories: 93   Protein: 4g   Carbohydrates: 13g
Fat: 4g   Cholesterol: 0mg   Sodium: 29mg
Dietary Fiber: 2g Calcium: 101mg Omega-3: 0.50g

HEALTH SALAD

Makes 4 luncheon-size servings

3-4   cups fresh spinach
1   carrot, shredded
2   ounces chopped cooked
      Canadian bacon
1/2   cup raisins
3   hard-cooked egg whites,
      chopped
1   cup fresh bean sprouts
1/4   cup sunflower seeds
1/2   cup SURPRISE DRESSING,
      (page 156)

Wash, dry and tear spinach into bite-size pieces. Combine spinach, carrot, bacon, raisins, egg whites, bean sprouts and sunflower seeds in a large bowl.

Just before serving, toss with dressing.

Nutrient Analysis: 1 serving
Exchanges: 1 very lean meat, 2 fruit,
*   1 vegetable, 1 fat*
Carbohydrate Choices: 2

Calories: 214   Protein: 11g   Carbohydrates: 33g
Fat: 5g   Cholesterol: 8mg   Sodium: 325mg
Dietary Fiber: 4g

COLE SLAW

Makes 7 cups; 14 servings

    4 cups shredded cabbage
  1/2 green pepper, chopped
    1 cup water
    1 teaspoon salt
    2 stalks celery, finely chopped
       Shredded carrots, as much as
          you like
1 1/2 cups BOILED DRESSING FOR
          COLE SLAW, *(page 155)*

Soak cabbage and green pepper a minimum of 20 minutes in a brine made of water and salt. Drain.

Add celery, carrots and cooled dressing. Cover and refrigerate overnight. Flavor is enhanced when made a day in advance.

Nutrient Analysis: 1/2 cup
Exchanges: 1 vegetable, 1 fat
Carbohydrate Choices: 1/2

Calories: 70   Protein: 0g   Carbohydrates: 9g
Fat: 4g   Cholesterol: 0mg   Sodium: 12mg
Dietary Fiber: 1g

CONFETTI APPLESLAW

Makes 7 cups; 14 servings

    2 tablespoons orange or apple juice
          concentrate, defrosted
    1 unpeeled red apple, cored and
          diced
    4 cups shredded cabbage
    2 small red onions, finely shredded
    1 red or green sweet pepper, thinly
          sliced
    3 tablespoons raisins
    1 tablespoon light mayonnaise
  1/2 cup plain low-fat yogurt
  1/2 teaspoon dry mustard
       Paprika to taste
       Freshly ground pepper to taste

Stir together juice concentrate and diced apple in a large bowl. Add cabbage, onion, pepper and raisins.

Stir together mayonnaise, yogurt, mustard, paprika and pepper in a small bowl. Add to vegetable mixture. Cover tightly and refrigerate until ready to serve.

Nutrient Analysis: 1/2 cup
Exchanges: 1 vegetable
Carbohydrate Choices: 1/2

Calories: 38   Protein: 1g   Carbohydrates: 8g
Fat: 1g   Cholesterol: 1mg   Sodium: 20mg
Dietary Fiber: 1g

VEGGIE SLAW

Makes 5 cups; 10 servings

1   large carrot, shredded
2   cups shredded cabbage
2/3   cup unsalted sunflower seeds or chopped nuts such as almonds, walnuts or pecans
1/2   cup raisins
1   apple, diced
1 1/2   cups BANANA-YOGURT DRESSING, *(page 163)*

Toss together carrot, cabbage, sunflower seeds, raisins and apple.

Add dressing and mix lightly.

Nutrient Analysis: 1/2 cup
Exchanges: 1 fruit, 1 vegetable, 1 fat
Carbohydrate Choices: 1

Calories: 125   Protein: 4g   Carbohydrates: 18g
Fat: 5g   Cholesterol: 1mg   Sodium: 63mg
Dietary Fiber: 2g

BROCCOLI-CORN SALAD

Makes 6 cups; 8 servings

1   bunch (about 1 1/2 pounds) broccoli
2   ears sweet corn (1 cup kernels)
1/2   cup chopped red onion
1/4   cup vegetable oil
5   tablespoons cider vinegar
2   teaspoons dried oregano, crushed
1 1/2   teaspoons ground cumin

Trim broccoli. If stalks are thick, peel off tough outer skin. Remove broccoli florets. Cut stalks into 1/4" thick slices. Steam florets and stems until crisp-tender but still bright green, about 5 minutes. Cool.

Husk and cook corn in boiling water until tender (about 7 minutes). Cool. Scrape kernels from cob into a large bowl. Add broccoli and onion.

In jar with a tight-fitting lid, combine oil, vinegar, oregano and cumin. Cover and shake well. Pour dressing over vegetables and toss well. Marinate at room temperature about 1 hour and then refrigerate about 1 hour or marinate in refrigerator several hours or overnight.

Nutrient Analysis: 3/4 cup
Exchanges: 2 vegetable, 1 fat
Carbohydrate Choices: 1/2

Calories: 108   Protein: 3g   Carbohydrates: 10g
Fat: 8g   Cholesterol: 0mg   Sodium: 23mg
Dietary Fiber: 3g

CARROT RAISIN SALAD

Adding a 1/4 cup crushed pineapple makes a tasty variation.

Makes 2 cups; 4 servings

4   medium carrots, shredded
1/4 cup raisins
2   teaspoons sugar
    Juice of 1 lemon

Thoroughly mix carrots, raisins, sugar and lemon in a medium bowl. Serve chilled.

Nutrient Analysis: 1/2 cup   Calories: 78   Protein: 1g   Carbohydrates: 19g
Exchanges: 1/2 fruit, 1 1/2 vegetable   Fat: 0g   Cholesterol: 0mg   Sodium: 41mg
Carbohydrate Choices: 1   Dietary Fiber: 3g

CAULIFLOWER SALAD

Tempting, even to those who usually shun cauliflower.

Makes 6 cups; 6 servings

4   cups thinly sliced cauliflower
    florets
1/2 cup sliced ripe olives, drained
2/3 cup chopped green pepper
2   tablespoons chopped pimiento
1/2 cup chopped onion
1/2 to 1 1/4 cups TANGY
    VINAIGRETTE DRESSING,
    (page 160)

Combine cauliflower, olives, green pepper, pimiento and onion in a medium bowl.

Pour well-blended dressing over vegetables. Mix well. Cover and refrigerate for 4 hours or overnight.

Toss again and drain thoroughly before serving.

Nutrient Analysis: 1 cup   Calories: 85   Protein: 2g   Carbohydrates: 7g
Exchanges: 1 vegetable, 1 fat   Fat: 6g   Cholesterol: 0mg   Sodium: 116mg
Carbohydrate Choices: 1/2   Dietary Fiber: 2g

CITRUS BEET SALAD

Makes 6 cups; 6 servings

4   medium beets
1   small head escarole
1   large grapefruit, peeled and
         sectioned
2   green onions, sliced
2   tablespoons walnut oil or other
         light salad oil
3   tablespoons red wine vinegar
1   teaspoon dried basil, crushed
1/4 teaspoon pepper

Cut off and discard beet tops. In medium saucepan, heat 1" water to boiling. Add beets and cook, covered, until tender (about 40 minutes). Drain and cool; remove skins. Cut beets into julienne strips.

Wash, dry and tear escarole into bite-sized pieces.

Just before serving, place torn escarole in a medium bowl. Arrange beets, grapefruit sections and onions on top of escarole.

In a jar with tight-fitting lid, combine oil, vinegar, basil and pepper. Cover and shake well. Drizzle dressing over salad and toss.

Nutrient Analysis: 1 cup
Exchanges: 2 vegetable, 1 fat
Carbohydrate Choices: 1/2

Calories: 92   Protein: 2g   Carbohydrates: 12g
Fat: 5g   Cholesterol: 0mg   Sodium: 62mg
Dietary Fiber: 5g   Omega-3: 0.49g

CUCUMBER TOMATO SALAD

Makes 6 cups; 6 servings

2   medium cucumbers
2   medium tomatoes
2   tablespoons olive oil
2   tablespoons lemon juice
1   teaspoon dried basil, crushed

Pare, score and cut cucumbers into 1/4" slices. Slice tomatoes thinly and cut slices in half. Arrange cucumbers and tomatoes in a shallow dish.

Combine oil, lemon juice and basil and mix well. Pour over cucumbers and tomatoes.

Nutrient Analysis: 1 cup
Exchanges: 1 vegetable, 1 fat
Carbohydrate Choices: 1/2

Calories: 70   Protein: 1g   Carbohydrates: 6g
Fat: 5g   Cholesterol: 0mg   Sodium: 2mg
Dietary Fiber: 1g

POTATO SALAD VINAIGRETTE

Best when served at room temperature.

Makes 7 cups; 14 servings

2 pounds small new potatoes, scrubbed
1/4 cup minced fresh parsley
1/2 cup diced green pepper
1/2 cup thinly sliced green onions
1/2 cup vegetable oil
1/4 cup red wine vinegar
1 tablespoon Dijon mustard
1 teaspoon sugar
1/2 teaspoon salt
1/2 teaspoon pepper

Boil unpeeled potatoes just until tender (15 to 20 minutes). Do not overcook. Drain.

Cut potatoes in quarters and arrange in a 11 x 7" glass dish. Sprinkle with parsley, green pepper and onions.

In a jar with a tight fitting lid, combine oil, vinegar, mustard, sugar, salt and pepper. Shake well and pour dressing over vegetables while potatoes are still warm. Toss gently.

Marinate several hours at room temperature before serving.

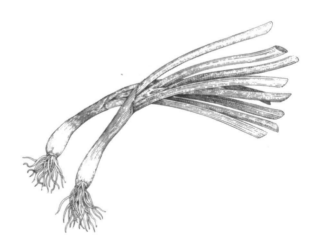

Nutrient Analysis: 1/2 cup
Exchanges: 1 starch, 1 fat
Carbohydrate Choices: 1

Calories: 117   Protein: 2g   Carbohydrates: 12g
Fat: 8g   Cholesterol: 0mg   Sodium: 96mg
Dietary Fiber: 2g

DRESSINGS
& SAUCES

What is sauce for the goose may be sauce for the gander but it is not necessarily sauce for the chicken, the duck, the turkey or the guinea hen.

Alice B. Toklas

DRESSINGS

SAUCES

DESSERT SAUCES

DRESSINGS & SAUCES

Dressings and sauces your heart will love.

Your nutritious and low-calorie salad needn't be compromised by a salty, high-calorie dressing. Two tablespoons of an oil, sour cream or mayonnaise-based dressing can add as many as 200 calories and 400 milligrams of sodium! Dressings and sauces are meant to "enhance" the flavors of meats, fish, greens and fruit. Never should they cover up the crispness nor freshness of the foods they are served upon.

Dressings and sauces can be good sources of unsaturated fats. Both types (monounsaturated and polyunsaturated) help to lower the amount of cholesterol in your blood. The recipes in this section are lower in fat than traditional recipes, have virtually no saturated fat nor cholesterol, and are very low in sodium. When fat is an essential part of the dressing or sauce, only unsaturated fats, the kinds that don't damage blood vessels, were used. Only three of the recipes in this section require salt.

Use the following chart to compare the amount of calories, total fat, cholesterol and sodium of various types of bases used in preparing dressings and sauces.

Table 18: Sauces & Dressings Comparison Chart

Type of Base: (Per Tablespoon)	Calories:	Total Fat: (grams)	Cholesterol: (mg)	Sodium: (mg)
Vegetable Oil	120	14	0	0
Margarine, liquid oil	100	11	0	125
Margarine, hydrogenated, stick	101	11	0	133
Tub Margarine, soft	100	11	0	105
Tub Margarine, diet	50	6	0	110
Shortening, vegetable	113	13	0	0
Butter	100	11	30	85
Sour Cream	30	3	8	8
Sour Cream, light	18	1	5	15
Cream Cheese	51	5	16	43
Light Cream Cheese	35	3	8	75
Mayonnaise	105	12	10	73
Mayonnaise-type salad dressing	57	5	4	105
Light Mayonnaise	50	5	5	125
Vinegar, cider	2	0	0	0
Wine, all types	10	0	0	1

Source: Food Processor SQL Nutrition Analysis Program, ESHA Research; © 2006-07, Salem, OR and manufacturer's data.

HERBED VINEGAR

Makes 1 1/4 cups; 20 servings

1	cup white wine vinegar
1/2	teaspoon dill weed
1/4	cup snipped chives
1	garlic clove
1/3	cup snipped fresh mint or 1 tablespoon dried mint, crushed

Combine vinegar, dill weed, chives, garlic and mint.

Refrigerate in a covered bottle for at least four days to allow flavors to blend. Strain before using.

TARRAGON VINEGAR:

Add a sprig of fresh tarragon to a bottle of white wine vinegar.

Nutrient Analysis: 1 tablespoon
Exchanges: free
Carbohydrate Choices: 0

Calories: 5   Protein: 0g   Carbohydrates: 1g
Fat: 0g   Cholesterol: 0mg   Sodium: 0mg

BOILED DRESSING FOR COLE SLAW

Makes 1 1/2 cups; 24 servings

1/2	cup sugar
1/2	cup water
1/2	cup vinegar
1	teaspoon mustard seed or celery seed or 1/2 teaspoon of each
1/4	cup vegetable oil

Combine sugar, water, vinegar, seeds and oil in small saucepan. Bring to a boil and boil about 1 minute. Cool.

Nutrient Analysis: 1 tablespoon
Exchanges: 1 fat
Carbohydrate Choices: 0

Calories: 58   Protein: 0g   Carbohydrates: 5g
Fat: 5g   Cholesterol: 0mg   Sodium: 0mg

SURPRISE DRESSING

Surprisingly delicious on greens or on citrus and greens combinations!

Makes 1 1/4 cups; 20 servings

1/2   cup evaporated skim milk
  1   (6-ounce) can frozen orange
        juice concentrate, thawed
      Pinch of ground ginger

Mix milk, orange juice concentrate and ginger. Shake well before using.

Nutrient Analysis: 1 tablespoon
Exchanges: free; 2 tablespoons = 1/2 fruit
Carbohydrate Choices: 0

Calories: 20   Protein: 1g   Carbohydrates: 4g
Fat: 0g   Cholesterol: 0mg   Sodium: 8mg

CELERY SEED DRESSING

A thick dressing, excellent on greens and fruit combinations. Keeps for several months in the refrigerator.

Makes 1 1/2 cups; 24 servings

1/3   cup honey or sugar
  1   teaspoon dry mustard
  1   teaspoon paprika
  1   small onion, minced
1/4   cup white wine vinegar
  1   tablespoon lemon juice
3/4   cup vegetable oil
  2   teaspoons celery seed

Place honey, mustard, paprika and onion in blender. Slowly add vinegar while blending at medium speed. Add the lemon juice and the oil, blending until creamy. Add celery seed and mix well. Refrigerate until ready to serve.

Nutrient Analysis: 1 tablespoon
Exchanges: 1 1/2 fat
Carbohydrate Choices: 0

Calories: 78   Protein: 0g   Carbohydrates: 5g
Fat: 7g   Cholesterol: 0mg   Sodium: 1mg

MAZATLAN LIME SALAD DRESSING

Delicious on mixed greens with slices of fresh orange and garnished with toasted almonds.
Also excellent on tossed lettuce, tomato and cucumber salad.

Makes 2/3 cups; 10 servings

1/4   cup extra-light olive oil
1/4   cup fresh lime juice
 1   teaspoon grated lime rind
 2   tablespoons sugar
1/4   teaspoon garlic powder
      (optional)

In a jar with a tight fitting lid, mix oil, lime juice, lime rind, sugar and garlic powder if desired. Shake well.

Refrigerate until ready to serve.

Nutrient Analysis: 1 tablespoon
Exchanges: 1 fat
Carbohydrate Choices: 0

Calories: 62   Protein: 0g   Carbohydrates: 3g
Fat: 6g   Cholesterol: 0mg   Sodium: 0mg

WESTERN DRESSING

This dressing can also be used as a marinade for meats.

Makes 1 1/2 cups; 24 servings

1/2   cup sodium-reduced ketchup
1/2   cup vegetable oil
1/3   cup sugar
 2   tablespoons lemon juice
1/4   teaspoon pepper
1/4   cup cider vinegar
 1   small onion, grated
      (optional)

In a jar with a tightly-fitting lid, combine ketchup, oil, sugar, lemon juice and pepper. Cover and shake vigorously. Add vinegar, and onion, if desired. Shake again. Refrigerate.

Shake well before each use.

Nutrient Analysis: 1 tablespoon
Exchanges: 1 fat
Carbohydrate Choices: 0

Calories: 58   Protein: 0g   Carbohydrates: 5g
Fat: 5g   Cholesterol: 0mg   Sodium: 1mg

SESAME DRESSING — SWEET

This light, sweet-sour Oriental-style dressing, enhanced by the nutty flavor of toasted sesame, is excellent with chicken or fresh spinach salad.

Makes 1/2 cup; 8 servings

4	tablespoons toasted sesame seeds
6	tablespoons rice wine vinegar
1/4	teaspoon salt
1/2	teaspoon sugar
1/2	teaspoon freshly ground black pepper

Toast sesame seeds in skillet over medium heat. Shake or stir and watch carefully! Sesame seeds can go from toasted to burned in the blink of an eye.

Add cooled seeds to vinegar, salt, sugar and pepper. Mix. Refrigerate until ready to use.

Nutrient Analysis: 1 tablespoon
Exchanges: free; 2 tablespoons = 1 fat
Carbohydrate Choices: 0

Calories: 31   Protein: 1g   Carbohydrates: 1g
Fat: 2g   Cholesterol: 0mg   Sodium: 73mg

VINAIGRETTE DRESSING

Just as the taste preference for certain oils and vinegars is very personal, so are the proportions in which they are combined. Experiment and adjust to suit your taste.

Makes 1 cup; 16 servings

1/2	cup oil (olive, canola)
1/2	cup vinegar (wine, tarragon, cider, etc.)
1	teaspoon dry mustard
1/2	teaspoon freshly ground pepper
1	teaspoon sugar
1/2	teaspoon paprika (optional)

In a jar with a tightly-fitting lid, combine oil, vinegar, mustard, pepper and sugar and paprika, if desired.

Cover and shake vigorously. Refrigerate. Shake again just before using.

Nutrient Analysis: 1 tablespoon
Exchanges: 1 1/2 fat
Carbohydrate Choices: 0

Calories: 67   Protein: 0g   Carbohydrates: 1g
Fat: 7g   Cholesterol: 0mg   Sodium: 0mg

DILLED VINAIGRETTE

Makes 1 1/4 cups; 20 servings

1/2   cup vegetable oil
1/2   cup red wine vinegar
 2   garlic cloves, minced
1/2   teaspoon dill weed
1/2   teaspoon dried oregano, crushed
1/4   teaspoon freshly ground pepper
1/2   teaspoon lemon juice

In a jar with a tightly-fitting lid, combine oil, vinegar, garlic, dill weed, oregano, pepper and lemon juice. Cover and shake vigorously.

Refrigerate. Shake again just before using.

Nutrient Analysis: 1 tablespoon
Exchanges: 1 fat
Carbohydrate Choices: 0

Calories: 49   Protein: 0g   Carbohydrates: 0g
Fat: 6g   Cholesterol: 0mg   Sodium: 0mg

HERBED VINAIGRETTE DRESSING

Makes 1 cup; 16 servings

1/2   cup olive oil
1/4   cup red wine vinegar
1-3   teaspoons Dijon mustard
 2   tablespoons lemon juice
 1   teaspoon sugar
1/2   teaspoon pepper
 1   teaspoon dried rosemary,
        crushed
 1   teaspoon dried tarragon,
        crushed

In a jar with a tightly-fitting lid, combine oil, vinegar, mustard, lemon juice, sugar, pepper, rosemary and tarragon. Cover and shake vigorously.

Refrigerate. Shake again just before using.

Nutrient Analysis: 1 tablespoon
Exchanges: 1 1/2 fat
Carbohydrate Choices: 0

Calories: 65   Protein: 0g   Carbohydrates: 0g
Fat: 7g   Cholesterol: 0mg   Sodium: 7mg

TANGY VINAIGRETTE DRESSING

Similar to traditional sour cream dressing. Experiment with different herbs and spices.

Makes 1 1/4 cups; 20 servings

1/2   cup olive oil
6   tablespoons lemon juice
6   tablespoons wine vinegar
1/4   teaspoon pepper
1   teaspoon sugar

In a jar with a tightly-fitting lid, mix oil, lemon juice, vinegar, pepper and sugar. Shake well.

Refrigerate. Shake again before using.

Nutrient Analysis: 1 tablespoon
Exchanges: 1 fat
Carbohydrate Choices: 0

Calories: 54   Protein: 0g   Carbohydrates: 1g
Fat: 6g   Cholesterol: 0mg   Sodium: 0mg

IMAGINATION VINAIGRETTE DRESSING

Good as a marinade too.

Makes 1 1/4 cups; 20 servings

3   tablespoons olive oil
5   tablespoons wine vinegar
2   tablespoons lemon juice
6   tablespoons water
1   teaspoon Dijon mustard
1   large garlic clove, crushed
2   tablespoons minced onions
1   tablespoon honey
1   teaspoon dried tarragon,
    crushed
1/4   teaspoon paprika
    Freshly ground pepper

In a jar with a tightly-fitting lid, combine oil, vinegar, lemon juice, water, mustard, garlic, onions, honey, tarragon, paprika and pepper. Cover and shake well.

Refrigerate until ready to use.

Nutrient Analysis: 1 tablespoon
Exchanges: 1/2 fat
Carbohydrate Choices: 0

Calories: 23   Protein: 0g   Carbohydrates: 1g
Fat: 2g   Cholesterol: 0mg   Sodium: 3mg

AMISH-STYLE SALAD DRESSING

A tart and lively dressing, exactly the right addition to vegetable and pasta salads.

Makes 1 cup; 16 servings

1 cup plain low-fat yogurt
1 tablespoon Dijon mustard
1 teaspoon dill weed
1 teaspoon sugar

Blend together yogurt, mustard, dill weed and sugar.

Refrigerate until ready to use.

Nutrient Analysis: 1 tablespoon
Exchanges: free
Carbohydrate Choices: 0

Calories: 12   Protein: 1g   Carbohydrates: 2g
Fat: 0g   Cholesterol: 1mg   Sodium: 23mg

CREAMY SALAD DRESSING

A good basic dressing for greens, vegetable and seafood salads.

Makes 1 1/2 cups; 24 servings

1 cup plain low-fat yogurt
1/4 cup light mayonnaise
1/2 teaspoon Dijon mustard
2 green onions, sliced
2 tablespoons minced fresh parsley

Combine yogurt, mayonnaise, mustard, onions and parsley in a blender. Blend until smooth.

Refrigerate until ready to use.

VARIATIONS:

CREAMY GARLIC DRESSING   Add 1 teaspoon garlic powder

CREAMY CUCUMBER DRESSING   Add 1/2 cup chopped cucumber

CREAMY HERB DRESSING   Add 2 to 4 tablespoons mixed fresh or 1 to 2 teaspoons dried herbs such as basil, rosemary, tarragon, chervil, dill.

Nutrient Analysis: 1 tablespoon
Exchanges: free
Carbohydrate Choices: 0

Calories: 17   Protein: 1g   Carbohydrates: 1g
Fat: 1g   Cholesterol: 1mg   Sodium: 30mg

HAWAIIAN DRESSING

Makes 1 cup; 16 servings

1/2	cup plain low-fat yogurt
1/2	cup light mayonnaise
2	teaspoons lemon juice
1	tablespoon honey
1	teaspoon grated fresh ginger
1/4	teaspoon paprika

Blend yogurt, mayonnaise, lemon juice, honey, ginger and paprika. Refrigerate until ready to use.

Nutrient Analysis: 1 tablespoon
Exchanges: free; 2 tablespoons = 1/2 carbohydrate   *Calories: 25   Protein: 1g   Carbohydrates: 3g*
Carbohydrate Choices: 0   *Fat: 1g   Cholesterol: 2mg   Sodium: 72mg*

FETA CHEESE DRESSING

Makes 1 1/4 cups; 20 servings

1	cup plain low-fat yogurt
2	ounces feta cheese, crumbled
1	garlic clove, minced
2	tablespoons chopped fresh parsley
1/4	teaspoon dried oregano, crushed

Combine yogurt, feta cheese, garlic, parsley and oregano.

Cover and refrigerate for at least 30 minutes before using.

Nutrient Analysis: 1 tablespoon
Exchanges: free   *Calories: 15   Protein: 1g   Carbohydrates: 1g*
Carbohydrate Choices: 0   *Fat: 1g   Cholesterol: 2mg   Sodium: 37mg*

BANANA YOGURT DRESSING

A creamy sweet-sour dressing that is particularly good on cabbage or fresh fruit. It doubles as a tasty dip for fruit.

Makes 1 1/3 cups; 20 servings

1/2   very ripe banana
1/2   cup low-fat cottage cheese
2   tablespoons honey
1/2   cup plain low-fat yogurt

Mix banana, cottage cheese, honey and yogurt in a blender or food processor, until smooth and creamy.

When used as a dip for fruit, mix banana, cottage cheese and honey in blender. Remove from blender and carefully stir in yogurt.

Refrigerate until ready to use.

Nutrient Analysis: 1 tablespoon
Exchanges: free; 2 tablespoons = 1/2 carbohydrate   *Calories: 17   Protein: 1g   Carbohydrates: 3g*
Carbohydrate Choices: 0   *Fat: 0g   Cholesterol: 1mg   Sodium: 28mg*

SPICY YOGURT FOR FRUIT

Makes 1 cup; 16 servings

1   cup sugar-free, nonfat
    vanilla yogurt
1/4   teaspoon ground cinnamon
1/8   teaspoon ground cardamon or
    nutmeg

Combine yogurt, cinnamon and cardamon or nutmeg in a small bowl. Chill.

Just before serving, add dressing to fruit and toss well.

Nutrient Analysis: 1 tablespoon
Exchanges: free   *Calories: 8   Protein: 0g   Carbohydrates: 1g*
Carbohydrate Choices: 0   *Fat: 0g   Cholesterol: 1mg   Sodium: 6mg*

WHITE (BÉCHAMEL) SAUCE

Use light sauce for creamed vegetables and as a soup base, medium for creamed and scalloped dishes, and heavy for croquettes or soufflés.

Makes 1 cup; 16 servings
(for all but Dugléré Sauce)

Light:
- 1   tablespoon soft margarine
- 1   tablespoon flour
- 1   cup skim milk
- 1/8   teaspoon white pepper

Medium:
- 2   tablespoons soft margarine
- 2   tablespoons flour
- 1   cup skim milk
- 1/8   teaspoon white pepper

Heavy:
- 4   tablespoons soft margarine
- 4   tablespoons flour
- 1   cup skim milk
- 1/8   teaspoon white pepper

Melt margarine in a saucepan. Add flour, stirring constantly, until mixture bubbles. Cook and stir an additional minute. DO NOT ALLOW TO BROWN.

Add skim milk and continue stirring until mixture comes to a boil and thickens. Add pepper.

VARIATIONS:

MORNAY SAUCE

Delicious with fish and vegetable dishes.

- 1   cup medium white sauce
- 1   tablespoon Parmesan cheese
- 1   tablespoon shredded part-skim brick cheese
- 1/8   teaspoon nutmeg or 1/2 teaspoon Dijon mustard

Cook over moderate heat, stirring until cheeses are melted.

WHITE SAUCE VARIATIONS, (continued)

VELOUTÉ SAUCE

For fish, veal or poultry. Slightly thinner and not as rich as traditional Velouté, which is topped with heavy cream.

Substitute one cup of reduced-sodium chicken broth for the skim milk in the white sauce recipe.

DUGLÉRÉ SAUCE

For fish.

Makes 1 3/4 cups; 28 servings

1/2 cup chopped tomatoes
1/4 cup sliced onions
  2 tablespoons white wine
  1 tablespoon lemon juice
  1 cup medium white sauce

Simmer the tomatoes, onions, wine and lemon juice for 12 to 15 minutes. Add to medium white sauce.

Nutrient Analysis: 1 tablespoon	Light	Medium	Heavy	Mornay	Velouté	Dugléré
Exchanges:	free	free	1/2 fat	free	free	free
Carbohydrate Choices:	0	0	0	0	0	0
Calories:	14	22	38	24	17	14
Protein:	1g	1g	1g	1g	0g	0g
Carbohydrates:	1g	2g	2g	2g	1g	1g
Fat:	1g	1g	3g	2g	1g	1g
Cholesterol:	0 mg	0 mg	0 mg	1 mg	0 mg	0 mg
Sodium:	15 mg	21 mg	33 mg	27 mg	39 mg	12 mg

PLUM SAUCE

Somewhere between a chutney and a sweet-sour sauce, this sauce is good with meats as well as with Oriental appetizers.

Makes 2 cups; 32 servings

1	(16-ounce) can plums, packed in own juice
3/4	cup plum juice
3	small pears, peeled, cored and diced
6	tablespoons red wine vinegar
3	slices fresh ginger, minced
3	garlic cloves, minced
1 1/2	teaspoons sodium-reduced soy sauce
3/4	teaspoon lemon juice
2	tablespoons cornstarch
6	tablespoons water

Drain plums and reserve juice. Remove and discard plum pits. Combine plums with juice, pears, vinegar, ginger, garlic, soy sauce and lemon juice in a food processor or blender. Process until smooth.

Pour mixture into small saucepan. Bring to a boil; reduce heat.

Dissolve cornstarch in water. Add to plum mixture. Simmer for about 10 minutes or until mixture thickens, stirring occasionally. Serve warm or at room temperature.

Nutrient Analysis: 1 tablespoon
Exchanges: free; 2 tablespoons = 1 fruit
Carbohydrate Choices: 0

Calories: 20   Protein: 0g   Carbohydrates: 5g
Fat: 0g   Cholesterol: 0mg   Sodium: 9mg

ORIENTAL SWEET-SOUR SAUCE

Particularly good with CHICKEN APPETIZERS, (see page 73).

Makes 1 1/2 cups; 24 servings

2	slices canned unsweetened pineapple, diced
1	tablespoon vegetable oil
2 1/2	teaspoons cornstarch
2	tablespoons vinegar*
1/2	tablespoon tomato sauce
1 1/2	teaspoons brandy (optional)
1 1/2	teaspoons sugar
1/2	teaspoon sodium-reduced soy sauce
1	cup water
2-3	green onions, chopped fine

Sauté pineapple in oil in a nonstick-sprayed or teflon pan.

Dissolve cornstarch in vinegar. Add tomato sauce, brandy, sugar and soy sauce. Stir mixture into pineapple. Add water. Bring to a boil; reduce heat and simmer 5 minutes. Cool.

Just before serving, stir in chopped onions. Serve with Oriental appetizers. Refrigerate any remaining sauce.

Flavored vinegars, such as raspberry or blueberry, are a delicious added touch.

Nutrient Analysis: 1 tablespoon
Exchanges: free
Carbohydrate Choices: 0

Calories: 10   Protein: 0g   Carbohydrates: 1g
Fat: 1g   Cholesterol: 0mg   Sodium: 7mg

SWEET-SOUR MUSTARD

Makes 1 1/4 cups; 20 servings

1/2	cup sugar
2	tablespoons all-purpose flour
3	tablespoons dry mustard
1/4	cup vinegar
3/4	cup water

Combine sugar, flour and dry mustard in a small saucepan. Add vinegar and water. Stir and heat over medium heat until mixture comes to a boil. Stir a few more minutes until thickened. Cool and store in refrigerator.

Nutrient Analysis: 1 tablespoon
Exchanges: 1/2 carbohydrate
Carbohydrate Choices: 1/2

Calories: 23   Protein: 0g   Carbohydrates: 6g
Fat: 0g   Cholesterol: 0mg   Sodium: 0mg

HOME-STYLE BARBECUE SAUCE

This tangy barbecue sauce is also delicious mixed with lean ground beef for grilled burgers.

Makes 1 1/2 cups; 24 servings

1/2 cup plain low-fat yogurt
1/2 cup sodium-reduced ketchup
1/4 cup sodium-reduced
    Worcestershire sauce
1/4 cup prepared mustard
1/4 cup firmly packed brown sugar
1/8 teaspoon Tabasco sauce
  1 teaspoon onion powder
1/2 teaspoon garlic powder

Combine yogurt, ketchup, Worcestershire, mustard, brown sugar, Tabasco, onion powder and garlic powder in a small bowl. Whisk until smooth.

Brush on chicken or ribs during the last 20 minutes of cooking, on steaks or pork chops for last 5 to 10 minutes of cooking.

Nutrient Analysis: 1 tablespoon
Exchanges: free; 2 tablespoons = 1/2 carbohydrate   *Calories: 20   Protein: 0g   Carbohydrates: 4g*
Carbohydrate Choices: 0   *Fat: 0g   Cholesterol: 0mg   Sodium: 37mg*

GARLIC SAUCE FOR CHOPS

A surprisingly mild, faintly sweet sauce similar to onion butter. Excellent served with pork, veal or lamb chops.

Makes 1/3 cup; 5 servings

10 garlic cloves
 3 mushrooms, sliced
    Pinch nutmeg
1/2 cup sodium-reduced chicken
    broth
 2 teaspoons chopped fresh parsley

Cover garlic with water in a small saucepan. Bring to a boil; drain. Repeat 3 times.

Mash garlic with fork and return to saucepan. Add mushrooms, nutmeg, chicken broth and parsley. Bring to a boil and reduce to desired consistency.

Nutrient Analysis: 1 tablespoon
Exchanges: free; 2 tablespoons = 1/2 carbohydrate   *Calories: 13   Protein: 1g   Carbohydrates: 3g*
Carbohydrate Choices: 0   *Fat: 0g   Cholesterol: 0mg   Sodium: 87mg*

GRAINS, PASTAS & LEGUMES

These were the staples that allowed humankind to survive and thrive throughout the ages.

Henry Blackburn

GRAINS, PASTAS & LEGUMES

The Dietary Guidelines recommend 3 servings of whole grains each day.

Once thought of only as side dishes, pasta, legumes and grains (such as barley, bulgur, and rice) now play a starring role on our plates as the main dish. These foods provide plenty of protein when combined with other grains, nuts and seeds, low-fat dairy products, or small amounts of lean meat, poultry or fish. To reduce our risk of heart disease, health experts advise us to use more whole grains and legumes to increase our soluble fiber intake, replace simple with complex carbohydrates, and reap the benefits of B vitamins that are nicely packaged in these wholesome foods. You'll find many tasty, heart-healthy dishes in this section. The following tables provide cooking tips for these three whole grains / vegetable groups, showing weights, dry measures, and cooking yields.

Table 19: Cooking Time and Yields for Rice & Grain

Uncooked Rice or Grain (1 cup)	Liquid (water)	Cooking Time (stovetop)	Yield (cooked)
GRAIN			
Barley, pearl	3 cups	50 minutes	3 1/2 cups
Buckwheat groats	2 cups	15 minutes	3 1/2 cups
Bulgur (cracked wheat)	2 cups	20 minutes	3 cups
Couscous, quick-cooking	2 cups	5 minutes	3 cups
Millet	2 cups	25 minutes	3 cups
Oats, quick, rolled	2 cups	1-5 minutes	2 cups
RICE			
Arborio (Risotto)	1 1/2 cups	20 minutes	3 cups
Basmati rice	2 cups	40 min soak/cook	3 cups
Brown (whole grain)	1 1/4 cups	40 - 45 minutes	3 to 4 cups
Brown (parboiled)	2 1/4 cups	30 minutes	3 to 4 cups
White, (precooked, instant)	1 cup	5 minutes	2 cups
White, long grain	2 cups	15 minutes	3 to 4 cups
White, medium grain	2 cups	15 minutes	3 cups
White, short grain	1 1/4 cups	15 minutes	3 cups
Wild (whole grain)*	3 cups, boiling	50-60 minutes	3 to 4 cups

Wild rice must be washed thoroughly before cooking.

Source: www.usarice.com/consumer/prep.html and www.mnwildrice.com, both accessed November 25, 2007 and TerMeer, M. and Gates, J., *Vegetarian Cooking for Healthy Living*. Mankato, MN: Appletree Press, 2008.

Oven

Cooking rice in the oven is an efficient use of energy as other foods are baking. Carefully combine rice and **boiling liquid** in a baking dish, stir. Cover tightly and bake at 350 degrees for 25 to 30 minutes for long grain white rice, (30-40 min for parboiled; 1-hour for whole grain brown rice). Remove carefully. Fluff with fork.

Microwave

Combine rice and liquid (see table above) in a 2 1/2 to 3-quart deep microwave-safe baking dish; cover tightly. For Medium or Long Grain rice, microwave on High *(100% power)* for 5 minutes or until boiling; reduce to Medium *(50% power)* and microwave 15 minutes (20 minutes for whole grain brown rice or parboiled rice; 30 minutes for wild rice) or until water is absorbed. Let stand 5 minutes.

Rice Cooker

Follow manufacturer's instructions. In general, all ingredients are combined in the rice cooker. Turn the rice cooker on; it will stop cooking automatically by sensing a rise in temperature and change in moisture content that occurs when rice has absorbed the liquid and is fully cooked. For proportion of rice to liquid, go to usarice.com.

Preparing the perfect pasta

To prepare the perfect pasta always boil the water first, then add the pasta, stirring, and return the water to a boil. Stir the pasta occasionally during cooking. Follow the package directions for cooking times for the type of pasta you enjoy. If the pasta is to be used as part of a dish that requires further cooking, undercook the pasta by one-third of the cooking time specified on the package. Taste the pasta to determine if it is done. Perfectly cooked pasta should be "al dente" or firm to the bite, yet cooked through.

Table 20: Weight, Dry Measure and Yields for Pasta

Type of Pasta	Weight	Dry Measure (uncooked)	Yield (cooked)
PASTA			
Egg noodles, 'short' elbow, shells, spirals, wagon wheels, ziti, etc	2 ounces	1/2 cup	just over 1/2 cup
Spaghetti, 'long' angel hair, vermicelli, linguine, etc	2 ounces	1/2 –inch bunch	1 cup
Egg noodles	1 pound	10 cups	12 cups
Macaroni	1 pound	4 cups	8 cups
Spaghetti	1 pound	4 cups	7 to 8 cups

Source: Ostmann, B. and Baker, J., *The Recipe Writer's Handbook.* New York: John Wiley & Sons, 2001.

How to Cook Legumes

Dried beans, split peas and lentils *must be cooked* before they are eaten in order to modify toxins that can cause stomach cramps, nausea and diarrhea.

Soaking Methods

Most legumes, except lentils, split peas and black-eyed peas, should be soaked in cold water for 6-8 hours or overnight at room temperature before cooking. This traditional method of soaking shortens the cooking time and improves the flavor, texture and appearance of the beans.

Another option of soaking legumes is the "quick-soak" method, in which 6-8 cups of hot water is added for each pound of dry beans. The water is heated to boiling and the legumes cooked for 2 minutes. Set them aside, cover and let stand to soak for 1 full hour. Drain and rinse the legumes and you're ready to cook.

Cooking Methods

Legumes can be cooked quickly in the pressure cooker, slowly in the slow cooker (crockpot), or on top the range. Legumes cooked in the pressure cooker will be done in 10-35 minutes at 15 pounds of pressure. In the slow cooker, legumes will take 10-12 hours at low heat or 5-6 hours at high heat.

Cooking Tips for Legumes

Follow the cooking requirements of legumes in the table below when cooking legumes on top the range. Be sure to use a large kettle or Dutch oven because legumes expand greatly when cooked. Adding a teaspoon of vegetable oil to the simmering legumes will help to prevent foaming. Don't add acidic ingredients such as lemon juice, vinegar or tomatoes to the cooking water until the beans are almost done as the acid slows the softening process.

Table 21: Cooking Yields of Legumes
(1 cup dry = 1/2 pound)

Legume:	Cooking Time: (in hours)	Minimum Water: (cups)	Yield: (cups)
Black beans	1 1/2	4	2
Black-eyed peas	1	3	2
Chickpeas (garbanzo)	3	4	4
Great Northern Beans	2	3 1/2	2
Kidney Beans	1 1/2	3	2
Lentils *	1	3	2 1/4
Lima beans	1 1/2	2	1 1/4
Navy beans	1 1/2	3	2
Pinto beans	2 1/2	3	2
Red beans	3	3	2
Soybeans	3 or more	3	2
Split peas	1	3	2 1/4

* Lentils are the one legume you can cook quickly (in fifteen minutes) even without soaking.

TerMeer, M. and Gates, J., *Vegetarian Cooking for Healthy Living.* Mankato, MN: Appletree Press, 2008.

WELLNESS GRANOLA*

Granola—honey-sweetened whole grains, nuts and dried fruit—makes a delicious, fiber and protein-packed snack or breakfast.

Makes 10 cups; 30 servings

1/2	cup vegetable oil
2/3	cup honey
5	cups uncooked old-fashioned oats
1	cup nonfat dry milk powder
1	cup wheat germ
1	cup sesame seeds
1	cup unsalted sunflower seeds
1	cup unsalted nuts (walnuts, almonds, or cashews)
1	cup raisins
1/2	cup chopped, dried apricots

* Be careful! Granolas are not a low-fat food.

Stir oil and honey over low heat in a small saucepan until combined thoroughly.

Mix together old-fashioned oats, dry milk powder, wheat germ, sesame seeds, sunflower seeds and unsalted nuts in a large bowl or roaster pan. Add oil and honey mixture and stir well.

Spread mixture on two nonstick-sprayed jelly roll pans or a large roaster pan. Bake, stirring occasionally. Remove from oven; stir in raisins and dried apricots. Cool. Store covered in refrigerator.

Oven: 250°
Time: 60 minutes

Nutrient Analysis: 1/3 cup
Exchanges: 1 starch, 1 fruit, 2 fat
Carbohydrate Choices: 2

Calories: 227   Protein: 6g   Carbohydrates: 26g
Fat: 12g   Cholesterol: 0mg   Sodium: 23mg
Dietary Fiber: 3g   Omega-3: 0.37g

CRUNCHY GRANOLA*

Delicious and hearty as a cereal or a snack. Make a batch and freeze half to keep fresh.

Makes 10 cups; 30 servings

5	cups uncooked old-fashioned oats
1	cup wheat germ
1	cup unsalted sunflower seeds
1/3	cup warm water
1/2	cup brown sugar
1/2	cup vegetable oil
2	tablespoons vanilla
1	cup Grape Nuts® cereal
1	cup All-Bran® cereal
1	cup chopped pecans
1	cup raisins

** Be careful! Granolas are not
a low-fat food.*

Mix oats, wheat germ and sunflower seeds in a large bowl.

Mix together water, sugar, oil and vanilla. Add to oat mixture and stir thoroughly. Spread in two 13 x 9" pans and bake at 325° for 20 minutes stirring every 10 mintues.

Add Grape Nuts, All-Bran and chopped pecans. Bake another 18 minutes, stir after 10 minutes and when finished. Remove from oven. When cool, add raisins.

Oven: 325°
Time: 38 minutes

Nutrient Analysis: 1/3 cup
Exchanges: 1 1/2 starch, 1 1/2 fat
Carbohydrate Choices: 1 1/2

Calories: 191   Protein: 5g   Carbohydrates: 24g
Fat: 10g   Cholesterol: 0mg   Sodium: 31mg
Dietary Fiber: 4g

OAT BRAN CEREAL

The soluble fiber in oat products appears to significantly lower blood cholesterol levels. For a tasty variation, cook cereals in apple juice instead of water.

Makes 3 cups; 4 servings

4 cups water
1/4 teaspoon salt
1 cup uncooked old-fashioned oats
1 cup oat bran
4 teaspoons raisins

Bring water to a boil in a medium saucepan. Add salt. Stir in old-fashioned oats and oat bran. Add raisins and cook over medium heat until thick.

Nutrient Analysis: 3/4 cup
Exchanges: 2 starch
Carbohydrate Choices: 2

Calories: 160   Protein: 7g   Carbohydrates: 32g
Fat: 3g   Cholesterol: 0mg   Sodium: 149mg
Dietary Fiber: 6g

CRISPY CEREAL SNACKS

A heart-healthy update of an old favorite.

Makes 6 cups; 18 servings

4 cups unsalted popped popcorn
2 cups bite-sized shredded wheat biscuits
4 cups puffed rice
1 cup unsalted peanuts
1/2 cup tub margarine
1/2 teaspoon paprika
1/4 teaspoon garlic powder
1/4 teaspoon curry powder
1 teaspoon sodium-reduced Worcestershire sauce.

Mix popcorn, shredded wheat, puffed rice and peanuts in a large roasting pan.

Melt margarine over low heat in a small saucepan. Stir in paprika, garlic powder, curry powder and Worcestershire.

Pour over cereal-nut mixture. Toss until well coated. Bake, uncovered, stirring every 15 minutes. Cool before serving. Store in an airtight container.

Oven: 250°
Time: 45 minutes

Nutrient Analysis: 1/3 cup
Exchanges: 1/2 starch, 2 fat
Carbohydrate Choices: 1/2

Calories: 130   Protein: 3g   Carbohydrates: 10g
Fat: 9g   Cholesterol: 0mg   Sodium: 44mg
Dietary Fiber: 2g

HONEY POPCORN BALLS

Makes 10 balls; 10 servings

3   quarts popped corn (about 1
       cup unpopped)
1/2   cup sugar, brown or white
1/2   cup honey or light corn syrup
2   tablespoons tub margarine
1   teaspoon vanilla

Pop corn and set aside in a large bowl.

Combine sugar and honey in a small saucepan. Heat and stir to dissolve sugar. Boil to hard ball stage (260°). Add margarine and vanilla. Stir the syrup slowly into the popped corn until every kernel is covered.

Shape the corn into balls with lightly oiled or floured hands as soon as it is cool enough to handle. Wrap balls in waxed paper or plastic wrap.

Nutrient Analysis: 1 ball
Exchanges: 2 starch, 1/2 fat
Carbohydrate Choices: 2

Calories: 147   Protein: 1 g   Carbohydrates: 31 g
Fat: 3 g   Cholesterol: 0 mg   Sodium: 20 mg
Dietary Fiber: 2 g

BARLEY PILAF

A nice change from potatoes or rice. Serve with meat or fish.

Makes 3 cups; 6 servings

3 tablespoons tub margarine
1/2 cup chopped onion
2 ribs celery, sliced
1 (4-ounce) can mushroom pieces, drained (or 4 oz. fresh, sliced)
1 cup uncooked pearl barley
3 teaspoons low-sodium, chicken-flavored bouillon granules
3 1/4 cups water
1/4 teaspoon pepper
1 bunch fresh spinach

Melt margarine in a large saucepan. Stir in onion, celery and mushrooms; sauté until tender (about 5 minutes).

Stir in barley and cook, stirring frequently, until lightly browned. Add bouillon, water and pepper; heat to boiling. Reduce heat to medium-low; cover and simmer 45 to 55 minutes or until liquid is absorbed and barley is tender. Or place barley mixture in covered casserole and bake at 325° until liquid is absorbed and barley is tender.

Meanwhile, wash spinach thoroughly. Steam 3 to 5 minutes. Remove from heat and stir into cooked barley mixture. Cook until heated through.

Nutrient Analysis: 1/2 cup
Exchanges: 1 1/2 starch, 1/2 vegetable, 1 fat
Carbohydrate Choices: 2

Calories: 189   Protein: 5g   Carbohydrates: 30g
Fat: 6g   Cholesterol: 0mg   Sodium: 231mg
Dietary Fiber: 6g

FRUITED BARLEY

A versatile dish suitable for brunch, a meat accompaniment or dessert.

Makes 4 cups; 8 servings

1/2	cup barley, dry
2 1/2	cups water, divided
1/2	cup raisins
1/2	cup dried plums
1/2	cup quartered apricots, dried or canned
1/2	cup quartered peaches, dried or canned
1/2	tablespoon brown sugar
1	tablespoon lemon juice

Soak barley in 1 1/2 cups of water in a medium saucepan overnight. When ready to cook barley, add remaining cup of water. Bring to a boil, cover and simmer 45 minutes.

Add fruit and simmer 5 more minutes or until fruit is soft. Just before serving, add brown sugar and lemon juice.

Nutrient Analysis: 1/2 cup
Exchanges: 1/2 starch, 2 fruit
Carbohydrate Choices: 2 1/2

Calories: 152   Protein: 3 g   Carbohydrates: 36 g
Fat: 0 g   Cholesterol: 0 mg   Sodium: 5 mg
Dietary Fiber: 4 g

BULGUR SAUTÉ

Bulgur, a cracked wheat product, and popular throughout the Middle East, is as versatile as rice or potatoes.

Makes 3 cups; 6 servings

2	tablespoons tub margarine
1	cup uncooked bulgur wheat
1/3	cup chopped onion
1/3	cup chopped celery
2	cups water
2 1/2	teaspoons low-sodium, beef-flavored bouillon
2	tablespoons chopped fresh parsley

Melt margarine in a medium saucepan. Stir in bulgur, onion and celery. Cook over low heat, 10 to 15 minutes. Stir in water and beef bouillon; bring to a boil. Reduce heat, cover and simmer for about 15 minutes or until bulgur is tender and water is absorbed. Stir in parsley.

Nutrient Analysis: 1/2 cup
Exchanges: 1 starch, 1 fat
Carbohydrate Choices: 1

Calories: 124   Protein: 3 g   Carbohydrates: 19 g
Fat: 4 g   Cholesterol: 0 mg   Sodium: 69 mg
Dietary Fiber: 5 g

RICE ALMOND BAKE

Serve as a side dish or use as a stuffing for poultry (enough to stuff one small turkey).

Makes 5 cups; 10 servings

2	tablespoons tub margarine
2	large onions, finely chopped
1	cup celery, finely chopped
2	cups defatted chicken broth
2/3	cup uncooked brown rice
1	cup raisins
2	teaspoons dried sage, crushed
1	teaspoon poultry seasoning
1/2	teaspoon pepper
1	cup sliced almonds

Heat margarine in a medium-sized saucepan. Add onion and celery and sauté until slightly soft.

Add chicken broth, rice and raisins and bring to a boil. Add seasonings and almonds. Place in a 1 1/2-quart casserole. Cover and bake.

If used as a poultry stuffing, simmer onion, celery, chicken broth, rice and raisins until most of the liquid is absorbed. Add sage, poultry seasoning, pepper and almonds; mix thoroughly. Stuff lightly into turkey cavity.

Oven: 350°
Time: 60 minutes

Nutrient Analysis: 1/2 cup
Exchanges: 1 starch, 1 fruit, 1 fat
Carbohydrate Choices: 2

Calories: 193　　Protein: 5g　　Carbohydrates: 27g
Fat: 8g　　Cholesterol: 1mg　　Sodium: 55mg
Dietary Fiber: 3g

RICE PILAF

Makes 3 cups; 6 servings

1   cup chopped onion
1/2   bay leaf
2   tablespoons tub margarine
3/4   cup uncooked long grain rice
1/4   cup white wine or vermouth
1 1/3 cups water
1   teaspoon low-sodium, chicken-
         flavored bouillon granules
2   tablespoons chopped fresh
         parsley or 1 tablespoon dried
         parsley flakes
       Freshly ground pepper

Sauté the onions and bay leaf in margarine in a medium saucepan until the onions are softened.

Add the rice and continue to cook over medium heat, stirring constantly, until rice is golden. Add wine, water, bouillon, parsley and pepper.

Bring to a boil. Reduce heat, cover and simmer for 25 minutes or until liquid is absorbed; OR place in covered casserole dish and bake in oven at 300° for about 40 minutes.

Nutrient Analysis: 1/2 cup
Exchanges: 1 starch, 1/2 vegetable, 1 fat
Carbohydrate Choices: 1 1/2

Calories: 139   Protein: 2g   Carbohydrates: 21g
Fat: 4g   Cholesterol: 0mg   Sodium: 45mg
Dietary Fiber: 1g

RICE WITH PINE NUTS

Makes 4 cups; 8 servings

1/4   cup pine nuts, roasted
2   tablespoons margarine, divided
1/4   cup chopped onion
1/2   teaspoon finely minced garlic
1   cup uncooked brown rice
3   cups water

Place pine nuts in skillet. Place over medium heat (300° in electric frying pan), cook and stir until lightly browned (approximately 7 minutes).

continued on next page

RICE WITH PINE NUTS, (continued)

Heat 1 tablespoon margarine in a saucepan; add onion and garlic and sauté until onion is wilted. Stir in the rice. Add water and pine nuts.

Bring to a boil. Reduce heat, cover tightly and simmer about 45 to 50 minutes or until water is absorbed and rice is tender.

Fluff the rice with a fork and stir in the remaining tablespoon of margarine.

Nutrient Analysis: 1/2 cup
Exchanges: 1 starch, 1 fat
Carbohydrate Choices: 1

Calories: 137   Protein: 3g   Carbohydrates: 19g
Fat: 6g   Cholesterol: 0mg   Sodium: 26mg
Dietary Fiber: 1g

GREEN RICE

Makes 2 1/2 cups; 5 servings

1	egg white
1	cup skim milk
1/2	cup finely chopped fresh parsley
1	garlic clove, minced
1	small onion, minced
2	cups cooked rice
1/2	cup shredded Cheddar cheese
1/8	teaspoon curry powder
1/4	teaspoon salt

Beat egg white. Add milk, parsley, garlic, onion, rice, cheese, curry powder and salt. Stir well.

Place in a nonstick-sprayed 7" ring mold and bake.

Oven: 325°
Time: 30 minutes

Nutrient Analysis: 1/2 cup
Exchanges: 1 1/2 starch, 1 very lean meat
Carbohydrate Choices: 1 1/2

Calories: 131   Protein: 8g   Carbohydrates: 22g
Fat: 1g   Cholesterol: 3mg   Sodium: 244mg
Dietary Fiber: 1g

ITALIAN RICE BAKE

Makes 4 cups; 6 servings

2/3 cup uncooked rice (or 2 cups leftover cooked rice)

1 1/3 cups water (if using uncooked rice)

1 onion, chopped

1 tablespoon tub margarine

1 (6-ounce) can tomato paste and

1 can water (to make tomato sauce)

1/2 teaspoon garlic powder

1 teaspoon sugar
Dash pepper

1/2 teaspoon whole thyme

1/2 teaspoon dried oregano, crushed

1 teaspoon parsley flakes

1 1/2 cups low-fat cottage cheese

1/2 cup grated part-skim mozzarella or farmer cheese

Cook rice in water.

Sauté onion in margarine in a skillet. Add tomato paste, water, garlic powder, sugar, pepper, thyme, oregano and parsley to onion mixture.

Add cottage cheese to the cooked rice.

Put 1/3 of rice mixture in nonstick-sprayed casserole dish. Top with 1/3 of tomato sauce. Continue to alternate layers, ending with tomato sauce. Top with grated mozzarella cheese. Bake until hot and bubbly.

Oven: 325°
Time: 30 minutes

Nutrient Analysis: 3/4 cup
Exchanges: 1 starch, 1 vegetable, 1 1/2 lean meat
Carbohydrate Choices: 2

Calories: 185   Protein: 12 g   Carbohydrates: 26 g
Fat: 4 g   Cholesterol: 8 mg   Sodium: 315 mg
Dietary Fiber: 2 g

WILD RICE

Wild rice, native to the North American continent, is actually the seed of an aquatic grass. It contains almost twice as much protein as white rice.

Makes 4 cups; 8 servings

1 cup uncooked wild rice
3 cups water
2 tablespoons low-sodium, chicken-flavored bouillon granules.

Rinse rice and put in a covered 1 1/2-quart baking dish. Add water and bouillon. Cover and bake. Check after 1 hour, fluffing with a fork and adding more water if necessary. Continue to bake until rice is tender but not dry.

OR in the top of a double boiler, bring rice, water and bouillon granules to a boil. Boil 5 minutes, then cover and place over simmering water in bottom of double boiler. Steam, stirring occasionally with a fork, until rice is tender and the water is absorbed (about 1 hour).

Do several batches at one time. Wild rice freezes well and is so handy to have on hand.

Oven: 350°
Time: 75 to 90 minutes

Nutrient Analysis: 1/2 cup
Exchanges: 1 starch
Carbohydrate Choices: 1

Calories: 83   Protein: 4g   Carbohydrates: 16g
Fat: 1g   Cholesterol: 1mg   Sodium: 49mg
Dietary Fiber: 1g

SPINACH LASAGNA

Makes 13 x 9" baking pan; 8 servings

8   whole wheat lasagna noodles
2   large bunches spinach, washed
      and trimmed
2   tablespoons oil
1   medium onion, chopped
2   garlic cloves, minced
1   (8-ounce) can no-salt-added
      tomato sauce
1   (6-ounce) can no-salt-added
      tomato paste
1   cup water
1   teaspoon honey
3/4   teaspoon dried basil, crushed
3/4   teaspoon dried oregano, crushed
      Freshly ground pepper
2   cups low-fat cottage or
      part-skim ricotta cheese
1   cup shredded part-skim
      mozzarella cheese
1   cup freshly grated Parmesan
      cheese

Cook lasagna noodles in boiling water until tender. Drain and set aside. Place spinach in steamer over medium heat and cook about 2 minutes. Drain well and set aside.

Heat oil in a medium skillet. Sauté onion until soft. Add garlic and sauté a few minutes more. Stir in tomato sauce, tomato paste, water, honey, basil, oregano and pepper. Reduce heat and simmer 20 minutes, stirring occasionally.

Lay 4 noodles on bottom of nonstick-sprayed 13 x 9" baking pan. Layer spinach, cottage or ricotta cheese and mozzarella cheese evenly over noodles. Top with half the sauce mixture. Cover with remaining noodles and sauce. Sprinkle with Parmesan. Cover and bake until lasagna is heated through and the cheeses are melted.

Oven: 350°
Time: 20 to 25 minutes

Nutrient Analysis: 1 serving   Calories: 298   Protein: 22g   Carbohydrates: 31g
Exchanges: 1 starch, 2 vegetable, 2 lean meat, 1 fat   Fat: 11g   Cholesterol: 18mg   Sodium: 573mg
Carbohydrate Choices: 2   Dietary Fiber: 7g   Calcium: 363mg

VEGETABLE LASAGNA

As pretty to look at as it is good to eat!

Makes 13 x 9" baking pan; 8 servings

3 cups diced zucchini (about 2 medium)
2 cups coarsely chopped broccoli (about 1/2 bunch)
1 cup chopped onion
2 garlic cloves, minced
1/2 teaspoon dried oregano, crushed
5 tablespoons tub margarine, divided
2 cups firmly packed spinach leaves (about 4 ounces), coarsely chopped
1 (15-ounce) container part-skim ricotta cheese
2 eggs
8 ounces whole wheat lasagna noodles (about 9 noodles)
1/4 cup all-purpose flour
2 1/2 cups skim milk
1/4 cup grated Parmesan cheese
8 ounces part-skim mozzarella cheese, sliced (8 slices)

Sauté zucchini, broccoli, onion, garlic and oregano in 2 tablespoons margarine in a medium skillet over medium heat until vegetables are crisp-tender (about 5 minutes). Add spinach and toss until wilted. Remove from heat.

In a medium bowl, mix ricotta and eggs; set aside.

Cook lasagna noodles according to package directions. Drain.

For white sauce: Melt 3 tablespoons margarine in a medium saucepan. Stir in flour. Gradually stir in milk and cook, stirring constantly, until sauce boils and thickens. Remove from heat and stir in Parmesan.

In a 13 x 9" baking pan, layer half the lasagna noodles, half the ricotta mixture, half the vegetable mixture, half the mozzarella and half the white sauce. Layer the remaining noodles, ricotta and vegetable mixture. Spoon remaining sauce over vegetables and top with sliced mozzarella cheese. Bake until hot and bubbly. Let lasagna stand 10 minutes before serving.

Oven: 350°
Time: 40 to 45 minutes

Nutrient Analysis: 1 serving
Exchanges: 1 1/2 starch, 2 vegetable, 2 lean meat, 3 fat
Carbohydrate Choices: 2

Calories: 403   Protein: 24g   Carbohydrates: 35g
Fat: 20g   Cholesterol: 93mg   Sodium: 453mg
Dietary Fiber: 6g   Calcium: 251mg

SPINACH LINGUINE WITH SPRING SAUCE

Makes 9 cups; 6 servings

3	tablespoons olive oil
1 1/2	cups diced zucchini
1	cup chopped onion
1	cup diced carrots
1	garlic clove, minced
2	cups skinned and chopped fresh tomatoes or 1 (16-ounce) can sodium-reduced tomatoes
1/2	teaspoon dried basil, crushed
1/4	teaspoon salt
1/2	teaspoon sugar
1	(8-ounce) package spinach linguine
3/4	cup grated Parmesan cheese

Heat oil in a large, deep skillet. Add zucchini, onion, carrots and garlic. Cook, stirring occasionally, until vegetables are crisp-tender.

Stir in tomatoes with juice, basil, salt and sugar. Cover and simmer over low heat 10 to 15 minutes, stirring occasionally to break up tomatoes.

Meanwhile, cook linguine according to package directions until al dente (about 8 to 10 minutes). Drain.

Add linguine and Parmesan to tomato mixture. Toss until well coated. Serve.

Nutrient Analysis: 1 1/2 cups
Exchanges: 2 starch, 1 1/2 vegetable, 2 fat
Carbohydrate Choices: 2 1/2

Calories: 280   Protein: 11 g   Carbohydrates: 37 g
Fat: 11 g   Cholesterol: 8 mg   Sodium: 299 mg
Dietary Fiber: 3 g   Calcium: 163 mg

PASTA PRIMAVERA

Makes 12 cups; 8 servings

1	cup zucchini, sliced
1 1/2	cups broccoli florets
1 1/2	cups snow peas
8	stalks asparagus
1	pound spaghetti or fettucine
16	cherry tomatoes
3	tablespoons olive oil, divided
2	teaspoons minced garlic
	Freshly ground pepper
1/4	cup chopped fresh parsley
1/4	cup pine nuts
10	large mushrooms, sliced
2	tablespoons tub margarine
1	cup evaporated skim milk
1/2	cup grated Parmesan cheese
1/4	cup chopped fresh basil
1/3	cup sodium-reduced chicken broth

Blanch zucchini, broccoli, snow peas and asparagus until crisp-tender. Drain and refresh under cold water.

Cook spaghetti or fettucine according to package directions. Drain and set aside.

Sauté tomatoes in 1 tablespoon oil with 1 teaspoon garlic, pepper and parsley for a minute or so. Set aside.

Heat remaining 2 tablespoons oil in a large pan and sauté pine nuts until golden. Add remaining garlic and all vegetables. Heat thoroughly.

In another large pan, melt margarine. Add evaporated milk, cheese and basil. Stir to blend and melt cheese. Stir in chicken broth. Add pasta and toss to coat. Add a third of the vegetables and toss.

Divide the pasta mixture among 8 plates. Top with remaining vegetables. Serve.

Nutrient Analysis: 1 1/2 cups
Exchanges: 3 starch, 1 vegetable, 2 fat
Carbohydrate Choices: 3 1/2

Calories: 384   Protein: 15g   Carbohydrates: 53g
Fat: 13g   Cholesterol: 5mg   Sodium: 172mg
Dietary Fiber: 4g   Calcium: 203mg

VEGETABLE NOODLE CASSEROLE

Resembles lasagna with a crunchy topping.

Makes 11 x 7" baking pan; 6 servings

2	tablespoons vegetable oil
2	green onions, sliced
2	garlic cloves, minced
3	tablespoons all-purpose flour
2	cups skim milk
1/4	cup chopped fresh parsley
1/4	teaspoon white pepper
1/4	teaspoon whole thyme
	Dash nutmeg
1	cup low-fat cottage cheese
1	(8-ounce) package wide egg noodles, cooked
3	cups diced, crisp-tender cooked vegetables (carrots, broccoli, mushrooms, celery)
1	cup shredded part-skim farmer cheese
1	cup whole grain bread crumbs

Sauté onions and garlic in oil in a medium saucepan until soft. Blend in flour and cook over medium heat several minutes, stirring constantly. Slowly add the milk, continuing to stir. Add the parsley, pepper, thyme, nutmeg and cottage cheese. Cook until sauce thickens.

Layer half the noodles, half the vegetables and half the sauce in a 11 x 7" nonstick-sprayed baking dish. Repeat with remaining noodles, vegetables and sauce. Top with cheese and bread crumbs.

Bake until piping hot and bubbly.

Oven: 350°
Time: 20 to 25 minutes

Nutrient Analysis: 1 serving
Exchanges: 2 starch, 1 vegetable, 2 lean meat, 1 fat
Carbohydrate Choices: 3

Calories: 343   Protein: 20g   Carbohydrates: 44g
Fat: 10g   Cholesterol: 53mg   Sodium: 321mg
Dietary Fiber: 3g   Calcium: 251mg

SPINACH PASTA CASSEROLE

6	ounces spinach noodles
1/2	cup sliced onion
1/4	cup chopped green pepper
2	tablespoons vegetable oil
1	cup low-fat cottage cheese
1	(6-ounce) container plain
	low-fat yogurt
1	tablespoon sodium-reduced
	Worcestershire sauce
1/4	teaspoon pepper
1/4	teaspoon garlic powder
1	cup shredded part-skim
	mozzarella cheese

Makes 1 1/2-quart casserole; 6 servings

Cook noodles according to package directions. Drain and set aside.

Sauté onion and green pepper in oil in a small skillet until onion is tender and golden.

Combine noodles, onion, green pepper, cottage cheese, yogurt, Worcestershire, pepper, garlic powder and shredded cheese in a large bowl. Toss to mix. Turn into a nonstick-sprayed 1 1/2-quart casserole. Cover and bake 25 minutes. Remove cover and bake an additional 15 minutes.

Oven: 350°
Time: 25 minutes covered and
15 minutes uncovered

Nutrient Analysis: 1 1/2 cups
Exchanges: 2 starch, 1 vegetable, 2 lean meat, 1 fat
Carbohydrate Choices: 2 1/2

Calories: 358   *Protein: 22g*   *Carbohydrates: 39g*
Fat: 13g   *Cholesterol: 21mg*   *Sodium: 393mg*
Dietary Fiber: 2g   *Calcium: 280mg*

SEAFOOD PASTA

Excellent dish to serve to guests. You'll receive raves. This dish can be prepared up to baking point a day ahead and refrigerated. If refrigerated, increase baking time by 15 minutes.

Makes 13 x 9" baking pan; 8 servings

1	cup medium WHITE SAUCE, *(page 164)*
12	ounces spaghetti noodles
1/2	red or green bell pepper, diced
6	ounces frozen crab or lobster meat
12	ounces frozen cooked shrimp
1	cup finely diced onion
1	cup sliced fresh mushrooms
1	cup frozen peas
1/4	cup diced pimiento
8	ounces part-skim farmer cheese, cubed

Make white sauce. Set aside.

Cook spaghetti in boiling water for 8 minutes. Drain and rinse with cold water.

Combine spaghetti, red or green pepper, crab or lobster, shrimp, mushrooms, onion, peas, pimiento and cheese. Turn into a nonstick-sprayed 13 x 9" baking pan and pour white sauce over the mixture. Cover and bake 30 minutes. Remove cover and bake an additional 15 minutes.

Oven: 350°
Time: 30 minutes covered and
*   15 minutes uncovered*

Nutrient Analysis: 1 1/2 cups

Exchanges: 1 1/2 starch, 2 1/2 very lean meat,
*   2 fat*
Carbohydrate Choices: 2

Calories: 305   Protein: 24g   Carbohydrates: 30g
Fat: 9g   Cholesterol: 80mg   Sodium: 314mg
Dietary Fiber: 2g   Calcium: 288mg   Omega-3: 0.31g

SPAGHETTI SAUCE

Makes 8 cups; 8 servings

1/2 cup onion slices
1 cup sliced fresh mushrooms
2 tablespoons olive oil
1 pound extra-lean ground beef
2 garlic cloves, minced
4 cups skinned and chopped fresh tomatoes or 2 (16-ounce) cans sodium-reduced tomatoes
2 (8-ounce) cans sodium-reduced tomato sauce
1/4 cup chopped fresh parsley
1 1/2 teaspoons dried oregano, crushed
Freshly ground pepper
1 bay leaf
1 cup water

Sauté onions and mushrooms in oil in a large saucepan. Add ground beef and garlic and brown lightly.

Add tomatoes, tomato sauce, parsley, oregano, pepper, bay leaf and water. Bring to a boil. Reduce heat, cover and simmer for 4 hours. Remove bay leaf.

Serve over cooked pasta of your choice and sprinkle with grated Parmesan.

Nutrient Analysis: 1 cup
Exchanges: 1 vegetable, 2 lean meat
Carbohydrate Choices: 1/2

Calories: 138   Protein: 13g   Carbohydrates: 10g
Fat: 6g   Cholesterol: 30mg   Sodium: 48mg
Dietary Fiber: 2g

DON'T COOK THE MANICOTTI

This dish can be prepared up to baking point a day ahead and refrigerated. If refrigerated, increase baking time by 15 minutes.

Makes 13 x 9" baking pan; 8 servings

1	pound extra-lean ground beef
1/2	cup chopped onion
1/4	teaspoon garlic powder
4	cups sodium-reduced tomato juice
1	(6-ounce) can no-salt-added tomato paste
2	teaspoons dried oregano, crushed
1	teaspoon sugar
1/8	teaspoon pepper
4	cups shredded part-skim mozzarella cheese, divided
1	(12-ounce) container low-fat cottage cheese
1	(10-ounce) package frozen chopped spinach, thawed and drained
1	egg
1	egg white
1/2	cup Parmesan cheese
1	(8-ounce) package large manicotti shells

Brown meat with onion and garlic powder in a skillet. Stir in 2 cups tomato juice, tomato paste, oregano, sugar, and pepper. Simmer 15 minutes.

Combine 2 cups mozzarella cheese, cottage cheese, spinach, egg, egg white and Parmesan in a large bowl. Stuff uncooked manicotti shells with cheese mixture. Arrange in a nonstick-sprayed 13 x 9" baking pan. Spread remaining stuffing mixture over the top and spoon meat sauce over shells. Pour remaining 2 cups tomato juice over all. Cover and bake.

Remove from oven and top with remaining 2 cups mozzarella cheese. Cover and let stand 15 minutes.

Oven: 350°
Time: 60 minutes

Nutrient Analysis: 1 serving
Exchanges: 1 1/2 starch, 2 vegetable, 5 lean meat
Carbohydrate Choices: 2 1/2

Calories: 428	*Protein: 40 g*	*Carbohydrates: 36 g*
Fat: 14 g	*Cholesterol: 95 mg*	*Sodium: 632 mg*
Dietary Fiber: 4 g	*Calcium: 529 mg*	

BAKED BEANS #1

Maple syrup adds that "something special" to these beans.

Makes 2-quart casserole; 8 servings

1	pound (about 2 1/2 cups) navy beans, dry
1/2	onion, chopped
2	cups sodium-reduced tomato juice
2/3	cup maple syrup
1	(6-ounce) can no-salt-added tomato paste
1	(6-ounce) can water
1/4	teaspoon black pepper

Sort and rinse beans. Cover with water in a 2-quart saucepan and bring to a boil. Turn off heat, cover and let beans sit in their cooking water for 1 hour. Return to heat and simmer the beans, covered, for 1 hour. Drain. Beans should be tender but firm. Do not stir beans.

Combine and heat onion, tomato juice, maple syrup, tomato paste, water and pepper in a medium saucepan. Layer beans and sauce in a nonstick-sprayed 2-quart casserole. Cover and bake.

Oven: 325°
Time: 2 1/2 hours

Nutrient Analysis: 3/4 cup
Exchanges: 3 starch, 2 vegetable
Carbohydrate Choices: 3

Calories: 276   Protein: 13 g   Carbohydrates: 57 g
Fat: 1 g   Cholesterol: 0 mg   Sodium: 35 mg
Dietary Fiber: 14 g   Calcium: 113 mg

BAKED BEANS #2

Long, slow cooking for these deep-brown, old-fashioned baked beans.

Makes 2 1/2-quart casserole; 8 servings

1	pound (about 2 1/2 cups) navy beans, dry
1/2	pound Canadian bacon
1/2	cup chili sauce
1	tablespoon vinegar
1	medium onion, chopped
1/2	teaspoon dry mustard
6	tablespoons molasses
1/4	cup brown sugar
2	cups bean water

Sort and rinse beans. Cover beans with water and soak overnight or, bring beans to a boil, turn off heat, cover and allow beans to sit in their cooking water for one hour. Return beans to heat. Add chunk of Canadian bacon and bring beans to a boil. Simmer, covered, for one hour or until beans are tender.

Remove Canadian bacon and dice. Drain beans reserving 2 cups bean water.

Combine chili sauce, vinegar, onion, mustard, molasses, brown sugar and bean water.

Place beans and diced Canadian bacon in a nonstick-sprayed 2 1/2-quart casserole and pour sauce over beans. Cover and bake in a slow oven.

Oven: 275°
Time: 4 to 5 hours

Nutrient Analysis: 3/4 cup
Exchanges: 3 starch, 1 lean meat
Carbohydrate Choices: 3

Calories: 293   Protein: 17g   Carbohydrates: 54g
Fat: 2g   Cholesterol: 14mg   Sodium: 783mg
Dietary Fiber: 13g   Calcium: 121mg

BLACK BEAN CHILI

Spicy-hot, meatless chili. Make a large pot and freeze for another occasion.

Makes 16 cups; 10 servings

2 pounds (about 4 cups)
   black beans, dry
2 tablespoons cumin seed
2 tablespoons dried oregano,
   crushed
2 large yellow onions,
   finely chopped
1 1/2 cups finely chopped green pepper
2 garlic cloves, minced
1/4 cup olive oil
1 teaspoon cayenne pepper
1 1/2 tablespoons paprika
3 cups canned sodium-reduced
   tomatoes, crushed
1/2 cup finely chopped jalapeño
   chilies (fresh or canned)
8 ounces (about 2 cups) part-skim
   farmer cheese or
   Lorraine Swiss, shredded
1 (6-ounce) container plain
   low-fat yogurt
1/2 cup green onions, finely chopped
8 sprigs fresh cilantro or parsley
   (optional)

Sort and rinse beans well. Place beans in a large pot and cover with water to several inches above top of beans. Cover pot and bring to a boil. Reduce heat and cook until beans are tender (about 1 hour) adding more water if beans begin to show above water level. Drain the beans reserving 1 cup of the bean water. Return beans and water to pot.

Place cumin seed and oregano in a small pan and bake in a 325° oven until the fragrance is toasty (10-12 minutes).

Sauté onions, green pepper and garlic in olive oil with cumin, oregano, cayenne pepper and paprika until onions are soft (about 10 minutes). Add onion mixture, tomatoes and chilies to the beans. Stir and heat thoroughly.

To serve: Place one ounce shredded cheese in heated bowl and cover with 1 1/2 cups hot chili. Top with a spoonful of yogurt and sprinkle with one tablespoon chopped green onion. Garnish with a sprig of cilantro or parsley.

Nutrient Analysis: 1 1/2 cups
Exchanges: 3 starch, 2 lean meat, 1 fat
Carbohydrate Choices: 2 1/2

Calories: 392   Protein: 24g   Carbohydrates: 55g
Fat: 10g   Cholesterol: 14mg   Sodium: 168mg
Dietary Fiber: 17g   Calcium: 297mg

SPANISH RED BEANS AND RICE

Makes 8 cups; 8 servings

1	cup kidney beans, dry
3	cups water
1	tablespoon dried basil, crushed
1	tablespoon dried marjoram, crushed
1	tablespoon black pepper
1	tablespoon jalapeño peppers, seeded and chopped
2	cups brown rice, dry
5 1/2	cups water
1	cup chopped green onions (optional)
	Lemon wedges (optional)

Sort and rinse beans. In a saucepan, soak kidney beans in 3 cups water overnight. Add basil, marjoram, pepper and chili peppers. Bring to a boil, reduce heat and simmer, covered until beans are tender (about 3 hours).

Combine rice and 5 1/2 cups water in a saucepan. Bring to a boil. Cover, reduce heat and simmer for 45 minutes. Remove from heat and let stand, covered, for 10 minutes.

To serve, dish rice onto individual serving plates, top with beans and garnish with onions and lemon wedge.

Nutrient Analysis: 1 cup
Exchanges: 3 starch
Carbohydrate Choices: 3

Calories: 252   Protein: 9g   Carbohydrates: 50g
Fat: 2g   Cholesterol: 0mg   Sodium: 11mg
Dietary Fiber: 8g

SAVORY BLACK BEANS

A good crock-pot recipe.

Makes 6 cups; 8 servings

1	pound (about 2 1/2 cups) black beans, dry
10	cups water
1/2	cup olive oil
1	large onion, sliced
1	green pepper, chopped
4	garlic cloves, minced

Sort, rinse and soak beans in water to cover overnight. Next morning, simmer beans, covered, in water for 1 hour.

Add oil, onion, green pepper, garlic, salt, pepper, oregano, bay leaf and sugar. Cook 1 hour.

continued on next page

SAVORY BLACK BEANS, (continued)

1/2   teaspoon salt
1/2   teaspoon pepper
1/4   teaspoon dried oregano,
        crushed
  1   bay leaf
  2   tablespoons sugar
  2   tablespoons vinegar

Add vinegar and cook over low heat or in crock-pot until tender (5 to 6 hours).

Serve with steamed rice.

Nutrient Analysis: 3/4 cup
Exchanges: 3 starch, 2 fat
Carbohydrate Choices: 2

Calories: 333   *Protein: 13 g*   *Carbohydrates: 41 g*
Fat: 14 g   *Cholesterol: 0 mg*   *Sodium: 159 mg*
Dietary Fiber: 12 g

GINGERED LENTILS

Makes 3 cups; 6 servings

  3   cups water
  1   cup lentils, dry
1/2   teaspoon salt
  3   tablespoons vegetable oil
  1   teaspoon grated fresh ginger
1/2   cup chopped green onions
1/3   cup chopped green pepper
  2   tablespoons white wine vinegar

Heat water, lentils and salt to boiling in a medium saucepan. Reduce heat, cover and simmer 20 to 25 minutes or until lentils are tender but not mushy. Drain lentils and set aside.

Heat oil and ginger in a medium skillet for 1 minute, stirring often. Add green onion and pepper. Stir-fry for 2 minutes.

Add lentils and vinegar. Heat thoroughly.

Nutrient Analysis: 1/2 cup
Exchanges: 1 1/2 starch, 1 fat
Carbohydrate Choices: 1

Calories: 173   *Protein: 9 g*   *Carbohydrates: 19 g*
Fat: 7 g   *Cholesterol: 0 mg*   *Sodium: 198 mg*
Dietary Fiber: 10 g

HERBED LENTILS AND RICE CASSEROLE

Makes 2 1/2-quart casserole; 6 servings

3   cups sodium-reduced,
      chicken-flavored broth
3/4   cup lentils, dry
3/4   cup chopped onion
1/2   cup brown rice, dry
1/4   cup white wine or water
1/2   teaspoon dried basil, crushed
1/4   teaspoon dried oregano,
      crushed
1/4   teaspoon whole thyme
1/4   teaspoon garlic powder
1/8   teaspoon pepper
1/2   cup shredded part-skim
      mozzarella cheese, divided

Combine broth, lentils, onion, rice, wine, basil, oregano, thyme, garlic powder and 1/4 cup of the grated cheese in a 2 1/2-quart casserole. Cover and bake 2 hours adding more broth if casserole becomes dry.

Top with the remaining cheese and bake another 2 to 3 minutes or until the cheese is melted.

Oven: 350°
Time: 2 hours

Nutrient Analysis: 1 cup   Calories: 185   Protein: 12 g   Carbohydrates: 28 g
Exchanges: 2 starch, 1/2 lean meat   Fat: 3 g   Cholesterol: 7 mg   Sodium: 102 mg
Carbohydrate Choices: 1 1/2   Dietary Fiber: 8 g

TOFU ITALIANO

No one suspects this dish is made from tofu! Tastes like lasagna.

Makes 13 x 9" baking dish; 8 servings

2	(1-pound) packages extra firm, silken tofu, diced
2	eggs
2	egg whites
1 1/2	cups sodium-reduced tomato sauce
1 3/4	cups sodium-reduced canned tomatoes, crushed
1/2	cup chopped onion
1/3	cup chopped green pepper
4	teaspoons garlic powder
2	tablespoons dried basil, crushed
1/8	teaspoon nutmeg
1 1/2	teaspoons onion powder
1/4	cup all-purpose flour
20	ounces (5 cups) shredded part-skim mozzarella cheese

Mix together the tofu, eggs, egg whites, tomato sauce, tomatoes, onion, green pepper, garlic powder, basil, nutmeg, onion powder and flour in a large bowl.

Spread half the mixture in a nonstick-sprayed 13 x 9" baking dish. Top with half the mozzarella. Cover with remaining tofu mixture.

Bake 40 minutes then remove from oven and cover with remaining cheese. Bake another 10 minutes or until the cheese is nicely browned.

Oven: 350°
Time: 50 minutes

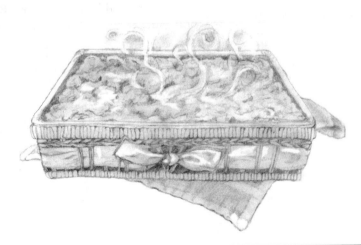

Nutrient Analysis: 1 serving
Exchanges: 1 starch, 4 lean meat
Carbohydrate Choices: 1

Calories: 308   Protein: 30g   Carbohydrates: 15g
Fat: 15g   Cholesterol: 94mg   Sodium: 459mg
Dietary Fiber: 2g   Calcium: 517mg

SUKIYAKI

Sukiyaki (pronounced "ski ya ke") is a great choice for casual entertaining. It is prepared at the table in a large skillet and guests help themselves to their choice of goodies from the simmering pot.

Makes 16 cups; 8 servings

1	(7-ounce) package cellophane (bean thread) noodles, dry
4	medium carrots, shredded
2	medium onions, thinly sliced in rounds
2	bunches green onions, 1" diagonal cuts
6	ribs bok choy or celery, 1" diagonal cuts
4	ounces mushrooms, 1/4" slices
1	(8-ounce) can no-salt-added sliced bamboo shoots
1	(8-ounce) package extra-firm, silken tofu, cut into 1/2" cubes
4	cups spinach leaves
1 1/2	pounds sirloin, sliced 2" x 1" x 1/4"
2	cups low-sodium beef broth
1/2	cup sodium-reduced soy sauce
1/4	cup sugar
3	tablespoons dry sherry
3	tablespoons oil

Soak bean thread in hot water for 20 minutes. Prepare vegetables and meat. In a pitcher, mix broth, soy sauce, sugar and sherry.

Arrange a row of bean thread down the center of a large platter and place meat slices on top. Place carrots in a row on one side, onions on the other.

Arrange the remainder of the vegetables in a similar manner.

Heat an electric skillet to 350°. Add enough oil just to coat skillet and when almost smoking, lay meat slices flat in the pan. Brown quickly on each side, 1 to 2 minutes and remove.

Add about a third of the broth mixture along with a third of the carrots, onions, bok choy, mushrooms and bamboo shoots. Bring to a boil. Add more broth if the pan seems dry.

Place a third of the bean thread, tofu and raw spinach over vegetables and top with a third of the meat.

When everything is boiling, have the guests help themselves. Repeat the above process as the skillet is emptied.

Nutrient Analysis: 2 cups
Exchanges: 2 starch, 2 vegetable,
3 lean meat, 1 fat
Carbohydrate Choices: 3

Calories: 368 *Protein: 26g* *Carbohydrates: 42g*
Fat: 11g *Cholesterol: 50mg* *Sodium: 700mg*
Dietary Fiber: 4g *Calcium: 120mg*

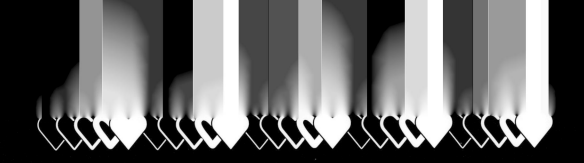

VEGETABLES

*It is nearly fifty years since I was
assured by a conclave of doctors
that if I did not eat meat I should
die of starvation.*

George Bernard Shaw

VEGETABLES

*Vegetables
are nutritional
bargains.*

Vegetables are naturally low in calories but loaded with natural antioxidants, such as Vitamins A, C, E, selenium, and certain dietary plant compounds called phytonutrients (phytochemicals), which provide many benefits to our overall health and well-being. Phytonutrients are regarded as nature's natural anti-cancer compounds and play a role in heart health. Antioxidants thwart heart disease by preventing oxidation of LDL cholesterol, fight chronic inflammation, can improve vascular function and discourage formation of blood clots. Researchers report that a higher consumption of fruits and vegetables can lower the risk of heart disease by 20 percent!

Eat the rainbow!

Vegetables have become the new "super heroes" to fighting various chronic diseases and their strength lies in their color pigments (which in turn, is often found in the skin or peel). Eating vegetables of different colors gives your body a wide range of valuable nutrients, like soluble fiber, folic acid, magnesium, potassium, plus antioxidants. So think "color groups" when you think vegetables. Strive to eat from each color group by varying the vegetables you eat and remember, the goal is to eat at least two and a half cups of vegetables a day. Visit 5aday.gov to learn how you can power pack your day with more fruits and vegetables.

Table 22: Antioxidants and Health Benefits found in Vegetable Color Groups

Color Group	Vegetables	Antioxidants	Health Benefits
Blue-Purple	Red Cabbage Eggplant Purple Peppers	Anthocyanins, Vitamin C, Ellagic acid, Phenolics Sulphoraphane	Maintains healthy blood pressure Improves vascular function Anticarcinogenic
Yellow-Orange	Corn, Squash, Carrots, Yellow Peppers Pumpkin, Rutabagas Sweet Potatoes	Beta-carotene, Lutein Alpha-carotene, Zeaxanthin	Reduces LDL-cholesterol Healthy vision Boosts immune system Anticarcinogenic
Red	Tomatoes, Beets, Radishes, Radicchio Red Peppers, Red potatoes	Anthocyanins, Lycopene, Vitamin C	Reduces inflammation Maintains healthy blood pressure Improves vascular function Anticarcinogenic

Table 22: Antioxidants and Health Benefits found in Vegetable Color Groups (Continued)

Color Group	Vegetables	Antioxidants	Health Benefits
White-Green	Cabbage, Garlic, Onions, Cauliflower Mushrooms, Parsnips Shallots, Turnips Bok Choy, Broccoli, Brussel Sprouts, Peas Asparagus, Kale, Spinach	Allicin, Thioallyls Flavonoids, Glucoraphanin Indoles, Sulforaphane Lutein, Selenium	Lowers blood cholesterol Maintains healthy blood pressure Prevents blood clots Anticarcinogenic

Sources: CDC, Fruits & Veggies Matter: Fruit & Vegetable Benefits/*ColorGuide* (2007); The Effect of Fruit and Vegetable Intake on Coronary Heart Disease, *Ann Int Med* 2001, 134:1106-1114 and Halvorsen, B.L., et al; Content of redox-active compounds (ie, antioxidants) in foods consumed in the United States, *Amer Jrnl Clin Nutrition* 2006, 84:95-135.

Preparation Methods

Proper storing and preparation preserves the nutrient content of vegetables. Pick or purchase vegetables at peak quality and refrigerate them unwashed and in air-tight containers. It's recommended that vegetables be used as quickly as possible. To maximize their flavor, texture and nutrients, cook vegetables with skins on and only until crisp-tender. Cooking liquid can be saved for soups and stews.

Steam   The preferred method, because vegetables do not come in direct contact with water which leaches nutrients.

Simmer   Add vegetables to a small amount of unsalted water. Simmer until crisp-tender.

Bake   Vegetables such as potatoes, rutabagas, squash and eggplant can be baked in skins with most nutrients retained. Pierce skins before baking to allow steam to escape.

Stir-fry   Add coarsely chopped vegetables to a small amount of hot liquid in a wok or skillet. Cook, stirring often, until vegetables are bright, glossy and crisp-tender.

Microwave   An excellent way to cook fresh or frozen vegetables, use only small amounts of water, don't add salt (salt toughens vegetables) and be sure to pierce vegetables with skins before cooking. Cover and cook until vegetables are slightly underdone (vegetables will continue to cook after being removed from the microwave) and serve immediately.

SEASONINGS FOR VEGETABLES *

Discover the world of herbs and spices which add interest and enhance the flavors of cooked and raw vegetables. Try the following suggestions as well as your own personal favorites.

Asparagus:	chives, lemon juice, caraway seed
Broccoli:	caraway seed, mustard, lemon, oregano, sesame seed, tarragon
Carrots:	cinnamon, curry, dill, ginger, lemon juice, mace, marjoram, mint, nutmeg, rosemary, savory, tarragon, thyme
Cauliflower:	nutmeg, oregano, savory, tarragon
Corn:	caraway seed, celery seed, curry, dill, mustard, green pepper, chives, parsley, onion
Green beans:	basil, dill, lemon juice, nutmeg, marjoram, mustard, onion, oregano, chives, rosemary
Peas:	basil, chili powder, dill, chives, marjoram, mint, mustard, nutmeg, orange rind, oregano, parsley, rosemary, sage, chervil, thyme
Potatoes:	basil, bay leaves, caraway seed, celery seed, chives, dill, mace, mustard, oregano, parsley, dill, rosemary, savory, sesame seed, thyme
Squash:	ginger, mace, onion, basil, chives
Tomatoes:	garlic, onion, parsley, basil, sage, Italian seasoning

* See SEASONINGS section for additional herb and spice blends.

ARTICHOKES

Artichokes are cooked whole and then served hot or cold, whole or cored. The leaves are pulled off one by one, dipped in a sauce and then the lower end is pulled through the teeth to extract the edible portion. When the outer leaves are gone, the light colored cone of immature leaves appears. With a spoon remove and discard the cone and the thistle-like center (the choke). Cut the heart into bite size pieces and dip in sauce.

Select green artichokes with leaves tight together. Discolored ones with loosely spreading leaves will be tough.

To prepare artichokes, cut off stem and 1/3 of the pointed top. Trim off the prickly points with a scissors. Rinse the trimmed artichokes in water.

Place artichokes upright in steamer basket or in about 2 inches of boiling water. Cook, covered, until tender (about 45 minutes) or pressure cook 15 minutes. Serve one artichoke for each person.

ARTICHOKES SMOTHERED WITH TOMATOES & HERBS

Serve one artichoke for each person as a vegetable or an appetizer.

TOPPING FOR EACH ARTICHOKE:

- 1   green onion, finely minced
- 1   small onion, thinly sliced
- 1   teaspoon olive oil
- 1   medium tomato, peeled, seeded and coarsely chopped
- 1/2   teaspoon tiny capers
  Freshly ground pepper

GARNISH:

Chopped fresh basil, oregano or marjoram or 1 teaspoon finely chopped jalapeño pepper (canned or fresh)

Makes 1 artichoke; 1 serving

Clean and rinse artichokes. Pry apart the center of the artichoke and scoop out the hairy core with a sharp teaspoon (a grapefruit spoon works well. This process takes a little practice but artichokes are very resilient and will take a lot of punishment). Do be careful not to tear off outer leaves. Stand artichokes upright in a deep, covered casserole, or 13 x 9" pan.

Combine onion, olive oil, tomato, capers and pepper. Spoon some of the mixture into center cavity of artichoke and sprinkle the rest over tops and in between outer leaves.

Add boiling water to cover bottom third of artichokes (or half way up the side of 13 x 9" pan). Cover and simmer gently on stove top or bake in oven until artichokes are tender but not mushy. Garnish and serve hot, warm or at room temperature.

Stove top: Simmer 30 to 45 minutes or
Oven: 350°
Time: 60 minutes

Nutrient Analysis: 1 artichoke
Exchanges: 5 vegetable, 1 fat
Carbohydrate Choices: 1

Calories: 165   Protein: 8g   Carbohydrates: 29g
Fat: 5g   Cholesterol: 0mg   Sodium: 262mg
Dietary Fiber: 12g   Calcium: 100mg

ASPARAGUS ORIENTAL

Makes about 4 cups; 6 servings

1 1/2	pounds fresh asparagus
1	tablespoon vegetable oil
1 1/2	teaspoons sodium-reduced soy sauce
1	teaspoon sesame oil
1	teaspoon water
1	garlic clove, pressed
1/4	teaspoon ground ginger
1	tablespoon sesame seed, toasted

Steam asparagus spears until crisp-tender (8 to 10 minutes).

In small jar with tight fitting lid, combine vegetable oil, soy sauce, sesame oil, water, garlic and ginger. Cover and shake. Pour over asparagus and marinate at room temperature or in refrigerator for at least an hour.

Serve cold or reheat in microwave. Just before serving, sprinkle asparagus with sesame seed.

Nutrient Analysis: 2/3 cup
Exchanges: 1 vegetable, 1 fat
Carbohydrate Choices: 0

Calories: 66   Protein: 4 g   Carbohydrates: 5 g
Fat: 4 g   Cholesterol: 0 mg   Sodium: 49 mg
Dietary Fiber: 2 g

GREEN BEANS CREOLE

Makes 4 cups; 4 servings

1	cup chopped onion
1	tablespoon olive oil
2	tomatoes, peeled and chopped
1	pound fresh green beans
1/2	teaspoon dried basil, crushed
1/2	teaspoon dried tarragon, crushed
1/4	teaspoon salt
	Freshly ground pepper
3	dashes Tabasco sauce

Sauté onion lightly in olive oil in a medium saucepan.

Add tomatoes and cook until juice is released.

Add beans, basil, tarragon, salt, pepper and Tabasco. Cook on low until beans are tender (15 to 20 minutes).

Nutrient Analysis: 1 cup
Exchanges: 2 vegetable, 1 fat
Carbohydrate Choices: 1/2

Calories: 98   Protein: 3 g   Carbohydrates: 15 g
Fat: 4 g   Cholesterol: 0 mg   Sodium: 157 mg
Dietary Fiber: 5 g

PINEAPPLE BEETS

Makes 3 cups; 4 servings

3/4T 1 1/2 tablespoons cornstarch
1/3 2/3 cup unsweetened pineapple
         juice, divided
1/6 1/3 cup sugar
p   2 tablespoons cider vinegar
1/2 1 (16-ounce) can small whole
         beets, drained
1/4 1/2 cup juice-packed pineapple
         tidbits, drained

Moisten the cornstarch and mix to a smooth paste using 2 tablespoons of the pineapple juice.

Mix remaining juice, sugar and vinegar in a medium saucepan and bring to a boil. Add the cornstarch mixture and cook, stirring to prevent lumping, until clear and thickened.

Add the beets and pineapple; heat thoroughly.

Nutrient Analysis: 3/4 cup
Exchanges: 1 starch, 1 fruit, 1 vegetable
Carbohydrate Choices: 2 1/2

Calories: 149   Protein: 1g   Carbohydrates: 37g
Fat: 0g   Cholesterol: 0mg   Sodium: 223mg
Dietary Fiber: 2g

ITALIAN BROCCOLI WITH TOMATOES

Makes 4 cups; 6 servings

4 cups broccoli florets
1 tablespoon water
1/2 teaspoon dried oregano, crushed
1/4 teaspoon pepper
1 tablespoon lemon juice
2 medium ripe tomatoes,
      cut in wedges
1 cup shredded part-skim
      mozzarella cheese

Wash and cut broccoli florets into 1/2" pieces. Place broccoli and water in a shallow, round microwave-safe dish. Cover with plastic wrap or lid. Microwave on HIGH for 6 to 8 minutes or until tender. Stir several times. Drain.

Stir in oregano, pepper, lemon juice and tomato wedges. Sprinkle cheese on top. Cover. Microwave to melt cheese. Let stand 2 minutes before serving.

Nutrient Analysis: 2/3 cup
Exchanges: 1 vegetable, 1 lean meat
Carbohydrate Choices: 1/2

Calories: 74   Protein: 6g   Carbohydrates: 6g
Fat: 3g   Cholesterol: 11mg   Sodium: 102mg
Dietary Fiber: 2g   Calcium: 151mg

BRUSSELS SPROUTS

Makes 4 cups; 6 servings

1 1/2	pounds Brussels sprouts
1	cup low-sodium chicken broth
1	tablespoon chopped onion
1/4	teaspoon fresh ground pepper
1	tablespoon tub margarine
1	tablespoon lemon juice

Remove wilted leaves, cut off stems and cut an X on the bottom of each sprout.

Bring chicken broth to a boil in a medium saucepan. Add sprouts and onions. Return to a boil and cook uncovered 5 minutes. Cover and cook another 5 to 8 minutes or until sprouts are crisp-tender. Drain.

Add pepper, margarine and lemon juice. Toss and serve immediately.

Nutrient Analysis: 2/3 cup
Exchanges: 2 vegetable, 1/2 fat
Carbohydrate Choices: 1

Calories: 72   Protein: 4g   Carbohydrates: 11g
Fat: 2g   Cholesterol: 1mg   Sodium: 62mg
Dietary Fiber: 4g

CRISP CABBAGE MEDLEY

A nice complement to pork.

Makes 6 cups; 6 servings

2	tablespoons tub margarine
3	cups shredded cabbage
1	medium onion, chopped
1	green pepper, chopped
1	cup thinly sliced celery
1/2	cup dry white wine

Melt margarine in a medium saucepan. Add cabbage, onion, green pepper, celery and wine. Cover and steam until vegetables are crisp-tender (about 5 minutes). Serve immediately.

Nutrient Analysis: 1 cup
Exchanges: 1 vegetable, 1 fat
Carbohydrate Choices: 1/2

Calories: 76   Protein: 1g   Carbohydrates: 7g
Fat: 4g   Cholesterol: 0mg   Sodium: 59mg
Dietary Fiber: 2g

RED CABBAGE

Makes 8 cups; 8 servings

1/4 cup sugar
1 teaspoon whole cloves
1/2 cup cider vinegar
1 medium onion, chopped
1/2 cup water
1 large head red cabbage,
      shredded (8 cups)

Combine sugar, vinegar and cloves in a small saucepan. Bring to a boil; reduce heat and simmer 6 minutes. Remove cloves.

Add onion and water and simmer 5 more minutes

Place shredded cabbage in a large saucepan and pour hot vinegar solution over cabbage. Cook until cabbage is hot and crisp-tender (5 to 6 minutes). Serve.

Nutrient Analysis: 1 cup
Exchanges: 1/2 starch, 2 vegetable
Carbohydrate Choices: 1

Calories: 72   Protein: 2g   Carbohydrates: 17g
Fat: 0g   Cholesterol: 0mg   Sodium: 16mg
Dietary Fiber: 3g

CARROTS ÉLÉGANT

Makes 4 1/2 cups; 6 servings

1 1/2 pounds carrots, scrubbed
        and sliced
2 tablespoons tub margarine
1/4 teaspoon cardamom
1/4 cup orange juice or 1 tablespoon
        frozen concentrate

Cook carrots until tender but not soft in a waterless cooker or steamer.

Melt together margarine, cardamom and orange juice in a small saucepan. Pour hot mixture over carrots and serve.

Nutrient Analysis: 3/4 cup
Exchanges: 2 vegetable, 1 fat
Carbohydrate Choices: 1

Calories: 89   Protein: 1g   Carbohydrates: 13g
Fat: 4g   Cholesterol: 0mg   Sodium: 91mg
Dietary Fiber: 3g

GLAZED CARROTS

Makes 4 1/2 cups; 6 servings

1 1/2	pounds carrots	
1	tablespoon olive oil	
3/4	teaspoon dried basil or oregano, crushed	
1	teaspoon brown sugar	
1/2	small garlic clove, minced	
1/2	cup water	
	Freshly ground pepper	

Scrub the carrots and cut on bias into slices 1/2" thick. Heat oil in frying pan. Add carrots, cover and cook over medium heat for 10 minutes, stirring occasionally.

Add basil or oregano, sugar, garlic, water and pepper. Cook uncovered, about 20 minutes until carrots are tender and liquid is reduced to a thin syrup.

Nutrient Analysis: 3/4 cup
Exchanges: 2 vegetable, 1/2 fat
Carbohydrate Choices: 1

Calories: 73   Protein: 1g   Carbohydrates: 12g
Fat: 2g   Cholesterol: 0mg   Sodium: 58mg
Dietary Fiber: 3g

STEAMED CARROTS WITH APRICOTS

Makes 4 cups; 8 servings

1	cup dried apricots	
3	cups carrots, cut into 1/2" rounds	
3	tablespoons water	
1	teaspoon tub margarine	
	Pinch of sugar	
	Chopped fresh parsley or dill for garnish (optional)	

Soak apricots in hot water for 1 1/2 hours. Pat dry and cut in julienne strips.

In a skillet with a tightly fitting lid, combine scraped carrots, water, margarine and sugar. Cover and cook over medium heat for 12 to 15 minutes or until carrots are fork tender. Shake occasionally to prevent sticking.

Stir in apricots and heat through. Serve garnished with parsley or dill.

Nutrient Analysis: 1/2 cup
Exchanges: 1 fruit, 1 vegetable
Carbohydrate Choices: 1

Calories: 78   Protein: 1g   Carbohydrates: 17g
Fat: 1g   Cholesterol: 0mg   Sodium: 21mg
Dietary Fiber: 2g

CARROTS & CUCUMBERS

An unusual but tasty combination.

Makes 6 cups; 6 servings

2   large cucumbers (about 1 1/4 pounds)
2   large carrots (about 1/2 pound)
1   cup boiling water
2   tablespoons tub margarine
1   tablespoon finely chopped green onion
1/4   teaspoon ground cumin
      Freshly ground pepper to taste

Peel cucumbers and cut lengthwise in half. Seed and slice thinly crosswise. There should be about 4 cups. Set aside.

Trim and scrub carrots. Cut carrots into 1 1/2" matchsticks. There should be about 2 cups.

Place carrots in a medium saucepan and add enough boiling water to cover. Cook about 4 minutes.

Add cucumber and cook about a minute more. Drain well.

In a skillet, heat margarine and add onion. Cook briefly, stirring.

Add carrots and cucumbers and sprinkle with cumin and pepper. Cook, stirring occasionally, about 2 minutes. Serve.

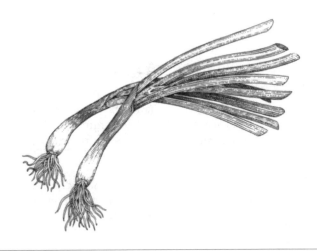

Nutrient Analysis: 1 cup
Exchanges: 1 vegetable, 1 fat
Carbohydrate Choices: 1/2

Calories: 65   Protein: 2g   Carbohydrates: 7g
Fat: 4g   Cholesterol: 0mg   Sodium: 46mg
Dietary Fiber: 2g

EGGPLANT CASSEROLE

This hearty vegetable casserole is a satisfying main dish.

Makes 6 cups; 4 servings

1	medium eggplant, peeled and diced (4 cups)
3	tablespoons tub margarine
3	tablespoons whole wheat flour
3	large tomatoes, diced
1	small green pepper, chopped
1	small onion, chopped
1	tablespoon brown sugar
1/2	bay leaf (optional)
2	whole cloves
1/2	cup bread crumbs

Cook eggplant in boiling water in a medium saucepan until tender but not mushy. Drain and place in a nonstick-sprayed casserole.

In the same saucepan, melt margarine and stir in the flour. Add the tomatoes, green pepper, onion, brown sugar, bay leaf and cloves. Cook 15 minutes. Remove bay leaf. Pour over eggplant and top with bread crumbs. Bake.

Oven: 350°
Time: 30 minutes

Nutrient Analysis: 1 1/2 cup
Exchanges: 1 starch, 2 vegetable, 2 fat
Carbohydrate Choices: 1

Calories: 196   Protein: 4g   Carbohydrates: 26g
Fat: 10g   Cholesterol: 0mg   Sodium: 112mg
Dietary Fiber: 6g

STUFFED PEPPERS

Makes 4 cups; 4 servings

2	medium green peppers
2	tomatoes, peeled, seeded and chopped
1/4	cup chopped onion
1/4	cup chopped fresh mushrooms
2	tablespoons chopped chives
1/8	teaspoon dried basil, crushed
1/4	teaspoon pepper
1/2	cup fresh bread crumbs
1	tablespoon margarine, melted

Cut peppers in half lengthwise; remove stems and seeds. Parboil 3 to 5 minutes. Remove from water and place cut side up in a shallow baking dish.

Combine tomatoes, onions, mushrooms, chives, basil and pepper and mix well. Divide mixture among the pepper shells.

continued on next page

STUFFED PEPPERS, (continued)

Mix bread crumbs with melted margarine and sprinkle over filled peppers. Pour 1/2" water into bottom of baking dish and bake uncovered.

Oven: 350°
Time: 25 to 30 minutes

Nutrient Analysis: 1 cup   *Calories: 85   Protein: 2g   Carbohydrates: 13g*
Exchanges: 2 vegetable, 1/2 fat   *Fat: 3g   Cholesterol: 0mg   Sodium: 59mg*
Carbohydrate Choices: 1   *Dietary Fiber: 2g*

BROCCOLI BAKED POTATOES

Makes 6 potatoes; 6 servings

6   medium Idaho potatoes
3   stalks broccoli
1/4   cup skim milk
1   cup shredded Cheddar cheese
1/8   teaspoon pepper

Scrub potatoes. Make shallow slits around the middle as if you were cutting the potatoes in half lengthwise. Bake until done, 30 to 60 minutes, depending on size.

Peel broccoli stems. Steam whole stalks just until tender and chop finely.

Carefully slice the potatoes in half and scoop the insides into a bowl with the broccoli. Add the milk, 3/4 cup cheese and pepper. Mash together until the mixture is pale green with dark green flecks.

Heap into the potato jackets and sprinkle with remaining cheese. Return to oven to heat through (about 15 minutes).

Oven: 350°
Time: 30 to 60 minutes;
     15 minutes to melt cheese or to reheat.

Nutrient Analysis: 1 potato   *Calories: 141   Protein: 10g   Carbohydrates: 28g*
Exchanges: 2 starch   *Fat: 1g   Cholesterol: 4mg   Sodium: 156mg*
Carbohydrate Choices: 2   *Dietary Fiber: 4g   Calcium: 103mg*

CAULIFLOWER WALNUT CASSEROLE

Because of the cheese and nuts, this is more appropriately considered a vegetable entrée than a vegetable side dish. Serve with a salad, French bread and a fruit dessert. For variety, substitute broccoli or cabbage for the cauliflower.

Makes 11 x 7" baking dish; 4 servings

1	medium head cauliflower, broken into florets
1	cup plain low-fat yogurt
1	cup shredded Cheddar cheese
1	tablespoon flour
2	teaspoons low-sodium, chicken-flavored bouillon granules
1	teaspoon dry mustard
1/2	cup chopped walnuts
1	tablespoon tub margarine
1/3	cup fine dry bread crumbs
1	teaspoon dried marjoram, crushed

Bring water to a boil in a medium sauce pan. Add cauliflower, reduce heat and simmer 15 minutes. Drain.

Mix yogurt, cheese, flour, bouillon granules and mustard. Place cauliflower in 11 x 7" baking dish and spoon yogurt mixture over cauliflower.

Mix together walnuts, bread crumbs, margarine, marjoram and sprinkle over cauliflower and sauce. Bake until casserole is bubbly.

Oven: 400°
Time: 20 minutes

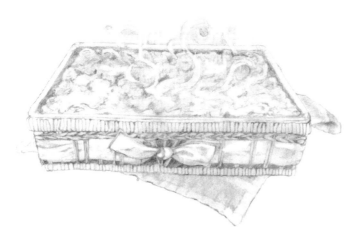

Nutrient Analysis: 1 1/2 cups
Exchanges: 1 starch, 2 vegetable,
*   1 1/2 lean meat, 2 fat*
Carbohydrate Choices: 1

Calories: 288   Protein: 19g   Carbohydrates: 24g
Fat: 15g   Cholesterol: 9mg   Sodium: 536mg
Dietary Fiber: 7g   Calcium: 267mg   Omega-3: 1.53g

BAKED POTATO TOPPINGS

A medium potato has only about 100 calories, but the toppings can be whopping calorie and fat contributors. Try the following low-calorie toppings on baked potatoes.

Toasted sesame seeds
A spoonful of stewed tomatoes and
   a bit of shredded cheese
Melted margarine thinned with
   lemon juice
Dried herb mixture: parsley,
   chives, basil, dill
MOCK SOUR CREAM, *(page 81)*
Chopped onion with freshly
   ground pepper
Chive-spiked yogurt
Lemon juice and freshly ground
   pepper
SALSA, *(page 226)*

PARMESAN POTATOES

Makes 3 cups; 4 servings

4   medium potatoes, scrubbed
2   tablespoons flour
2   tablespoons Parmesan cheese
     Pepper to taste
2   tablespoons tub margarine

Cut each potato into 4 to 6 chunks.

Combine flour, Parmesan and pepper in a plastic bag. Shake potatoes, a few at a time, in cheese mixture.

Melt the margarine in a 13 x 9" baking pan. Place potatoes in a single layer and bake turning once during baking.

Oven: 350°
Time: 60 minutes

Nutrient Analysis: 3/4 cup
Exchanges: 1 starch, 1 fat
Carbohydrate Choices: 1

Calories: 116   Protein: 4g   Carbohydrates: 19g
Fat: 4g   Cholesterol: 1mg   Sodium: 63mg
Dietary Fiber: 2g

SWEET POTATOES & APPLES

Makes 6 cups; 6 servings

1-c	1 1/2	pounds sweet potatoes (about 4 sweet potatoes, 3 cups sliced)
1-c	3	tart apples, unpeeled, cored and sliced (about 3 cups)
1/4 c	3/4	cup orange juice
1/4 hp	3/4	teaspoon grated fresh ginger
1/8	1/2	teaspoon cinnamon
1/16	1/4	teaspoon allspice
1/16	1/4	teaspoon nutmeg

Cook unpeeled potatoes in boiling water in a medium saucepan for 25 minutes.

Heat apples and orange juice with ginger, cinnamon, allspice and nutmeg in a medium skillet, over high heat. Cover and cook until apples soften, 3 to 5 minutes. Uncover and reduce heat; simmer apples a few minutes longer.

Peel and slice cooked sweet potatoes and add to apple mixture. Mix gently and heat thoroughly

Nutrient Analysis: 1 cup
Exchanges: 1 1/2 starch, 1 fruit
Carbohydrate Choices: 2 1/2

Calories: 174　　Protein: 2g　　Carbohydrates: 41g
Fat: 1g　　Cholesterol: 1mg　　Sodium: 18mg
Dietary Fiber: 5g

SPAGHETTI SQUASH SAUTÉ

Makes 6 cups; 6 servings

2	pounds spaghetti squash (3-4 medium, 6 cups, sliced)
2	tablespoons vegetable oil
1/2	cup chopped green onions
2	garlic cloves, minced
1/2	cup chopped fresh parsley
1	tablespoon lemon juice
1/4	cup grated Parmesan cheese

Place whole spaghetti squash in baking dish. Prick skin several times with fork. Bake in preheated 350° oven 45 to 60 minutes or until tender; cool. Cut squash in half lengthwise; remove seeds. With fork, scoop out flesh into medium bowl, separating into spaghetti-like strands.

Heat oil in a large skillet over medium-high heat. Cook green onions and garlic in oil about 3 minutes, stirring constantly. Add squash and stir-fry 3 to 5 minutes more until heated through. Stir in parsley and lemon juice; mix well. Add cheese and toss to coat.

Nutrient Analysis: 1 cup
Exchanges: 1 vegetable, 1 fat
Carbohydrate Choices: 0

Calories: 69　　Protein: 2g　　Carbohydrates: 3g
Fat: 6g　　Cholesterol: 3mg　　Sodium: 69mg
Dietary Fiber: 1g

SQUASH STUFFED WITH RICE

The RICE ALMOND BAKE, (page 181) also makes a tasty stuffing for squash.

Makes 6 stuffed acorn halves; 6 servings

1 1/2	cups cooked brown rice
1/2	cup chopped walnuts
1/4	cup cracker crumbs
1	medium onion, finely chopped
2	egg whites, slightly beaten
1/2	teaspoon ground sage
1/2	teaspoon nutmeg
1	tablespoon chopped fresh parsley
2	tablespoons brown sugar
	Freshly ground pepper
3	small acorn or buttercup squash, halved and seeded

Combine rice, walnuts, cracker crumbs, onion, egg whites, sage, nutmeg, parsley, brown sugar and black pepper.

Spoon mixture loosely into squash halves. Bake in foil-covered pan until squash is tender.

Oven: 350°
Time: 60 minutes

Nutrient Analysis: 1 acorn half
Exchanges: 1 starch, 4 vegetable, 1 fat
Carbohydrate Choices: 2 1/2

Calories: 254   Protein: 6g   Carbohydrates: 44g
Fat: 8g   Cholesterol: 0mg   Sodium: 91mg
Dietary Fiber: 5g   Omega-3: 0.97g

BAKED GARLIC TOMATOES

The baking time is correct!

Makes 4 cups; 8 servings

4	ripe tomatoes
1/4	cup olive oil
4	garlic cloves, minced
2	tablespoons chopped fresh basil or 1 tablespoon chopped fresh rosemary
1/4	teaspoon salt
	Freshly ground pepper

Core tomatoes and slice in half crosswise. Place in baking dish, cut side up.

Mix olive oil, garlic, basil or rosemary, salt and pepper. Pour over tomatoes. Bake.

Oven: 325°
Time: 2 hours

Nutrient Analysis: 1/2 cup
Exchanges: 1 vegetable, 1 fat
Carbohydrate Choices: 0

Calories: 77   Protein: 1g   Carbohydrates: 4g
Fat: 7g   Cholesterol: 0mg   Sodium: 75mg
Dietary Fiber: 1g

HOW TO PREPARE TOMATOES FOR STUFFING

Makes 6 stuffed tomatoes; 6 servings

6 tomatoes

Prepare tomatoes by slicing 1/2" from the stem end of medium to large tomatoes and a thin sliver from the bottom if necessary to make the tomato stand upright. Scoop out the seeds and pulp, leaving a 1/4" shell. Drain pulp well and reserve the pulp for stuffing. Invert the tomatoes to drain while preparing stuffing. Stuff shells with filling and arrange in a baking pan. Bake until shells and stuffing are thoroughly heated, usually 20-30 minutes in a moderate oven.

STUFFED TOMATO VARIATIONS:

CURRIED RICE STUFFED TOMATOES

6	tomatoes
1/4	teaspoon salt
1/8	teaspoon pepper
1/4	cup diced green pepper
1/3	cup minced onion
1	teaspoon sodium-reduced Worcestershire sauce
1	teaspoon curry powder
2	cups cooked brown rice
1/4	cup fine soft bread crumbs

Prepare tomatoes as in STUFFED TOMATOES, *(above)*.

Mash drained pulp in a medium saucepan and combine with salt, pepper, green pepper, onion, Worcestershire and curry powder. Cook over low heat for 5 minutes.

Add rice and stir. Stuff tomato shells and sprinkle with bread crumbs. Bake.

Oven: 375°
Time: 15 to 20 minutes

MUSHROOM STUFFED TOMATOES

  6   tomatoes
  1   tablespoon tub margarine
1/2 pound coarsely chopped
      mushrooms
1/3 cup minced onion
  1   teaspoon minced garlic
1 1/2 cups HERB SEASONED
      CROUTONS, *(page 124)*

Prepare tomatoes as in STUFFED TOMATOES.

Melt margarine in a large, nonstick-sprayed skillet. Sauté mushrooms, onion and garlic for 5 minutes.

Stir in tomato pulp and croutons. Stuff tomato shells and bake.

Oven: 375°
Time: 15 to 20 minutes

CHEESE STUFFED TOMATOES

  6   tomatoes
  1   cup low-fat cottage cheese
  1   tablespoon lemon juice
  2   tablespoons tub margarine
  8   ounces fresh mushrooms, sliced
      (about 1 1/2 cups)
  3   green onions with tops, sliced
      thinly
  1   tablespoon minced fresh parsley
  1   tablespoon all-purpose flour
1/2 cup coarse, whole wheat bread
      crumbs

Prepare tomatoes as in STUFFED TOMATOES.

Whip cottage cheese with lemon juice in a blender or food processor.

Melt margarine in a large skillet. Add mushrooms and onions and sauté 5 minutes.

Blend parsley and flour and stir into mushroom-onion mixture.

Stir in cottage cheese and cook about 5 minutes. DO NOT BOIL. Stuff tomato shells and bake.

Oven: 375°
Time: 15 to 20 minutes

Nutrient Analysis: 1 stuffed tomato	*Rice*	*Mushroom*	*Cheese*
Exchanges:	*1 starch, 1 1/2 vegetable*	*1/2 starch, 2 vegetable, 1 fat*	*2 vegetable, 1 very lean meat, 1 fat*
Carbohydrate Choices:	*1 1/2*	*1*	*1*
Calories:	*114*	*140*	*123*
Protein:	*3g*	*4g*	*7g*
Carbohydrates:	*23g*	*17g*	*13g*
Fat:	*1g*	*7g*	*5g*
Cholesterol:	*0g*	*1mg*	*2mg*
Sodium:	*116mg*	*138mg*	*213mg*
Dietary Fiber:	*2g*	*3g*	*2g*

TOMATOES ROCKEFELLER

Makes 6 tomato halves; 6 servings

3   large tomatoes, cut in half
1   tablespoon margarine, melted
3   tablespoons finely chopped onion
2   tablespoons finely chopped fresh
  parsley
2   cups chopped fresh spinach
1   tablespoon light mayonnaise
  Freshly ground pepper
  Paprika
3   tablespoons Italian seasoned
  bread crumbs

Place tomatoes cut-side up in a nonstick-sprayed baking dish.

Melt margarine in a medium skillet. Sauté onion slowly until tender but not brown.

Add parsley and spinach. Cover pan and "sweat" spinach 1 to 2 minutes until wilted.

Mix in mayonnaise, pepper and paprika.

Top tomato halves with mounds of the spinach mixture. Sprinkle with crumbs and bake.

Oven: 375°
Time: 15 to 20 minutes

Nutrient Analysis: 1 tomato half
Exchanges: 2 vegetable, 1/2 fat
Carbohydrate Choices: 1/2

Calories: 68 Protein: 2g Carbohydrates: 9g
Fat: 3g Cholesterol: 1mg Sodium: 140mg
Dietary Fiber: 2g Calcium: 124mg

HOMEMADE TOMATO SAUCE

Use on any meat, pasta or pizza calling for tomato sauce. This sauce freezes well.

Makes 2 cups; 4 servings

1/3 cup onion, finely chopped
2 tablespoons olive oil
4 parsley sprigs
1 small bay leaf
1/4 teaspoon thyme
2 teaspoons all-purpose flour
4 cups fresh tomatoes, peeled,
    seeded and chopped
    (about 4 tomatoes)
1/8 teaspoon sugar
2 garlic cloves, mashed
1/8 teaspoon fennel
1/8 teaspoon basil
    Pinch coriander

Cook onion in olive oil in a heavy 3-quart saucepan over low heat until tender but not browned.

Make herb bouquet by tying parsley, bay leaf and thyme in cheesecloth or place in a spice infuser.

Stir flour into onion and cook slowly for 3 minutes.

Add herb bouquet, tomatoes, sugar, garlic, fennel, basil and coriander. Cover and cook slowly for 10 minutes.

Uncover and simmer for 30 minutes, stirring often. If sauce becomes too thick, add a small amount of water. When the sauce is thick enough to mound in a spoon, remove the herb bouquet.

Nutrient Analysis: 1/2 cup
Exchanges: 2 vegetable, 1 fat
Carbohydrate Choices: 1

Calories: 107   Protein: 2g   Carbohydrates: 11g
Fat: 7g   Cholesterol: 0mg   Sodium: 17mg
Dietary Fiber: 2g

SALSA

SALSA is an all-purpose topping for everything from rice or tacos to baked potatoes or salad greens. It will keep for two weeks in the refrigerator. It can also be made with fresh tomatoes, although it doesn't keep as long (2 to 3 days). If using fresh tomatoes, add a tablespoon of vinegar or lemon juice.

Makes 2 cups; 4 servings

3 tablespoons chopped cilantro
1 medium onion, finely chopped
2 green chilies or jalapeño
     peppers, finely chopped
1 (28-ounce) can sodium-reduced
     tomatoes, drained
    Freshly ground pepper
1/4 teaspoon ground coriander

Chop cilantro, onion, chilies or peppers and tomatoes in a food processor, one ingredient at a time.

Return all ingredients to food processor, add pepper and coriander and process for a few seconds.

Nutrient Analysis: 1/2 cup
Exchanges: 2 vegetable
Carbohydrate Choices: 1/2

Calories: 57   Protein: 2g   Carbohydrates: 10g
Fat: 0g   Cholesterol: 0mg   Sodium: 50mg
Dietary Fiber: 3g

FRESH TOMATO-PINEAPPLE SALSA

A favorite from the California tomato growers.

Makes 4 cups; 8 servings

3 cups fresh tomatoes, diced
1 cup fresh diced pineapple
1 cup sliced green onions
1 fresh jalapeño pepper, seeded
     and finely chopped
3 tablespoons chopped
     fresh cilantro
3 tablespoons fresh lemon juice
2 cloves garlic, finely chopped

Combine all ingredients in large bowl. Stir gently until evenly mixed. Serve salsa with grilled or broiled fish or chicken.

Nutrient Analysis: 1/2 cup
Exchanges: 1 1/2 vegetable
Carbohydrate Choices: 1/2

Calories: 34   Protein: 1g   Carbohydrates: 8g
Fat: 0g   Cholesterol: 0mg   Sodium: 6mg
Dietary Fiber: 1g

STEAMED VEGETABLE MEDLEY

Makes 4 1/2 cups; 6 servings

2 cups cauliflower florets
  (about 1 medium head)
1 cup carrots, sliced diagonally
1 medium red onion, sliced and
  separated into rings
1 cup sliced fresh mushrooms
1 1/2 tablespoons tub margarine
1 tablespoon lemon juice
1/4 teaspoon dried basil, crushed
1/4 teaspoon dried marjoram,
  crushed

Place the cauliflower, carrots and onion in steamer basket. Cover and steam over boiling water for 10 minutes.

Add mushrooms and steam 5 minutes more or until vegetables are just tender.

Meanwhile, melt margarine. Add lemon juice, basil and marjoram.

To serve, place vegetables in serving bowl. Pour lemon mixture over vegetables and toss to coat.

Nutrient Analysis: 3/4 cup
Exchanges: 1 vegetable, 1/2 fat
Carbohydrate Choices: 1/2

Calories: 55   Protein: 2g   Carbohydrates: 6g
Fat: 3g   Cholesterol: 0mg   Sodium: 41mg
Dietary Fiber: 2g

AUTUMN VEGETABLE STEW

Makes 9 cups; 6 servings

2 tablespoons vegetable oil
1 large onion, sliced
2 carrots or parsnips, peeled and
  sliced (1 1/2 cups)
1/2 pound green beans, trimmed
  and halved (2 cups)
2 cups shredded green cabbage
2 cups low-sodium tomato juice
1 teaspoon ground coriander
1 teaspoon chili powder
1 teaspoon turmeric

Heat oil in a large skillet or Dutch oven. Add onion and sauté 3 minutes, stirring frequently.

Stir in carrots or parsnips, green beans, cabbage, tomato juice, coriander, chili powder and turmeric. Heat to boiling. Reduce heat to medium; cover and simmer 20 to 30 minutes or until vegetables are tender.

Nutrient Analysis: 1 1/2 cups
Exchanges: 2 vegetable, 1 fat
Carbohydrate Choices: 1

Calories: 93   Protein: 2g   Carbohydrates: 12g
Fat: 5g   Cholesterol: 0mg   Sodium: 29mg
Dietary Fiber: 4g

TURNIP CASSEROLE

This colorful vegetable casserole is even better the next day.

Makes 4 cups; 4 servings

1   pound fresh white turnips
      (3 medium, 3 cups cubed)
2   tablespoons margarine, melted
1/4 cup chopped onion
1   cup peeled, chopped, fresh
      tomatoes
1/2 cup chopped celery
1/2 teaspoon sugar
1/4 teaspoon dried sage, crushed
1/8 teaspoon pepper

Peel and cube the turnips. Place in 1" of boiling water in a medium saucepan and simmer, covered, about 5 to 7 minutes or until barely tender.

Mix turnips, margarine, onion, tomatoes, celery, sugar, sage and pepper and turn into a nonstick-sprayed 1-quart casserole. Cover and bake until vegetables are hot and tender.

Oven: 350°
Time: 15 to 20 minutes

Nutrient Analysis: 1 cup		
Exchanges: 2 vegetable, 1 fat		
Carbohydrate Choices: 1		

Calories: 99	*Protein: 2g*	*Carbohydrates: 11g*
Fat: 6g	*Cholesterol: 0mg*	*Sodium: 142mg*
Dietary Fiber: 3g		

ZUCCHINI MEDLEY

As colorful as a Mexican fiesta.

Makes 8 cups; 8 servings

3   tablespoons vegetable oil
4   cups thinly sliced zucchini
      (about 2 large)
1   cup coarsely shredded carrot
1   medium onion, chopped
3/4 cup chopped celery
1/2 green pepper, cut in thin strips
1/2 teaspoon garlic powder
1/2 teaspoon dried basil, crushed

Heat oil in a large skillet. Add zucchini, carrot, onion, celery, green pepper, garlic powder, basil, pepper, dry mustard and taco sauce. Toss to mix well. Cover and cook over medium heat 4 minutes, stirring occasionally.

continued on next page

ZUCCHINI MEDLEY, (continued)

Dash of pepper
2 teaspoons dry mustard
1/3 cup taco sauce
2 tomatoes, cut in wedges
1/4 cup grated Parmesan cheese

Add tomato wedges and cook, uncovered, 3 to 5 minutes or until tomatoes are heated through Sprinkle with Parmesan and serve.

Nutrient Analysis: 1 cup
Exchanges: 1 1/2 vegetable, 1 fat
Carbohydrate Choices: 1/2

Calories: 96   Protein: 3 g   Carbohydrates: 8 g
Fat: 6 g   Cholesterol: 2 mg   Sodium: 126 mg
Dietary Fiber: 2 g

RATATOUILLE

Versatile ratatouille—hot vegetable entrée or side dish, cold salad, condiment, stuffing or seasoning. Make plenty while vegetables are in season and freeze.

Makes 8 cups; 8 servings

1 pound eggplant (about 1 medium)
1 large zucchini
3 tablespoons olive oil
1 green pepper, seeded and cut in squares
1 large onion, cut in squares and separated
2 garlic cloves, minced
2 cups cubed fresh tomatoes
3 tablespoons tomato paste
1 bay leaf
1/2 teaspoon whole thyme
   Pepper to taste
1/4 cup Parmesan cheese

Trim and peel the eggplant. Cut into 3/4" cubes.

Trim the ends of the zucchini but do not peel. Cut into 1/2" cubes.

Heat the oil in a heavy skillet until it is very hot. Add the eggplant and zucchini and cook, stirring often, for about 2 minutes.

Add the green pepper and onion and cook for 6 minutes, stirring gently.

Add garlic, tomatoes, tomato paste, bay leaf, thyme and pepper. Bring to a boil, stirring.

Pour the mixture into a nonstick-sprayed 13 x 9" baking dish. Bake 20 minutes. Sprinkle with Parmesan and bake an additional 10 minutes. Serve immediately.

Oven: 400°
Time: 20 minutes, 10 minutes

Nutrient Analysis: 1 cup
Exchanges: 2 vegetable, 1 fat
Carbohydrate Choices: 1/2

Calories: 100   Protein: 3 g   Carbohydrates: 10 g
Fat: 6 g   Cholesterol: 2 mg   Sodium: 108 mg
Dietary Fiber: 3 g

VEGETABLE SHEPHERD'S PIE

Makes 11 x 7" baking pan; 6 servings

4	large potatoes (about 2 1/2-3 cups mashed)
1/2	cup plain low-fat yogurt
1/2	cup chopped fresh or 4 teaspoons dried chives
1/2	cup chopped fresh or 4 teaspoons dried parsley
1 1/2	cups chopped onion
1	large garlic clove, minced
1 1/2	tablespoons tub margarine
1	stalk celery, chopped
1	eggplant (about 1 pound), peeled and cubed
1	green pepper, chopped
1	(14-ounce) can whole tomatoes, drained and cut in pieces
1/4	teaspoon whole thyme, crushed
1/2	teaspoon dried basil, crushed
1/2	teaspoon dried oregano, crushed
1/2	cup shredded Cheddar cheese
1	tablespoon cider vinegar

Cook and drain potatoes. Mash potatoes with yogurt, chives and parsley until fluffy. Set aside.

Sauté onions and garlic in margarine in a medium saucepan.

Add celery, eggplant and green pepper. Cook until eggplant is soft, stirring occasionally and covering pan between stirrings.

Add tomato, thyme, basil and oregano. Cook 5 minutes longer. Toss with cheese and vinegar and turn into a nonstick-sprayed baking pan.

Top with potato mixture to form a crust. Bake.

Oven: 350°
Time: 15 to 20 minutes

Nutrient Analysis: 2 cups
Exchanges: 1 starch, 2 vegetable, 1 fat
Carbohydrate Choices: 2

Calories: 179   *Protein: 9g*   *Carbohydrates: 33g*
Fat: 4g   *Cholesterol: 3mg*   *Sodium: 224mg*
Dietary Fiber: 6g   *Calcium: 120mg*

STIR-FRY VEGETABLES

The following recipe is basic for most vegetables or combination of vegetables. It works well for asparagus, sliced broccoli, bean sprouts, green beans, carrots or celery.

Makes 6 cups; 6 servings

1	**pound bok choy (about 6 cups sliced)**
2	**tablespoons peanut oil**
1/4	**teaspoon salt**
1	**thin slice fresh ginger**
1/4	**cup low-sodium chicken broth**
1/4	**teaspoon sugar**
	Dash pepper

Slice bok choy diagonally (1/8").

Heat wok over high heat. Add oil, salt and ginger. Stir for 30 seconds.

Add bok choy and stir-fry 1 minute.

Add chicken broth, sugar and pepper. Cover for 1 1/2 minutes. Uncover and cook an additional 15 seconds.

Nutrient Analysis: 1 cup
Exchanges: 1/2 vegetable, 1 fat
Carbohydrate Choices: 0

Calories: 52   Protein: 1g   Carbohydrates: 2g
Fat: 5g   Cholesterol: 0mg   Sodium: 151mg
Dietary Fiber: 1g

SPINACH QUICHE

Makes 9" pie; 6 servings

CRUST:

1 1/2	cups fine bread crumbs
3	tablespoons melted margarine

FILLING:

8-10	sliced fresh mushrooms
1	garlic clove, minced
1/4	cup chopped onions
1	teaspoon vegetable oil
3/4	cup torn fresh spinach or chopped broccoli
1/2	teaspoon dried basil
	Freshly ground pepper
1	cup shredded part-skim farmer cheese
1	cup plain low-fat yogurt
5	egg whites or 1 1/4 cups HOMEMADE EGG SUBSTITUTE, *(page 234)*

For crust: Mix bread crumbs and margarine and pat into pie tin.

For filling: Sauté mushrooms, garlic and onion in oil.

Mix together sautéd vegetables, spinach or broccoli, basil and pepper. Place in pie shell.

Sprinkle cheese over vegetables.

Blend together yogurt and egg whites and pour over cheese. Bake.

Oven: 425° for 10 minutes
350° for 20 to 25 minutes

Nutrient Analysis: 1/6 pie
Exchanges: 1 1/2 starch, 1 very lean meat, 2 fat
Carbohydrate Choices: 1 1/2

Calories: 268   Protein: 15 g   Carbohydrates: 25 g
Fat: 11 g   Cholesterol: 13 mg   Sodium: 428 mg
Dietary Fiber: 2 g   Calcium: 274 mg

VEGETABLE QUICHE

Can be sliced very thin and served as an appetizer. Make rice crust at least 8 hours ahead.

Makes 9" pie; 6 servings

RICE CRUST:

1	cup cooked brown rice, hot
1	egg, beaten
2/3	cup shredded part-skim farmer cheese

FILLING:

1/2	cup chopped onion
1/2	cup sliced fresh mushrooms
2/3	cup shredded part-skim farmer cheese
1/2	teaspoon safflower oil
1	cup EGG SUBSTITUTE, *(page 234)*
1	cup evaporated skim milk
1/4	teaspoon salt
1/4	teaspoon pepper
1	large tomato, sliced thin
1	tablespoon fresh chopped basil or 1/2 teaspoon dried basil, crushed

For crust: Mix hot rice, egg and cheese. Press into a deep 9" pie tin. Refrigerate for about 8 hours or overnight.

For filling: Sauté onion and mushrooms in oil in a nonstick-sprayed pan.

Sprinkle vegetables and cheese evenly on the bottom of the rice crust.

Beat egg substitute, milk, salt and pepper until well blended. Pour into pie shell and top with tomato slices. Sprinkle with basil.

Bake until a knife inserted near the center comes out clean. Let stand for 10 minutes before serving.

Oven: 375°
Time: 50 to 60 minutes

Nutrient Analysis: 1/6 pie
Exchanges: 1 starch, 2 lean meat, 1/2 fat
Carbohydrate Choices: 1

Calories: 217   Protein: 17 g   Carbohydrates: 19 g
Fat: 8 g   Cholesterol: 51 mg   Sodium: 375 mg
Dietary Fiber: 1 g   Calcium: 332 mg

HOMEMADE EGG SUBSTITUTE

A whole egg contains 213 mg cholesterol while the egg substitute contains only 1 mg. The egg substitute will keep for a week in the refrigerator. It also freezes well.

Makes 1 cup; 4 servings

8   egg whites
1/3   cup nonfat dry milk powder
1   tablespoon vegetable oil
6   drops yellow food coloring
    (optional)

Combine all ingredients in a mixing bowl and blend until smooth. Refrigerate until used.

Nutrient Analysis: 1/4 cup (equivalent to 1 whole egg)
Exchanges: 1 very lean meat, 1 fat   *Calories: 83*   *Protein: 9g*   *Carbohydrates: 4g*
Carbohydrate Choices: 0   *Fat: 4g*   *Cholesterol: 1 mg*   *Sodium: 140 mg*

THE EGG YOLK DILEMMA

What to do with extra egg yolks.

While we may be totally convinced that we should reduce cholesterol, we still have difficulty throwing away perfectly good egg yolks. Limiting egg yolks to four a week (advised for those with high cholesterol) would be a lot easier if we weren't so concerned about wasting food.

The every-other-yolk rule: In preparing recipes that call for a number of whole eggs, use one whole egg, one white, one whole egg and so on. If the recipe calls for eight eggs, use four whole eggs and four whites. Since egg yolks freeze well, save them in the freezer, and then use them in the recipes on the next page.

Make hand lotions and skin softeners with extra egg yolks.

You can feed egg yolks to your dog since dogs are not bothered by cholesterol and clogged arteries. Egg yolk is good for them and promotes a shiny coat.

You can make all-natural cosmetics with egg yolk.

HAIR AND SCALP CONDITIONER #1

1   tablespoon wheat germ oil
1   tablespoon glycerin
1   egg yolk, beaten

Mix the oil, glycerin and egg in the top of a double boiler. Heat until warm over hot water.

Apply to hair and scalp. Leave on for 30 minutes. Rinse well with cool water.

HAIR AND SCALP CONDITIONER #2

1/2   cup yogurt
1   egg yolk, beaten
1   teaspoon grated lemon rind

Mix together yogurt, egg yolk and lemon rind. Rub into scalp and leave on for 10 minutes. Rinse and shampoo hair.

HAND LOTION AND SKIN SOFTENER

1   egg yolk
3   tablespoons glycerin
3   tablespoons lemon juice

Mix together yolk, glycerin and lemon juice in a small saucepan. Cook over low heat until thickened. Do not boil. Cool and place in a jar. Use regularly as hand lotion and skin softener.

FISH & SEAFOOD

Buy the best fish you can find, preferably from Byzantium, sprinkle with marjoram. Wrap fish in fig leaves. Bake. Have slaves serve it on silver platters.

Archestratus, 330 B.C.

FISH & SEAFOOD

SEASONINGS

Also See:

FISH & SEAFOOD

Create a seafood habit.

Fish and shellfish are an important part of a healthy diet. Most fish (with the exception of fish sticks and 'fast-food' fish sandwiches) are low in saturated fat and sodium, and contain healthy, long-chain omega-3 fatty acids (EPA and DHA).

The American Heart Association (AHA) recommends that everyone eat fish at least twice a week. (Research suggests that two fish meals a week could cut heart attack risk by 25 to 50 percent or more!) We've already established from **Chapter 1** that the healthiest seafood for your heart is cold-water fish (i.e., salmon, sardines, tuna, mackerel, herring, rainbow trout, and anchovies). The AHA recommends that people with documented coronary heart disease consume about 1 gram (1,000 milligrams) of long-chain omega-3 fatty acids per day. While other seafood may not have as many omega-3s, all types of seafood are good sources of lean protein and a host of other beneficial nutrients such as vitamin B6, niacin, iron, calcium, magnesium, fluorine, iodine and selenium.

Your heart loves a healthy fish dinner.

Eating seafood has its concerns and we'd like to address three of them. One such concern is the high cholesterol content of some fish such as lobster and shrimp. Although it's true that these popular crustaceans have higher cholesterol values than other fish; it doesn't seem to adversely affect blood cholesterol. Perhaps that's because it is packaged with healthy omega-3 fatty acids and is low in saturated fat. These fish still fit a heart-healthy eating pattern.

Addressing the mercury dilemma

Another health concern about eating fish on a regular basis is the level of mercury. Nearly all fish and shellfish contain traces of mercury. For most people, the risk from mercury by eating fish and shellfish is not a health concern. Yet, some fish and shellfish contain higher levels of mercury that may harm an unborn baby or young child's developing nervous system.

Levels of mercury in fish are expressed in terms of parts per million (ppm). The U.S. Food & Drug Administration (FDA) and the U.S. Environmental Protection Agency (EPA) have established a maximum permissible level of one part of mercury in a million parts of seafood (1 ppm), which is equal to one milligram of mercury per 2.2 pounds of fish.

Benefits still outweigh the risks

Children, pregnant and nursing women may be at higher risk of exposure to excessive mercury from fish. They can still receive the benefits of eating fish and shellfish and be confident that they have reduced their exposure to the harmful effects of mercury by following these guidelines established by the FDA and the EPA.

1. Do <u>not</u> eat Shark, Swordfish, King Mackerel or Tilefish because they contain high levels of mercury (0.73 to 1.45 ppm per 3 ounces).
2. Eat up to 12 ounces (2 average meals) a week of a variety of fish and shellfish that are lower in mercury. Five of the most commonly eaten fish that are low in mercury are Shrimp, canned light Tuna, Salmon, Pollock and Catfish. Albacore ("white") tuna has more mercury than canned light tuna so choose this less often (no more than 6 ounces) per week.
3. Check local advisories about the safety of fish caught in local lakes, rivers and coastal areas. If no advice is available, eat up to 6 ounces (one average meal) per week of fish you catch from local waters, but don't consume any other fish during the week.

For environmental impact, visit oceansalive.org

Finally, there is concern about the environmental impact our fish consumption is having on the marine ecosystem. Some fish and shellfish species have been severely depleted by overfishing, or unnecessarily eliminated as a bycatch from trawlers, or their habitat has been damaged, making them endangered. The Environmental Defense Network has an Oceans Alive campaign that focuses on protecting ecosystems and fisheries to stem the tide of decline in our seas. We encourage you to visit oceansalive.org for more information and to learn how you can help safeguard our seas and their marine life.

To help you select eco-healthy fish whether dining out or purchasing to make the recipes in this section, we've put together Table 22 listing the omega-3 fatty acids, mercury levels, and the ecological impact of various commonly eaten fish. If an ecological grade of 'best' is given, it means this species of fish is well managed, naturally replenishable, or constructive marine regulations are enforced. If an ecological grade of 'worst' is given, it means the species is severely depleted or endangered.

Table 23: Omega-3 Fatty Acids, Mercury Content & Ecological Impact of Commonly Eaten Fish

Fish (3 ounce serving)	Omega-3 Fatty Acids (1000 Milligrams = 1 gram)	Mercury Level (Parts per million)	Ecological Impact (Best / Worst)
Anchovies	1,750 mg	0.04 ppm	Best
Catfish	150 –200 mg	0.05 ppm	Best
Clams (quahogs)	240 mg	0.00 ppm*	Best
Cod (Pacific cod from Alaska is a better ecological choice.)	130-240 mg	0.10 ppm	Worst
Crab (U.S. King, Snow)	340 - 400 mg	0.06 ppm	Best
Flounder (Sole, Flatfish)	430 mg	0.05 ppm	Best
Grouper	210 mg	0.47 ppm	Worst
Haddock	200 mg	0.02 ppm	Best
Halibut	470 – 1000 mg	0.26 ppm	Best-Pacific Worst-Atlantic
Herring, Atlantic	1,830 mg	0.04 ppm	Best
Lobster (Northern, American)	70 – 410 mg	0.31 ppm	Best
Mahi Mahi (Dolphinfish)	120 mg	0.19 ppm	Best
Orange Roughy	30 mg	0.56 ppm	Worst
Oysters	1,240 mg	0.13 ppm	Best
Pollock, Pacific (used for imitation crab and fish sticks)	460 mg	0.04 ppm	Best
Salmon, canned wild Alaska farm, (labeled "Atlantic")	 1,230 mg 1,570 mg 1,830 mg	 0.00 ppm* 0.01 ppm 0.01 ppm	 Best Best Worst
Sardines, Atlantic	830 mg	0.02 ppm	Best
Scallops	170 mg	0.05 ppm	Best-Bay Worst-Atlantic Calico
Shrimp (US farmed is well managed and sold as Spot prawns, Northern, Pink, and White shrimp.) Worst-Tiger and Giant prawns; Blue, Brown, and Whiteleg shrimp	270 mg	0.00 ppm*	Best-US farmed Worst-Foreign caught
Tilapia	50 mg	0.01 ppm	Best
Snapper	340 mg	0.19 ppm	Worst
Trout, rainbow sea	 840 – 980 mg 410 mg	 0.07 ppm 0.26 ppm	 Best, esp. Arctic char NA
Tuna bluefin fillet canned, Albacore canned, light	 1,280 mg 730 mg 280 mg	 0.38 ppm 0.35 ppm 0.12 ppm	 Worst Good Best
Whitefish, mixed species	1,380 mg	0.07 ppm	NA

*Mercury concentration below the Level of Detection (LOD=0.01ppm)   NA = not available

Sources: USDA Nutrient Databank, websites accessed on November 23, 2007: cfsan.fda.gov/~frf/sea-mehg.html; americanheart.org/presenter.jhtml?identifier=3013797; and oceansalive.org/eat.cfm?subnav=fishpage&group

Eat a wide variety of fish.

If you choose carefully, the benefits of eating fish far outweigh the health risks. And, remember, eating a variety of fish will help minimize any potentially adverse effects due to environmental pollutants. It also prevents any one species of fish from becoming over fished. All recipes in this section call for fish that are low in mercury and are not endangered.

How to Prepare Fish

Timing is all important when it comes to cooking fish and seafood. Perfectly cooked fish is moist and has a delicate flavor; overcooked fish is dry and tasteless. Fish is done when it has just turned opaque and is easily separated with a fork. The 10-Minute Rule is a good guide to cooking seafood properly. Here's how to use it:

10-Minute Rule

1. Measure the fish at its thickest part. Fold thin parts under to make the fish as evenly thick as possible.
2. Cook thawed or fresh fish 10 minutes per inch of thickness.
3. Cook frozen fish for 20 minutes per inch of thickness.
4. Add 5 minutes to the total cooking time if you are cooking the fish in foil or if fish is cooked in a sauce.

Microwave Directions

When preparing fish in the microwave, the 10-minute rule does not apply. Place the fish in a shallow dish and cover with plastic wrap leaving one corner turned back for venting. Microwave on High (*100 percent power*) for 3 minutes per pound of boneless fish. Rotate the dish once during cooking time to ensure even cooking. Remove from microwave when the edges of the fish are firm and opaque and the center is slightly translucent. Let the fish stand, still covered for 3 to 5 minutes. It will continue to cook by retained heat.

Preparing fish in the microwave helps to prevent fishy odors from spreading in the house. To remove the fishy odor from the microwave, combine 2 tablespoons of lemon juice with a cup of water. Place in the microwave and let boil for 1-2 minutes.

SEASONING FOR FISH

The delicate flavor of fish is enhanced by the addition of the following: bay leaf, curry powder, dry mustard, fennel, green pepper, lemon juice, marjoram, mushrooms, paprika and tarragon.

SPICE BLEND FOR FISH

Makes 5 tablespoons

1   tablespoon dried basil
1   tablespoon dried chervil
1   tablespoon dried marjoram
1   tablespoon parsley flakes
1   tablespoon dried tarragon

Crush dried herbs and blend thoroughly. Sprinkle on fish during cooking or use in shaker on table. Store extra in tightly covered glass container.

See SEASONINGS for additional herb and spice blends.

HERBED LEMON SPREAD

A zesty spread for baked, broiled or poached fish.

Makes 6 tablespoons; 9 servings

1/4   cup tub margarine
1   tablespoon grated lemon rind
1/2   teaspoon dried basil, crushed
1   teaspoon parsley flakes
1   teaspoon chopped chives
1/2   teaspoon chervil

Cream margarine and lemon rind until well mixed. Stir in basil, parsley, chives and chervil. Spread lightly (about 1 teaspoon a serving) on very hot fish.

Nutrient Analysis: 2 teaspoons
Exchanges: 1 fat
Carbohydrate Choices: 0

Calories: 45   Protein: 0g   Carbohydrates: 0g
Fat: 5g   Cholesterol: 0mg   Sodium: 43mg

SOLE ROLLS

An attractive, delicious fish dish suitable for family or guests.

Makes 6 (4-ounce) fillets; 6 servings

3   (8-ounce) fillets of sole or
6 (4-ounce) any white fish fillets

FILLING:

1 1/2   tablespoons tub margarine
1 1/2   tablespoons all-purpose flour
1/2   cup skim milk
1/2   cup cooked, chopped shrimp
1/2   cup flaked, boned crab
1/4   cup finely chopped celery
1/4   cup finely chopped green onions
1   tablespoon chopped fresh parsley
1/2   to 1 teaspoon *SPICE BLEND FOR FISH (page 243)*

SAUCE:

1   tablespoon tub margarine
1   tablespoon all-purpose flour
1   cup skim milk
1   tablespoon light mayonnaise
1   tablespoon fresh lemon juice
1   teaspoon chopped fresh parsley

6   cooked whole shrimp, for garnish

Defrost fish if frozen. Divide into six equal portions.

For filling: Melt margarine in a medium saucepan. Add flour and stir with whisk to combine thoroughly. Add milk and cook, stirring constantly, until sauce is thick. Remove from heat and stir in shrimp, crab, celery, onions, parsley and spiceblend.

Spread filling on fillets. Roll and secure with toothpicks. Place in a nonstick-sprayed baking dish. Bake until fish turns from translucent to opaque flakes. If browning too fast, cover with foil.

Meanwhile, make sauce. Melt margarine and stir in flour. Add milk and cook, stirring constantly, until sauce is thick. Remove from heat and stir in mayonnaise, lemon juice and parsley.

At serving time, carefully transfer sole rolls to serving plate. Remove wooden picks. Pour sauce over sole rolls and garnish with whole shrimp.

Oven: 375°
Time: 20 minutes

Nutrient Analysis: 1 fillet with sauce | *Calories: 251*   *Protein: 35g*   *Carbohydrates: 7g*
Exchanges: 1/2 starch, 4 very lean meat, 1 fat | *Fat: 8g*   *Cholesterol: 134mg*   *Sodium: 293mg*
Carbohydrate Choices: 1/2 | *Omega-3: 0.50g*

FISH FLORENTINE

Makes 6 (4-ounce) fillets; 6 servings

1 1/2 (10-ounce) packages frozen chopped spinach, thawed and drained
3/4 cup shredded part-skim mozzarella cheese
1 1/2 tablespoons grated Parmesan cheese
1 tablespoon lemon juice
3/4 teaspoon pepper
1/4 teaspoon salt
1/4 teaspoon dried oregano, crushed
2 teaspoons dill weed
3 fresh or frozen sole fillets (about 8 ounces each)
1 tablespoon tub margarine

Thaw spinach in a saucepan over low heat, then cook on high until liquid is almost evaporated. Drain.

Stir together spinach, mozzarella, Parmesan, lemon juice, pepper, salt, oregano and dill weed in a medium bowl.

Cut fillets into 6 portions. Place in a single layer in a nonstick-sprayed baking dish. Spread filling over each portion, dividing equally. Dot each fillet with 1/2 teaspoon margarine.

Cover pan loosely with aluminum foil. Bake.

With a spatula, carefully transfer fillets to serving plate.

Oven: 425°
Time: 10 minutes

Nutrient Analysis: 1 fillet
Exchanges: 3 very lean meat, 1/2 vegetable, 1 fat
Carbohydrate Choices: 0

Calories: 179   Protein: 27 g   Carbohydrates: 3 g
Fat: 6 g   Cholesterol: 64 mg   Sodium: 390 mg
Dietary Fiber: 2 g   Omega-3: 0.26 g

FISH FILLETS WITH CUCUMBER DILL SAUCE

Makes 6 (4-ounce) fillets; 6 servings

1 1/2   pounds Pacific halibut, flounder
or tilapia fillets
2   tablespoons lemon juice

SAUCE:
1   medium cucumber, unpared
and sliced
1/2   teaspoon dill weed
4   green onions, chopped
1   cup plain low-fat yogurt
Lemon wedges (optional)

Place fish in shallow, nonstick-sprayed baking pan. Sprinkle with lemon juice. Bake.

Meanwhile, make sauce. Puree cucumber, dill weed and onions in a blender. Combine with yogurt. Pour into a small saucepan and heat over low heat just to simmer. DO NOT BOIL.

When fish is done, drain liquid from pan. Top with sauce and garnish with lemon wedges. Serve.

Oven: 400°
Time: 20 minutes

Nutrient Analysis: 1 fillet
Exchanges: 1 vegetable, 3 very lean meat
Carbohydrate Choices: 1/2

Calories: 132   Protein: 23g   Carbohydrates: 6g
Fat: 1g   Cholesterol: 51mg   Sodium: 95mg
Dietary Fiber: 1g   Omega-3: 0.21g   Calcium: 102mg

VEGETABLE TILAPIA BAKE

Makes 4 (4-ounce) fillets; 4 servings

1   pound frozen tilapia fillets
3   tablespoons lemon juice
1/2   teaspoon paprika
1/2   cup sliced fresh mushrooms
1/4   cup chopped tomato
1/4   cup chopped green pepper
1   tablespoon chopped fresh
parsley
Freshly ground pepper
Lemon wedges (optional)

Thaw fillets. Cut into 4 portions and place in nonstick-sprayed baking dish. Sprinkle with lemon juice and paprika.

Combine mushrooms, tomato, green pepper, parsley and pepper. Spread over fish. Cover and bake. Serve with lemon wedges.

Oven: 350°
Time: 25 minutes

Nutrient Analysis: 1 fillet
Exchanges: 3 very lean meat
Carbohydrate Choices: 0

Calories: 103   Protein: 21g   Carbohydrates: 2g
Fat: 1g   Cholesterol: 49mg   Sodium: 63mg
Omega-3: 0.21g

FILLETS AU GRATIN

Makes 4 (4-ounce) fillets; 4 servings

4 (4-ounce) fish fillets (sole,
    halibut, haddock, flounder)
1/4 teaspoon pepper
2 small zucchini, sliced
2 medium tomatoes, sliced
3 tablespoons sliced green onions
1/2 cup fresh bread crumbs
2 tablespoons melted margarine
2 tablespoons lemon juice
1/2 cup freshly grated Parmesan
    cheese

Place fillets in nonstick-sprayed baking dish. Season with pepper. Cover with zucchini, tomatoes and onions.

Combine bread crumbs, margarine and lemon juice in a small bowl. Toss together and spread over vegetables. Top with cheese and bake.

Oven: 425°
Time: 20 to 30 minutes

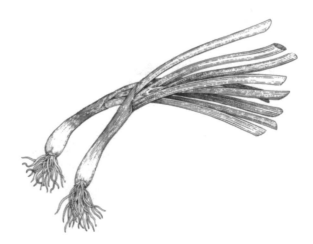

Nutrient Analysis: 1 fillet
Exchanges: 1 starch, 3 very lean meat, 2 fat
Carbohydrate Choices: 1

Calories: 277   Protein: 28g   Carbohydrates: 15g
Fat: 11g   Cholesterol: 62mg   Sodium: 435mg
Dietary Fiber: 1g Omega-3: 0.28g Calcium: 193mg

HADDOCK WITH MOCK SOUR CREAM

Makes 6 (4-ounce) fillets; 6 servings

1 1/2 pounds haddock, tilapia or any
        white fish
        Freshly ground pepper
  2 tablespoons tub margarine
1/4 teaspoon whole thyme
  1 bay leaf
  1 tablespoon finely chopped onion
  1 tablespoon finely chopped fresh
        dill or 1/2 teaspoon dried
        dill weed
1/4 teaspoon sugar
1/4 cup light mayonnaise
1/4 cup plain low-fat yogurt
        Parsley, for garnish
        Lemon wedges, for garnish

Season haddock with pepper and place in shallow nonstick-sprayed baking dish.

Melt margarine in saucepan or in microwave. Add thyme, bay leaf, onion, dill, sugar, mayonnaise and yogurt. Pour over fillets and bake. Remove bay leaf. Garnish with parsley and lemon wedges. Serve.

Oven: 350°
Time: 25 minutes

Nutrient Analysis: 1 fillet
Exchanges: 3 very lean meat, 1 1/2 fat
Carbohydrate Choices: 0

Calories: 174   Protein: 22 g   Carbohydrates: 3 g
Fat: 8 g   Cholesterol: 69 mg   Sodium: 200 mg
Omega-3: 0.21 g

SALMON STEAKS

A winner served with steamed new potatoes, fresh peas and a crisp salad.

Makes 4 (5-ounce) fillets; 4 servings

4   (5-ounce) salmon steaks
3   tablespoons lemon juice
1   tablespoon dry vermouth or
    white wine
1   teaspoon onion powder
1/2   teaspoon dried oregano, crushed
    Freshly ground pepper
    Paprika
    Chopped fresh parsley, for garnish
    Lemon wedges, for garnish

Rinse fish in water and pat dry. Arrange steaks close together in nonstick-sprayed, shallow baking dish.

Stir together lemon juice, vermouth, onion powder and oregano. Pour evenly over fish. Sprinkle with pepper and paprika. Bake.

Spoon the juices over fish and garnish with chopped parsley and lemon wedges. Serve.

Oven: 350°
Time: 10 to 15 minutes

Nutrient Analysis: 1 fillet
Exchanges: 4 very lean meat, 1 1/2 fat
Carbohydrate Choices: 0

Calories: 210   Protein: 28 g   Carbohydrates: 1 g
Fat: 9 g   Cholesterol: 78 mg   Sodium: 63 mg
Omega-3: 2.45 g

SUMMER LAKE BAKE

Makes 6 (4-ounce) fillets; 6 servings

1 1/2	pounds walleye fillets
2	teaspoons lemon juice
1/4	teaspoon salt
1/4	teaspoon pepper
2	large fresh tomatoes, sliced
1	green pepper, sliced in rings
1 1/2	cups fresh or frozen corn
1/4	cup dry bread crumbs
2	teaspoons chopped fresh basil or 1/2 teaspoon dried basil, crushed
1/2	teaspoon dried oregano, crushed
1	tablespoon vegetable oil
	Chopped fresh parsley, for garnish
	Lemon wedges, for garnish

Place fillets in nonstick-sprayed, shallow baking dish. Sprinkle with lemon juice, salt and pepper. Layer tomato and green pepper slices over fish and cover with corn.

Combine bread crumbs, basil, oregano and oil. Spread bread crumb mixture over corn. Bake.

Serve hot garnished with chopped parsley and lemon wedges.

Oven: 350°
Time: 20 minutes

Nutrient Analysis: 1 fillet
Exchanges: 1/2 starch, 2 vegetable, 3 very lean meat
Carbohydrate Choices: 1

Calories: 203   Protein: 24 g   Carbohydrates: 16 g
Fat: 5 g   Cholesterol: 98 mg   Sodium: 192 mg
Dietary Fiber: 3 g   Omega-3: 0.37 g   Calcium: 141 mg

FLOUNDER FILLETS WITH MUSTARD

Makes 6 (4-ounce) fillets; 6 servings

1 1/2	pounds flounder fillets
2	tablespoons light mayonnaise
1	tablespoon Dijon mustard
1	tablespoon chopped fresh parsley
	Freshly ground pepper
	Lemon wedges, for garnish

Arrange fillets on nonstick-sprayed broiler pan. Combine mayonnaise, mustard, parsley and pepper. Spread evenly over fillets. Broil 3 to 4 inches from heat.

Serve garnished with lemon wedges.

Oven: Broil
Time: 4 to 5 minutes

Nutrient Analysis: 1 fillet
Exchanges: 3 very lean meat, 1/2 fat
Carbohydrate Choices: 0

Calories: 120   Protein: 21 g   Carbohydrates: 1 g
Fat: 3 g   Cholesterol: 56 mg   Sodium: 166 mg
Omega-3: 0.23 g

HADDOCK WITH TOMATO CHEESE SAUCE

Makes 6 (4-ounce) fillets; 6 servings

1 1/2	pounds haddock fillets (or sole, pollock, etc.)
1	tablespoon tub margarine
1/2	cup no-salt-added tomato paste
1/2	cup water
1	medium onion, finely chopped
1/2	cup shredded Cheddar cheese

Place fish in nonstick-sprayed broiler pan. Dot with margarine. Broil on middle shelf for about 8 minutes.

Blend tomato paste and water until smooth. Sprinkle fish with chopped onion, and pour tomato sauce over all. Broil another 3 to 4 minutes.

Top with shredded cheese, and broil until bubbly.

Oven: Broil
Time: About 15 minutes

Nutrient Analysis: 1 fillet
Exchanges: 1 vegetable, 3 very lean meat, 1/2 fat
Carbohydrate Choices: 1/2

Calories: 160   Protein: 25g   Carbohydrates: 6g
Fat: 3g   Cholesterol: 66mg   Sodium: 186mg
Dietary Fiber: 2g   Omega-3: 0.21g

WALLEYE ALMONDINE

Makes 4 (4-ounce) fillets; 4 servings

4	walleye fillets (1 pound)
1	egg white
1/4	cup plain low-fat yogurt
1/4	cup toasted sliced almonds
1-2	teaspoons grated orange rind

Poach fillets 4 minutes in simmering water. Drain and dry thoroughly on paper toweling.

Whip egg white until stiff. Fold in yogurt, almonds and orange rind. Coat the drained fillets with egg white mixture.

Broil until brown and puffy (about 2 to 3 minutes).

Oven: Broil
Time: 2 to 3 minutes

Nutrient Analysis: 1 fillet
Exchanges: 3 very lean meat, 1/2 fat
Carbohydrate Choices: 0

Calories: 128   Protein: 20g   Carbohydrates: 3g
Fat: 4g   Cholesterol: 24mg   Sodium: 97mg
Dietary Fiber: 1g

BROILED SALMON STEAK

Makes 4 (4-ounce) fillets; 4 servings

4   (4-ounce) salmon steaks
    Freshly ground pepper
2   tablespoons tub margarine
1   tablespoon finely chopped fresh
        dill or 1 teaspoon dill weed
2   tablespoons lemon juice
    Lemon wedges, for garnish
    Fresh dill sprigs, for garnish

Preheat broiler. Season both sides of salmon with pepper.

Melt margarine in a small saucepan or microwave; add dill and lemon juice. Brush steaks with mixture.

Place salmon on broiler pan and broil 3 inches from heat for 3 to 5 minutes. Turn salmon, brush with margarine mixture. Broil an additional 3 to 5 minutes or until fish turns from translucent to opaque.

Garnish steaks with lemon wedges and dill. Serve on heated plates.

Oven: Broil
Time: 3 to 5 minutes a side

Nutrient Analysis: 1 fillet
Exchanges: 3 lean meat, 1 fat
Carbohydrate Choices: 0

Calories: 214   Protein: 23 g   Carbohydrates: 1 g
Fat: 13 g   Cholesterol: 63 mg   Sodium: 98 mg
Omega-3: 1.96 g

THAI-STYLE FRIED FISH

Some like it hot — a spicy fish dish!

Makes 8 (4-ounce) fillets; 8 servings

2   pounds fish fillets
1/4 cup vegetable oil
6   green onions cut into 1" pieces
4   garlic cloves, minced
3   teaspoons finely grated
        fresh ginger

Wash fish and pat dry. Fry in hot oil on both sides until lightly browned and cooked through. Remove fish to serving platter and keep warm.

continued on next page

THAI-STYLE FRIED FISH, (continued)

2 tablespoons sodium-reduced
    soy sauce
1 tablespoon sugar
1 tablespoon lemon juice
1/4 teaspoon freshly ground pepper
2 tablespoons chopped fresh
    cilantro
1 fresh red chili pepper, seeded
    and sliced

Let oil cool slightly, then fry green onions until soft. Add garlic and ginger and cook on low heat, stirring until soft and golden.

Add soy sauce, sugar, lemon juice and pepper. Simmer the mixture for 1 minute. Pour over fish. Garnish with cilantro and chili. Serve at once with steamed rice.

Nutrient Analysis: 1 fillet without rice
Exchanges: 3 very lean meat, 1 1/2 fat
Carbohydrate Choices: 0

Calories: 178   Protein: 22g   Carbohydrates: 3g
Fat: 8g   Cholesterol: 54mg   Sodium: 227mg
Omega-3: 0.24g

CHARCOAL GRILLED TROUT

Makes 4 trout; 4 servings

4 whole medium trout with heads
1 lemon, thinly sliced
    Olive oil

Wash trout and pat dry. Place several slices of lemon in body cavity. Brush both sides liberally with olive oil.

Grill over high heat 5 to 7 minutes a side. Serve whole trout. The slightly charred skin peels off easily. Run knife along back bone. Open fish. Lift off head and back bone.

Charcoal grill or broil
Time: 5 to 7 minutes a side

Nutrient Analysis: 1 trout
Exchanges: 2 very lean meat, 1 fat
Carbohydrate Choices: 0

Calories: 113   Protein: 16g   Carbohydrates: 1g
Fat: 4g   Cholesterol: 46mg   Sodium: 29mg
Omega-3: 0.78g

POACHING FISH

Poach fish in court bouillon, a light stock or water. Lower small or cut pieces of fish into boiling liquid and reduce heat to simmer. Start with larger pieces or whole fish in cold liquid. Allow 5 to 8 minutes to the pound, depending on the size of the fish.

MICROWAVE: Place fish and liquid in shallow dish. Cover with plastic wrap. Microwave on High (*100 percent power*) for 2 minutes. Remove wrap, turn fish and return plastic wrap cover. Let sit until cool. Fish turns from translucent to opaque when done. If not done, microwave in 30-second increments.

COURT BOUILLON

Makes 8 cups

1 quart water
1 cup dry white wine
1 carrot, chopped
1 rib celery with leaves, chopped
1 small onion, chopped

Bring water, wine, carrot, celery and onion to a boil. A large shallow pan such as an electric fry pan works well. Add fish and reduce heat immediately to simmer.

Time: 5 to 8 minutes to the pound.

DOVER SOLE WITH TOMATO & BASIL SAUCE

Makes 4 (4-ounce) fillets; 4 servings

4   Dover sole fillets*, or any firm
       white fish without skin
4   cups COURT BOUILLON,
       (page 254)

SAUCE:
1   cup court bouillon
1   carrot, shredded
1   small onion, shredded
1   teaspoon no-salt-added
       tomato paste
1/2 teaspoon dried basil, crushed
2   tablespoons low-fat cottage
       cheese, pureed

** Other suggested fish include perch,
northern pike, striped bass, lake trout,
lake herring and Pollack.*

Poach fish in COURT BOUILLON about 5 minutes. Remove to serving platter and keep warm.

Strain bouillon. Combine 1 cup of strained bouillon with carrot and onion in small saucepan. Bring to a boil and reduce to one half. Add tomato paste and basil. Stir in cottage cheese. Serve hot over fillets.

Nutrient Analysis: 1 fillet with sauce
Exchanges: 1 vegetable, 3 very lean meat
Carbohydrate Choices: 0

Calories: 135   Protein: 25g   Carbohydrates: 4g
Fat: 2g   Cholesterol: 42mg   Sodium: 113mg
Dietary Fiber: 1g   Omega-3: 0.36g

STEAMED HALIBUT STEAKS

Makes 4 (4-ounce) steaks; 4 servings

1   leek or mild onion, thinly sliced
1   tablespoon grated fresh ginger
1   teaspoon dried tarragon, crushed
4   halibut steaks, cut about
        1/2" thick (1 pound)
        Lemon wedges, for garnish

Combine leek or onion, ginger and tarragon in small bowl. Spread half the leeks on a large, nonstick-sprayed, heat-proof plate. Lay halibut steaks on top. Sprinkle remaining leeks over top.

Fill large saucepan or Dutch oven with 1" water and place steamer rack in water. Place plate with halibut on top of rack and cover pan tightly. Steam over medium-high heat 7 to 10 minutes or until fish turns opaque.

Serve garnished with lemon wedges.

Nutrient Analysis: 1 steak
Exchanges: 1 vegetable, 3 very lean meat
Carbohydrate Choices: 0

Calories: 139   Protein: 24 g   Carbohydrates: 3 g
Fat: 3 g   Cholesterol: 36 mg   Sodium: 62 mg
Dietary Fiber: 1 g   Omega-3: 0.49 g

STEAMED FISH & VEGETABLES

Makes 4 (4-ounce) fillets; 4 servings

1 1/2   pounds haddock fillets or
            (sole, pollock, etc.)
2   tablespoons lemon juice
        Freshly ground pepper
        Water
2   sprigs parsley
6   peppercorns

Pat the fish dry and cut into serving portions. Sprinkle with 1 tablespoon of the lemon juice and freshly ground pepper.

Measure and combine 1-inch water, remaining tablespoon lemon juice, parsley sprigs, peppercorns and bay leaf in bottom of steamer. Bring to a boil.

Separate onion slices into rings and place half the rings on steamer rack.

continued on next page

STEAMED FISH & VEGETABLES, (continued)

1   bay leaf
1   small onion, thinly sliced
3   carrots, julienne strips
1/4   pound green beans, French cut
2   potatoes, julienne cut

Place fish on onions and cover with carrots, beans, potatoes and remaining onion rings.

Reduce heat to simmer. Cover and steam about 10 minutes for each inch of thickness or until fish turns from translucent to opaque. Remove bay leaf. Transfer fish and vegetables to heated serving plate. Serve hot.

Nutrient Analysis: 1 fillet
Exchanges: 1 starch, 1 vegetable,
*   3 very lean meat, 1 fat*
Carbohydrate Choices: 1 1/2

Calories: 255   Protein: 26 g   Carbohydrates: 23 g
Fat: 7 g   Cholesterol: 62 mg   Sodium: 82 mg
Dietary Fiber: 4 g   Omeg-3: 1.97 g

SCALLOPS & MUSHROOMS IN WINE SAUCE

Makes about 42 sea scallops; 6 servings

1 1/2   pounds sea scallops
         (about 42 scallops)
1   cup dry white wine
1/4   cup chopped fresh parsley
     Water
1   cup sliced fresh mushrooms
2   green onions, chopped
5   tablespoons tub margarine,
         divided
3   tablespoons all-purpose flour
1/2   cup evaporated skim milk
1   cup whole wheat bread crumbs

Simmer scallops 8 minutes in the wine, parsley and enough water to cover. Remove scallops and reserve 1 cup liquid.

Sauté mushrooms and onions in a saucepan in 1 tablespoon margarine. Remove from pan.

Melt 2 tablespoons margarine, stir in flour. Add reserved water and cook until thickened. Stir in milk, scallops, mushrooms, and onions. Heat until bubbling. Place in a nonstick-sprayed casserole dish.

Melt remaining 2 tablespoons margarine and toss with bread crumbs. Sprinkle over scallop mixture and broil 5 inches from heat until crumbs are toasted (about 3 minutes).

Nutrient Analysis: 7 scallops
Exchanges: 2 starch, 3 very lean meat, 2 fat
Carbohydrate Choices: 1 1/2

Calories: 318   Protein: 24 g   Carbohydrates: 22 g
Fat: 11 g   Cholesterol: 37 mg   Sodium: 432 mg
Dietary Fiber: 1 g   Omega-3: 0.22 g

SALMON LOAF

Don't discard the salmon backbone; mix it in for added calcium.

Makes 9 x 5" loaf pan; 5 servings

3/4	cup bulgur, dry
1 1/2	cups very hot water
1/2	cup chopped onion
1/2	cup chopped celery
1/4	cup chopped green pepper (optional)
1	tablespoon tub margarine
1	egg or 1/4 cup egg substitute
3	tablespoons lemon juice
1	tablespoon Dijon mustard
2	tablespoons fresh chopped parsley
1/4	teaspoon dried tarragon, crushed
1	(16-ounce) can salmon, drained and flaked
1/2	cup liquid (salmon water plus skim milk)
	Lemon wedges, for garnish

Combine bulgur and hot water in a large bowl. Let stand until water is absorbed and bulgur is tender (about 30 minutes).

Sauté onion, celery and green pepper in margarine. Thoroughly mix sautéd vegetables, lemon juice, mustard, parsley, tarragon and reserved salmon liquid with bulgur.

Add salmon and mix lightly. Place in a nonstick-sprayed 9 x 5" loaf pan. Bake.

Serve with lemon wedges and DUGLÉRÉ SAUCE *(page 165)*.

Oven: 350°
Time: 60 minutes

Nutrient Analysis: 1 slice
Exchanges: 1 starch, 3 very lean meat, 1 1/2 fat
Carbohydrate Choices: 1

Calories: 247   Protein: 24g   Carbohydrates: 19g
Fat: 9g   Cholesterol: 78mg   Sodium: 522mg
Dietary Fiber: 5g   Calcium: 249mg   Omega-3: 1.13g

SHRIMP CASSEROLE (MICROWAVE)

Makes 6 cups; 6 servings

8 ounces fresh mushrooms, sliced
2 tablespoons tub margarine
1 cup medium **WHITE SAUCE**,
    (page 164)
2 tablespoons chopped green pepper
2 tablespoons chopped onion
2 tablespoons lemon juice
2 cups cooked brown rice
1/2 teaspoon sodium-reduced
    Worcestershire sauce
1/2 teaspoon dry mustard
1/4 teaspoon pepper
1 pound frozen cooked shrimp,
    thawed
1/4 cup bread crumbs
    Paprika

Sauté mushrooms in 1 tablespoon margarine.

Make white sauce in a medium saucepan. Add mushrooms, green pepper, onion, lemon juice, rice, Worcestershire, mustard, pepper and shrimp to sauce.

Place in nonstick-sprayed casserole. Sprinkle with bread crumbs and dot with remaining tablespoon of margarine. Sprinkle with paprika.

Cover and microwave, turning dish around halfway through baking time. Uncover for last 2 minutes.

Microwave: High
Time: 10 minutes

Nutrient Analysis: 1 cup
Exchanges: 1 1/2 starch, 2 very lean meat, 2 fat
Carbohydrate Choices: 1 1/2

Calories: 276   Protein: 21g   Carbohydrates: 26g
Fat: 10g   Cholesterol: 116mg   Sodium: 240mg
Dietary Fiber: 2g   Omega-3: 0.38g

SHRIMP JAMBALAYA

Jambalaya is a Creole dish consisting of rice cooked with fish, poultry or meat and vegetables and spices.

Makes 9 cups; 6 servings

4	ounces fresh mushrooms, sliced
1	ounce Canadian bacon, chopped
1 1/2	teaspoons tub margarine
1	small onion, chopped
1/2	green pepper, chopped
1	rib celery, chopped
2	garlic cloves, minced
2	large fresh tomatoes, diced
1	(6-ounce) can no-salt-added tomato paste
1	can water
1/4	teaspoon Tabasco sauce (or to taste)
1/2	teaspoon sodium-reduced Worcestershire sauce
1	tablespoon chopped fresh parsley
1	large or 2 small bay leaves
3	cups water
1	cup uncooked brown rice
1/8	teaspoon salt
	Freshly ground pepper to taste
12	ounces shrimp, shelled and deveined (about 24 small)
1	tablespoon lemon juice

Sauté mushrooms and bacon in margarine in a 4-quart saucepan. Add onion, green pepper, celery and garlic; sauté on low heat for 10 to 12 minutes or until golden brown.

Add tomatoes, tomato paste, water, Tabasco, Worcestershire, parsley, and bay leaves. Bring to a boil, reduce heat, cover and simmer 8 to 10 minutes.

Add 3 cups water and bring to a boil again. Add rice, reduce heat, cover and simmer 15 minutes. When rice begins to swell, add salt, pepper and shrimp. Stir, cover and cook over very low heat until rice is done. Add more water if thinner consistency is desired. Just before serving, remove bay leaf and stir in lemon juice.

Nutrient Analysis: 1 1/2 cups
Exchanges: 1 1/2 starch, 2 vegetable,
2 very lean meat
Carbohydrate Choices: 2

Calories: 236   Protein: 17 g   Carbohydrates: 34 g
Fat: 4 g   Cholesterol: 89 mg   Sodium: 302 mg
Dietary Fiber: 3 g   Omega-3: 0.30 g

LEMON SHRIMP

A light, tasty stir-fry that's ready in minutes.

Makes 6 cups; 6 servings

2 tablespoons cornstarch
1 tablespoon sugar
1/8 teaspoon pepper
1 teaspoon low-sodium, chicken-flavored bouillon granules
1 cup water
1/2 teaspoon grated lemon rind
3 tablespoons lemon juice
2 tablespoons vegetable oil
1 green pepper, sliced in strips
1 1/2 cups diagonally sliced celery
1/4 cup sliced green onion
2 cups sliced mushrooms
6 ounces snow peas
1 pound fresh shrimp, peeled and deveined

Combine cornstarch, sugar, bouillon and pepper. Blend in water, lemon rind and lemon juice. Set aside.

Heat wok on high. Add 1 tablespoon oil. Add green pepper, celery and onion. Stir-fry 3 minutes.

Add mushrooms and pea pods. Stir-fry 3 minutes. Remove vegetables and keep warm.

Heat wok on high and add remaining tablespoon oil. Add shrimp and stir-fry 7 to 8 minutes.

Stir lemon-cornstarch mixture and add to wok. Cook and stir until bubbly. Add vegetables, cover and cook 1 minute.

Serve over steamed rice.

Nutrient Analysis: 1 cup (without rice)
Exchanges: 2 vegetable, 2 very lean meat
1 fat
Carbohydrate Choices: 1

Calories: 171   Protein: 17g   Carbohydrates: 12g
Fat: 6g   Cholesterol: 115 mg   Sodium: 171 mg
Dietary Fiber: 2g   Omega-3: 0.38g

POULTRY

Health is the thing that makes you
feel that now is the best time
of the year.

Franklin P. Adams

POULTRY

SEASONINGS

Also See:

POULTRY

Chicken and turkey easily fit into a heart-healthy eating plan.

The good taste, versatility and low-fat content of poultry make it an excellent addition to your meal plans. For example, a three-ounce serving of chicken breast has only 3 grams of total fat, less than 1 gram of saturated fat, 1.1 grams of heart-healthy monounsaturated fat and is an excellent source of protein and vitamin B6.

This section contains a wide range of recipes for family fare as well as for elegant entertaining. You won't need a wishbone to bring you exciting ideas for preparing poultry. As shown in the table below, fat, saturated fat and cholesterol content varies between light and dark meat as well as eating or not eating the skin.

Table 24: Fat, Saturated Fat and Cholesterol Content of Poultry

Poultry Item: *(3 ounces, roasted)*	Total Fat *(grams)*	Saturated Fat *(grams)*	Cholesterol *(milligrams)*
Chicken			
White meat, no skin	3	0.9	72
White meat, with skin	7	1.9	71
Dark meat, no skin	9	2.6	81
Dark meat, with skin	13	3.7	79
Turkey			
White meat, no skin	1	0.2	71
Dark meat, no skin	6	2.1	75
Ground	13	3.4	102
Ground, extra-lean	2	0.5	45
Duck			
Domestic, no skin	10	3.5	76
Domestic, with skin	19	8.2	77
Wild, no skin	4	1.1	65
Wild, with skin	13	4.3	68
Goose			
White & dark, no skin	11	3.9	82
White & dark, with skin	19	5.8	77

Source: USDA Nutrient Database for Standard Reference, Release 20 (2007). Available online at www.nal.usda.gov/fnic/foodcomp.

Select either fresh or frozen poultry and use within three days when stored in the refrigerator. Poultry keeps well frozen for about six months. Cook poultry to a safe temperature to kill microorganisms. Use a meat thermometer to make sure that the meat is cooked all the way through. Ground poultry (such as ground turkey) should cook to an internal temperature of 165°F; poultry breasts, to 170°F; and whole poultry to 180°F.

STIR-FRY

Stir-frying helps you use smaller portions of meat while using several vegetables.

Although the wok is the favored cooking utensil for stir-fry, a large, heavy skillet or an electric fry pan will do very well. The wok's advantage is that very little oil is needed as the flaring sides of the wok allow tossing the ingredients and searing them in a single layer.

One of the benefits of stir-fry and wok cookery is that it is fast. The food is cut into bite-sized pieces and tossed in sequence with a small amount of hot liquid (oil, broth, or water). Ingredients are moved rapidly over the hot surface, making the vegetables translucent for a minute or two, and then their natural color intensifies. At that point, they are done and should be removed from the wok. They will finish cooking from their retained heat.

Many stir-fry recipes end with the addition of cornstarch dissolved in broth or water to thicken the pan juices. Remember, the sauce is intended as a glaze, not a gravy.

Cutting the ingredients properly for stir-fry is important. Diagonally cut tubular vegetables such as celery and green beans. Slice meat, poultry, fish, or other vegetables into thin strips 2" long by 1" wide; 1/8" to 1/4" thick. Shred hard vegetables such as carrots or turnips into cuts 1" to 2" long; 1/8" wide, and 1/8" thick. (If you don't have the patience for this, a coarse grater or a food processor works nicely.)

Try any one of the eight stir-fry recipes contained in **Cooking À La Heart**. You'll find them in the **VEGETABLES, GRAINS & LEGUMES; FISH;** and **MEAT** Sections. You'll not want to miss the CHICKEN ALMOND STIR-FRY recipe in this section located on *page 283.*

SEASONING

A number of spices and herbs complement poultry and reduce the need for salt. Experiment with the following flavor enhancers: basil, bay leaf, chervil, curry powder, garlic, green pepper, dried ground lemon peel, lemon juice, lemon verbena, marjoram, mushrooms, paprika, parsley, pepper, poultry seasoning, rosemary, sage and thyme.

HERB BLEND FOR POULTRY

1 tablespoon dried basil
1 tablespoon dried chervil
1 tablespoon dried marjoram
1 tablespoon parsley flakes
1 teaspoon whole thyme
1 teaspoon dried lemon verbena

Crush herbs and blend thoroughly. Sprinkle on poultry during cooking or use in a shaker at the table. Store extra in a tightly-covered glass container.

See SEASONINGS for additional herb and spice blends.

EASY OVEN-BAKED CHICKEN

Try our easy, tasty SHAKE AND MAKE as an alternative to high sodium commercial preparations.

Makes 1 whole chicken; 4 servings

1 broiler chicken, disjointed and
     skinned
2/3 cup SHAKE & MAKE,
     (page 381)

Shake chicken pieces in SHAKE & MAKE mixture. Place in nonstick-sprayed baking pan and bake until chicken is tender.

Oven: 375°
Time: 45 to 60 minutes

Nutrient Analysis: 1/4 chicken
Exchanges: 3 1/2 very lean meat,
*   1/2 skim milk, 1 fat*
Carbohydrate Choices: 1/2

Calories: 182   Protein: 29g   Carbohydrates: 6g
Fat: 4g   Cholesterol: 81mg   Sodium: 180mg
Calcium: 159mg

CHICKEN WITH HERBS

Makes 2 whole chickens; 8 servings

2 broiler chickens, quartered and
   skinned
  Freshly ground pepper
1 garlic clove, crushed
1/2 cup skim milk
3/4 cup fine dry bread crumbs
1 teaspoon dried rosemary, crushed
1/4 cup fresh chopped parsley
1/2 teaspoon dry mustard

Sprinkle chicken pieces lightly with pepper.

Combine garlic and milk in a small bowl. On a piece of waxed paper, combine bread crumbs, rosemary, parsley and mustard. Dip chicken in milk, then roll in bread crumbs to coat well.

Place in a foil-lined baking pan and bake, uncovered.

Oven: 375°
Time: 60 minutes

Nutrient Analysis: 1/4 chicken
Exchanges: 1/2 starch, 3 very lean meat, 1 fat
Carbohydrate Choices: 1/2

Calories: 181   Protein: 27 g   Carbohydrates: 8 g
Fat: 4 g   Cholesterol: 79 mg   Sodium: 172 mg

LEMON CHICKEN

Makes 1 whole chicken; 4 servings

2 1/2 pound fryer chicken, disjointed
    and skinned
1/4 cup vegetable oil
1/4 cup lemon juice
2 teaspoons dried oregano or
   tarragon, crushed
1/8 teaspoon garlic powder
2 tablespoons chopped fresh
   parsley
1/4 teaspoon paprika

Arrange chicken in single layer in a baking dish.

Combine oil, lemon juice, oregano or tarragon and garlic powder and brush on chicken.

Cover and bake for 35 minutes. Remove cover and brush again with lemon-oil mixture. Bake another 20 minutes. Sprinkle with parsley and paprika. Serve.

Oven: 350°
Time: 35 minutes covered and
       20 minutes uncovered

Nutrient Analysis: 1/4 chicken
Exchanges: 3 very lean meat, 2 fat
Carbohydrate Choices: 0

Calories: 197   Protein: 25 g   Carbohydrates: 1 g
Fat: 10 g   Cholesterol: 78 mg   Sodium: 85 mg

CURRY-GLAZED CHICKEN

Makes 1 whole chicken; 4 servings

2	tablespoons tub margarine
1/4	cup honey
3	tablespoons Dijon mustard
2	teaspoons curry powder
2 1/2	pounds fryer chicken, disjointed and skinned

Place margarine in 13 x 9" baking dish and heat in oven until melted.

Stir in honey, mustard, and curry powder. Add chicken, turning to coat.

Bake, turning after 20 minutes.

Oven: 375°
Time: 40 to 45 minutes

Nutrient Analysis: 1/4 chicken

Exchanges: 1 starch, 3 very lean meat, 1 1/2 fat		
Carbohydrate Choices: 1		
Calories: 247	*Protein: 27g*	*Carbohydrates: 18g*
Fat: 7g	*Cholesterol: 66mg*	*Sodium: 249mg*

BREADED CHICKEN BREASTS

Makes 8 breaded half-breasts; 8 servings

1	cup evaporated skim milk
4	teaspoons lemon juice
1 1/2	tablespoons sodium-reduced Worcestershire sauce
1	teaspoon paprika
1 1/2	garlic cloves, minced
1/4	teaspoon pepper
4	whole chicken breasts, boned, split and skinned (about 1 1/2 pounds)
2	cups fine whole wheat bread crumbs
1/4	cup melted soft margarine

Combine the milk, lemon juice, Worcestershire, paprika, garlic, pepper in a large bowl. Add the chicken breasts. Cover and refrigerate overnight to marinate.

When ready to bake, roll breasts in crumbs and place on jelly roll pan. Drizzle 2 tablespoons of the margarine over the chicken. Bake 30 minutes, turn and drizzle remaining margarine over chicken. Bake an additional 15 to 20 minutes until brown and tender.

Oven: 350°
Time: 45 to 50 minutes

Nutrient Analysis: 1 breaded half-breast

Exchanges: 1 1/2 starch, 3 very lean meat, 1 fat		
Carbohydrate Choices: 1 1/2		
Calories: 281	*Protein: 26g*	*Carbohydrates: 23g*
Fat: 8g	*Cholesterol: 49mg*	*Sodium: 357mg*
Dietary Fiber: 1g	*Calcium: 130mg*	

GINGER CHICKEN BREASTS

Makes 4 stuffed half-breasts; 4 servings

GINGER MARINADE:

2	teaspoons grated fresh ginger
3	dashes Tabasco sauce or cayenne pepper
2	large garlic cloves, minced
1	teaspoon dried rosemary, crushed
1/4	cup dry vermouth (or orange juice)
1/2	cup sodium-reduced chicken stock
1	tablespoon wine vinegar
1	tablespoon vegetable oil
1	tablespoon minced fresh parsley
2	whole chicken breasts, skinned (about 1 pound)
2	tart green apples, peeled, cored and finely diced
2	tablespoons minced fresh parsley
1	bay leaf, crushed

In a jar with a tightly-fitting lid, combine ginger, Tabasco or cayenne pepper, garlic, rosemary, vermouth, stock, vinegar, oil and parsley. Shake well to blend.

Rinse the chicken and pat dry. Place in large bowl and pour marinade over chicken, turning to coat. Cover tightly and refrigerate overnight. Remove chicken from refrigerator 1 hour before baking.

Drain chicken, reserving marinade. Pat chicken lightly with paper toweling. Split breast in half. Bone or make a pocket. Stuff half-breasts with apple, parsley and bay leaf. Secure with string or skewer. Bake, basting 4 to 5 times with marinade.

Oven: 350°
Time: 30 to 45 minutes

Nutrient Analysis: 1 stuffed half-breast
Exchanges: 1 fruit, 3 very lean meat, 1 fat
Carbohydrate Choices: 1

Calories: 212   Protein: 27g   Carbohydrates: 11g
Fat: 5g   Cholesterol: 66mg   Sodium: 91mg
Dietary Fiber: 1g

CHICKEN BREASTS IN MUSHROOM SAUCE

Makes 4 half-breasts; 4 servings

2	whole chicken breasts, boned, split and skinned (about 1 pound)
1/2	cup evaporated skim milk
1	cup fine whole wheat bread crumbs
2	cups sliced fresh mushrooms
2	tablespoons diced green onions
1/2	cup dry white wine
1	teaspoon fresh lemon juice
1/8	teaspoon whole thyme
1/8	teaspoon dried marjoram, crushed

Flatten chicken breasts. Dip in milk, then in bread crumbs, coating well. Roll up and arrange, seam down, in nonstick-sprayed baking pan. Cover and bake 25 minutes.

While chicken is baking, simmer the mushrooms and onions in wine and lemon juice. Add thyme and marjoram.

Uncover chicken and spoon mushroom mixture over chicken. Bake, uncovered, 10 to 15 minutes longer, or until chicken is tender and brown.

Oven: 350°
Time: 25 minutes, covered and
10 to 15 minutes, uncovered

Nutrient Analysis: 1 half-breast
Exchanges: 1 1/2 starch, 1 vegetable,
3 very lean meat
Carbohydrate Choices: 2

Calories: 258   Protein: 27g   Carbohydrates: 25g
Fat: 3g   Cholesterol: 49mg   Sodium: 309mg
Dietary Fiber: 2g   Calcium: 136mg

ORANGE BAKED CHICKEN BREASTS

Makes 5 half-breasts; 5 servings

5	chicken breast halves, skinned (about 1 1/4 pounds)
1/4	cup onion, chopped
1/4	teaspoon dried rosemary, crushed
1/2	teaspoon paprika
1/8	teaspoon pepper
2	tablespoons all-purpose flour
2	cups orange juice

Place chicken in shallow pan, meat side up. Sprinkle onion, rosemary, paprika and pepper over chicken.

Blend flour with orange juice and pour over chicken. Bake uncovered until done, basting often with juice.

Oven: 350°
Time: 60 minutes

Nutrient Analysis: 1 half-breast
Exchanges: 1 fruit, 3 very lean meat
Carbohydrate Choices: 1

Calories: 152   Protein: 20g   Carbohydrates: 14g
Fat: 1g   Cholesterol: 49mg   Sodium: 66mg

CHICKEN TANDOORI

Grand Prize Winner Heart's Delight Recipe Contest—Senior Division

Makes 8 half-breasts; 8 servings

4   whole chicken breasts, boned,
      split and skinned (about 2
      pounds)
1   (6-ounce) container plain
      low-fat yogurt
1   tablespoon fresh lemon juice
4   garlic cloves, crushed
1   tablespoon grated fresh ginger
1 1/2   teaspoons ground coriander
1/2   teaspoon ground cumin
1   teaspoon paprika
1/4   teaspoon cayenne pepper
1/4   teaspoon whole cumin seed or
      caraway seed
1/4   cup margarine, melted
      Lettuce leaves
      Green chilies, for garnish
      Lime wedges, for garnish
      Radishes, for garnish

Lightly score breasts.

Combine yogurt, lemon juice, garlic, ginger, coriander, cumin, paprika, cayenne pepper and whole cumin or caraway in a small bowl. Blend thoroughly. Using a pastry brush, brush generously over breasts. Cover and refrigerate 8 hours or overnight.

Place breasts on a nonstick-sprayed shallow baking pan and drizzle with melted margarine. Bake at 400° for 8 to 10 minutes then at 350° until breasts are done (25 to 30 minutes).

Arrange breasts on lettuce leaves and garnish with chilies, lime wedges and radishes.

*Oven: 400°, 10 minutes and
      350°, 25 to 30 minutes*

Nutrient Analysis: 1 half-breast
Exchanges: 3 very lean meat, 1 fat
Carbohydrate Choices: 0

Calories: 159   Protein: 21 g   Carbohydrates: 2 g
Fat: 7 g   Cholesterol: 51 mg   Sodium: 121 mg

WAIKIKI CHICKEN

Entertaining a group? Easy, quick and delicious WAIKIKI CHICKEN, steamed rice and a green garden salad is a real crowd pleaser.

Makes 12 chicken quarters; 12 servings

12   chicken quarters, skinned
        (3 whole chickens)
1   cup all-purpose flour
1/2   tablespoon freshly ground pepper

Wash and dry chicken.

Mix flour and pepper in a paper or plastic bag. Shake chicken in mixture to coat. Arrange in shallow baking pan.

continued on next page

WAIKIKI CHICKEN, (continued)

SAUCE:

1	(16-ounce) can mandarin oranges
1 3/4	cups orange syrup, plus water
1/2	cup sugar
3	tablespoons cornstarch
1/3	cup cider vinegar
1 1/2	tablespoons sodium-reduced soy sauce
1/2	teaspoon ginger
1 1/2	tablespoons low-sodium, chicken-flavored bouillon granules
1	green pepper, seeded and cut into julienne strips

Brown in 425° oven for 10 minutes. Reduce oven to 350°.

In the meantime, drain oranges, reserving syrup. Set orange segments aside for garnish. Add water to the orange syrup to equal 1 3/4 cups.

Combine sugar and cornstarch in a medium saucepan. Add mandarin orange syrup, vinegar, soy sauce, ginger and bouillon. Bring to a boil stirring constantly. Boil for 3 minutes.

Pour over chicken. Bake uncovered, 30 minutes.

Arrange mandarin orange slices and green pepper attractively over chicken. Cover. Bake for an additional 20 to 30 minutes or until chicken is tender. Serve with steamed rice.

Oven: 425° for 10 minutes and
350° for 50 to 60 minutes

Nutrient Analysis: 1 chicken quarter no rice   Calories: 186   Protein: 20g   Carbohydrates: 21g
Exchanges: 1 starch, 1/2 fruit, 3 very lean meat   Fat: 2g   Cholesterol: 59mg   Sodium: 133mg
Carbohydrate Choices: 1 1/2   Dietary Fiber: 1g

CHICKEN QUICK-FRY

Heart-healthy "Nuggets" are a big favorite with kids.

Makes 4 (4-ounce) servings

2	whole chicken breasts, boned, split and skinned (about 1 pound)
1/2	cup crushed bran flakes
1/2	teaspoon dried tarragon, crushed
1/3	cup skim milk
2	tablespoons safflower oil

Cut chicken in chunks or strips.

Mix bran flakes and tarragon. Dip chicken pieces in milk, then roll in bran flakes.

Heat oil in a heavy skillet or wok. Fry chicken pieces quickly (about 10 to 15 minutes), turning once.

Nutrient Analysis: 4 ounces   Calories: 182   Protein: 21g   Carbohydrates: 6g
Exchanges: 1/2 starch, 3 very lean meat, 1 fat   Fat: 8g   Cholesterol: 50mg   Sodium: 124mg
Carbohydrate Choices: 1/2   Dietary Fiber: 1g

SESAME CHICKEN

Makes 8 chicken thighs; 4 servings

  8 chicken thighs, skinned
       (about 1 pound)
1/2 cup calorie-reduced Russian
       salad dressing
1/4 cup sodium-reduced soy sauce
1/2 onion, minced
  1 tablespoon sesame seeds
  2 tablespoons water
1/2 teaspoon ground ginger
  1 garlic clove, minced
1/8 teaspoon red pepper

Place chicken in a large, shallow baking dish.

In a jar with a tightly-fitting lid, combine salad dressing, soy sauce, onion, sesame seeds, water, ginger, garlic and red pepper. Shake well and pour over chicken, turning chicken to coat well. Cover and refrigerate at least 8 hours, turning occasionally.

Remove chicken from marinade and grill over slow coals 45 to 50 minutes or until chicken is tender. Turn and baste with marinade every 15 minutes.

Or broil in oven. Place thighs on nonstick-sprayed broiler rack, and broil 8 inches from heat. Turn and baste every 10 minutes until tender.

Nutrient Analysis: 2 chicken thighs
Exchanges: 1 starch, 3 lean meat
Carbohydrate Choices: 1

Calories: 252   Protein: 24 g   Carbohydrates: 12 g
Fat: 12 g   Cholesterol: 83 mg   Sodium: 896 mg
Dietary Fiber: 1 g   Omega-3: 0.24 g

CHICKEN TERIYAKI

Makes 4 half-breasts; 4 servings

MARINADE:
  2 tablespoons sugar
1/4 cup sodium-reduced soy sauce
1/3   cup water
1/4 cup sherry
  1 teaspoon grated fresh ginger
1/8 teaspoon garlic powder
1/8 teaspoon white pepper

Mix together sugar, soy sauce, water, sherry, ginger, garlic powder and pepper for marinade in a large bowl.

continued on next page

CHICKEN TERIYAKI, (continued)

2 whole chicken breasts, boned,
   split and skinned (about 1
   pound)
1 green bell pepper, seeded and cut
   in julienne strips
2 cups cooked brown or wild rice

Place chicken in marinade and marinate for 2 hours or longer, turning occasionally.

Over low heat, poach chicken in marinade until tender (about 20 minutes). Add green pepper strips and cook until crisp-tender.

Serve chicken breasts over rice topped with green pepper strips. Serve marinade on the side as a sauce.

Nutrient Analysis: 1 half-breast
Exchanges: 2 starch, 3 very lean meat
Carbohydrate Choices: 2

Calories: 256   Protein: 24g   Carbohydrates: 33g
Fat: 2g   Cholesterol: 49mg   Sodium: 595mg
Dietary Fiber: 3g

CHICKEN CUTLETS

Makes 8 half-breasts; 8 servings

2 pounds chicken breasts, boned,
   split and skinned, pounded
   thin
   Freshly ground pepper
1 tablespoon vegetable oil
1 tablespoon tub margarine
4 tablespoons all-purpose flour
1/2 cup skim milk
1/2 cup unsalted chicken stock, or
   1 teaspoon low-sodium,
   chicken-flavored bouillon
   granules in 1/2 cup water
1 cup white wine
1/2 teaspoon dried tarragon or basil,
   crushed
1 teaspoon dried parsley flakes
1/2 cup sliced fresh mushrooms

Sprinkle cutlets with pepper.

Melt the oil and margarine in a large skillet and sauté chicken over medium heat 5 to 8 minutes on each side. Remove from pan and keep warm.

Blend flour with milk and stock. Add to pan drippings and cook and stir over medium heat until thick. Reduce heat and add wine, tarragon or basil, parsley and mushrooms. Heat thoroughly and serve immediately over cutlets.

Nutrient Analysis: 1 half-breast
Exchanges: 3 very lean meat, 1 fat
Carbohydrate Choices: 0

Calories: 162   Protein: 21g   Carbohydrates: 4g
Fat: 4g   Cholesterol: 49mg   Sodium: 78mg

ITALIAN CHICKEN

Makes 1 whole chicken; 4 servings

2 1/2 to 3 pound fryer chicken, disjointed and skinned
1 tablespoon vegetable oil
1/2 cup sliced green onions (with some green tops), divided
1 (35-ounce) can unsalted tomatoes, drained
3/4 cup buttermilk
1 tablespoon snipped fresh dill or 1 teaspoon dried dill weed
1/2 teaspoon sugar
1/8 to 1/4 teaspoon freshly ground pepper
Dash Tabasco sauce
1 (6-ounce) container plain low-fat yogurt
1/4 cup grated Parmesan cheese
1/2 cup minced fresh parsley

Lightly brown the chicken pieces in oil in a large skillet with a cover. Add 1/4 cup of the green onions and cook the chicken and onions until the onion is wilted. Remove from heat.

Combine the tomatoes, buttermilk, dill, sugar, pepper and Tabasco in a blender or food processor. Blend until the mixture is smooth.

Pour the sauce over the chicken and bring the contents of the skillet to a boil. Reduce the heat, cover pan and simmer the chicken for about 20 minutes or until it is tender.

Stir in the yogurt and the Parmesan and heat thoroughly but do not boil.

To serve, garnish the chicken with the remaining 1/4 cup onions and parsley.

Nutrient Analysis: 1/4 chicken
Exchanges: 1 starch, 1 vegetable,
3 very lean meat, 1 fat
Carbohydrate Choices: 1 1/2

Calories: 259   Protein: 27g   Carbohydrates: 20g
Fat: 8g   Cholesterol: 68mg   Sodium: 344mg
Dietary Fiber: 4g   Calcium: 249mg

CHICKEN BROCCOLI CASSEROLE

Makes 2-quart casserole; 6 servings

1	(10-ounce) package cut broccoli
2 1/2	cups diced cooked chicken
3	tablespoons tub margarine
3	tablespoons all-purpose flour
3/4	cup skim milk
1	tablespoon lemon juice
1	cup sliced fresh mushrooms
1/2	cup sliced water chestnuts
1	cup plain croutons

Cook broccoli until crisp-tender. Layer chicken and broccoli in a nonstick-sprayed baking dish.

Melt margarine in a saucepan. Stir in flour and add milk. Cook and stir over medium heat until mixture comes to a boil and thickens.

Add lemon juice, mushrooms and water chestnuts. Pour over chicken and broccoli and top with croutons. Bake.

Oven: 350°
Time: 25 minutes

Nutrient Analysis: 1 cup
Exchanges: 1/2 starch, 1 vegetable
*   3 very lean meat, 1 fat*
Carbohydrate Choices: 1

Calories: 223   Protein: 27g   Carbohydrates: 12g
Fat: 7g   Cholesterol: 60mg   Sodium: 163mg
Dietary Fiber: 2g

COTTAGE BROCCOLI CASSEROLE

Makes 1 1/2-quart casserole; 4 servings

1 (10-ounce) package broccoli cuts
    or 2 cups fresh broccoli cuts
1 cup diced cooked chicken or
    turkey
1 cup low-fat cottage cheese
1/2 cup EGG SUBSTITUTE,
    (page 234)
1 teaspoon instant onion flakes
1/8 teaspoon paprika
1/8 teaspoon garlic powder
1/8 teaspoon curry powder
1/8 teaspoon celery seed
1/4 teaspoon pepper
1/4 teaspoon dried sage or marjoram,
    crushed

TOPPING:

2 tablespoons vegetable oil
1/3 cup whole wheat bread crumbs
2 tablespoons sesame seeds

Cook broccoli until crisp-tender. Layer broccoli and chicken in a nonstick-sprayed casserole.

Blend together cottage cheese, egg substitute, onion, paprika, garlic powder, curry powder, celery seed, pepper and sage or marjoram in blender. Pour over broccoli and chicken.

Combine oil, bread crumbs and sesame seeds in small bowl. Sprinkle over top of casserole. Bake.

Oven: 325°
Time: 30 to 40 minutes

Nutrient Analysis: 1 cup
Exchanges: 1/2 starch, 1 vegetable,
         3 very lean meat, 2 fat
Carbohydrate Choices: 1

Calories: 261   Protein: 28 g   Carbohydrates: 12 g
Fat: 11 g   Cholesterol: 38 mg   Sodium: 405 mg
Dietary Fiber: 3 g   Calcium: 110 mg   Omega-3: 0.10 g

ENCHILADA CASSEROLE

Makes 13 x 9" baking dish; 8 servings

1   cup heavy WHITE SAUCE,
    (page 164)
2   teaspoons low-sodium chicken-
    flavored bouillon granules
1   cup water
4   ounces fresh mushrooms, sliced
1   medium onion, chopped
2   cups plain low-fat yogurt
1   (4-ounce) can chopped green
    chilies
8   6-inch corn tortillas
2-3 cups diced cooked chicken or
    turkey (about 1 pound)
8   ounces part-skim farmer cheese,
    shredded (2 cups)
6   green onions, chopped

Make white sauce. Add bouillon granules dissolved in water, mushrooms, onion, yogurt and chilies. Heat.

Layer tortillas, chicken, and sauce in a nonstick-sprayed 13 x 9" baking pan. Repeat until pan is filled.

Top with grated cheese and onion. Bake until cheese is melted and casserole is heated through.

Oven: 350°
Time: 30 minutes

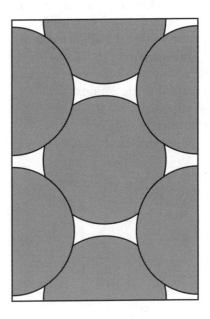

Nutrient Analysis: 1 serving
Exchanges: 1 1/2 starch, 1 vegetable,
    3 lean meat, 1 fat
Carbohydrate Choices: 2

Calories: 372   Protein: 32 g   Carbohydrates: 29 g
Fat: 14 g   Cholesterol: 64 mg   Sodium: 449 mg
Dietary Fiber: 2 g   Calcium: 188 mg

CHICKEN MARENGO

A good buffet dish which can be made a day ahead.

Makes 12 cups; 8 servings

1	onion, thinly sliced
1/4	cup olive oil
2	fryer chickens, skinned and quartered
1/2	cup dry white wine
2	garlic cloves, minced
1/2	teaspoon whole thyme
1	bay leaf
1	cup low-sodium CHICKEN STOCK, *(page 329)* or 2 teaspoons low-sodium chicken-flavored bouillon granules in 1 cup water
2	cups canned Italian tomatoes
2	tablespoons tub margarine
1	pound fresh mushrooms, sliced
16-20	small white onions, whole
1/4	cup sliced black olives
1	ounce brandy
	Chopped fresh parsley

Sauté onion in olive oil until soft and transparent in a heavy skillet. Remove onion and set aside.

Sauté chicken in same pan, browning well on all sides. Remove chicken and drain. Pour off olive oil from pan and discard.

Add wine, garlic, thyme, bay leaf, chicken stock and tomatoes in their juice to the pan. Mix well and return chicken to the sauce. Cover and simmer about 30 minutes or bake 30 minutes at 300°.

In a separate pan, melt margarine and sauté sliced mushrooms. Add whole onions and sauté lightly. Set aside.

When chicken is tender, remove meat and keep warm. Strain tomato sauce and reduce it by boiling rapidly for 5 minutes.

Arrange chicken, onions, mushrooms and olives in a deep earthenware casserole. Sprinkle with brandy. Pour tomato sauce over all and reheat 15 to 20 minutes at 350°.

Sprinkle with chopped parsley and serve with steamed rice or pasta.

Oven: 300°, 30 minutes and
Time: 350°, 15 to 20 minutes

Nutrient Analysis: 1 1/2 cups
Exchanges: 1/2 starch, 3 vegetable,
*   2 1/2 lean meat, 1 fat*
Carbohydrate Choices: 1 1/2

Calories: 318   Protein: 23 g   Carbohydrates: 23 g
Fat: 13 g   Cholesterol: 59 mg   Sodium: 369 mg
Dietary Fiber: 4 g   Omega-3: 0.11 g

WILD RICE CHICKEN CASSEROLE

Makes 6 cups; 6 servings

4   tablespoons tub margarine
5   tablespoons all-purpose flour
1   cup low-sodium CHICKEN
     BROH, *(page 329)* or 2
     teaspoons low-sodium,
     chicken-flavored bouillon
     granules in 1 cup water
1 1/2   cups evaporated skim milk
1/4   teaspoon salt
1   cup wild rice, uncooked
2   cups diced cooked chicken
3/4   cup sliced fresh mushrooms
1/4   cup diced pimiento
1/3   cup chopped green pepper
1/2   cup sliced almonds

Melt margarine in a heavy saucepan. Add flour and blend. Add chicken broth, milk and salt. Cook over medium-high heat until thick, stirring constantly.

Mix together uncooked rice, chicken, mushrooms, pimiento and green pepper. Place in a nonstick-sprayed 11 x 7" baking dish. Pour sauce over casserole and top with almonds. Cover and bake until rice is tender, about 1 hour. Add more chicken broth if casserole becomes dry during baking.

Oven: 350°
Time: 1 hour

Nutrient Analysis: 1 cup
Exchanges: 2 starch, 1 vegetable,
*   3 lean meat, 1 fat*
Carbohydrate Choices: 2 1/2

Calories: 380   Protein: 30 g   Carbohydrates: 36 g
Fat: 13 g   Cholesterol: 48 mg   Sodium: 351 mg
Dietary Fiber: 3 g   Calcium: 198 mg   Omega-3: 0.11 g

CHICKEN COUSCOUS

Couscous is a North African dish made of crushed grain with various meats, vegetables and spices.

Makes 12 cups; 6 servings

2 1/2 to 3 pound broiler/fryer chicken
1/4 cup vegetable oil
3 medium onions, sliced (about 2 cups)
2 garlic cloves, minced
2 teaspoons turmeric
1/2 teaspoon allspice
1/4 teaspoon cayenne pepper
2 tablespoons low-sodium, chicken-flavored bouillon granules
3 cups warm water
1 cup bulgur, dry
1/2 cup dried apricots
1 cup dark seedless raisins
3 small zucchini, sliced (about 3 cups)
1/2 cup slivered almonds, toasted

Disjoint, skin and cut whole chicken into 6 pieces. Set aside.

Heat oil in Dutch oven or large, deep skillet. Add onions and garlic and sauté until limp. Reduce heat. Add turmeric, allspice and pepper. Cook, stirring constantly, for 5 minutes.

Add chicken pieces and cook 5 minutes on each side. Dissolve bouillon granules in water and add to chicken. Heat to boiling, reduce heat to low. Cover and cook 10 minutes. Stir in bulgur, cover and cook 10 minutes.

Add apricots, raisins and zucchini. Cover and cook 10 minutes more or until chicken and bulgur are tender and liquid is absorbed. If some liquid remains, cook uncovered until evaporated but not dry. Stir in almonds and heat through. Serve.

Nutrient Analysis: 2 cups
Exchanges: 1 1/2 starch, 2 fruit, 3 lean meat, 1 fat
Carbohydrate Choices: 3

Calories: 460   Protein: 25 g   Carbohydrates: 56 g
Fat: 16 g   Cholesterol: 59 mg   Sodium: 180 mg
Dietary Fiber: 9 g

CHICKEN ALMOND STIR-FRY

Makes 6 cups; 4 servings

2 whole chicken breasts, split, boned and skinned (about 1 pound)
1 tablespoon cornstarch
2 tablespoons sherry
1/2 cup diced green pepper
1/2 cup diced sweet red pepper
4 green onions sliced including some of the tops
1/4 cup sliced water chestnuts
2 tablespoons vegetable oil
1 (8-ounce) can pineapple chunks in natural juices, drain and reserve juice
3 tablespoons slivered almonds

SAUCE:

1 1/2 tablespoons sherry
1 teaspoon sesame oil
1 teaspoon sugar
1/4 cup low-sodium chicken broth
1 1/2 tablespoons sodium-reduced soy sauce
1 teaspoon cornstarch
1 teaspoon reserved pineapple juice

Cube chicken. Stir with 1 tablespoon cornstarch and 2 tablespoons sherry. Set aside while preparing vegetables and combining sauce ingredients.

Heat oil in wok or heavy skillet. Add chicken and stir-fry until lightly browned.

Add green and red peppers, onions and water chestnuts. Stir-fry 2 minutes.

Add pineapple, slivered almonds and sauce mixture. Cook 2 more minutes or until sauce is thickened and smooth. If sauce is too thick, thin with reserved pineapple juice.

Serve over steamed rice.

Nutrient Analysis: 1 1/2 cups (without rice)
Exchanges: 1 vegetable, 1 fruit,
*   3 very lean meat, 2 fat*
Carbohydrate Choices: 1

Calories: 274   Protein: 22g   Carbohydrates: 18g
Fat: 12g   Cholesterol: 50mg   Sodium: 272mg
Dietary Fiber: 2g

TURKEY THIGHS FLORENTINE

Makes 2 stuffed thighs; 6 servings

1/2 cup chopped onion
1 garlic clove, minced
1/2 teaspoon Italian seasoning
1 tablespoon tub margarine
2 egg whites
1/2 cup chopped cooked spinach
1/2 cup fine soft bread crumbs
1/2 cup grated Parmesan cheese
Pepper to taste
2 turkey thighs (about 2 pounds)

Sauté onion, garlic and Italian seasoning in margarine in a small skillet until soft, but not browned.

Combine egg whites, spinach, bread crumbs, cheese and pepper. Add onion mixture and mix well. Set aside.

Skin and debone turkey thighs. Pound as flat as possible. Divide filling mixture between two flattened thighs. Bring edges together to enclose filling and skewer or tie with string.

Place in shallow, nonstick-sprayed baking pan and cover with foil. Bake. Open foil after 1 hour and bake an additional 30 minutes to brown.

Serve either hot or cold cut into slices.

Oven: 325°
Time: 60 minutes covered and
30 minutes uncovered

Nutrient Analysis: 1/3 stuffed thigh   Calories: 203   Protein: 23 g   Carbohydrates: 8 g
Exchanges: 1/2 starch, 3 very lean meat, 1 1/2 fat   Fat: 8 g   Cholesterol: 64 mg   Sodium: 296 mg
Carbohydrate Choices: 1/2   Dietary Fiber: 1 g   Calcium: 147 mg

TURKEY SCALLOPS À LA ORANGE

Easy but elegant!

Makes 3 3/4 cups; 5 servings

 2   tablespoons tub margarine
 1/2 teaspoon minced garlic
 1 1/4 pounds boneless turkey breast,
       skinned and cut into 1/4" slices

SAUCE:
 1/2 cup orange juice
 2   tablespoons lemon juice
     White pepper to taste
 2   teaspoons cornstarch

Cook margarine with garlic in a large skillet over medium heat until foamy.

Add turkey slices and cook until opaque and no longer pink (about 2 minutes a side). Remove to platter and keep warm.

For sauce: Stir orange juice, lemon juice, pepper and cornstarch in a small bowl, until smooth. Stir orange mixture into skillet, scraping up browned bits on bottom. Boil 1 minute, stirring constantly, until thickened. Pour over turkey and serve.

Nutrient Analysis: 3/4 cup
Exchanges: 3 very lean meat, 1 fat
Carbohydrate Choices: 0

Calories: 155   Protein: 20g   Carbohydrates: 4g
Fat: 6g   Cholesterol: 51 mg   Sodium: 95 mg

TURKEY & FRUIT KABOBS

Makes 4 (10-inch) skewers; 4 servings

 3/4 pound cooked boneless turkey
       breast, cut in 12, 1" cubes
 1   orange, cut in wedges
 1   firm pear, cut in wedges
 1   green pepper, cut in squares
 4   small spiced crab apples
 1/2 cup jellied cranberry sauce
 1/2 cup sugar-free apricot preserves
 1/4 cup lemon juice
 2   tablespoons tub margarine
 1/4 teaspoon ground cinnamon
     Dash ground cloves

Thread pieces of turkey, orange, pear, green pepper and a crab apple onto four 10" skewers.

Combine cranberry sauce, apricot preserves, lemon juice, margarine, cinnamon and cloves in a saucepan. Bring to a boil, stirring occasionally. Brush sauce over turkey and fruit.

Grill about 4" above medium-hot coals, turning and basting until meat and fruit are hot and well glazed (about 10 minutes).

Nutrient Analysis: 1 skewer
Exchanges: 1 starch, 2 fruit, 2 very lean meat, 1 fat
Carbohydrate Choices: 3

Calories: 299   Protein: 21g   Carbohydrates: 44g
Fat: 7g   Cholesterol: 51 mg   Sodium: 111 mg
Dietary Fiber: 3g

ORIENTAL CASSEROLE

Reheats well.

Makes 1 1/2-quart casserole; 4 servings

1	cup heavy WHITE SAUCE, *(page 164)*
2	teaspoons low-sodium, chicken- flavored bouillon granules
1/2	pound fresh broccoli
1	pound extra-lean ground turkey
1	tablespoon sodium-reduced soy sauce
1	small onion, chopped
1	garlic clove, minced
1	cup sliced celery
1	cup bean sprouts
1/2	cup chow mein noodles

Make heavy WHITE SAUCE and stir in bouillon granules.

Separate the broccoli florets and cut the stems into 1/8" slices.

Brown turkey quickly in sprayed skillet, stirring constantly and sprinkling with soy sauce.

Add broccoli, onion, garlic, celery and bean sprouts to the turkey and stir-fry for 2 to 3 minutes.

Mix together white sauce, turkey and vegetables and chow mein noodles and pour into nonstick-sprayed casserole dish. Bake.

Oven: 350°
Time: 30 minutes

Nutrient Analysis: 1 1/2 cups
Exchanges: 1 starch, 1 vegetable,
3 lean meat, 1 fat
Carbohydrate Choices: 1 1/2

Calories: 314   Protein: 28 g   Carbohydrates: 21 g
Fat: 15 g   Cholesterol: 35 mg   Sodium: 541 mg
Dietary Fiber: 4 g Calcium: 112 mg Omega-3: 0.19 g

SWEET & SOUR TURKEY

Makes 9 cups; 6 servings

3   cups cubed turkey breast
        tenderloin (about 1 pound)
1/2 cup chopped green onion
1   garlic clove, minced
2   tablespoons vegetable oil
2   (14-ounce) cans unsweetened
        pineapple chunks
2   tablespoons red wine vinegar
2   tablespoons sodium-reduced soy
        sauce
1   cup water
1   tablespoon brown sugar
2   teaspoons low-sodium, chicken-
        flavored bouillon granules
3   tablespoons cold water
2   tablespoons cornstarch
1   green pepper, cut in strips
1/3 cup toasted slivered almonds

Sauté turkey cubes, onion and garlic in hot oil in a large skillet until meat is lightly browned and onion is tender.

Drain pineapple reserving juice. Add reserved juice, vinegar, soy sauce, brown sugar, bouillon granules and 1 cup water to turkey. Simmer, covered, for 15 minutes.

Blend together cold water and cornstarch. Stir into turkey mixture and cook until thick and bubbly, stirring often.

Add pineapple and green pepper, continue cooking 2 to 3 minutes or until pepper is crisp-tender.

Sprinkle with toasted almonds and serve over steamed rice.

Nutrient Analysis: 1 1/2 cups (without rice)   Calories: 254   Protein: 19g   Carbohydrates: 27g
Exchanges: 1 starch, 1 fruit, 2 very lean meat, 1 fat   Fat: 8g   Cholesterol: 28mg   Sodium: 360mg
Carbohydrate Choices: 2   Dietary Fiber: 2g

MEAT

We often live as if our habits don't matter. They do.

John Farquhar

BEEF

VEAL

PORK

LAMB

SEASONINGS

MEAT

Lean red meat in modest amounts can be part of a heart-healthy eating pattern.

The USDA MyPyramid Food Guide and the DASH Diet (Dietary Approaches to Stop Hypertension) both emphasize nutrient-rich foods, which qualifies lean red meats to be included in a heart-healthy eating pattern. Portion sizes count and a serving is considered 3 ounces, with no more than 5.5 ounces of lean meat to be consumed per day. Low-fat cooking methods such as roasting on a rack, broiling, grilling, braising, or stir-frying keep beef, pork, veal and lamb at acceptable levels of total fat, saturated fat and cholesterol. While beef is a source of saturated fat, a third of it is stearic acid, which has a neutral effect on blood cholesterol levels.

A 3-ounce portion of lean beef contributes less than 10 percent of calories to a 2,000-calorie diet and is an "excellent source" of protein, vitamin B_{12}, zinc and selenium and a "good" source of vitamin B_6, riboflavin, niacin and iron. A 3-ounce portion of pork tenderloin is an "excellent" source of protein, thiamin, vitamin B_6, and niacin and a "good" source of potassium, riboflavin and zinc, yet contributes only 6 percent of calories to a 2,000-calorie diet.

Choose wisely; read the label!

In selecting beef, pork, veal or lamb, look for "loin" on the label as in pork tenderloin, or veal loin, or beef sirloin because "loin" means "lean". When choosing red meat cuts at the meat counter, look for these claims on the package for a 3-ounce serving:

Label Claim	Total fat	Saturated fat	Cholesterol
Extra lean	<5 g	<2.0 g	<95 mg
Lean	<10 g	<4.5 g	<95 mg

Both the beef and pork industry have responded to the consumer's desire for lean meats. Table 25 compares the amount of total fat, saturated fat and cholesterol in various cuts of lean red meat to a skinless chicken breast. Six of the most common cuts of pork (which on average have 16% less fat and 27% less saturated fat than 15 years ago) fall below 10 grams of total fat in a 3-ounce serving and more than twenty cuts of lean beef meet the grade.

Table 25: Fat, Saturated Fat and Cholesterol Content of Lean Red Meat
(in comparison to a skinless chicken breast)

Cut of Meat: (3 ounces, cooked)	Total Fat (grams)	Saturated Fat (grams)	Cholesterol (milligrams)
Skinless Chicken Breast	3.0 g	0.9 g	72 mg
Pork, Tenderloin	2.7 g	0.9 g	48 mg
Pork, Boneless Top Loin chop	3.0 g	1.0 g	44 mg
Beef, Eye of Round roast & steak	4.0 g	1.5 g	46 mg
Beef, Bottom Round roast & steak	4.5 g	1.6 g	61 mg
Beef, Sirloin Tip steak	4.5 g	1.8 g	63 mg
Pork, Cured Ham, boneless extra-lean (note, the sodium is 1,023 mg/3-ounce serving)	4.7 g	1.5 g	45 mg
Beef, Top Round roast & steak	4.8 g	1.7 g	66 mg
Beef, Top Sirloin steak	4.9 g	1.9 g	49 mg
Pork, Boneless Top Loin roast	5.3 g	1.6 g	67 mg
Ground Beef, 95% lean	5.6 g	2.5 g	65 mg
Beef, Chuck Arm pot roast	5.7 g	1.9 g	48 mg
Veal, Loin	5.9 g	2.2 g	90 mg
Beef, Brisket-flat half	5.9 g	2.3 g	59 mg
Pork, Bone-in Center Loin chop	6.2 g	1.8 g	71 mg
Lamb, domestic, Loin	8.2 g	3.0 g	81 mg

Source: US Dept of Agriculture, Agriculture Research Service, 2006. USDA Nutrient Database for Standard Reference, Release 20 (2007). Available online at www.nal.usda.gov/fnic/foodcomp.

Low-fat cooking tips.

The following preparation suggestions will help you keep the fat content of your meal low:

- Trim all visible fat from meat prior to cooking.
- Use nonstick pans to brown meat.
- Use vegetable cooking sprays instead of fat to brown meat.
- Prepare meats by roasting, baking, broiling or braising. When roasting meat, use a rack so fat can be easily drained. Low-temperature roasting (325°-350°F) is recommended because more of the fat will come out of the meat. Higher temperatures will seal the fat in.
- After making soup or stew containing meat, refrigerate until the fat congeals on the surface so that it can be easily removed.

The recipes in this chapter include combination dishes using smaller amounts of meat with pasta, vegetables and grains. We know you'll enjoy the adventuresome variety.

SEASONING

Reduce your dependency on salt by discovering the subtleties of herbs and spices. The following additions enhance the flavor of beef: bay leaf, chili powder, dry mustard, garlic, ginger, green pepper, sage, marjoram, mushrooms, nutmeg, onion, oregano, pepper and thyme.

HERB BLEND FOR BEEF

1 tablespoon dried marjoram
1 tablespoon dried basil
1 tablespoon dried parsley
1 tablespoon dried celery leaves
1/4 teaspoon dried summer savory
1/4 teaspoon whole thyme

Crush dried herbs and blend thoroughly. Sprinkle on beef during cooking or use in a shaker at the table. Store extra in a tightly-covered glass container.

See SEASONINGS for additional herb and spice blends.

MARINATED FLANK STEAK

Carve flank steak very thin, diagonally across the grain.

Makes 4 (4-ounce) servings

1/4 cup orange juice
1 teaspoon grated orange peel
1/4 cup vegetable oil
1 1/2 tablespoons sodium-reduced soy sauce
2 garlic cloves, minced
2 tablespoons sodium-reduced ketchup
1/8 teaspoon Tabasco sauce
1 pound flank steak
1 medium orange, sliced

In shallow baking dish, combine orange juice, peel, oil, soy sauce, garlic, ketchup and Tabasco. Mix well.

Add flank steak, turning to coat both sides. Arrange orange slices on top of meat, cover and marinate several hours or overnight in refrigerator.

Prepare charcoal grill or preheat broiler. Remove steak from marinade and set orange slices aside. Grill or broil steak 4 to 6 minutes a side or until desired doneness. During last 2 minutes of cooking, grill or broil orange slices until heated through.

Serve steak thinly sliced and garnished with orange slices.

Nutrient Analysis: 1 serving
Exchanges: 3 medium-fat meat
Carbohydrate Choices: 0

Calories: 247   Protein: 23g   Carbohydrates: 3g
Fat: 15g   Cholesterol: 57mg   Sodium: 186mg

STEAK & VEGETABLES

Makes 4 (4-ounce) servings

1   pound boneless beef round steak,
    cut 1/2" thick
    Freshly ground pepper
1   tablespoon vegetable oil
2   cups water
1   (6-ounce) can no-salt-added
    tomato paste
2   teaspoons sodium-reduced
    Worcestershire sauce
1/4   teaspoon dried basil, crushed
1/4   teaspoon whole thyme
1/4   teaspoon dried marjoram, crushed
4   medium carrots, cut in 1/4" strips
1   medium green pepper, cut in 1/4"
    strips
2   cups sliced fresh mushrooms

Trim excess fat from steak and cut into 4 portions. Sprinkle with pepper.

Brown meat on both sides in oil in a 3-quart saucepan. Stir in water, tomato paste, Worcestershire, basil, thyme and marjoram. Bring to boil; reduce heat. Cover and simmer 30 minutes.

Add carrots, green pepper and mushrooms. Cover and simmer 15 minutes or until meat and vegetables are tender. Transfer meat and vegetables to a serving dish and pour tomato sauce over all.

Serve with rice or noodles.

Nutrient Analysis: 1 serving
Exchanges: 4 vegetable, 3 very lean meat, 1 fat
Carbohydrate Choices: 1

Calories: 231   Protein: 28 g   Carbohydrates: 20 g
Fat: 7 g   Cholesterol: 50 mg   Sodium: 138 mg
Dietary Fiber: 5 g

BEEF SHISH KABOBS

Makes 6 (8-inch) skewers

1 1/2   pounds round steak or sirloin
    tip
2   tablespoons vegetable oil
2   tablespoons fresh lemon juice
1   teaspoon dried oregano, crushed

Trim excess fat from steak and cut into 1 1/2" cubes.

Combine oil, lemon juice, oregano, bay leaf and pepper in a mixing bowl. Add beef and cover, turning occasionally, for at least 3 hours.

continued on next page

BEEF SHISH KABOBS, (continued)

1 bay leaf
    Freshly ground pepper
1 sweet red pepper cut into 1 1/2"
    chunks
1 green pepper cut into 1 1/2"
    chunks
2 large tomatoes, quartered
1 onion, quartered and separated
12 large fresh mushrooms

Thread beef cubes on skewers alternately with vegetables. Grill kabobs over medium-hot coals, three minutes a side for rare or until desired doneness. Baste with marinade during cooking.

Nutrient Analysis: 1 skewer
Exchanges: 2 vegetable, 3 very lean meat, 1 fat
Carbohydrate Choices: 1/2

Calories: 195   Protein: 26 g   Carbohydrates: 9 g
Fat: 8 g   Cholesterol: 50 mg   Sodium: 60 mg
Dietary Fiber: 2 g

GROUND BEEF STROGANOFF (CROCK POT)

Makes 8 cups; 8 servings

2 pounds extra-lean ground beef
2 medium onions, chopped
2 garlic cloves, minced
8 ounces fresh mushrooms, sliced
2 teaspoons sodium-reduced, beef-
    flavored bouillon granules
1 cup water
1 1/2 cups plain low-fat yogurt
4 tablespoons all-purpose flour
3 tablespoons tomato paste
1/4 teaspoon salt
1/4 teaspoon pepper

Brown meat in skillet; drain fat.

Add onions, garlic and mushrooms and sauté until onion is golden. Place in slow cooker (crock pot).

Dissolve bouillon granules in water. Mix together yogurt and flour. Add bouillon, yogurt, tomato paste, salt and pepper to slow cooker. Cover and cook on low for 6 hours*.

Serve hot over noodles or rice.

* Simmer in Dutch oven for about 1 hour or bake at 350° for 1 hour.

Nutrient Analysis: 1 cup (without noodles)
Exchanges: 2 vegetable, 3 very lean meat, 1 fat
Carbohydrate Choices: 1

Calories: 204   Protein: 27 g   Carbohydrates: 13 g
Fat: 5 g   Cholesterol: 63 mg   Sodium: 195 mg
Dietary Fiber: 1 g

BEEF STROGANOFF

Makes 4 cups; 4 servings

1 pound lean round steak, thinly sliced into strips
3 tablespoons all-purpose flour
1 1/2 teaspoons paprika
1 tablespoon vegetable oil
1 onion, chopped
1 garlic clove, crushed or 1/4 teaspoon garlic powder
1/4 teaspoon pepper
8 ounces fresh mushrooms, sliced*
1/3 cup water or wine *
1 teaspoon low-sodium, beef-flavored bouillon granules
1 (6-ounce) container plain low-fat yogurt

May substitute 1 (4-ounce) can mushrooms with liquid and omit the water or wine.

Shake beef strips in mixture of flour and paprika.

Heat oil in a large skillet or Dutch oven. Over high heat, brown beef, onion, garlic, pepper and mushrooms.

Stir in water or wine, beef bouillon and yogurt. Bring to a boil stirring constantly. Reduce heat, cover and simmer for 12 to 15 minutes.

Serve over rice or noodles.

Nutrient Analysis: 1 cup (without noodles)   Calories: 211   Protein: 28g   Carbohydrates: 13g
Exchanges: 1 starch, 3 very lean meat, 1 fat   Fat: 8g   Cholesterol: 53mg   Sodium: 102mg
Carbohydrate Choices: 1   Dietary Fiber: 1g

SWEDISH MEAT BALLS

The secret to making Swedish meat balls is good meat—finely ground, finely chopped onion and thorough mixing of ingredients.

Makes 30 meatballs; 10 servings

1	large onion, very finely chopped
1	tablespoon water
1 1/2	pounds extra-lean ground beef
1/2	pound ground pork
1/4	teaspoon ground allspice
1/3	teaspoon ground cloves
1/2	teaspoon salt
2	cups whole wheat bread crumbs
3	tablespoons all-purpose flour
2	cups skim milk
1 1/2	tablespoons low-sodium, beef-flavored bouillon granules

Heat onion and water in a covered saucepan until onion pieces are soft.

Mix onion, beef, pork, allspice, cloves, salt and bread crumbs thoroughly. Form into 30 medium balls.

In skillet (or in oven at 350°), brown meat balls. Remove balls to casserole dish.

Make gravy by mixing together flour, milk, bouillon granules and drippings in the same skillet. Cook until thickened. Pour gravy over meat balls. Bake or simmer.

Oven: 350°
Time: 45 minutes

Nutrient Analysis: 3 meatballs
Exchanges: 1 1/2 starch, 2 1/2 lean meat
Carbohydrate Choices: 1 1/2

Calories: 262   Protein: 23 g   Carbohydrates: 21 g
Fat: 9 g   Cholesterol: 54 mg   Sodium: 376 mg
Dietary Fiber: 1 g

GRILLED HERBED HAMBURGERS

Makes 8 (4-ounce) servings

1/2 cup finely chopped onion
1/4 teaspoon garlic powder
 1   tablespoon chopped fresh parsley
1/2 tablespoon vegetable oil
 2   pounds extra-lean ground beef
1/4 teaspoon dried marjoram,
       crushed
1/4 teaspoon dried basil, crushed
 2   tablespoons lemon juice

Sauté onion, garlic and parsley in oil in a small skillet until soft.

Add onion mixture to ground beef along with marjoram, basil and lemon juice. Mix well and form into 8 patties.

Grill over medium-high heat to desired degree of doneness.

Nutrient Analysis: 1 serving
Exchanges: 3 very lean meat, 1 fat
Carbohydrate Choices: 0

Calories: 142   Protein: 22g   Carbohydrates: 1g
Fat: 5g   Cholesterol: 60mg   Sodium: 65mg

NEVADA ANNIE CHILI

Hot! Hot! Hot!

Makes 8 cups; 8 servings

 1   cup chopped onion
1/2 cup chopped green pepper
1/2 cup chopped celery
 1   garlic clove, minced
 1   tablespoon canned green chilies,
       diced
 1   tablespoon tub margarine
 2   pounds extra-lean ground beef
 1   cup no-salt-added tomato sauce
 1   (6-ounce) can no-salt-added
       tomato paste
 2   teaspoons chili powder
3/4 teaspoon ground cumin
1/8 teaspoon garlic powder
1/4 teaspoon pepper
     Dash Tabasco sauce
 1   (12-fluid ounces) bottle beer
 1   cup water

Sauté onions, green pepper, celery, garlic and green chilies in margarine.

Add ground beef and brown.

Add tomato sauce, tomato paste, chili powder, cumin, garlic powder, pepper, Tabasco, beer and water. Simmer about 3 hours.

Nutrient Analysis: 1 cup
Exchanges: 2 vegetable, 3 very lean meat, 1 fat
Carbohydrate Choices: 1/2

Calories: 199   Protein: 24g   Carbohydrates: 10g
Fat: 6g   Cholesterol: 60mg   Sodium: 112mg
Dietary Fiber: 2g

MINNESOTA CHILI

Make a double batch of meat sauce and freeze. Add beans when ready to use.

Makes 18 cups; 12 servings

1	pound extra-lean ground beef
3	garlic cloves, minced
2	cups chopped onion
2	cups chopped celery with leaves
2	(28-ounce) cans no-salt-added whole tomatoes
3	tablespoons chili powder
1/4	cup chopped parsley
1/2	teaspoon pepper
2	(16-ounce) cans dark red kidney beans

Brown meat in a heavy saucepan or Dutch oven.

Add garlic, onion and celery and cook until onion is golden.

Break tomatoes into pieces and add along with juice to meat mixture. Add chili powder, parsley and pepper. Bring to a boil, reduce heat, cover and simmer for 2 hours.

Shortly before serving, add kidney beans with liquid and heat thoroughly.

Nutrient Analysis: 1 1/2 cups
Exchanges: 1 starch, 1 1/2 vegetable,
1 very lean meat
Carbohydrate Choices: 1

Calories: 159   Protein: 14g   Carbohydrates: 22g
Fat: 2g   Cholesterol: 20mg   Sodium: 244mg
Dietary Fiber: 7g

MEAT LOAF

Makes 9 x 5" loaf pan; 6 servings

1	(8-ounce) can sodium-reduced tomato sauce
2	teaspoons SEASONING BLEND #1 or #2, *(page 377)*
1/4	teaspoon pepper
1 1/2	pounds extra-lean ground beef
1	large onion, finely chopped
1	egg white
1	cup Wheatena, farina, or bran cereal, uncooked
1/2	cup chopped green pepper
1/4	cup chopped fresh parsley

Mix tomato sauce, SEASONING BLEND and pepper.

Combine the ground beef, onion, egg white, uncooked cereal, green pepper, parsley and half the seasoned tomato sauce.

Pat into 9 x 5" loaf pan. Spread remaining tomato sauce on top. Bake.

Oven: 350°
Time: 50 to 60 minutes

Nutrient Analysis: 1 slice
Exchanges: 1 starch, 1 vegetable,
3 very lean meat, 1 fat
Carbohydrate Choices: 1 1/2

Calories: 241   Protein: 27g   Carbohydrates: 24g
Fat: 5g   Cholesterol: 60mg   Sodium: 83mg
Dietary Fiber: 4g

BEEF STEW

A tasty, easy-to-prepare stew.

Makes 12 cups; 6 servings

1	pound extra-lean top round steak, cubed
1	tablespoon whole wheat flour
1	quart water
1	onion, coarsely chopped
3	garlic cloves, minced
1/8	teaspoon pepper
3	carrots, diced (about 1 3/4 cups)
3	potatoes, diced (about 2 1/4 cups)
1/2	cup sliced fresh mushrooms
1	green pepper, cut in 1" squares
1	tomato, peeled and cut in eighths
4	sprigs parsley, chopped
1/2	cup red wine

Trim all visible fat from meat. Shake in flour.

Brown beef at high heat in a nonstick-sprayed pan.

Bring water to a boil in a heavy saucepan. Add beef, onion, garlic and pepper. Simmer for 2 hours, stirring occasionally. Remove beef. Strain and chill broth. Skim and discard fat.

Thirty minutes before serving, combine beef, broth, carrots and potatoes. Simmer for 15 minutes.

Add mushrooms, green pepper, tomato, parsley and wine. Simmer another 10 to 15 minutes or until vegetables are tender.

Nutrient Analysis: 2 cups
Exchanges: 1 starch, 2 vegetable, 2 very lean meat
Carbohydrate Choices: 1 1/2

Calories: 184   Protein: 20g   Carbohydrates: 24g
Fat: 3g   Cholesterol: 33mg   Sodium: 60mg
Dietary Fiber: 4g

OLD-FASHIONED BEEF STEW

A hearty stew chock-full of meat and vegetables.

Makes 16 cups; 8 servings

1/2	cup all-purpose flour
1/2	teaspoon pepper
1 1/2	pounds beef stew meat, cubed
2	tablespoons vegetable oil
1 1/2	tablespoons low-sodium, beef-flavored bouillon granules
3 1/2	cups water
1/2	cup dry red wine
1	(16-ounce) can low-sodium tomatoes, drained (reserve juice) and chopped
1/2	teaspoon dried marjoram, crushed
1/4	teaspoon salt
4	carrots, sliced (about 2 1/2 cups)
1	(1-pound) package frozen pearl onions
1 1/2	pounds potatoes, cubed (about 4 cups)
1	(9-ounce) package frozen cut green beans

In a paper or plastic bag, combine flour and pepper. Add meat and toss until well-coated.

In Dutch oven, heat oil over medium-high heat. Brown meat in several batches and set aside.

Mix flour remaining in bag with bouillon and water and stir into pan drippings, scraping up brown bits from pan. Return meat to pot.

Add red wine, tomato liquid and marjoram and salt. Bring to a boil. Reduce heat, cover and simmer 1 1/2 hours.

Add carrots, onions, potatoes and tomatoes. Cook, uncovered, 30 minutes, stirring occasionally.

Add green beans and cook 10 minutes longer, stirring to separate beans.

Nutrient Analysis: 2 cups

Exchanges: 1 starch, 3 vegetable, 2 medium-fat meat, 1 fat
Carbohydrate Choices: 2 1/2

Calories: 354   Protein: 20 g   Carbohydrates: 36 g
Fat: 14 g   Cholesterol: 52 mg   Sodium: 194 mg
Dietary Fiber: 4 g

BASIC STIR-FRY RECIPE

Makes 6 cups; 6 servings

1/4   cup sodium-reduced soy sauce
1   tablespoon cornstarch
1   tablespoon grated fresh ginger
    (optional)
1-2   tablespoons olive oil
1   pound poultry, fish, or lean
    meat, cut in 1/4" slices
    Garlic clove (optional)
2   cups sliced vegetable or
    combination of vegetables such
    as carrots, broccoli, bok choy,
    celery, onion, green or red
    peppers
2-3   cups vegetable or combination of
    vegetables such as bean sprouts,
    sliced mushrooms, snow peas
1/2   cup bamboo shoots or water
    chestnuts

Mix soy sauce, cornstarch and ginger for marinade. Toss with meat and set aside while you prepare the vegetables.

When all ingredients are prepared, drain poultry, fish or meat, reserving marinade.

Heat wok over high heat for 30 seconds. Swirl in 1 tablespoon oil and count to 30. Add poultry, fish, or meat and stir-fry until blanched (about 2 minutes). Add vegetables, beginning with the first group which require longer cooking, and toss quickly. (You may have to add another tablespoon of oil with the vegetables.)

Push solid ingredients up side of wok. Cook only until vegetables are hot but still crisp-tender.

To reserved marinade, add water or sodium-reduced stock to equal one cup. Add mixture to wok and stir until sauce thickens and clears. Mix all ingredients together. Serve with steamed rice, bean or rice thread noodles.

Nutrient Analysis: 1 cup (without rice)
Exchanges: 2 vegetable, 2 1/2 very lean meat,
1/2 fat
Carbohydrate Choices: 1

Calories: 156   Protein: 20 g   Carbohydrates: 11 g
Fat: 4 g   Cholesterol: 44 mg   Sodium: 427 mg
Dietary Fiber: 3 g

STIR-FRY BEEF WITH VEGETABLE

This recipe can be varied by using broccoli, cauliflower, snow peas, mushrooms or a combination of vegetables. Although the cooking time will vary depending on the vegetables used, the secret to a tasty stir-fry is to avoid overcooking.

Makes 6 cups; 6 servings

MARINADE:

1	tablespoon cornstarch
1	tablespoon sodium-reduced soy sauce
	Dash of pepper
1 1/2	teaspoons sugar
1 1/2	teaspoons sesame oil
1	tablespoon dry sherry

1	pound extra-lean top round steak
1 1/2	pounds bok choy (about 6–8 cups)
3	tablespoons peanut oil, divided
2	thin slices fresh ginger
3/4	cup water
1 1/2	teaspoons sodium-reduced soy sauce
1	teaspoon cornstarch
3	tablespoons water

For marinade: Combine cornstarch, soy sauce, pepper, sugar, sesame oil and sherry.

Slice the beef across the grain in thin (1/4") slices. Toss the beef with the marinade and allow it to marinate for an hour.

Slice the bok choy diagonally. Heat the wok over high heat. Add 1 1/2 tablespoons of the oil and ginger. Add the bok choy and stir-fry for 1 minute.

Add water. Cover and cook for 1 minute. Remove the bok choy and set aside.

Heat the wok over high heat and add the remaining oil. Stir-fry the beef for 1 minute. Add the bok choy and soy sauce. Stir-fry for 2 minutes. Mix the cornstarch and water and add to wok. Cook until liquid is slightly thickened. Serve with steamed rice or Chinese noodles.

Nutrient Analysis: 1 cup (without rice)   Calories: 160   Protein: 18g   Carbohydrates: 5g
Exchanges: 1 vegetable, 2 very lean meat, 1 1/2 fat   Fat: 10g   Cholesterol: 33mg   Sodium: 199mg
Carbohydrate Choices: 0   Dietary Fiber: 1g   Calcium: 120mg

ONE-DISH MEAL

A quick and easy one-dish supper.

Makes 12 cups; 6 servings

1	pound extra-lean ground beef (or sliced extra-lean top round steak)
1	onion, chopped
2	pounds potatoes, scrubbed and sliced (about 6 medium)
3	cups chopped fresh tomatoes
1/4	teaspoon salt
4	cups sliced zucchini (about 2 large)
	Water
	Parmesan cheese (optional)

Brown meat and onion in a heavy nonstick-sprayed skillet. Drain well.

Add potatoes, tomatoes and salt. Cook 15 minutes.

Add zucchini and simmer until potatoes and squash are tender. Add water if needed.

Serve sprinkled with Parmesan, if desired.

Nutrient Analysis: 2 cups

Exchanges: 1 1/2 starch, 1 vegetable, 2 very lean meat
Carbohydrate Choices: 2

Calories: 224   Protein: 20 g   Carbohydrates: 34 g
Fat: 3 g   Cholesterol: 40 mg   Sodium: 146 mg
Dietary Fiber: 5 g

EGGPLANT HAMBURGER CASSEROLE

Makes 8 x 8" baking dish; 4 servings

1	eggplant (about 3/4 pound)
1/2	pound extra-lean ground beef
1/2	cup chopped onion
1/2	pound extra-firm silken tofu, cubed
1	large tomato, diced
1	cup (4-ounces) shredded part-skim farmer cheese
1/2	cup sodium-reduced tomato sauce
1/2	teaspoon dried oregano, crushed

Peel eggplant and cut into 1/2" cubes.

Sauté eggplant, ground beef and onion in a medium skillet over medium-high heat for 5 minutes.

Remove from heat and stir in tofu, tomato, half the cheese, tomato sauce and oregano.

Spoon into a nonstick-sprayed 8 x 8" baking dish. Sprinkle remaining cheese on top. Bake.

Oven: 375°
Time: 25 to 30 minutes

Nutrient Analysis: 1 serving
Exchanges: 1 starch, 3 lean meat
Carbohydrate Choices: 1

Calories: 223   Protein: 24 g   Carbohydrates: 15 g
Fat: 8 g   Cholesterol: 46 mg   Sodium: 208 mg
Dietary Fiber: 4 g   Calcium: 221 mg

VEGETABLE BEEF CASSEROLE

Makes 13 x 9" baking dish; 8 servings

1	pound extra-lean ground beef
1	egg white
1	cup bread crumbs
1/2	teaspoon garlic powder
2/3	cup skim milk
1/2	(10-ounce) package frozen spinach, thawed and drained
2-3	zucchini, thinly sliced
1	medium onion, sliced and separated into rings
1	medium green pepper, thinly sliced
1	(6-ounce) can no-salt-added tomato paste
1	(8-ounce) can no-salt-added tomato sauce
1/4	cup water
1/2	teaspoon dried basil, crushed
1/2	teaspoon dried oregano, crushed
	Freshly ground pepper
1 1/2	cups (6 ounces) shredded part-skim mozzarella cheese

Mix together ground beef, egg white, bread crumbs, garlic powder and milk. Pat into a 13 x 9" baking dish. Bake at 350° for 15 minutes. Pour off any accumulated fat.

Spread spinach over meat. Layer zucchini over spinach; layer onion and green pepper over zucchini.

Mix together tomato paste, tomato sauce, water, basil, oregano and pepper. Pour over layered casserole. Cover with foil and return to oven. Bake until vegetables are tender, about 30 minutes. During last 10 minutes of baking time, remove foil and top with shredded cheese.

Oven: 350°
Time: 15 minutes beef mixture and
*   30 minutes casserole*

Nutrient Analysis: 1 serving
Exchanges: 1 starch, 2 vegetable, 2 lean meat
Carbohydrate Choices: 1 1/2

Calories: 234   Protein: 22g   Carbohydrates: 22g
Fat: 7g   Cholesterol: 43mg   Sodium: 306mg
Dietary Fiber: 4g   Calcium: 237mg

SEASONING FOR VEAL

The following herbs add to the delicate flavor of veal: bay leaf, curry, dill, lemon, marjoram, and oregano.

The HERB BLEND FOR POULTRY, (page 267) is excellent with veal.

VEAL LOAVES

Makes 8 mini-loaves; 8 servings

3/4	cup soft bread crumbs
1/2	cup skim milk
1/2	pound extra-lean ground ham
1 1/2	pounds extra-lean ground veal
1/2	teaspoon pepper
1/2	teaspoon onion powder
1	egg white
1/4	cup finely chopped parsley
1/4	teaspoon poultry seasoning
2	tablespoons brown sugar
2	tablespoons prepared mustard

Pour milk over bread crumbs. Let stand 5 minutes.

Mix ham, veal, pepper, onion powder, egg white, parsley and poultry seasoning in a large bowl. Thoroughly combine bread and milk mixture with meat mixture.

Form into 8 loaves and place in shallow pan. Bake.

Mix brown sugar and mustard and baste loaves occasionally during last 15 minutes of baking.

Oven: 325°
Time: 45 to 60 minutes

Nutrient Analysis: 1 mini-loaf

Exchanges: 1/2 starch, 3 very lean meat, 1 fat   *Calories: 192   Protein: 24g   Carbohydrates: 6g*
Carbohydrate Choices: 1/2   *Fat: 7g   Cholesterol: 78mg   Sodium: 473mg*

SAUTÉ OF VEAL WITH MUSHROOMS

A great make-ahead dinner dish. Reheat just before serving. Pork tenderloin may be substituted for the veal.

Makes 8 x 8" baking dish; 4 servings

1 1/2	pounds lean veal cut in 3/4" slices
2	tablespoons tub margarine
1	tablespoon vegetable oil
1	(8-ounce) can of mushrooms, stems and pieces, or 1/2 pound fresh mushrooms
1/2	teaspoon dried tarragon, thyme, or mixed fine herbs, crushed
1/4	teaspoon salt
	Freshly ground pepper
1-2	garlic cloves, pressed (optional)
2-3	tablespoons finely minced green onions
1/4	cup Madeira or dry white Vermouth

Dry the veal on paper towels.

Heat oil and margarine in a heavy skillet. Sauté the meat over high heat, browning lightly on all sides. Lower heat and continue cooking until meat has stiffened when pressed with finger (7 to 10 minutes).

Drain mushrooms, reserving liquid. Add mushrooms to veal along with herbs, salt and pepper. Add garlic and onions. Toss and cook for one minute.

Add mushroom liquid and wine. Cook uncovered until liquid is reduced by half.

Serve over rice or noodles.

Nutrient Analysis: 1 serving
Exchanges: 1 vegetable, 3 lean meat
Carbohydrate Choices: 0

Calories: 206   Protein: 24g   Carbohydrates: 3g
Fat: 9g   Cholesterol: 94mg   Sodium: 229mg
Dietary Fiber: 1g

VEAL PARMESAN

Makes 8 (4-ounce) servings

2 tablespoons all-purpose flour
1/2 teaspoon paprika
1/8 teaspoon pepper
1 egg white
1 tablespoon water
1/2 cup dry bread crumbs
3 tablespoons Parmesan cheese
2 pounds veal rump roast cut in
  1/3-1/2" slices
2 tablespoons olive oil
1 (8-ounce) can sodium-reduced
  tomato sauce
1/4 teaspoon dried basil, crushed
6 ounces part-skim mozzarella
  cheese, sliced

Mix flour, paprika and pepper together; set aside. Beat egg white with water in a separate bowl. Mix bread crumbs and Parmesan together in a third bowl.

Dredge veal in flour mixture. Dip dredged veal into the egg white mixture and then into the bread crumb and cheese mixture. Chill in refrigerator for at least 1 hour.

Heat the olive oil in a large skillet. Sauté the breaded veal until nicely browned on both sides. Transfer meat to a shallow casserole or baking dish.

Mix tomato sauce with basil and drizzle around the veal slices. Top veal with thin slices of mozzarella. Bake.

Oven: 350°
Time: 25 to 30 minutes

Nutrient Analysis: 4 ounces (with sauce)   Calories: 308   Protein: 30g   Carbohydrates: 9g
Exchanges: 1/2 starch, 4 lean meat, 1 fat   Fat: 17g   Cholesterol: 106 mg   Sodium: 333 mg
Carbohydrate Choices: 1/2   Dietary Fiber: 1g

VEAL SCALLOPINI

Makes 8 (4-ounce) servings

2 tablespoons all-purpose flour
1/2 teaspoon paprika
1/8 teaspoon pepper
2 pounds veal (rump roast or round steak) cut into scallops 1/3-1/2" thick
2 tablespoons vegetable oil
4 green onions with some of the tops, chopped
2 cups sliced fresh mushrooms (about 1 pound)
1 tablespoon chopped fresh parsley
1/4 teaspoon dried tarragon, crushed
2 tablespoons lemon juice

Mix together flour, paprika and pepper. Dredge veal in mixture.

Heat 1 tablespoon oil in a large skillet. Sauté veal until brown on both sides.

Remove to a heated casserole or pan to keep warm.

Add the remaining tablespoon of oil to the skillet and sauté the onions and mushrooms until lightly browned.

Return the veal to the skillet and heat through. Sprinkle veal with tarragon and parsley. Sprinkle lemon juice over all and serve.

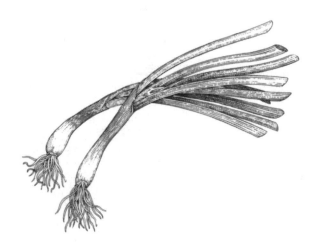

Nutrient Analysis: 4 ounces
Exchanges: 3 very lean meat, 1 fat
Carbohydrate Choices: 0

Calories: 170   *Protein: 24g*   *Carbohydrates: 3g*
Fat: 7g   *Cholesterol: 94mg*   *Sodium: 99mg*

SEASONINGS FOR PORK

Reach for the spice rack instead of the salt shaker when preparing pork. You will find the following seasonings particularly good with pork: basil, lemon, marjoram, onion, paprika, parsley, poultry seasonings, sage, and summer savory.

HERB BLEND FOR PORK

1   tablespoon dried basil
1   tablespoon dried marjoram
1   tablespoon dried sage
1   tablespoon dried summer savory

Crush dried herbs and blend thoroughly. Sprinkle on steaks, chops or roasts during cooking or use in a shaker at the table. Store extra in tightly covered glass container.

See SEASONINGS for additional herb and spice blends.

PORK CHOPS WITH CARAWAY RICE

Makes 4 (4-ounce) pork chops; 4 servings

  1   cup sliced celery
1/2   cup thinly sliced onion
  1   tablespoon canola oil
1 1/4   cups long grain brown rice, uncooked
2 1/2   cups water
  2   teaspoons caraway seed
1/4   teaspoon salt
  4   lean center-cut pork chops (about 1 pound edible meat)
  1   teaspoon lemon juice

Cook celery and onion in oil in a large skillet until crisp-tender (about 2 minutes). Stir in rice, water, caraway seed and salt. Bring to a boil, reduce heat and cover. Simmer 20 minutes or until liquid is absorbed. Stir in lemon juice and fluff with a fork.

While the rice is cooking, trim any visible fat from pork chops and place on broiler pan rack. Broil 4 to 5" from heat turning every 5 minutes until chops are done (about 20 minutes).

Arrange chops on top of rice mixture and serve.

Nutrient Analysis: 1 pork chop with
  3/4 cup rice
Exchanges: 1 starch, 3 very lean meat, 2 fat
Carbohydrate Choices: 1

Calories: 278   Protein: 20 g   Carbohydrates: 17 g
Fat: 14 g   Cholesterol: 60 mg   Sodium: 232 mg
Dietary Fiber: 2 g

STIR-FRY PORK

Makes 6 cups; 4 servings

1	pound lean boneless pork, cut in 1/4" slices
1	tablespoon vegetable oil
1	small onion, sliced in rounds
1	garlic clove, minced
1/2	pound fresh broccoli, diagonally sliced (about 1 1/2 cups florets or slices)
1/2	pound carrots, diagonally sliced (about 1 1/2 cups)
1	tablespoon sodium-reduced soy sauce

Quickly brown pork strips in hot oil in a wok or large skillet over high heat.

Add onion, garlic, broccoli stems and carrots. Cook and stir constantly until vegetables are hot but crisp.

Add broccoli florets and soy sauce. Cook and stir 1 to 2 minutes.

Serve with steamed rice or bean or rice thread noodles.

Nutrient Analysis: 1 1/2 cups (without rice)   Calories: 228   Protein: 19g   Carbohydrates: 11g
Exchanges: 2 vegetable, 2 very lean meat, 2 fat   Fat: 12g   Cholesterol: 53mg   Sodium: 229mg
Carbohydrate Choices: 1   Dietary Fiber: 4g

MARINATED PORK CUBES

Makes 8 skewers; 8 servings

MARINADE:

8	brazil nuts, shelled
1/4	cup sodium-reduced soy sauce
3	tablespoons lemon juice
2	tablespoons finely chopped onion
2	tablespoons ground coriander seed
1	tablespoon brown sugar
1	garlic clove, minced
1/4	teaspoon black pepper
1/8	teaspoon red pepper

1 1/2   pounds lean boneless pork, cut in 1 1/2" cubes

For marinade: Grind brazil nuts and mix with soy sauce, lemon juice, onion, coriander, sugar, garlic, black and red pepper.

Add pork cubes and mix well. Marinate pork 2 to 3 hours.

Skewer meat and grill slowly over low heat. Baste once or twice with marinade. Serve with rice.

Nutrient Analysis: 1 skewer (without rice)
Exchanges: 3 very lean meat, 2 fat
Carbohydrate Choices: 0

Calories: 190   Protein: 19g   Carbohydrates: 2g
Fat: 11g   Cholesterol: 60mg   Sodium: 191mg

FRUITED PORK CHOPS

Makes 6 pork chops; 6 servings

6 lean center-cut pork chops
    (about 1 1/2 pounds edible meat)
2/3 cup apple juice
1/4 teaspoon curry powder
1/4 teaspoon pepper
1 large apple, unpeeled
1/4 cup raisins

Trim the fat from chops. Brown the chops in a nonstick pan; remove to a large baking dish when the chops are nicely browned.

Pour the apple juice over the chops. Sprinkle with curry powder and pepper.

Core the apple and slice into 6 rings. Put one slice on each pork chop and fill the center hole of apple with raisins. Cover and bake until chops are tender.

Oven: 350°
Time: 60 minutes

Nutrient Analysis: 1 pork chop
Exchanges: 1 fruit, 2 very lean meat, 1 1/2 fat
Carbohydrate Choices: 1

Calories: 195   Protein: 16g   Carbohydrates: 12g
Fat: 9g   Cholesterol: 53mg   Sodium: 54mg
Dietary Fiber: 1g

CHOP & SQUASH BAKE

Makes 4 pork chops; 4 servings

4 lean center-cut pork chops,
    (about 1 pound edible meat)
1/2 teaspoon whole thyme
1 tablespoon canola oil
1 large onion, chopped
1 garlic clove, minced
1 small acorn squash
1/2 cup apple juice
1 1" slice of orange peel, 1" wide
1 teaspoon ground ginger
1/4 teaspoon ground allspice
1/4 teaspoon cayenne pepper

Trim fat from chops. Rub chops with thyme. Brown pork chops lightly in oil in a large skillet, adding onion and garlic after turning chops over to brown the second side. Pour off any remaining oil.

Cut squash in half, seed, quarter, peel and slice thick. Add to skillet.

Combine apple juice, orange peel, ginger, allspice, cayenne and honey. Pour over chops and squash and bring to a boil.

continued on next page

CHOP AND SQUASH BAKE, (continued)

1 tablespoon honey
1 large apple, peeled, cored and
   thickly sliced
4 orange slices (optional)

Cover and bake, turning chops after 30 minutes. Bake an additional 25 minutes, adding apples for last 10 minutes of cooking time.

Serve garnished with orange slices.

Oven: 375°
Time: 55 minutes

Nutrient Analysis: 1 pork chop w/1/4 squash
Exchanges: 2 starch, 2 very lean meat, 2 fat
Carbohydrate Choices: 2

Calories: 302   Protein: 18 g   Carbohydrates: 32 g
Fat: 13 g   Cholesterol: 53 mg   Sodium: 58 mg
Dietary Fiber: 4 g

PORK MEDALLIONS WITH PESTO

Makes 8 medallions; 4 servings

PESTO:

1/4 cup chopped fresh basil
2 tablespoons chopped fresh parsley
2 tablespoons grated Parmesan
   cheese
1 garlic clove, minced
1 tablespoon lemon juice
   Freshly ground pepper
1 tablespoon sunflower seeds or
   pine nuts

1 pound lean pork tenderloin,
   trimmed
1 teaspoon olive oil

For pesto: Process basil, parsley, Parmesan, garlic, lemon juice, pepper and seeds or nuts in a food processor until blended.

Cut tenderloin lengthwise; open and lay flat. Spread all but 1 tablespoon of pesto on cut side of pork.

Fold edges of tenderloin together and tie with string at 1" intervals. Slice into eight medallions and place cut side up on rack in broiler pan. Spread with remaining tablespoon of pesto.

Broil 2 to 3" from heat for 6 to 7 minutes a side, brushing occasionally with olive oil.

Oven: Broil
Time: 12 to 14 minutes

Nutrient Analysis: 2 medallions
Exchanges: 3 very lean meat, 2 fat
Carbohydrate Choices: 0

Calories: 196   Protein: 25 g   Carbohydrates: 1 g
Fat: 9 g   Cholesterol: 73 mg   Sodium: 104 mg

PORK STEW

Makes 9 cups; 6 servings

1 pound lean boneless pork, cut into 1" cubes

4 carrots, diagonally sliced (about 2 1/2 cups)

2 celery ribs, diagonally sliced (about 1 1/2 cups)

1 onion, coarsely chopped

2 potatoes, cut into 1" cubes (about 1 1/2 cups)

1 (6-ounce) can no-salt-added tomato paste

2 cups water

1/4 teaspoon pepper

1/2 teaspoon garlic powder

1 teaspoon sugar

1/2 teaspoon HERB BLEND for PORK, *(page 310)*

2 tablespoons cold water

1 tablespoon all-purpose flour

Brown pork cubes in a large, heavy saucepan over medium heat.

Add carrots, celery, onion, potatoes, tomato paste, water, pepper, garlic powder, sugar and spice blend. Bring to a boil. Cover and reduce heat. Simmer meat and vegetables until tender (about 30 minutes).

Blend cold water and flour and stir into stew. Cook and stir until thickened and bubbly. Serve.

Nutrient Analysis: 1 1/2 cups
Exchanges: 1 starch, 1 vegetable,
*   2 very lean meat, 1 fat*
Carbohydrate Choices: 1 1/2

Calories: 211   Protein: 16 g   Carbohydrates: 24 g
Fat: 7 g   Cholesterol: 40 mg   Sodium: 109 mg
Dietary Fiber: 4 g

SEASONINGS FOR LAMB

Traditional seasonings for lamb range from spicy curries [HOMEMADE CURRY POWDER, (page 380)] to a subtle hint of mint. Try your choice of the following with lamb: basil, curry powder, garlic, marjoram, mint, parsley, rosemary, and savory.

HERB BLEND FOR LAMB*

1 tablespoon dried basil
1 tablespoon dried marjoram
1 tablespoon parsley flakes
1 teaspoon dried rosemary
1 teaspoon dried savory

Blend crushed herbs thoroughly. Sprinkle on lamb during cooking or use in a shaker at the table. Store extra in a tightly covered glass container.

* See SEASONINGS for additional herb and spice blends.

LAMB SHISH KABOBS

Kabobs are probably of Turkish origin, but are served throughout the Middle East. Few people could afford meat more than perhaps once a week, or for special feast days. Their daily diet of soups, vegetable stew, black bread, cheese and fruit still contributes to their low incidence of heart disease.

Makes 8 skewers; 8 servings

MARINADE:

6	tablespoons olive oil
4	tablespoons sherry
1/2	cup vinegar or white wine
1-2	garlic cloves, minced
1/4	large onion, minced
4	tablespoons finely chopped parsley
1	teaspoon oregano, crushed
1/2	teaspoon salt
	Freshly ground pepper

2	pounds lean boneless lamb
4	green peppers, seeded
4	medium onions
24	cherry tomatoes
8	ounces fresh mushrooms
1	tablespoon olive oil

For marinade: Combine olive oil, sherry, vinegar or wine, garlic, onion, parsley, oregano, salt and pepper in a large bowl. Cut lamb into 1 1/2" cubes. Place lamb in marinade, making sure all cubes are covered. Cover bowl and refrigerate for 4 hours or overnight. Turn meat several times.

When ready to cook, cut onion and green pepper into 1 1/2" pieces. Divide meat, green pepper, onions and cherry tomatoes into 8 portions. Alternate vegetables and lamb cubes on skewer beginning with a cherry tomato.

Brush skewers with marinade and cook over medium-hot gas grill or under broiler, turning several times until desired degree of doneness (15 to 20 minutes for medium).

Shortly before kabobs are done, sauté mushrooms lightly in olive oil. Remove kabobs to large serving platter and cover with mushrooms.

This dish is excellent when served with RICE PILAF, *(page 182)* and a mixed-greens salad dressed with lemon juice and fresh mint.

Oven: Gas grill or broil, medium-hot in oven
Time: About 8 to 10 minutes, each side for medium; more for well-done.

Nutrient Analysis: 1 skewer (without rice)   Calories: 268   Protein: 24g   Carbohydrates: 13g
Exchanges: 2 1/2 vegetable, 3 very lean meat, 2 fat   Fat: 13g   Cholesterol: 67mg   Sodium: 135mg
Carbohydrate Choices: 1   Dietary Fiber: 3g   Omega-3: 0.15g

LAMB CURRY

Curry is better if made a day ahead and then reheated allowing the flavors to "marry". A traditional curry recipe has about 20g of fat whereas this modified version has less than 10g.

Makes 8 cups; 8 servings

1 1/2	pounds lean boneless lamb
1	tablespoon vegetable oil
2	large onions, chopped
4	garlic cloves, chopped
2	tablespoons CURRY POWDER, *(page 380)*
1/2	cup hot water
1/3	cup seedless raisins
2	large tomatoes, chopped
2	fresh green chilies

Cut lamb into 3/4" cubes. Heat oil and sauté lamb cubes in a heavy saucepan, until well browned. Remove lamb.

Gently sauté onion and garlic in the same pan until soft and transparent but not brown. Add curry powder to the onion mixture making sure to "fry" the spices so their full flavor comes out. Return the lamb and stir until lamb is coated with spice mixture.

Add water, raisins, tomatoes and chilies. Cover and cook over low heat for 1 hour or until lamb is tender. Skim the fat from the curry and stir occasionally while it simmers.

Curry is traditionally served over steamed rice with some or all of the following condiments: chutney, chopped onion, diced pineapple, chopped banana, chopped apple, chopped peppers, chopped nuts, diced tomato.

Nutrient Analysis: 1 cup (without rice)   Calories: 219   Protein: 24g   Carbohydrates: 11g
Exchanges: 2 vegetable, 3 very lean meat, 1 1/2 fat   Fat: 9g   Cholesterol: 72mg   Sodium: 60mg
Carbohydrate Choices: 1   Dietary Fiber: 1g

LAMB PIE (BOBOTIE)

Makes 11 x 7" baking pan; 8 servings

2 large onions, finely chopped
2 garlic cloves, crushed
2 tablespoons olive oil
1 tablespoon CURRY POWDER,
  (page 380)
1 slice day-old bread
1 cup skim milk
1 egg white
1 tablespoon sugar
1/2 teaspoon freshly ground pepper
1/2 teaspoon turmeric
  Juice of 1 lemon
3 tablespoons hot mango chutney
5 tablespoons blanched almonds,
  chopped
1/2 cup raisins
4 strips lemon rind, 1/2 inch wide
1 1/2 pounds lean, coarsely ground
  lamb
1 egg

Sauté onion and garlic lightly in oil. Add curry powder.

Soak bread in the milk and squeeze dry, saving the milk.

Combine the bread, onion mixture, egg white, sugar, pepper, turmeric, lemon juice, chutney, almonds, raisins, lemon rind and ground lamb in a large bowl. Mix well.

Pat meat mixture into a 11 x 7" nonstick-sprayed baking pan. Bake 60 minutes and remove from oven. The mixture will have shrunk leaving lots of liquid. Skim off the fat leaving the other juices in pan.

Beat the whole egg with the reserved milk and pour over the meat. Bake an additional 15 to 20 minutes or until the custard is set and the top golden.

Serve with rice and a green salad.

Oven: 350°
Time: 60 minutes, meat mixture and
  15 to 20 minutes, custard

Nutrient Analysis: 1 serving
Exchanges: 1 starch, 1 vegetable
            3 medium-fat meat
Carbohydrate Choices: 1

Calories: 321   Protein: 19 g   Carbohydrates: 19 g
Fat: 19 g   Cholesterol: 83 mg   Sodium: 103 mg
Dietary Fiber: 2 g   Omega-3: 0.18 g

STUFFED CABBAGE ROLLS *

A delicious Lebanese dish that is definitely worth the extra preparation time.

Makes 24 cabbage rolls; 12 servings

1   medium cabbage head

LAMB FILLING:
1   pound lean ground lamb
1   cup brown rice, uncooked
1/4   teaspoon cinnamon
1/4   teaspoon pepper
1/4   teaspoon salt
2   tablespoons lemon juice

SAUCE:
    Water to cover rolls
1   (28-ounce) can no-salt-added
        whole tomatoes or 4 cups
        peeled and seeded fresh
        tomatoes
4   large garlic cloves, peeled and cut
        in half

SAUCE VARIATIONS:
    Beef broth flavored with juice of
        one lemon
    Beef or chicken broth and 1/2
        cup tomato juice

Wash the cabbage and core it deeply enough that the outer leaves begin to separate from the head. In a pan large enough to hold the head of cabbage, bring water to a boil. Dip the head of cabbage in boiling water. As the leaves loosen, remove them. Continue removing leaves until you have at least 12. Blanch the 12 leaves in boiling water for 2 minutes. Cool. Cut the cooked leaves in half, removing the center ribs.

Knead together the lamb, rice, cinnamon, pepper, salt and lemon juice.

Place half a cabbage leaf with the cut side toward you. Place 1 or 2 tablespoons of filling on the center of the cabbage leaf. Fold the left and right sides of the cabbage over filling. Roll the leaf away from you starting with the cut side.

Arrange filled rolls tightly in a nonstick-sprayed 13 x 9" baking pan. Break the tomatoes into small pieces and pour tomatoes with juice over the tops of rolls. Place the garlic over the tomatoes. Add water to the top of the rolls. Bake, uncovered.

Oven: 350°
Time: 45 minutes

* Nutrient Analysis follows the recipe for Spicy Rice Filling for Cabbage Rolls on the next page.

SPICY RICE FILLING FOR CABBAGE ROLLS

Makes 24 cabbage rolls; 12 servings

1 cup brown rice, uncooked
1/2 cup chopped onion
2 tablespoons chopped fresh parsley
2 tablespoons olive oil
2 tablespoons sodium-reduced
    tomato sauce
1 teaspoon chopped fresh mint
1/2 teaspoon ground allspice
1/2 teaspoon pepper
1/4 teaspoon salt

Mix together rice, onion, parsley, olive oil, tomato sauce, mint, allspice, pepper and salt. Stuff, roll, cover with sauce and bake as above.

Nutrient Analysis: 2 cabbage rolls	Lamb Cabbage Rolls	Spicy Rice Cabbage Rolls
Exchanges:	1 starch, 1 vegetable, 1 lean meat	1 starch, 1 1/2 vegetable
Carbohydrate Choices:	1	1 1/2
Calories:	169	119
Protein:	9g	3g
Carbohydrates:	20g	21g
Fat:	6g	3g
Cholesterol:	25 mg	0 mg
Sodium:	86 mg	66 mg
Dietary Fiber:	3g	3g

SOUPS,
SANDWICHES
& PIZZA

*Soup of the evening,
beautiful soup!*

Lewis Carroll

SOUPS

Soup is good food.

Soup is nothing short of remarkable in its variety. Choices range from rich and tasty stocks to chunky vegetable, thick "cream" and chilled soups. Whether you choose a light or a hearty soup, it can provide protein, complex carbohydrates and fiber, vitamins A and C and essential minerals to your diet. Soups have an added bonus of making you feel full, thus helping curb your appetite and control calories.

Commercial soups, while tasty, are generally a source of fat and saturated fat with a considerable amount of sodium. Check the table below for a comparison of fat and sodium between commercial soups and the soups in **Cooking À La Heart**.

Table 26: Fat and Sodium Comparison of Soup

Commercial Soup: *(1 cup)*	Fat: *(g)*	Sodium: *(mg)*	Cooking À La Heart Soup: *(1 cup)*	Fat: *(g)*	Sodium: *(mg)*
Chicken Noodle soup	2	890	Chicken Noodle soup	2	60
Chicken Stock	1	770	Chicken or Turkey Stock	1	20
Campbell's® Chunky Vegetable	4	870	Chicken or Turkey Vegetable Soup	2	38
Cream of Mushroom	7	870	Cream of Morel	6	176
New England Clam Chowder (with milk)	7	1022	Hearty Chowder	2	266
Healthy Choice® Split Pea & Ham	3	430	Hearty Pea	4	143

Source: The Food Processor SQL Nutrition Analysis Program, Version 9.9 (ESHA Research); Salem, OR. and manufacturer's data.

Soup is for all seasons and all ages.

You'll enjoy the thick and robust soups on cool days; the savory light soups to serve as a first course; the hearty bean or pea soup to serve as a main dish and chilled soups to refresh your summer guests. You can further enhance your homemade specialty by serving soup in creative containers such as tureens, two-handled cups, mugs, soup plates, and, for chilled soups, frosted glasses. Soups are a good way to nourish children and they will be encouraged to eat soup if its served in an imaginative manner such as in a playware bowl, plastic construction hat or coffee mug.

SANDWICHES & PIZZA

Pizza is a popular food evidenced by the fact that on the average, Americans eat an estimated 22.5 pounds of pizza each year. Pizza appears to be a national staple, more popular by far than any other food. With supermarket shelves and freezer cases providing us with an alluring array of options and the local pizzeria offering to deliver more quickly than you can say "cheese", you may wonder if all the pizza we're eating is healthy for us.

Pizza can be a good source of protein, calcium, iron, riboflavin and vitamin C. But it can also be a source of a great deal of fat, saturated fat, calories and sodium. In fact, pepperoni, a particular high-fat meat, is the favorite topping preferred by pizza lovers.

Sandwiches, like pizza, can offer much nutrition but they can also be a source of hidden fat and contain high-sodium ingredients. Table 27 shows the amount of calories, fat, saturated fat and sodium contained in selected pizzas and sandwiches.

Table 27: Fat and Sodium Content of Selected Pizzas and Sandwiches

Item:	Calories:	Fat: (g)	Saturated Fat: (g)	Sodium: (mg)
Sandwiches:				
KFC™ Chicken Sandwich (original recipe)	450	22	5	940
Cooking À La Heart Meat/Seafood Pockets	197	9	2	214
Wendy's® Grilled Chicken Sandwich	300	7	2	740
Cooking À La Heart Hot Chicken Pockets	130	3	0	158
Denny's® Tuna Melt	640	39	13	1438
Cooking À La Heart Taste O' the Sea Sandwich	269	15	1	270
Taco John's® Taco (soft shell)	278	11	4	556
Cooking À La Heart Turkey Taco	178	7	2	139
Taco Bell® Tostada	250	10	4	710
Cooking À La Heart Tostada	222	5	1	75
Pizza:				
Pizza Hut® Cheese (2 slices, hand-tossed crust)	480	20	10	1300
Cooking À La Heart Three Cheese (2 slices, yeast crust)	480	20	10	532
Pizza Hut® Pepperoni (2 slices, hand-tossed crust)	560	26	12	1580
Cooking À La Heart Heart Healthy Pizza Topping (2 slices, yeast crust)	482	18	6	340

Source: The Food Processor SQL Nutrition Analysis Program, Version 9.9 (ESHA Research); Salem, OR and manufacturer's data.

BOUQUET GARNI

For the well-seasoned soup or stew—a bouquet of fresh herbs. Bouquet garni also makes a fragrant package decoration or room freshener.

FRESH HERB BOUQUET GARNI

2 sprigs parsley
1 sprig marjoram
1 sprig basil
1 sprig thyme
1 bay leaf
1 branch tarragon
2 garlic cloves, sliced (optional)

Tie the fresh sprigs together with string or place in a cheesecloth bag and add to soup or stock.

Remove at the end of cooking time.

DRIED HERB BOUQUET GARNI

1 tablespoon parsley flakes
1/4 teaspoon dried marjoram
1/4 teaspoon dried basil
1/4 teaspoon whole thyme
1/4 teaspoon dried tarragon
1 bay leaf

Place dried herbs in a cheesecloth bag and use as above.

BEEF STOCK

Ready-to-use canned stocks contain approximately 1300 mg sodium a cup whereas this homemade stock contains only 10 mg sodium a cup. Stock freezes well. For convenience sake, freeze in pre-measured containers.

Makes about 2 quarts; 8 servings

5-6   pounds soup bones
  4   quarts water
  2   large onions, quartered
  1   medium carrot, halved
  2   celery ribs with leaves, halved
  1   cup drained or fresh tomatoes, diced
  1   BOUQUET GARNI, *(see preceding page)*
8-10   whole peppercorns

Brown the bones in a large Dutch oven or stock pot.

Add water, onion, carrot, celery, tomatoes, bouquet garni and peppercorns. Bring to a boil, reduce heat and simmer, uncovered for about 3 hours.

Strain stock through cheesecloth or fine sieve into large pan or bowl. Let stand 15 minutes. Refrigerate until fat congeals on surface. Skim off and discard fat.

Storing: Stock can be stored in refrigerator for up to one week or frozen in ice cube trays or other containers up to 4 months. If you use ice cube trays, remove cubes once they are frozen and store in tightly closed freezer container.

Nutrient Analysis: 1 cup
Exchanges: 1/2 vegetable, 1/2 fat
Carbohydrate Choices: 0

Calories: 44   Protein: 0g   Carbohydrates: 3g
Fat: 3g   Cholesterol: 0mg   Sodium: 10mg

CHICKEN OR TURKEY STOCK

Ready-to-use canned stocks contain approximately 1300 mg sodium a cup whereas this homemade stock contains only 20 mg sodium a cup. Stock freezes well. For convenient use, freeze in small, pre-measured amounts.

Makes 2 quarts; 8 servings

3	quarts water
3	pounds uncooked chicken or turkey parts (backs, necks, wing tips) or cooked carcass with some meat left on bones
2	large onions, quartered
1	medium carrot, halved
2	celery ribs with leaves, halved
1	BOUQUET GARNI, *(page 327)*
8-10	whole peppercorns

Combine water, poultry parts, onions, carrot and celery in a large Dutch oven or stockpot. Bring to a boil; add bouquet garni and peppercorns. Reduce heat to low. Cover and simmer about 3 hours.

Strain stock through cheesecloth or fine sieve into large pan or bowl. Let stand 15 minutes. Refrigerate until fat congeals on surface. Skim off and discard fat.

Storing: Stock can be stored in refrigerator for up to one week or frozen in ice cube trays or other containers up to 4 months. If you use ice cube trays, remove cubes once they are frozen and store in tightly closed freezer container.

Nutrient Analysis: 1 cup

Exchanges: 1/2 vegetable, 1/2 very lean meat · *Calories: 40   Protein: 4g   Carbohydrates: 2g*
Carbohydrate Choices: 0 · *Fat: 1g   Cholesterol: 12 mg   Sodium: 20 mg*

GRANDMA'S CHICKEN SOUP*

Makes 2 1/2 quarts; 10 servings

3	quarts water
2 1/2 to 3	pound chicken, cut up
2	large onions, quartered
1	medium carrot, halved
2	celery ribs with leaves, halved
1	BOUQUET GARNI, *(page 327)*
8-10	whole peppercorns
1	tablespoon tub margarine
2	medium carrots, diced
2	medium celery ribs, diced

Combine the water and the chicken in a large Dutch oven or stockpot. Bring to a boil; reduce heat and simmer, uncovered, 1 hour.

Add quartered onions, halved carrot and celery. Simmer, covered for 1 hour. Remove chicken pieces and cool.

Remove skin and bones from chicken and return them to stockpot. Simmer broth for another hour. Shred meat and set aside.

Strain stock through cheesecloth or fine sieve into large pan or bowl. Let stand 15 minutes. Refrigerate until fat congeals on surface. Skim fat and discard.

Meanwhile, in small skillet, melt margarine. Add carrots and celery. Sauté until tender, 5 to 10 minutes. Add carrots, celery and shredded chicken to broth and heat thoroughly.

VARIATIONS:

GRANDMA'S CHICKEN SOUP, QUICK VERSION*

Makes 3 quarts; 12 servings

1	tablespoon tub margarine
2	medium carrots, diced
2	medium celery ribs, diced
2	quarts CHICKEN OR TURKEY STOCK, *(see preceding page)*
2	cups diced cooked chicken or turkey

Melt margarine in a small skillet. Add carrots and celery. Sauté until tender, 5 to 10 minutes.

In a large saucepan, combine sautéd vegetables, STOCK and diced chicken or turkey. Heat thoroughly.

* Nutrient Analysis follows the recipes on the next page.

VARIATIONS, (continued):

CHICKEN RICE SOUP

Makes 3 quarts; 12 servings

2 1/2   quarts **GRANDMA'S CHICKEN SOUP,** *(see preceding page)*
  2   cups cooked long grain brown rice
1/4   cup chopped fresh parsley
1/4   cup white wine (optional)

Bring GRANDMA'S CHICKEN SOUP to a boil in a large saucepan.

Add rice, parsley and wine. Season to taste with herbs.

CHICKEN NOODLE SOUP

Makes 2 1/2 quarts; 10 servings

  2   quarts **GRANDMA'S CHICKEN SOUP,** *(see preceding page)*
  2   cups uncooked wide noodles
1/4   cup chopped fresh parsley

Bring GRANDMA'S CHICKEN SOUP to a boil in a large saucepan.

Add noodles and boil until tender, about 8 to 10 minutes. Stir in chopped parsley.

Season to taste with herbs.

Nutrient Analysis: 1 cup	*Grandma's*	*Grandma's (Quick)*	*Chicken Rice*	*Chicken Noodle*
Exchanges:	*1/2 vegetable, 1 1/2 very lean meat*	*1 vegetable, 2 very lean meat*	*1/2 starch, 1 1/2 very lean meat*	*1/2 starch, 2 very lean meat*
Carbohydrate Choices:	*0*	*0*	*1/2*	*1/2*
Calories:	*69*	*97*	*93*	*103*
Protein:	*11 g*	*11 g*	*10 g*	*12 g*
Carbohydrates:	*2 g*	*5 g*	*9 g*	*8 g*
Fat:	*2 g*	*3 g*	*2 g*	*2 g*
Cholesterol:	*26 mg*	*31 mg*	*22 mg*	*36 mg*
Sodium:	*58 mg*	*66 mg*	*50 mg*	*60 mg*
Dietary Fiber:	*1 g*	*1 g*	*1 g*	*1 g*

CHICKEN OR TURKEY VEGETABLE SOUP

Makes 4 quarts; 16 servings

2   quarts **CHICKEN OR TURKEY STOCK,** *(page 329)*

1   cup **whole grain or starchy vegetable (uncooked brown rice, barley, pasta or potatoes)**

1   cup **highly flavored vegetable (celery, onion, Chinese cabbage or rutabaga)**

3   cups **vegetable (carrots, green beans, okra, tomatoes, corn, or peas)**

2   cups **diced cooked chicken or turkey**

Follow steps for CHICKEN OR TURKEY STOCK. Bring stock to a boil.

Add other ingredients in order of required cooking time (barley – 60 minutes; rice, potatoes and vegetables-20 minutes; pasta and meat-10 minutes).

Nutrient Analysis: 1 cup
Exchanges: 1 starch, 1 very lean meat
Carbohydrate Choices: 1

Calories: 118   Protein: 10 g   Carbohydrates: 15 g
Fat: 2 g   Cholesterol: 23 mg   Sodium: 38 mg
Dietary Fiber: 2 g

MULLIGATAWNY SOUP

A great use of left-over holiday turkey and it freezes well.

Makes 1 1/2 quarts; 6 servings

1/4	cup chopped onion
1 1/2	teaspoons curry powder
2	tablespoons vegetable oil
1	tart apple, peeled, cored and chopped
1/4	cup chopped carrots
1/4	cup chopped celery
2	tablespoons chopped green pepper
3	tablespoons all-purpose flour
2	tablespoons low-sodium, chicken-flavored bouillon granules
4	cups water
1	(16-ounce) can tomatoes, cut up
1	tablespoon chopped fresh parsley
2	teaspoons fresh lemon juice
1	teaspoon sugar
2	whole cloves
1/4	teaspoon salt
	Dash of pepper
1	cup diced cooked turkey or chicken

Cook onion and curry powder in oil in a large saucepan until onion is tender. Add apple, carrot, celery and green pepper, stirring occasionally until vegetables are crisp-tender (about 5 minutes).

Sprinkle flour over mixture, stirring to mix well.

Add bouillon granules, water, undrained tomatoes, parsley, lemon juice, sugar, cloves and pepper. Bring to a boil and add chicken or turkey. Simmer for 30 minutes, stirring occasionally.

Nutrient Analysis: 1 cup
Exchanges: 1 starch, 1 lean meat
Carbohydrate Choices: 1

Calories: 126   Protein: 7g   Carbohydrates: 13g
Fat: 5g   Cholesterol: 14mg   Sodium: 154mg
Dietary Fiber: 2g

TURKEY TOMATO VEGETABLE SOUP

Heart's Delight Recipe Contest Grand Prize Winner—Junior Division.

Makes 4 quarts; 16 servings

1	quart CHICKEN OR TURKEY STOCK, *(page 329)*
1	quart stewed, unsalted tomatoes
1/2	cup barley, dry
4	teaspoons low-sodium, chicken-flavored bouillon granules
1/2	teaspoon garlic powder
1/4	teaspoon black pepper
1/2	teaspoon dried oregano, crushed
1	tablespoon parsley flakes
1/2	teaspoon dried basil, crushed
2	cups diced cooked turkey
1 1/2	cups sliced carrots
1 1/2	cups sliced celery
1	cup chopped onions
1	cup chopped green pepper
1	(10-ounce) package frozen okra

Simmer stock, tomatoes, barley, bouillon granules, garlic powder, pepper, oregano, parsley and basil in a large saucepan for 1 hour.

Add turkey, carrots, celery, onions, green pepper, and okra. Simmer 30 minutes or until vegetables are tender.

Nutrient Analysis: 1 cup
Exchanges: 1 starch, 1 very lean meat
Carbohydrate Choices: 1

Calories: 95   Protein: 9g   Carbohydrates: 13g
Fat: 1g   Cholesterol: 18mg   Sodium: 64mg
Dietary Fiber: 4g

MUSHROOM SOUP

The fresh, light flavor is a pleasant alternative to heavier, cream-style mushroom soup.

Makes 3 quarts; 12 servings

1   pound fresh mushrooms
        (2-3 cups sliced)
3   tablespoons tub margarine
2   cups chopped carrots
2   cups chopped celery
1   cup chopped onion
1   garlic clove, minced
6   cups BEEF STOCK, *(page 328)*
        or 4 tablespoons low-sodium,
        beef-flavored bouillon
        granules in 6 cups water
3   tablespoons tomato paste
     Freshly ground pepper to taste
6   sprigs parsley
3   celery rib tops with leaves
1   bay leaf
1/4 cup dry sherry
     Lemon slices or parsley sprigs,
        for garnish

Rinse and chop half the mushrooms. Slice the remaining half and set aside.

Melt 2 tablespoons of margarine in a large, heavy saucepan. Add the chopped mushrooms and sauté 5 minutes. Add carrots, celery, onion and garlic and sauté 5 minutes longer. Stir in beef stock, tomato paste and pepper.

Form a bouquet garni by tying together with a string: parsley, celery tops and bay leaf. Add to soup. Bring to a boil, cover, reduce heat and simmer for 1 hour. Remove the bouquet garni.

In a blender or food processor, puree soup 1 cup at a time. Return pureed soup to pan. In a medium skillet, melt remaining tablespoon of margarine. Add reserved sliced mushrooms and sauté gently for 5 minutes. Add mushrooms and sherry to soup and heat thoroughly. Serve garnished with lemon slices or parsley sprigs.

Nutrient Analysis: 1 cup
Exchanges: 1/2 starch, 1 fat
Carbohydrate Choices: 1/2

Calories: 78   Protein: 2g   Carbohydrates: 8g
Fat: 5g   Cholesterol: 0mg   Sodium: 60mg
Dietary Fiber: 2g

SPICED TOMATO BOUILLON

Delicious served either hot or cold.

Makes 3 quarts; 12 servings

3/4   cup diced celery
3/4   cup diced carrots
1/2   cup diced onion
3   tablespoons chopped fresh
      parsley
8   cups unsalted tomato juice
1/2 to 1 teaspoon white pepper
10   whole cloves
2   bay leaves
1/4   teaspoon whole thyme
4   cups hot CHICKEN OR
      TURKEY STOCK, *(page 329)*

Simmer celery, carrots, onion, parsley, tomato juice, pepper, cloves, bay leaves and thyme about an hour, covered.

Strain and add broth. Heat to serving temperature.

Nutrient Analysis: 1 cup
Exchanges: 2 vegetable
Carbohydrate Choices: 1

Calories: 61   Protein: 4g   Carbohydrates: 10g
Fat: 1g   Cholesterol: 8mg   Sodium: 39mg
Dietary Fiber: 2g

TOMATO & CLAM SOUP

Makes 4 quarts; 16 servings

3   small onions, sliced
3   ribs celery, finely diced
1   sweet red pepper, finely diced
2   tablespoons tub margarine
6   cups no-salt-added
      canned tomatoes
4   cups water
2   bay leaves
1/2   tablespoon dried basil, crushed
1/2   teaspoon whole black peppers
3/4   teaspoon curry powder
2   (6 1/2-ounce) cans minced clams,
      undrained
1/3   cup plain low-fat yogurt, for garnish

Sauté onion, celery and pepper in margarine in a large saucepan until soft.

Add tomatoes, water, bay leaves, basil, pepper, curry and clams. Simmer 1 hour. Remove bay leaves.

Serve garnished with a dollop of yogurt.

Nutrient Analysis: 1 cup
Exchanges: 2 vegetable
Carbohydrate Choices: 1/2

Calories: 54   Protein: 3g   Carbohydrates: 8g
Fat: 2g   Cholesterol: 4mg   Sodium: 160mg
Dietary Fiber: 2g

FRENCH ONION SOUP, GRATINÉE

Makes 2 quarts; 8 servings

1 1/2   pounds (5 cups) thinly sliced
      yellow onions
2   tablespoons tub margarine
1   teaspoon vegetable oil
1   teaspoon sugar
3   tablespoons all-purpose flour
2   quarts boiling BEEF STOCK,
      (page 328) or 5 tablespoons
      low-sodium, beef-flavored
      bouillon granules dissolved in
      2 quarts water
1/2   cup dry white wine
      Pepper to taste
8   slices hard toasted French bread
1 1/2   cups shredded part-skim farmer
      or Swiss cheese

In a large, heavy, covered saucepan, cook onions slowly with the margarine and oil for 15 minutes. Uncover, raise heat to medium and add sugar. Cook 30 to 40 minutes, stirring frequently, until the onions have turned a deep golden brown.

Sprinkle the flour over the onions. Cook and stir for about 2 minutes. Remove from heat and stir in the beef stock, wine and pepper.

Return to heat. Simmer, partially covered, for 30 to 40 minutes, skimming occasionally.

Bring soup to a boil and pour into oven-proof tureen or individual bowls. Top with toasted French bread and cheese. Bake at 350° for 20 minutes, then set under broiler for 2 minutes or until the cheese is lightly browned. Serve immediately.

Nutrient Analysis: 1 cup
Exchanges: 1 1/2 starch, 1 lean meat, 1 fat
Carbohydrate Choices: 1 1/2

Calories: 232   Protein: 8 g   Carbohydrates: 23 g
Fat: 11 g   Cholesterol: 12 mg   Sodium: 234 mg
Dietary Fiber: 3 g

SCOTCH BROTH

Makes 3 quarts; 12 servings

  3 pounds meaty lamb bones
12 cups water
  1 onion, quartered
  2 celery ribs with leaves, cut in thirds
1/2 teaspoon salt
1/2 cup barley, dry
  1 onion, chopped
  2 ribs celery, sliced
  2 carrots, sliced
     Freshly ground pepper

Brown the lamb bones in a heavy saucepan. Add water, quartered onion, celery ribs with leaves and salt. Bring to a boil, reduce heat and simmer covered, for 2 to 3 hours.

Strain the broth and cool until the fat congeals on the top. Skim and discard. Remove meat from the bones, dice and reserve.

Bring defatted broth to a boil. Add barley and simmer for 30 minutes. Add chopped onion, sliced celery, carrots, reserved meat and pepper. Simmer another 30 to 40 minutes.

Nutrient Analysis: 1 cup
Exchanges: 1/2 starch, 1 very lean meat
Carbohydrate Choices: 1/2

Calories: 74   *Protein: 6g*   *Carbohydrates: 8g*
Fat: 2g   *Cholesterol: 16 mg*   *Sodium: 127 mg*
Dietary Fiber: 2g

CONDENSED CREAM SOUP MIX

*Use as a casserole sauce mix or as a base for cream soups such as mushroom, asparagus, broccoli, cauliflower, etc. A can of Campbell's® Cream of Mushroom Soup contains 2175 mg sodium, and a can of Campbell's® Healthy Request® Cream of Mushroom Soup contains 1175 mg sodium; while our **Cooking À La Heart** equivalent contains 88 mg sodium.*

Makes 3 cups dry mix (equivalent to 9 cans of soup); 9 servings

2	**cups nonfat dry milk powder**
3/4	**cup cornstarch**
1/4	**cup sodium-reduced, chicken-flavored bouillon granules**
2	**tablespoons dried onion flakes**
1	**teaspoon dried basil, crushed**
1	**teaspoon whole thyme**
1/2	**teaspoon white pepper**

Mix together dry milk, cornstarch, bouillon granules, onion flakes, basil, thyme and pepper. Store in an airtight container.

To substitute for one can condensed soup, combine 1/3 cup dry mix with 1 1/4 cup water. Heat to boiling, cook and stir until thickened.

Nutrient Analysis: 1/3 cup dry mix (equivalent to 1 can of soup)
Exchanges: 1 starch, 1 very lean meat
Carbohydrate Choices: 1

Calories: 104   Protein: 5 g   Carbohydrates: 19 g
Fat: 0 g   Cholesterol: 3 mg   Sodium: 88 mg
Calcium: 186 mg

CREAM OF MOREL SOUP

Should you be fortunate enough to procure fresh or dried morels, there are none finer for mushroom soup.

Makes 1 quart; 4 servings

10	dried morels
1 1/2	tablespoons tub margarine
2	tablespoons finely chopped onion
2	tablespoons finely chopped celery
1	teaspoon dried parsley flakes or 1 tablespoon chopped fresh parsley
1	tablespoon all-purpose flour
1 1/2	cups water (reserve water from soaking morels)
4	teaspoons low-sodium, chicken-flavored bouillon granules
	Freshly ground pepper to taste
1 1/2	cups evaporated skim milk
1 1/2	tablespoons sherry
	Parsley or chives, for garnish

Soak dried morels in tepid water until soft (about an hour). Drain; reserving liquid. Squeeze out remaining water and chop stems and caps.

Heat margarine in a medium saucepan and sauté onion, celery and parsley until limp. Add mushrooms to vegetable mixture and sauté a few more minutes. Stir in flour.

Add water, bouillon granules and pepper. Bring to a boil and simmer 15 to 20 minutes. Remove from heat and let stand several hours.

Just before serving, add the milk and sherry and heat. Serve steaming hot, garnished with chopped fresh parsley or chives.

Nutrient Analysis: 1 cup
Exchanges: 2 starch, 1 very lean meat, 1 fat
Carbohydrate Choices: 2

Calories: 255   Protein: 15 g   Carbohydrates: 33 g
Fat: 6 g   Cholesterol: 0 mg   Sodium: 176 mg
Dietary Fiber: 5 g   Calcium: 266 mg

CREAM OF BROCCOLI SOUP

A good basic recipe for any cream of vegetable soup such as asparagus, cauliflower, carrot, etc.

Makes 2 quarts; 8 servings

1   bunch fresh broccoli
1   tablespoon tub margarine
1/3   cup finely chopped onion
4   cups CHICKEN STOCK,
   (page 329)
1   bay leaf
1/8   teaspoon whole thyme
1/8   teaspoon dried tarragon, crushed
1/8   teaspoon dried rosemary, crushed
1/4   teaspoon salt
1/4   teaspoon white pepper
1   large potato, peeled and thinly
   sliced
1   (12-ounce) can evaporated skim
   milk

Remove tips of broccoli florets and reserve. Peel broccoli stalks and slice very thinly into rounds.

Melt margarine in a large saucepan. Sauté onions slowly until translucent.

Add chicken stock and herbs to saucepan and bring to a boil. Add potato and broccoli stalks to broth and simmer, covered, 20 minutes or until vegetables are tender.

Reserve 1/2 cup of florets. Add the remainder to the soup and simmer 5 minutes.

In a blender or processor, puree the soup mixture. Return to saucepan. Add skim milk and heat to simmering.

In a separate small pan, blanch reserved 1/2 cup of florets in boiling water for one minute. Plunge florets into cold water, drain and chop coarsely. Add to soup just before serving.

Nutrient Analysis: 1 cup
Exchanges: 1 starch, 1 lean meat
Carbohydrate Choices: 1

Calories: 127   Protein: 10g   Carbohydrates: 16g
Fat: 3g   Cholesterol: 12mg   Sodium: 185mg
Dietary Fiber: 3g   Calcium: 172 mg Omega-3: 0.13 g

CREAMY ASPARAGUS SOUP

Makes 1 1/2 quarts; 6 servings

1   cup chopped onion
1/2 cup chopped celery
1   tablespoon tub margarine
2   cups cooked fresh asparagus
     or 1 (10-ounce) package frozen
     asparagus
1   cup cooked white rice
1   cup CHICKEN STOCK,
     (page 329)
3   cups evaporated skim milk
     Nutmeg
     Freshly ground pepper

Cook onion and celery in margarine in a heavy 3 to 4-quart saucepan until soft, about 5 minutes. Reserve 1/3 cup asparagus. Chop and set aside.

Add remaining asparagus, rice and stock. Cover and simmer 10 minutes. Puree in batches in food processor or blender. Return to saucepan. Add milk and reserved asparagus. Heat to boiling point. Season with nutmeg and pepper.

Nutrient Analysis: 1 cup
Exchanges: 2 starch, 1 very lean meat
Carbohydrate Choices: 2

Calories: 192   Protein: 12 g   Carbohydrates: 29 g
Fat: 3 g   Cholesterol: 4 mg   Sodium: 200 mg
Dietary Fiber: 2 g   Calcium: 348 mg

LEEK AND POTATO SOUP (VICHYSSOISE)

Makes 2 quarts; 8 servings

3   medium leeks
1   medium onion, thinly sliced
1   tablespoon tub margarine
4   medium potatoes, peeled and
        thinly sliced
4   cups CHICKEN STOCK,
        (page 329) **or 3 tablespoons
        low-sodium, chicken-favored
        bouillon in 4 cups water**
1 1/2   cups evaporated skim milk
1/4   teaspoon salt
1/4   teaspoon white pepper
        Chopped chives, for garnish

Clean leeks (separate each piece, for leeks can be very sandy). Mince the white part.

Sauté leeks and onion in margarine in a medium saucepan until soft but not brown.

Add potatoes and chicken stock and simmer covered, 15 minutes or until the vegetables are very tender.

Puree in small batches in blender or food processor. Return to saucepan. Add milk, salt and pepper.

Serve either hot or very cold garnished with chopped chives.

Nutrient Analysis: 1 cup
Exchanges: 1 starch, 1 vegetable, 1 very lean meat
Carbohydrate Choices: 1

Calories: 137   Protein: 9 g   Carbohydrates: 20 g
Fat: 3 g   Cholesterol: 12 mg   Sodium: 165 mg
Dietary Fiber: 2 g   Calcium: 145 mg

CURRIED SQUASH & APPLE BISQUE

1   medium acorn squash
1 1/2 tablespoons tub margarine
3/4   cup chopped onion
1   large apple, diced
2   teaspoons CURRY POWDER,
         (page 380)
1/2   cup apple cider
4   teaspoons low-sodium, chicken-
         flavored bouillon granules
1 1/2 cups water
1 1/2 cups evaporated skim milk
       Apple slices, for garnish
       Paprika or cayenne pepper,
         for garnish

Makes 1 quart; 4 servings

Prick squash all over with fork and place on a microwave-safe plate. Microwave for 5-7 minutes until tender. Cool. Cut in half and remove seeds. Scoop out flesh and set aside.

Melt margarine in a medium saucepan. Stir in onion, apple and curry powder. Cook 5 minutes, stirring frequently.

Add squash, cider, bouillon granules and water. Heat to boiling. Reduce heat, cover and simmer 30 minutes or until vegetables and apples are tender.

In food processor or blender, puree in small batches until smooth. Return to saucepan and stir in milk. Cook over low heat until heated through.

Serve garnished with apple slices, paprika or cayenne pepper.

Nutrient Analysis: 1 cup
Exchanges: 2 starch, 1 vegetable, 1 fat
Carbohydrate Choices: 2 1/2

Calories: 212   Protein: 7g   Carbohydrates: 37g
Fat: 5g   Cholesterol: 0mg   Sodium: 168mg
Dietary Fiber: 3g   Calcium: 284mg

HEARTY CHOWDER

Makes 3 quarts; 12 servings

4 ounces Canadian bacon, diced
1 tablespoon tub margarine
1 medium onion, chopped
2 cups water
1 cup diced celery (with leaves)
1 medium potato, diced
2 carrots, diced
3 sprigs parsley, chopped
2 tablespoons low-sodium, chicken-flavored bouillon granules
1/4 teaspoon dried basil, crushed
2 dashes Tabasco sauce
   Freshly ground pepper to taste
1/4 cup all-purpose flour
3 cups skim milk, divided
1 (7-ounce) can clams, drained
1 (15.5-ounce) can corn, drained

Lightly sauté the Canadian bacon in margarine in a heavy saucepan.

Add the onions and cook until onions are wilted.

Add the water, celery, potato, carrots, parsley, bouillon granules, basil, Tabasco and pepper. Bring to a boil and simmer until the vegetables are tender (about 15 minutes).

Dissolve the flour in one cup of milk. Add to vegetable mixture and bring to a boil. Cook a minute or two until chowder is slightly thickened. Add the remaining milk, clams and corn. Heat thoroughly and serve.

Nutrient Analysis: 1 cup
Exchanges: 1 starch, 1 very lean meat
Carbohydrate Choices: 1

Calories: 129   Protein: 9g   Carbohydrates: 19g
Fat: 2g   Cholesterol: 14mg   Sodium: 266mg
Dietary Fiber: 2g

ONE-OF-IT-SOUP

An often-requested recipe shared by the food editor of Tokyo Asahi Evening News.

Makes 1 1/2 quarts; 6 servings

1   banana
1   apple, cored
1   potato
1   onion
1   large celery rib
2   cups CHICKEN STOCK,
      (page 329)
1/2   teaspoon curry powder
1 1/2 to 2 cups evaporated skim milk
      Shredded carrots
      Chives, parsley or lemon thyme

Quarter the banana, apple, potato, onion and celery. Place in a medium saucepan with chicken stock. Bring to a boil. Reduce heat and simmer until the vegetables are soft.

Put vegetable mixture through food mill or blend in blender or food processor and return to saucepan. Add curry and milk (start with 1 1/2 cup).

Serve hot or cold garnished with shredded carrots and chives, parsley or lemon thyme.

Nutrient Analysis: 1 cup   Calories: 136   Protein: 8g   Carbohydrates: 25g
Exchanges: 1 starch, 1 vegetable, 1 very lean meat   Fat: 1g   Cholesterol: 8 mg   Sodium: 103 mg
Carbohydrate Choices: 1 1/2   Dietary Fiber: 3g   Calcium: 183 mg

BLACK BEAN SOUP

This soup is very black. The yogurt and green onion garnish provides a colorful contrast.

Makes 2 quarts; 8 servings

1	pound dry black beans, navy beans or red beans (about 2 1/2 cups)
8	cups water
1	tablespoon vegetable oil
1	medium onion, diced
2	carrots, diced
1/2	teaspoon salt
1	teaspoon ground nutmeg
2	tablespoons lemon juice
1/2	cup plain low-fat yogurt, for garnish
2	green onions, sliced, for garnish

Rinse beans and place in Dutch oven or large saucepan with water. Cover and let stand overnight. (Or heat to boiling and boil 2 minutes; cover and let stand 1 hour).

Heat oil in a small skillet. Add onion and carrots; sauté until crisp-tender. Stir into beans with salt and nutmeg. Heat to boiling; reduce heat to low and simmer, covered, 1 1/2 to 2 hours or until beans are very tender. Stir occasionally.

Spoon 2 cups of bean mixture into food processor or blender. Process or blend until finely chopped and almost smooth. Pour into large bowl and repeat with remaining beans. Stir in lemon juice.

To serve, spoon steaming soup into soup bowls and top each serving with 1 tablespoon yogurt and sliced green onions.

Nutrient Analysis: 1 cup
Exchanges: 2 starch, 2 very lean meat
Carbohydrate Choices: 2

Calories: 230   Protein: 14 g   Carbohydrates: 40 g
Fat: 3 g   Cholesterol: 1 mg   Sodium: 180 mg
Dietary Fiber: 12 g   Calcium: 109 mg

CHICKEN LENTIL SOUP

First Prize Heart's Delight Recipe Contest - Junior Division

Makes 2 1/2 quarts; 10 servings

2 1/2   pounds chicken, skinned, and
        cut in pieces
1 1/2   cups lentils, dry
1/2   cup split peas, dry
3   quarts water
1   cup chopped celery
1   cup chopped carrots
1/2   cup chopped onion
1   teaspoon parsley flakes
1/2   teaspoon whole thyme
1/2   teaspoon pepper
1/2   teaspoon ground turmeric
1/4   teaspoon ground sage
1/4   teaspoon poultry seasoning

Bring skinned, defatted chicken, lentils and split peas to a boil in water. Reduce heat to low, cover and simmer 2 hours.

Remove chicken; bone, dice, and refrigerate. Cool soup and refrigerate for 4 hours or overnight.

Remove and discard any congealed fat. Add celery, carrots, onion, parsley, thyme, pepper, turmeric, sage and poultry seasoning. Simmer 1 1/4 hours.

Just before serving, add diced chicken and heat thoroughly.

Nutrient Analysis: 1 cup
Exchanges: 1 starch, 3 very lean meat
Carbohydrate Choices: 1

Calories: 191   Protein: 21 g   Carbohydrates: 25 g
Fat: 1 g   Cholesterol: 26 mg   Sodium: 49 mg
Dietary Fiber: 12 g

LENTIL SOUP VARIATION:

VEGETARIAN LENTIL OR SPLIT PEA SOUP

Makes 2 quarts; 8 servings

Use CHICKEN LENTIL SOUP recipe omitting the chicken and decreasing the water to 2 quarts. Use either 2 cups lentils or 2 cups split peas and add 2 extra-large vegetarian vegetable bouillon cubes if desired.

Nutrient Analysis: 1 cup
Exchanges: 1 1/2 starch, 2 1/2 very lean meat
Carbohydrate Choices: 1 1/2

Calories: 233   Protein: 17 g   Carbohydrates: 41 g
Fat: 1 g   Cholesterol: 0 mg   Sodium: 332 mg
Dietary Fiber: 19 g

BEEF LENTIL SOUP

Makes 2 quarts; 8 servings

1 pound extra-lean beef stew meat, diced
2 tablespoons tub margarine
1 medium onion, chopped
2 celery ribs, chopped
2 quarts water
1 (10-ounce) package frozen leaf spinach
1 whole tomato
3/4 cup lentils, dry
1/4 teaspoon salt
Pepper to taste
3 tablespoons red wine vinegar

Brown beef in margarine in a Dutch oven. Add onions and celery and sauté lightly.

Add water, spinach, tomato, lentils, salt and pepper. Simmer for 2 to 3 hours.

To serve, ladle soup into individual serving bowls. Stir a teaspoon of vinegar into each bowl just before serving.

Nutrient Analysis: 1 cup
Exchanges: 1/2 starch, 3 very lean meat
Carbohydrate Choices: 1/2

Calories: 163   Protein: 19g   Carbohydrates: 15g
Fat: 5g   Cholesterol: 25mg   Sodium: 174mg
Dietary Fiber: 7g

CREOLE-STYLE LENTIL STEW

Makes 2 1/2 quarts; 10 servings

1	tablespoon vegetable oil
1/2	pound lean boneless pork, cut in 1/2" cubes
2	garlic cloves, minced
1	large onion, chopped
4	cups water
1	cup dry lentils, rinsed
1	(6-ounce) can no-salt-added tomato paste
2	bay leaves
1	(10-ounce) package frozen okra
2	medium tomatoes, peeled and chopped
2	teaspoons sodium-reduced Worcestershire sauce
1	teaspoon dried oregano, crushed
1	teaspoon sugar
1/2	teaspoon cayenne pepper
1/4	teaspoon salt
2	cups cooked rice or bulgur
4	teaspoons vinegar

Heat oil in a Dutch oven or large saucepan. Add pork cubes, garlic and onion and cook until meat is browned and onion is tender.

Stir in water, lentils, tomato paste and bay leaves. Bring to a boil; reduce heat, cover and simmer about an hour, stirring occasionally.

Add okra, tomatoes, Worcestershire, oregano, sugar, pepper and salt. Simmer another 30 minutes or until lentils and okra are tender.

To serve, ladle mixture into individual soup bowls. Stir 1/2 teaspoon of vinegar into each serving. Top with a mound of rice or bulgur.

Nutrient Analysis: 1 cup
Exchanges: 1 starch, 1 vegetable, 2 very lean meat
Carbohydrate Choices: 1

Calories: 188   Protein: 13g   Carbohydrates: 28g
Fat: 4g   Cholesterol: 14mg   Sodium: 92mg
Dietary Fiber: 8g

HEARTY PEA SOUP

Makes 2 1/2 quarts; 10 servings

2	tablespoons vegetable oil
1	onion, diced
2	bay leaves
1	teaspoon celery seed
1/4	cup barley, dry
1	cup green split peas, dry
3/4	cup dry lima beans
10	cups water
6	ounces (3/4 cup) diced lean ham
1	carrot, chopped
3	ribs celery, diced
1	potato, diced
1/2	cup chopped fresh parsley
	Dash pepper
1/2	teaspoon dried basil, crushed
1/4	teaspoon garlic powder
1/4	teaspoon whole thyme

Heat oil in a Dutch oven or large saucepan. Sauté onion, bay leaves and celery seed until onion is soft.

Add peas, barley, lima beans and water and bring to a boil. Reduce heat, cover and simmer for about 1 1/2 hours.

Add ham, carrot, celery, potato, parsley, pepper, basil, garlic powder and thyme. Simmer for another 30 to 45 minutes. Remove bay leaf before serving.

Nutrient Analysis: 1 cup
Exchanges: 2 starch, 1 very lean meat
Carbohydrate Choices: 2

Calories: 198   Protein: 12 g   Carbohydrates: 31 g
Fat: 4 g   Cholesterol: 4 mg   Sodium: 143 mg
Dietary Fiber: 5 g

ORIENTAL HOT POT

The Oriental fondue (a tradition dating back to the 13th century) is an attractive, low-calorie, low-cholesterol choice for entertaining. You will need: a fondue pot or saucepan on a hot plate, wooden skewers, chopsticks or fondue forks, individual plates for each guest, platters for uncooked foods, and dipping bowls for soy sauce, sherry or other sauces.

Makes 2 quarts; 8 servings

5	cups sodium-reduced chicken or beef broth
1/2	pound lean beef, cut into paper thin slices (partially frozen meat is easiest to slice)
1/2	pound boneless, skinless chicken, cut into thin slices
1/2	pound raw fish or seafood, cut into bite-sized pieces
12	whole small mushrooms
1	(8-ounce) package of tofu, cut into bite-sized pieces
6	green onions (green tops only) cut into 2" lengths (reserve the white part)
24	spinach or kale leaves, washed and trimmed of their stems
4	cups hot cooked rice

Arrange uncooked beef, chicken, fish, mushrooms, tofu, onion tops and spinach or kale attractively on a platter.

Fill cooking pot two-thirds full of broth (have extra broth ready to add if necessary during cooking). Heat broth to boiling and place in center of table over heat source.

Using skewers, chopsticks or fondue forks, dip pieces of raw meat, beef, chicken, fish and vegetable into the boiling broth, cooking to the desired doneness. Serve with rice and dipping sauces such as: ORIENTAL SWEET-SOUR, PLUM, or SWEET-SOUR MUSTARD, all found in the *Dressings and Sauces Section.*

Nutrient Analysis: 1 cup
Exchanges: 1 1/2 starch, 3 very lean meat
Carbohydrate Choices: 1 1/2

Calories: 230   Protein: 25 g   Carbohydrates: 25 g
Fat: 4 g   Cholesterol: 44 mg   Sodium: 139 mg
Dietary Fiber: 2 g

PEACH & CANTALOUPE SOUP

Makes 1 1/2 quarts; 6 servings

1	medium ripe cantaloupe, peeled, seeded and cubed
1	medium ripe peach, peeled, pitted and cubed
1/2	cup dry white wine
1/4	cup orange juice
1	tablespoon sugar
1 1/2	cups buttermilk
	Fresh peach slices, for garnish

Place cantaloupe, peach, wine, orange juice and sugar in food processor or blender. Process or blend until almost smooth.

Add buttermilk and process until well blended. Refrigerate several hours or overnight to blend flavors.

To serve, pour into chilled bowls and garnish with sliced peaches.

Nutrient Analysis: 1 cup
Exchanges: 1 skim milk
Carbohydrate Choices: 1

Calories: 98   Protein: 3g   Carbohydrates: 18g
Fat: 1g   Cholesterol: 4mg   Sodium: 86mg
Dietary Fiber: 1g

MINTED PEA SOUP

The mint is a must! Good heated, also.

Makes 2 1/2 quarts; 10 servings

2	tablespoons chopped onion
1/2	cup shredded Boston lettuce
1	(10-ounce) package frozen tiny baby peas
1	sprig fresh mint (18 leaves)
	Dash nutmeg
1	tablespoon low-sodium, chicken-flavored bouillon granules
1 1/2	cups water
1/2	cup buttermilk

Combine onion, lettuce, peas, mint, nutmeg, bouillon granules and water in a medium saucepan. Heat to boiling; reduce heat, cover and simmer 15 minutes or until vegetables are very tender.

Place soup in food processor or blender and puree until smooth. Strain, pressing out all the liquid.

Stir in buttermilk and refrigerate several hours or overnight.

Nutrient Analysis: 1 cup
Exchanges: 1 starch
Carbohydrate Choices: 1

Calories: 79   Protein: 5g   Carbohydrates: 13g
Fat: 1g   Cholesterol: 2mg   Sodium: 117mg
Dietary Fiber: 4g

COOL SHRIMP SOUP

This is wonderful for lunch on a hot summer day.

Makes 2 quarts; 8 servings

1 large cucumber, peeled and seeded
6 green onions, chopped, with some
   of the green tops
12 sprigs fresh dill, chopped, or 1/2
   teaspoon dried dill weed
   Freshly ground pepper to taste
1 pound shrimp, fresh or frozen,
   cooked, cleaned and deveined
   Juice of one lemon
1 quart buttermilk
   Paprika, for garnish
   Parsley sprigs, for garnish

Slice the cucumber into the bottom of a
4-quart ceramic or glass casserole dish.

On top of cucumbers, layer onions, then dill
and finally, shrimp. Grind pepper to taste
and sprinkle lemon juice over shrimp. Pour
buttermilk over all ingredients and cover.

Refrigerate overnight or at least 6 hours. Just
before serving, garnish with paprika and parsley
sprigs.

Nutrient Analysis: 1 cup
Exchanges: 1 skim milk, 1 very lean meat
Carbohydrate Choices: 1/2

Calories: 127   Protein: 17g   Carbohydrates: 10g
Fat: 2g   Cholesterol: 94mg   Sodium: 221mg
Dietary Fiber: 1g   Calcium: 174mg

GAZPACHO

This is the traditional Spanish gazpacho thickened with bread. Make "instant gazpacho" from left-over greens and vegetable salads. In food processor or blender, process left-over salad with sodium-reduced tomato or V-8® juice.

Makes 1 1/2 quarts; 6 servings

4	ripe tomatoes, peeled and chopped
1/2	cucumber, halved, seeded and chopped
1	rib celery, chopped
2	crosswise slices onion
1/2	green pepper, chopped
1	garlic clove
3	tablespoons white vinegar
2	tablespoons olive oil
3	slices French bread
1	cup water
1	cup no-salt-added tomato juice
1/8	teaspoon Tabasco sauce

Mix tomatoes, cucumber, celery, onion, green pepper, garlic, vinegar, olive oil, French bread, water, tomato juice and Tabasco in a large bowl.

Puree half of the mixture in a blender or food processor and then the other half. Chill thoroughly.

Serve the soup in individual bowls and pass small dishes of diced green pepper, cucumber, tomato, celery and croutons for garnish.

GARNISH:

1/2	green pepper, diced
1/2	cucumber, seeded and diced
1	small tomato, peeled and chopped
1/4	cup diced celery
1/2	cup croutons

Nutrient Analysis: 1 cup
Exchanges: 1/2 starch, 2 vegetable, 1 fat
Carbohydrate Choices: 1

Calories: 133   Protein: 3g   Carbohydrates: 19g
Fat: 6g   Cholesterol: 0mg   Sodium: 115mg
Dietary Fiber: 3g

CURRIED PEACH SOUP

Makes 1 1/2 quarts; 6 servings

1 pound ripe fresh peaches,
   peeled and pitted, (4 large)
1/2 cup chopped onion
3/4 teaspoon curry powder
1 bay leaf
2 tablespoons tub margarine
2 tablespoons whole wheat flour
2 cups CHICKEN STOCK,
   (page 329) **or 2 tablespoons
   low-sodium, chicken-flavored
   bouillon granules dissolved in
   2 cups water**
   Dash of white pepper
1/4 cup plain low-fat yogurt
   Fresh mint leaves, for garnish

Cut up peaches and puree in blender.

Sauté onion, curry powder and bay leaf in margarine for 3 minutes or until onions are tender.

Remove from heat and stir in flour until smooth. Return to heat. Gradually add chicken stock, pepper and peaches. Bring to a boil, reduce heat and simmer 3 minutes. Remove bay leaf and discard.

Refrigerate soup.

Serve chilled with a dollop of yogurt and fresh mint leaf garnish.

Nutrient Analysis: 1 cup
Exchanges: 1 fruit, 1 fat
Carbohydrate Choices: 1

Calories: 115   Protein: 4g   Carbohydrates: 14g
Fat: 5g   Cholesterol: 9mg   Sodium: 53mg
Dietary Fiber: 2g

DATE SANDWICHES

For canapés, cut date sandwiches into small triangles and garnish with a slice of green pepper or sprig of parsley.

Makes 6 sandwiches; 6 servings

3   tablespoons tub margarine
3   tablespoons honey
3   cups shredded lettuce
1   cup sliced, pitted dates
1/2   cup thinly sliced celery
1/2   cup light mayonnaise
2   teaspoons lemon juice
12   slices multigrain, low-calorie, high fiber bread

Beat together margarine and honey in a small bowl until creamy.

Toss shredded lettuce with dates, celery, mayonnaise and lemon juice in a medium bowl.

Spread each slice of bread with honey mixture. Top with lettuce-date filling and another slice of bread. Press lightly, cut in half, and serve.

Nutrient Analysis: 1 sandwich   *Calories: 331   Protein: 5 g   Carbohydrates: 55 g*
Exchanges: 3 starch, 2 fat   *Fat: 14 g   Cholesterol: 11 mg   Sodium: 463 mg*
Carbohydrate Choices: 3   *Dietary Fiber: 8 g*

BETTER PEANUT BUTTER

Extra-good on plain or toasted 7-grain bread.

Makes 1 1/4 cups; 20 servings

2   cups roasted, unsalted peanuts
3   tablespoons vegetable oil
1   tablespoon honey

Place peanuts in food processor equipped with metal blade. Process on high until peanuts form a ball which will whirl briefly around bowl before breaking apart (about 2 minutes).

Remove cover and scrape down. Replace cover and continue processing, adding oil in a steady stream.

Add honey and blend until smooth and creamy.

Nutrient Analysis: 1 tablespoon spread
Exchanges: 2 fat
Carbohydrate Choices: 0

Calories: 101   Protein: 3g   Carbohydrates: 4g
Fat: 9g   Cholesterol: 0mg   Sodium: 1mg
Dietary Fiber: 1g

CARROT NUT RAISIN SANDWICHES

Makes 4 open-face sandwiches; 4 servings

1   cup shredded part-skim
      mozzarella cheese
1   cup shredded carrots
1/4   cup chopped nuts
2   tablespoons raisins
4   tablespoons light mayonnaise
4   slices multigrain, low-calorie,
      high fiber bread

Combine cheese, carrots, nuts and raisins in a bowl. Moisten with mayonnaise. Spread filling on bread.

Nutrient Analysis: 1 sandwich
Exchanges: 1 1/2 starch, 1 lean meat, 2 fat
Carbohydrate Choices: 1 1/2

Calories: 245   Protein: 10g   Carbohydrates: 21g
Fat: 15g   Cholesterol: 24mg   Sodium: 384mg
Dietary Fiber: 4g   Calcium: 218mg   Omega-3: 0.74g

CARROT & CHEESE SANDWICHES

Makes 4 open-face sandwiches; 4 servings

1   large carrot, shredded
1   cup shredded part-skim
    farmer cheese
2   tablespoons finely diced
    green pepper
1   tablespoon diced onion
1/2 cucumber, diced
2   tablespoons light mayonnaise
2   tablespoons plain low-fat yogurt
1   tablespoon Italian dressing
4   slices multigrain, low-calorie,
    high fiber bread
    Fresh sprouts

Combine carrot, cheese, green pepper, onion and cucumber in a medium bowl.

Stir together mayonnaise, yogurt and Italian dressing in a small bowl. Toss vegetable-cheese mixture with dressing and spread on bread. Top with sprouts.

Nutrient Analysis: 1 sandwich
Exchanges: 1 starch, 1 lean meat, 1 fat
Carbohydrate Choices: 1

Calories: 168   Protein: 10g   Carbohydrates: 17g
Fat: 8g   Cholesterol: 22mg   Sodium: 388mg
Dietary Fiber: 4g   Calcium: 229mg

GRILLED ZUCCHINI PARMESAN SANDWICHES

Makes 4 open-face sandwiches; 4 servings

1/2 cup chopped onion
1   garlic clove, crushed
1/2 teaspoon dried basil, crushed
1/2 teaspoon dried oregano, crushed
    Freshly ground pepper to taste
2   tablespoons olive oil
2   cups grated fresh zucchini
4   slices multigrain, low-calorie,
    high fiber bread, toasted
1   tomato, thinly sliced
4   tablespoons Parmesan cheese

Sauté onion, garlic, basil, oregano and pepper in olive oil in a skillet until onion is translucent.

Add zucchini and sauté until soft.

Spread vegetable mixture on toast. Top each sandwich with thin slices of tomato and a sprinkling of 1 tablespoon Parmesan. Broil until cheese turns golden.

Nutrient Analysis: 1 sandwich
Exchanges: 1 starch, 2 fat
Carbohydrate Choices: 1

Calories: 156   Protein: 5g   Carbohydrates: 16g
Fat: 9g   Cholesterol: 6mg   Sodium: 214mg
Dietary Fiber: 4g   Calcium: 105mg

HOT CHICKEN POCKETS

Makes 12 half pockets; 12 servings

3/4   cup plain low-fat yogurt
1/2   cucumber, peeled and seeded
1/2   teaspoon dill weed
2   whole chicken breasts, boned
     and skinned
1 1/2   tablespoons vegetable oil
2   medium garlic cloves, chopped
6   whole wheat pita breads
6   radishes, thinly sliced
2   green onions, thinly sliced

Combine yogurt, cucumber and dill weed in a blender or food processor. Blend until smooth. Set aside.

Slice chicken breasts across the muscle 1/4" thick. Slice these into 1/4"-wide matchsticks.

Heat the oil in a heavy skillet. Add the chopped garlic and chicken strips. Cook and stir over high heat until no pink remains.

Cut pockets in half. Fill with chicken, radishes and onion. Top with sauce and serve immediately.

Nutrient Analysis: 1 half pocket
Exchanges: 1 starch, 2 very lean meat
Carbohydrate Choices: 1

Calories: 130   Protein: 12g   Carbohydrates: 14g
Fat: 3g   Cholesterol: 23mg   Sodium: 158mg
Dietary Fiber: 2g

TOFU SALAD SANDWICHES

Described by one fan as "an egg salad sandwich only better." Tofu, once found only in Oriental food stores, is now available in the produce section of most grocery stores.

Makes 6 sandwiches; 6 servings

1	(16-ounce) package extra-firm, silken, light tofu
1/4	cup light mayonnaise
1	tablespoon prepared mustard
1	teaspoon sodium-reduced Worcestershire sauce
1/8	teaspoon ground cumin
1/8	teaspoon ground turmeric
1/4	teaspoon paprika
1	green onion, minced
1/4	cup shredded carrot
1/4	cup minced celery
2	tablespoons minced green pepper
12	slices multigrain, low-calorie, high fiber bread
2	cups fresh sprouts (bean, lentil or alfalfa)

Crumble tofu with a fork or pastry blender to small lumps in a medium bowl.

Stir in mayonnaise, mustard and Worcestershire.

Sprinkle cumin; turmeric and paprika over salad mixture. Stir well.

Add green onion, carrot, celery and green pepper; stir.

Divide filling among six slices of bread and spread to edges. Top salad with generous layer of sprouts and another slice of bread. Cut in half to serve.

Nutrient Analysis: 1 sandwich
Exchanges: 1 starch, 1 vegetable, 1 medium-fat meat
Carbohydrate Choices: 1

Calories: 172   Protein: 11g   Carbohydrates: 26g
Fat: 5g   Cholesterol: 8mg   Sodium: 430mg
Dietary Fiber: 7g

VEGETABLE & CHEESE POCKETS

6 whole wheat pita breads
6 cups shredded lettuce or a
      combination of lettuce and
      fresh sprouts (alfalfa or bean)
1 1/2 cups shredded part-skim farmer
      or mozzarella cheese
2 cups vegetables (1/3 cup each
      of the following or any
      proportion you choose)
1/3 cup diced green pepper
1/3 cup sliced green onion
1/3 cup sliced radishes
1/3 cup shredded carrots
1/3 cup diced cucumber
1/3 cup diced celery
1/3 cup seeded, chopped tomato
1/3 cup sliced fresh mushrooms
1/3 cup unsalted sunflower seeds

CREAMY YOGURT DRESSING:
3 tablespoons light mayonnaise
2 tablespoons plain low-fat yogurt
1 teaspoon lemon juice
1/2 teaspoon mixed, crushed herbs
      (oregano, basil, marjoram,
      savory)

Makes 12 half pockets; 12 servings

Cut pita breads in half and set aside. Combine shredded lettuce and sprouts together; add shredded cheese and your selection of vegetables in a large bowl.

To prepare Creamy Yogurt Dressing: Combine mayonnaise, yogurt, lemon juice and herbs. Toss with vegetable-cheese mixture, fill pockets and serve immediately.

Dressing Variation: In place of the creamy dressing, we suggest using 6 tablespoons DILLED VINAIGRETTE DRESSING *(page 158)*. Fill pockets first, then drizzle 1/2 tablespoon dressing over vegetables in pockets.

Nutrient Analysis: 1 half pocket
Exchanges: 1 starch, 1 lean meat
Carbohydrate Choices: 1

Calories: 123   Protein: 7g   Carbohydrates: 16g
Fat: 4g   Cholesterol: 10mg   Sodium: 228mg
Dietary Fiber: 3g   Calcium: 108mg

MEAT OR SEAFOOD POCKETS

Makes 8 half pockets; 8 servings

2 cups diced cooked chicken, pork, beef or seafood
1 1/2 cups shredded lettuce
1 cup alfalfa or bean sprouts
1 medium tomato, seeded and chopped
2 green onions with tops, thinly sliced
1 cup shredded part-skim farmer or mozzarella cheese
3 tablespoons olive oil
2 tablespoons red wine vinegar
1 teaspoon parsley flakes
1/4 teaspoon dried basil, crushed
1/4 teaspoon dried oregano, crushed
1/4 teaspoon garlic powder
1/4 teaspoon dry mustard
1/4 teaspoon sugar
1/8 teaspoon pepper
4 whole wheat pita breads
Lemon wedges (optional)

Combine meat or seafood, lettuce, sprouts, tomato, green onion and cheese in a medium bowl.

In a jar with a tight fitting lid, combine oil, vinegar, parsley, basil, oregano, garlic powder, mustard, sugar and pepper. Shake well and toss with meat and vegetables.

Cut pockets in half and spoon mixture into bread. Garnish each with a lemon wedge.

Nutrient Analysis: 1 half pocket
Exchanges: 1 starch, 2 lean meat, 1 fat
Carbohydrate Choices: 1

Calories: 197   Protein: 15g   Carbohydrates: 15g
Fat: 9g   Cholesterol: 30mg   Sodium: 214mg
Dietary Fiber: 2g   Calcium: 106mg

TASTE O' THE SEA SANDWICHES

Makes 4 open-face sandwiches; 4 servings

1 (7-ounce) can no-salt-added
   water-packed tuna, drained
1/2 cup chopped roasted, unsalted
   peanuts
1/2 cup finely chopped tomato
1/4 cup chopped green onion
1/4 cup light mayonnaise
2 tablespoons lemon juice
2 tablespoons chopped fresh
   parsley
1 teaspoon dried basil, crushed
1 teaspoon dried marjoram,
   crushed
4 slices multigrain, low-calorie,
   high fiber bread

Combine tuna, peanuts, tomato, green onion, mayonnaise, lemon juice, parsley, basil and marjoram in a medium mixing bowl. Mix well.

Spread tuna mixture on bread slices. Serve immediately.

Nutrient Analysis: 1 sandwich
Exchanges: 1 starch, 2 lean meat, 2 fat
Carbohydrate Choices: 1

Calories: 269   Protein: 19 g   Carbohydrates: 18 g
Fat: 15 g   Cholesterol: 22 mg   Sodium: 270 mg
Dietary Fiber: 5 g   Omega-3: 0.16 g

HOT TUNA PINEAPPLE TOAST

Makes 4 open-face sandwiches; 4 servings

1 (7-ounce) can no-salt-added
   water-packed tuna, drained
1 (8-ounce) can unsweetened
   crushed pineapple, drained
1/4 cup light mayonnaise
4 slices multigrain, low-calorie,
   high fiber bread

Combine tuna, pineapple and mayonnaise. Mix well.

Spread mixture over bread and place on baking sheet. Bake until hot. Serve immediately.

Oven: 450°
Time: 5 minutes

Nutrient Analysis: 1 sandwich
Exchanges: 1 1/2 starch, 1 very lean meat, 1 fat
Carbohydrate Choices: 1 1/2

Calories: 185   Protein: 14 g   Carbohydrates: 21 g
Fat: 6 g   Cholesterol: 21 mg   Sodium: 270 mg
Dietary Fiber: 3 g   Omega-3: 0.15 g

TOSTADAS

Makes 12 tostadas; 12 servings

FRIJOLES (REFRIED BEANS):

1 1/2	cups dry pinto beans
5	cups water or unsalted stock
1	cup chopped onions
2	medium tomatoes, chopped
1	garlic clove, minced
1	teaspoon chili powder
	Pinch cayenne pepper
2	tablespoons vegetable oil

SALSA:

6	medium tomatoes, seeded and chopped
1	cup finely chopped onions
1	teaspoon dried oregano, crushed
1/2	teaspoon minced garlic
1	teaspoon honey
1/2	cup red wine vinegar

TOPPING:

3	cups shredded lettuce
3/4	cup chopped green onion
3/4	cup shredded part-skim mozzarella cheese
3/4	cup plain low-fat yogurt (optional)

TORTILLAS:

12	tostada shells

FRIJOLES: Soak beans in 5 cups of water overnight. Cook in the water with half the onion, half of the tomato, half the garlic, the chili powder and the cayenne until tender, about 3 hours.

Heat 2 tablespoons vegetable oil in a large frying pan. Sauté the remaining onions and garlic.

Add the remaining tomatoes. Add beans gradually, mashing as they are added. Heat and stir until they have a thick consistency.

SALSA: Combine tomatoes, onion, oregano, garlic, honey and vinegar in a medium bowl.

To assemble tostadas: Spread each tostada shell with about 1/3 cup frijoles. Top with 1/4 cup shredded lettuce, a tablespoon of green onion, 1/4 cup salsa, and a tablespoon of shredded cheese. Garnish with a tablespoon of yogurt and chopped chives if desired.

Nutrient Analysis: 1 tostada
Exchanges: 2 starch, 1 very lean meat, 1 fat
Carbohydrate Choices: 2

Calories: 222   Protein: 9g   Carbohydrates: 36g
Fat: 5g   Cholesterol: 4mg   Sodium: 75mg
Dietary Fiber: 6g   Calcium: 108mg

TURKEY TACOS

Makes 12 tacos; 12 servings

3	tablespoons vegetable oil
1 1/2	pounds extra-lean ground turkey
3/4	cup chopped onions
1	(6-ounce) can low-sodium tomato paste
1	(6-ounce) can water
3/4	teaspoon ground cumin
1	tablespoon chili powder
1	teaspoon garlic powder
12	taco shells
4	ounces mozzarella cheese, shredded (1 cup)

Heat oil in a large skillet. Add turkey and chopped onion and sauté until meat loses its pink color.

Add tomato paste, water, cumin, chili powder and garlic powder. Simmer for 10 minutes.

Spoon into taco shells and top with cheese.

Nutrient Analysis: 1 taco
Exchanges: 1 starch, 2 lean meat
Carbohydrate Choices: 1

Calories: 178   Protein: 18 g   Carbohydrates: 12 g
Fat: 7 g   Cholesterol: 28 mg   Sodium: 139 mg
Dietary Fiber: 2 g

CORN CRUST FOR PIZZA

Makes 15 x 10" pizza crust; 10 slices

1 1/2   cups all-purpose flour
1/2   cup cornmeal
1/2   teaspoon baking powder
1/3   cup tub margarine
1/2   cup cold water

Sift flour, cornmeal, and baking powder into a bowl. Cut in margarine. With a fork, gradually stir in cold water adding only enough to bind the crumbly mixture together.

Turn dough onto a floured board and knead briefly. Roll out into a rectangle measuring 15 x 10". Place dough on ungreased baking sheet. Turn up edges and flute. Prick crust with tines of fork. Bake.

Add topping and return to oven to melt cheese.

Oven: 425°
Time: 12 minutes

Nutrient Analysis: 1 slice (crust only)
Exchanges: 1 starch, 1 fat
Carbohydrate Choices: 1

Calories: 138   Protein: 2g   Carbohydrates: 19g
Fat: 6g   Cholesterol: 0mg   Sodium: 71mg
Dietary Fiber: 1g

YEAST PIZZA CRUST #1

Makes 12" pizza crust; 8 slices

1   tablespoon or 1 package active
   dry yeast
1   cup warm water
2   tablespoons vegetable oil
1/4 teaspoon salt
1   cup all-purpose flour
1   cup whole wheat flour

Combine yeast and water in a large bowl. Add oil and salt.

Stir in the all-purpose flour. Add the whole wheat flour gradually until the dough is no longer sticky. Knead lightly. Cover and put in a warm place to rise for 20 minutes.

Roll out crust on lightly floured surface. Place crust on pizza pan and press firmly to edges to get a good seal.

Add sauce and toppings and cheese of your choice. Bake.

Oven: 400°
Time: 20 minutes

Nutrient Analysis: 1 slice (crust only)   Calories: 142   Protein: 4g   Carbohydrates: 24g
Exchanges: 1 1/2 starch, 1/2 fat   Fat: 4g   Cholesterol: 0mg   Sodium: 73mg
Carbohydrate Choices: 1 1/2   Dietary Fiber: 3g

YEAST PIZZA CRUST #2

VEGETABLE NUT PIZZA TOPPING, (see next page) is a winner.

Makes 2 (12-inch) pizza crusts; 16 slices

2	cups whole wheat flour
2	cups all-purpose flour
1	package dry yeast
1 1/4	cups water
3	tablespoons tub margarine
2	tablespoons vegetable oil

Combine 1/4 cup flour and yeast in a large bowl.

Heat water and margarine in microwave until very warm (120-130 degrees). Add to flour and yeast and beat 2 minutes. Stir in enough flour, alternating whole wheat and all-purpose, to form a soft dough.

Turn out on floured board and knead 6 to 8 minutes. Place in oiled bowl. Turn dough so it is completely coated with oil. Cover and let rise until doubled (about 50 minutes).

Punch dough down. Divide in half. On floured surface, roll out into two 12 1/2" rounds. Press into pizza pans, forming dough over rims. Cover; let rise 30 minutes. Top with favorite pizza toppings and bake.

Nutrient Analysis: 1 slice (crust only)
Exchanges: 1 1/2 starch, 1/2 fat
Carbohydrate Choices: 1 1/2

Calories: 145   Protein: 4 g   Carbohydrates: 24 g
Fat: 4 g   Cholesterol: 0 mg   Sodium: 18 mg
Dietary Fiber: 2 g

VEGETABLE NUT PIZZA TOPPING

Makes 2 (12-inch) pizzas; 16 slices

2 cups shredded part-skim mozzarella cheese
1 teaspoon minced garlic
2 (16-ounce) cans low-sodium tomatoes, drained and coarsely chopped
1 cup chopped green pepper
1/2 cup chopped onion
1 teaspoon dried oregano, crushed
1 teaspoon dried basil, crushed
2 cups sliced fresh mushrooms
1 cup thinly sliced zucchini
2/3 cup unsalted cashews

Sprinkle 3/4 cup cheese over two 12" pizza crusts.

Mix together garlic, tomatoes, green pepper, onion, oregano and basil in a bowl. Spread the vegetable mixture evenly over the two pizzas.

Arrange the mushrooms and zucchini over the vegetable mixture and sprinkle with remaining cheese and cashews. Bake.

Oven: 400°
Time: 30 to 35 minutes

Nutrient Analysis: 1 slice (topping only)
Exchanges: 1 vegetable, 1 fat
Carbohydrate Choices: 1/2

Calories: 88   Protein: 5g   Carbohydrates: 7g
Fat: 5g   Cholesterol: 8mg   Sodium: 90mg
Dietary Fiber: 2g   Calcium: 106mg

THREE CHEESE PIZZA TOPPING

Makes 1 (14-inch) pizza; 10 slices

1 (15-ounce) container part-skim ricotta cheese
1 egg, beaten
1 small zucchini, sliced
1 small red or green pepper, sliced
4 mushrooms, sliced
1/2 teaspoon dried oregano, crushed
8 ounces part-skim mozzarella cheese, shredded
2/3 cup grated Parmesan cheese

Combine ricotta and egg in a small bowl. Spoon onto a 14" pizza crust.

Arrange zucchini, pepper and mushroom slices over ricotta. Sprinkle with oregano. Bake 20 minutes.

Sprinkle pizza with mozzarella and Parmesan. Bake 15 minutes more or until cheese is lightly browned.

Oven: 400°
Time: 30 to 35 minutes

Nutrient Analysis: 1 slice (topping only)
Exchanges: 1 vegetable, 1 lean meat, 1 fat
Carbohydrate Choices: 0

Calories: 128   Protein: 11g   Carbohydrates: 4g
Fat: 8g   Cholesterol: 53mg   Sodium: 208mg
Calcium: 248mg

HEART-HEALTHY PIZZA TOPPING

Makes 1 (12-inch) pizza; 8 slices

1   (6-ounce) can low-sodium
      tomato paste
1/4 cup water
1/2 teaspoon dried basil, crushed
1/2 teaspoon dried oregano, crushed
1/2 teaspoon garlic powder
1/2 teaspoon dried crushed red
      peppers
3/4 cup chopped green pepper
3/4 cup sliced fresh mushrooms
1/2 cup chopped or sliced onions
      Other vegetables in season as
      desired
8   ounces shredded part-skim
      mozzarella cheese (2 cups)

Mix thoroughly tomato paste, water, basil, oregano, garlic powder and red peppers in a bowl. Spread evenly over an unbaked 12" pizza crust.

Layer green pepper, mushrooms, onions and other vegetables, if desired, evenly over sauce. Cover with shredded cheese. Bake.

Oven: 400°
Time: 20 minutes or until cheese is melted and crust lightly browned.

Nutrient Analysis: 1 slice (topping only)   Calories: 99   Protein: 8g   Carbohydrates: 7g
Exchanges: 1 vegetable, 1 medium-fat meat   Fat: 5g   Cholesterol: 16mg   Sodium: 152mg
Carbohydrate Choices: 1/2   Dietary Fiber: 1g   Calcium: 194mg

HAM HEALTHWICHES

An attractive, colorful choice for brunches or luncheons.

Makes 4 open-face sandwiches; 4 servings

1	(10-ounce) package frozen chopped broccoli
1/2	cup chopped celery
1/4	cup chopped green pepper
1/4	cup chopped onion
1	hard-cooked egg, chopped
1/8	teaspoon pepper
1/2	package ranch-style dressing mix
1	cup plain low-fat yogurt
4	ounces extra-lean ham, thinly sliced in 8 slices
1	tomato, cut into 8 slices
4	slices multigrain, low-calorie, high fiber bread

Combine broccoli, celery, green pepper, onion, egg and pepper. Combine dressing mix and yogurt.

Toss vegetables with 1/2 cup dressing. Chill remaining dressing.

Place 3 rounded tablespoons of vegetable mixture on each ham slice and roll up.

Arrange 2 tomato slices on each bread slice. Top with 2 ham rolls and 1 tablespoon chilled dressing.

Nutrient Analysis: 1 sandwich
Exchanges: 1 1/2 starch, 2 very lean meat
Carbohydrate Choices: 1 1/2

Calories: 173   Protein: 15 g   Carbohydrates: 22 g
Fat: 4 g   Cholesterol: 67 mg   Sodium: 569 mg
Dietary Fiber: 6 g   Calcium: 155 mg   Omega-3: 0.12 g

SEASONINGS

*Condiments are like old friends—
highly thought of , but often taken
for granted.*

Marilyn Kaytor

SEASONINGS

Also See:

SEASONINGS

We eat too much salt.

Our dependence on salt as a seasoning is not healthful. According to the guidelines for a more healthful eating pattern, we need to reduce our daily sodium intake. Fortunately, our taste for salt is acquired and it is possible to cut back on salt without feeling the pinch. In its place, the wonderful subtleties of spices and herbs remain to be discovered. The natural flavors of foods can often be masked by over-salting. These flavors can be enhanced by spices and herbs, which add a whole new zest to food.

Reduce salt gradually while using more herbs and spices.

Since our appetite for salt is acquired, it is important to reduce the salt intake gradually allowing our taste buds to adapt to new, more subtle flavors. Here are some tips to help reduce our dependence on salt:

Tips to reduce salt intake

- Replace the salt shaker at the table with a spice shaker containing one of the many seasonings from this section. It is estimated that as much as a third of the salt we eat comes from adding salt to foods.

- Begin to reduce foods that are noticeably salty, such as bacon, luncheon meats, hot dogs, sausage, potato chips, snack crackers, sauerkraut, olives and salted nuts. An extra bonus in reducing use of these foods is that you will also reduce the amount of fat in your diet.

- In preparing main dishes and vegetables, consider salt's actual contribution. Highly seasoned dishes generally do not need salt and the natural flavors of fresh, quickly cooked foods can stand alone or be enhanced with a little lemon juice. Be creative with spices, herbs and other flavorings.

- Become a sodium-wise food buyer. Nearly all processed foods are much higher in sodium than fresh foods. Use the Nutrition Facts panel and select foods with a low %DV value. Use Table 13 on page 44 to help you recognize sodium (and salt) contained in the foods you are purchasing.

Due to the increased consumer demand for lower sodium products, many manufacturers are offering sodium-reduced alternatives in several types of packaged or canned foods, sauces, condiments and beverages.

*Experiment
with herbs
and spices.*

Various blends of herbs and spices complementing beef, pork, veal and other meats and certain vegetables are provided in the **MEAT** and **VEGETABLE** sections. This section of **Cooking À La Heart** contains additional spice and herb blends. We encourage you to experiment with herbs and spices to determine which ones you like best. Begin using them in a few dishes and gradually increase, allowing your palate to be the best guide.

Fresh herbs add a particularly pleasing taste to foods and as a result their use has increased dramatically. They have become widely available in markets as well as in home gardens, where it has been found that they can be easily grown. Better yet, herbs will flourish in pots inside the home and provide attractive greenery in many a kitchen window. Either raised or purchased, herbs can be successfully dried for later use.

Use fresh herbs when they are available and dried or ground herbs when they're not. The rule of thumb for substituting one for another is:

*Rule of thumb
for converting
fresh herb to dried
or powdered:*

> For every 1 Tablespoon of fresh herb, substitute 1 teaspoon dried herb or 1/3 teaspoon powdered herb.

Extended cooking diminishes the flavor of spices and herbs. They are generally added to meats, soups and stews about 45 minutes before serving and allowed to cook with the food. Spices and herbs should be added to vegetables during the last few minutes of cooking or just before serving.

The flavor in herbs and spices comes from their oils which will evaporate with time and exposure to light and/or heat. Store herbs and spices in tightly covered containers away from heat and light, keeping in mind they will not retain their freshness indefinitely. A few kernels of raw rice added to spice containers help to absorb moisture and prevent caking. It is wise to label and date your spice containers.

DESSERT SPICE BLEND

A spicy concoction to use in cakes and cookies or to sprinkle on toast.

Makes about 1/3 cup

2   teaspoons ground cinnamon
2   teaspoons ground nutmeg
1   teaspoon ground ginger
1/2 teaspoon ground allspice
1/2 teaspoon ground cardamom
1/4 teaspoon ground cloves

Mix ingredients together and store in shaker bottle for toast. Substitute mixture for spices in your favorite cookie or cake recipe.

SEASONING BLEND #1

A good "all-purpose" seasoning for meats and vegetables. Also try on broiled tomatoes.

Makes about 1/2 cup

2   tablespoons dry mustard
2   tablespoons onion powder
2   tablespoons paprika
2   teaspoons garlic powder
2-3 teaspoons white pepper
2   teaspoons ground thyme
1/2 teaspoon ground basil

Blend thoroughly. Use in shaker on table. Store extra in tightly covered glass container.

SEASONING BLEND #2

An "all-purpose" seasoning guaranteed to pep up chicken, hamburger and tomato based dishes.

Makes about 3/4 cup

4   tablespoons onion powder
4   tablespoons parsley flakes,
      crushed
2   tablespoons garlic powder
2   tablespoons paprika
1   tablespoon ground basil

Blend thoroughly. Use in shaker on table. Store extra in tightly covered glass container.

SEASONING BLEND #3

A blend for meats, poultry and vegetables.

Makes about 1/2 cup

3　tablespoons onion powder
3　tablespoons dry mustard
3　tablespoons paprika
4　teaspoons white pepper

Blend thoroughly. Use in shaker on table. Store extra in tightly covered glass container.

SEASONING BLEND #4

Sprinkle this aromatic blend on grilled meats.

Makes about 1/2 cup

2　tablespoons garlic powder
1　tablespoon ground basil
1　tablespoon ground anise seed
1　tablespoon ground oregano
1　tablespoon powdered lemon rind

Blend thoroughly. Store in tightly covered glass container.

SEASONING BLEND #5

The cumin in this blend gives a peppery hotness associated with Far Eastern and Mexican dishes.

Makes about 1/2 cup

2　tablespoons dried basil
4　teaspoons dried savory
4　teaspoons celery seed
4　teaspoons ground cumin
4　teaspoons dried sage
4　teaspoons dried marjoram
2　teaspoons dried lemon thyme

Combine. Use mortar and pestle, food processor or blender to reduce to powder. Use in shaker on table. Store extra in tightly covered glass bottle.

SEASONING BLEND #6

An excellent seasoning for pork. Sprinkle on roasts or add to hamburger patties allowing time for the seasoning to permeate the meat.

Makes about 3/4 cup

- 4 tablespoons citric acid
- 2 tablespoons parsley flakes, crushed
- 2 tablespoons black pepper
- 2 tablespoons paprika
- 1 tablespoon garlic powder
- 1 tablespoon ground ginger
- 1 tablespoon onion powder

Mix together. Use in shaker on table. Store extra in tightly covered glass container.

SEASONING BLEND #7

Sprinkle this aromatic blend on grilled meats.

Makes about 3/4 cup

- 1 teaspoon chili powder
- 2 teaspoons ground oregano
- 1 tablespoon garlic powder
- 2 teaspoons black pepper
- 6 tablespoons onion powder
- 3 tablespoons paprika
- 1 tablespoon poultry seasoning

Blend thoroughly. Use in shaker on table. Store extra in tightly covered glass container.

ITALIAN SEASONING BLEND

Try this in your favorite pasta sauce or in Italian meat balls.

Makes about 1/2 cup

- 4 tablespoons dried parsley, crushed
- 4 teaspoons dried minced onion
- 1 teaspoon ground oregano
- 2 teaspoons dried basil, crushed
- 1 teaspoon ground thyme or marjoram
- 2 teaspoons celery seed
- 1 teaspoon garlic powder
- 1/4 teaspoon black pepper

Blend thoroughly. Use in shaker on table. Store extra in tightly covered glass bottle.

HOMEMADE CURRY POWDER

Curry-lovers—it's worth the effort to make your own!

Makes about 1 cup

- 1 tablespoon ground fenugreek seeds
- 3 tablespoons ground turmeric
- 4 tablespoons ground coriander
- 2 tablespoons ground cumin
- 1 tablespoon ground black pepper
- 1 tablespoon ground ginger
- 2 teaspoons ground cardamom
- 2 teaspoons ground nutmeg
- 2 teaspoons ground cinnamon
- 2 teaspoons cayenne or Spanish paprika
- 1 teaspoon ground cloves
- 1 teaspoon dry mustard

Mix all seasonings together and put through a fine sieve. Store in an airtight container.

SHAKE AND MAKE

Use as a crispy coating for fish, poultry, meats and vegetables.

Makes about 2/3 cup, enough for one chicken or several fish fillets.

2/3 cup nonfat dry milk powder
1/2 teaspoon pepper
1/2 teaspoon dry mustard
 2   teaspoons paprika
 2   teaspoons low-sodium, chicken-
     flavored bouillon granules
1/2 teaspoon poultry seasoning

Mix all ingredients thoroughly. Moisten meat slightly and shake in mixture. (If using chicken, remove the skin first.)

Bake according to recipe.

FRUIT DESSERTS & MORE

Winter or summer, I think the best dessert in the world, after no matter how plain or elaborate a meal, is what is at its peak of ripening from the fields and orchards.

M.F.K. Fisher

FRUITS & FRUIT DESSERTS

Prepare desserts with less fat, sugar and calories.

Desserts are an American institution. To insist that we give up sweets to attain a healthy diet would be an unattainable goal. However, it is possible to cater to the sweet tooth without creating an upwardly mobile bathroom scale. It is also possible to prepare desserts that are delicious and nutritionally rich without excess fat, sugar, and calories.

Our guidelines in **Chapter 1** discuss maintaining desirable body weight, avoiding too much fat and limiting nutritionally-empty calories. The recipes in **FRUITS & FRUIT DESSERTS** feature fruits that are low in fat and contain natural sugar. Cakes and pies are included in this section because fruits or vegetables are basic ingredients in the recipes.

Fruit Desserts

A little extra-special preparation (BAKED PEARS or BERRIES 'N CANNOLI CREAM) or an interesting, new combination, such as CHESNUT FRUIT PUDDING, transforms ordinary fruit into extraordinary treats. Combinations of several different fruits make a simple and satisfying dessert.

Cakes

Cakes and pies contain fruits or vegetables as basic ingredients.

Classic cakes and crisps containing fruits or vegetables have the added bonus of supplying fiber. The two torte recipes are delicious when topped with your favorite fresh or frozen fruit.

Pies

Filling and crust recipes are printed separately to enable you to use these recipes in a variety of combinations. In matching crust and filling, take into account the fat and calorie content of both. A single pastry crust contains 140 to 160 calories and 7.5 grams of fat per slice. Adding a top crust adds another 80 to 100 calories and 6 grams of fat. Crumb crusts can be prepared with less fat than traditional pastry crusts and are somewhat lower in fat and calories. To reduce fat and calories still further, serve the fillings as crustless pies, chiffons and fruit desserts.

COOKIES, BARS, PUDDINGS & TOPPINGS

Curb the desire for sweetness by gradually reducing sugar intake.

We have modified traditional recipes for cookies, bars, puddings and toppings by reducing the sugar, limiting total fat and using unsaturated fat when needed. The desire for sweets can be curbed by gradually reducing sugar intake. You will find that reducing the sugar in most recipes by one-third to one-half and substituting unsaturated fat for shortening will affect neither the taste nor the texture of your product. Follow the guidelines given in the *Recipe Modification Guidelines* in **Chapter 2**. Gradually, you will find that you prefer less sugary sweets.

Cookies & Bars

Delicious and nutritionally sound treats will appeal to family and guests alike. Although our cookies and bars contain less fat, sugar and sodium than commercial or traditional home-baked varieties, cookie monsters should remember that bite for bite, even healthful cookies are relatively high in fat and sugar.

Puddings

Cooking À La Heart puddings are tastier and more filling than commercial boxed pudding mixes.

The CHOCOLATE MOUSSE will satisfy any chocoholic! The RICE and VANILLA PUDDINGS are tasty, streamlined versions of old favorites and the CRANBERRY STEAMED PUDDING lacks none of the taste but a lot of the calories, fat and sodium of its ancestors.

Sauces

Rich sauces are often the culprits in turning an otherwise healthful dish into a nutritional disaster. Our CARAMEL, HONEY FUDGE and LEMON SAUCE recipes fulfill that anticipated richness without the added fat, making them all low calorie.

HOT CITRUS FRUIT COMPOTE

Delightful for a special brunch. Notching the edges of the grapefruit shells adds a festive touch.

Makes 6 filled grapefruit halves; 6 servings

3	medium grapefruit
2	medium oranges
1/3	cup honey
1	tablespoon tub margarine, melted
1/8	teaspoon curry powder
1/2	cup plumped raisins* or 1/2 cup chopped unsalted mixed nuts
	Fresh mint leaves (optional)

* To plump raisins: bring raisins to a boil in 1 cup water. Let stand 2 minutes. Drain before using.

Cut grapefruit in half; remove sections and reserve. Remove and discard membrane from grapefruit shells; set shells aside. Peel and section oranges.

Mix honey, margarine and curry powder in a medium bowl. Fold in grapefruit, orange sections, and raisins or nuts. Spoon fruit mixture into grapefruit shells and place in shallow baking dish. Bake. Serve warm, garnished with fresh mint leaves if desired.

Oven: 450°
Time: 15 minutes or until hot

Nutrient Analysis: 1 filled grapefruit half
Exchanges: 3 fruit
Carbohydrate Choices: 3

Calories: 174   Protein: 2g   Carbohydrates: 41g
Fat: 2g   Cholesterol: 0mg   Sodium: 19mg
Dietary Fiber: 4g

CURRIED FRUIT

Serve as a dessert, a brunch dish or as accompaniment with meat or poultry.

1	cup dried plums
1 1/2	cups dried apricots
1	(29-ounce) can water-packed peaches
1	(29-ounce) can water-packed pears
1	(29-ounce) can juice-packed pineapple
1	cup water-packed sweet cherries

SAUCE:

1/2	cup boiling water
1/4	cup tub margarine
1/4	cup brown sugar (or equivalent no-calorie sweetener)
1-2	teaspoons curry powder

Makes 12 cups; 24 servings

Combine fruits and their juices and soak overnight in a large bowl. Drain fruit and arrange in a large ovenproof glass baking dish.

Heat water, margarine, sugar and curry powder in a small saucepan until margarine is melted and sugar is dissolved. Pour over fruit. Bake. Serve hot.

Oven: 350°
Time: 60 minutes

Nutrient Analysis: 1/2 cup
Exchanges: 1 1/2 fruit
Carbohydrate Choices:
  sauce made with brown sugar 1 1/2
  sauce made with no-calorie sweetener 1

Calories: 102   Protein: 1g   Carbohydrates: 21g
Fat: 2g   Cholesterol: 0mg   Sodium: 20mg
Dietary Fiber: 2g

CHESTNUT FRUIT PUDDING

A tasty accompaniment with a pasta casserole or meat dish.

Makes 6 cups; 12 servings

1 cup dried apricots
1 cup water
1 (15.5-ounce) can pineapple chunks in natural juices
1 cup liquid (reserved pineapple juice and apricot juice plus water to equal 1 cup)
1 teaspoon tub margarine
1/4 cup sliced water chestnuts
4 teaspoons cornstarch
1/4 cup frozen orange juice concentrate
1 small cinnamon stick
Dash ginger
3/4 teaspoon lemon rind
2 teaspoons lemon juice

Soak dried apricots in water until soft, about an hour. Drain the apricots and pineapple, reserving the juice. Place fruit in a bowl. Add water to reserved juice to equal 1 cup.

Heat margarine in a small skillet and sauté the drained water chestnuts.

Dissolve cornstarch in 1/4 cup of the juice and water in a small saucepan. Add the remaining 3/4 cup liquid, orange juice concentrate, cinnamon stick, ginger and lemon rind. Heat and stir over medium heat until clear and thickened, 5 to 10 minutes. Remove the cinnamon stick. Add the lemon juice and sautéd water chestnuts. Pour over fruit and stir gently. Chill before serving.

Nutrient Analysis: 1/2 cup
Exchanges: 1 starch
Carbohydrate Choices: 1

Calories: 74   Protein: 1g   Carbohydrates: 17g
Fat: 0g   Cholesterol: 0mg   Sodium: 7mg
Dietary Fiber: 1g

PEAR & GRAPEFRUIT TOSS WITH MINT

A hint of mint for a fresh taste.

Makes 8 cups; 16 servings

2 grapefruit, peeled and sectioned
4 fresh pears, peeled and cut in
   wedges
1 (8.75-ounce) can apricot halves,
   drained
1 cup seedless grapes

GRAPEFRUIT MINT DRESSING:

1 (6-ounce) container plain low-fat
   yogurt
2 tablespoons honey
1 tablespoon fresh grapefruit rind,
   grated
1 tablespoon grapefruit juice,
   reserved from sections
2 tablespoons chopped fresh mint
   leaves, or 1 teaspoon dried mint
   leaves, crushed

Combine grapefruit, pears, apricot halves and grapes in a medium bowl. Cover and chill.

Combine yogurt, honey, grapefruit rind, grapefruit juice and mint in a small bowl. Mix well. Cover and chill.

To serve, arrange the fruit in individual serving bowls. Serve the mint dressing on the side.

Nutrient Analysis: 1/2 cup
Exchanges: 1 fruit
Carbohydrate Choices: 1

Calories: 60   Protein: 1g   Carbohydrates: 15g
Fat: 0g   Cholesterol: 1mg   Sodium: 10mg
Dietary Fiber: 2g

APPLESAUCE

Makes about 8 cups; 16 servings

6-8 large Granny Smith apples
      (3 1/2 pounds)
      Juice and rind of 1 lemon
1/2 teaspoon cinnamon
1/2 cup sugar (or equivalent
      no-calorie sweetener), sweeten
      to taste
1/2 teaspoon vanilla

Wash and quarter apples. Core and halve the quarters but do not peel. Place apples in heavy pan along with juice and rind of the lemon, cinnamon and sugar. Cover pan and set over moderately low heat. Apples will slowly soften and render their juices. Stir and mash frequently until tender throughout (about 30 minutes).

Puree through a vegetable mill or sieve. Return to pan: simmer, stirring for a few minutes, adding more sugar or sweetener if necessary. The applesauce should be thick enough to hold its shape in spoon. Stir in vanilla.

Nutrient Analysis: 1/2 cup
Exchanges: 1 fruit
Carbohydrate Choices: made with sugar`1
*   made with no-calorie sweetener 1/2*

Calories: 52   Protein: 0g   Carbohydrates: 14g
Fat: 0g   Cholesterol: 0mg   Sodium: 1mg
Dietary Fiber: 1g

FRUIT TOPPING

A delicious topping for pancakes or waffles with only 4 calories a tablespoon as compared with 60 calories a tablespoon in commercial syrup.

Makes about 2 cups; 8 servings

2 cups unsweetened fresh or frozen
      fruit: strawberries, raspberries,
      peaches, etc.
2 teaspoons frozen apple juice
      concentrate

Process 1 cup of fruit and the apple juice concentrate in a blender or food-processor until smooth. Cut remaining cup of fruit into small pieces. Pour the sauce over the cut fruit. Spoon over pancakes or waffles.

Nutrient Analysis: 1/4 cup
Exchanges: free
Carbohydrate Choices: 0

Calories: 16   Protein: 0g   Carbohydrates: 4g
Fat: 0g   Cholesterol: 0mg   Sodium: 0mg
Dietary Fiber: 1g

BAKED APPLES

Makes 4 baked apples; 4 servings

4	medium-sized baking apples
1/2	teaspoon grated orange rind
3/4	cup unsweetened orange juice
1	tablespoon raisins or currants
1	teaspoon cinnamon
1/2	teaspoon allspice

Wash and core apples. Make several slits on upper portion of apples. Place in shallow baking dish.

Mix orange rind, orange juice, raisins, cinnamon and allspice in a small saucepan. Bring to a boil; reduce heat and simmer for 5 minutes. Pour sauce over apples and cover with aluminum foil. Bake until apples are tender, basting apples 3 times during baking. Serve warm or chilled.

Oven: 350°
Time: 45 minutes

Nutrient Analysis: 1 baked apple
Exchanges: 2 fruit
Carbohydrate Choices: 2

Calories: 111   Protein: 0 g   Carbohydrates: 28 g
Fat: 1 g   Cholesterol: 0 mg   Sodium: 5 mg
Dietary Fiber: 4 g

BERRIES 'N CANNOLI CREAM

Makes 3 cups; 6 servings

1	pint sliced fresh strawberries, blueberries, or raspberries
2	teaspoons sugar
1	(12-ounce) container low-fat cottage cheese
1/3	cup powdered sugar
1	teaspoon vanilla
1 1/2	tablespoons grated orange rind
1/2	square (1/2 ounce) semisweet chocolate, grated, for garnish

Toss berries with sugar in a small bowl; set aside.

Whip cottage cheese in blender until fluffy. Add powdered sugar and vanilla and whip until smooth and light. Stir in orange rind.

Divide berries among 6 dessert dishes. Top with cheese mixture and garnish with grated chocolate.

Nutrient Analysis: 1/2 cup
Exchanges: 1 fruit, 1 very lean meat
Carbohydrate Choices: 1

Calories: 99   Protein: 8 g   Carbohydrates: 15 g
Fat: 1 g   Cholesterol: 2 mg   Sodium: 231 mg
Dietary Fiber: 1 g

FRUIT FILLED ORANGE

This colorful and refreshing recipe was a Grand Prize Winner in the Heart's Delight Recipe Contest. For a salad, substitute CELERY SEED DRESSING, (page 156) for HONEYBERRY GLAZE.

Makes 8 stuffed orange halves; 8 servings

4 large oranges
1 medium banana, peeled and
     sliced
4 fresh plums, pitted and sliced or
     1 grapefruit, sectioned
1 cup seedless green grapes

HONEYBERRY GLAZE:

1/2 cup jellied cranberry sauce
2 tablespoons honey
1 tablespoon orange juice
     Fresh mint sprigs (optional)

Cut oranges in half. Remove orange sections and combine with banana, plums or grapefruit and grapes. Refill orange with the fruit mixture.

Beat cranberry sauce until smooth. Stir in honey and orange juice and pour over fruit. Garnish with fresh mint sprigs if desired.

Nutrient Analysis: 1 stuffed orange half   Calories: 161   Protein: 2g   Carbohydrates: 42g
Exchanges: 2 1/2 fruit   Fat: 0g   Cholesterol: 0mg   Sodium: 6mg
Carbohydrate Choices: 2 1/2   Dietary Fiber: 6g

SPARKLING FRUIT

A Grand Prize Winner (Elementary Division) Heart's Delight Recipe Contest.

Makes 12 cups; 12 servings

3 medium peaches
2 cups sliced strawberries
2 cups blueberries
2 cups melon balls
3 medium bananas
1 (25.6-ounce) bottle pink
     sparkling catawba grape juice,
     chilled

Slice peaches into bowl. Top peach slices with strawberries, blueberries and melon balls. Cover and refrigerate. Just before serving, slice bananas into fruit mixture. Pour chilled catawba over fruit.

Nutrient Analysis: 1 cup   Calories: 85   Protein: 1g   Carbohydrates: 21g
Exchanges: 1 1/2 fruit   Fat: 0g   Cholesterol: 0mg   Sodium: 4mg
Carbohydrate Choices: 1 1/2   Dietary Fiber: 3g

BAKED GLAZED PEARS

An elegant dessert.

Makes 8 glazed pears; 8 servings

8	fresh small pears, firm and slightly underripe
	Juice of 1/2 lemon
	Water to cover pears
1/2	cup sugar
1	stick cinnamon
2	whole cloves
2	strips lemon peel
1 1/2	cups Port wine
2/3	cup WHIPPED TOPPING, *(page 410)*
1	tablespoon Kirsch (optional)

Peel pears, but leave on stems. Place them in a bowl containing the lemon juice, plus enough water to cover.

In a saucepan large enough to hold the pears upright, combine 2/3 cup lemon water in which pears are soaking, sugar, cinnamon, cloves and lemon peel. Bring to a boil, stirring to dissolve sugar.

Add pears and simmer, covered, for 15 minutes. Add all but 1/4 cup of the wine and continue simmering, covered, until pears are tender. With a slotted spoon, carefully transfer pears to serving dishes.

At a rapid boil, reduce liquid to the consistency of a light syrup. Stir in remaining wine. Spoon syrup over pears several times to glaze them. Allow to cool, then chill thoroughly.

Serve with WHIPPED TOPPING flavored with Kirsch, if desired.

Nutrient Analysis: 1 glazed pear
Exchanges: 1 starch, 1 1/2 fruit
Carbohydrate Choices: 2 1/2

Calories: 153   Protein: 1g   Carbohydrates: 36g
Fat: 1g   Cholesterol: 0mg   Sodium: 10mg
Dietary Fiber: 3g

NORWEGIAN FRUIT SOUP

For a meat accompaniment resembling chutney, omit the raspberries.

Makes 10 cups; 20 servings

1 cup dried plums, cut into quarters
1 cup raisins
1 cup peeled, chopped apple
1 tablespoon grated orange rind
1 orange, cut up
4 cups water
1 tablespoon lemon juice
1 stick cinnamon
1/4 teaspoon salt
2 tablespoons quick-cooking tapioca
1 (10-ounce) package frozen raspberries

Combine plums, raisins, apple, orange rind, orange, water, lemon juice, cinnamon and salt in a large saucepan. Bring to a boil, reduce heat, cover and simmer for 1 hour.

Sprinkle tapioca over mixture stirring to avoid lumping. Cook another 15 minutes. Add frozen raspberries and stir occasionally until they are thawed. Serve either hot or cold in bowls.

Nutrient Analysis: 1/2 cup
Exchanges: 1 starch
Carbohydrate Choices: 1

Calories: 73   Protein: 1g   Carbohydrates: 18g
Fat: 0g   Cholesterol: 0mg   Sodium: 32mg
Dietary Fiber: 2g

STRAWBERRY PINEAPPLE FROZEN YOGURT

Use this recipe with any fresh fruit (except pineapple and kiwi fruit) as well as with all fruits canned in fruit juices. For a refreshing molded salad, serve squares on lettuce leaves.

Makes 4 cups; 8 servings

1	**tablespoon unflavored gelatin (1 envelope)**
1/4	**cup cold water**
1/2	**cup sugar**
2	**cups plain low-fat yogurt**
1	**cup fresh strawberries, mashed**
1	**cup crushed pineapple, drained**

Sprinkle gelatin over water in a small saucepan. Let stand 5 minutes. Heat gelatin over low heat until dissolved. Add sugar and stir until dissolved. Let cool.

Stir in yogurt. Refrigerate in shallow dish until thickened (about 45 minutes).

Add strawberries and pineapple and whip until light and fluffy (about 2 minutes with electric mixer). Pour into freezer tray (without dividers) or cupcake papers and freeze until firm (about 2 hours).

Let stand at room temperature about 10 minutes before serving.

Nutrient Analysis: 1/2 cup
Exchanges: 1 fruit, 1/2 skim milk
Carbohydrate Choices: 1 1/2

Calories: 114	Protein: 4g	Carbohydrates: 23g
Fat: 1g	Cholesterol: 4mg	Sodium: 52mg
Dietary Fiber: 1g	Calcium: 103mg	

FROZEN FRUIT POPS

Fruit pops are a big favorite with kids.

BANANA POPS

1 banana
1 tablespoon toasted wheat germ
1 tablespoon crunchy peanut butter
    (optional)

Makes 2 pops; 2 servings

Peel and cut banana in half crosswise. Insert stick into end of fruit. Roll in wheat germ. Stand in jar or muffin tin and freeze. For a nutty treat, freeze banana for about an hour, roll in melted peanut butter and then in wheat germ. Stand in jar and freeze

PINEAPPLE POPS

1 pineapple wedge (1/8 pineapple)
1 tablespoon toasted wheat germ

Makes 1 pop; 1 serving

Peel, core and cut pineapple wedge in half crosswise. Insert stick into end of fruit. Roll in wheat germ. Stand in jar and freeze.

ORANGE YOGURT POPS

1 (6-ounce) can frozen orange
    juice concentrate
1 pint plain low-fat yogurt
2 teaspoons vanilla
    Honey to sweeten, if desired

Makes 6 pops; 6 servings

Beat orange juice concentrate, yogurt and vanilla together until well blended. Fill molds or paper cups and insert sticks.

Freeze 24 hours.

Nutrient Analysis: 1 popsicle	Banana	w/ Peanut Butter	Pineapple	Orange Yogurt
Exchanges:	1 fruit	1 fruit, 1 fat	1 fruit	1 fruit 1/2 skim milk
Carbohydrate Choices:	1	1	1	1 1/2
Calories:	68	115	56	110
Protein:	2g	4g	2g	6g
Carbohydrates:	16g	17g	11g	21g
Fat:	1g	5g	1g	1g
Cholesterol:	0mg	0mg	0mg	5mg
Sodium:	1mg	40mg	1mg	64mg
Dietary Fiber:	2g	2g	2g	0mg
Calcium:	5mg	5mg	7mg	145mg

RICE CRUST

A boon to pie lovers who can't eat wheat! Delicious when filled with fresh sliced strawberries, peaches or raspberries and VANILLA PUDDING, (page 421).

Makes 1 (9-inch) pie crust; 8 servings

1   cup cooked brown rice
         (or white rice)
1/2 teaspoon vanilla
1   egg white
1   teaspoon tub margarine

Mix together rice, vanilla, and egg white in a medium bowl with a fork.

Coat 9" pie pan with margarine. Spread rice mixture evenly over bottom and halfway up the side of pan. Do not leave any holes! Bake. Cool and fill. Garnish filling with berries if desired.

Oven: 350°
Time: 5 minutes

Nutrient Analysis: 1 slice
Exchanges: 1/2 starch
Carbohydrate Choices: 1/2

Calories: 33   Protein: 1 g   Carbohydrates: 6 g
Fat: 1 g   Cholesterol: 0 mg   Sodium: 12 mg

NUT CRUST

A light, crispy crust delicious filled with RASPBERRY CHIFFON, (page 402) or other fruit filling.

Makes 1 (9-inch) pie crust; 8 servings

1   cup all-purpose flour
1/3 cup tub margarine, softened
1/4 cup finely chopped walnuts or
         pecans
1/4 cup confectioners' sugar

Mix flour, margarine, nuts and sugar together to form a soft dough.

Press firmly and evenly against the bottom and sides of a 9" pie pan. Bake. Cool and fill.

Oven: 400°
Time: 12 to 15 minutes

Nutrient Analysis: 1 slice
Exchanges: 1 starch, 2 fat
Carbohydrate Choices: 1

Calories: 156   Protein: 2 g   Carbohydrates: 16 g
Fat: 10 g   Cholesterol: 0 mg   Sodium: 64 mg
Dietary Fiber: 1 g

GINGERSNAP CRUST

For an attractive, refreshing dessert, fill with a mixture of 1 pint each softened vanilla ice milk and your favorite sherbet. Freeze and top with fresh fruit.

Makes 1 (9-inch) pie crust; 8 servings

1/4   cup tub margarine, melted
1/4   cup sugar
22   gingersnaps, crushed (about 1 1/2 cups crumbs)

Mix margarine, sugar and gingersnap crumbs in a medium bowl.

Pat into a 9" pie pan. Bake. Cool and fill with favorite filling.

Oven: 350°
Time: 5 to 8 minutes

Nutrient Analysis: 1 slice
Exchanges: 1 starch, 1 1/2 fat
Carbohydrate Choices: 1

Calories: 148   Protein: 1g   Carbohydrates: 20g
Fat: 7g   Cholesterol: 0mg   Sodium: 163mg

CRUMB CRUSTS
(VANILLA, CHOCOLATE, GRAHAM CRACKER)

Makes 1 (9-inch) pie crust; 8 servings

1/4   cup tub margarine
1 1/2 cups crushed vanilla or chocolate wafers or graham crackers*

*30 vanilla wafers = 1 cup fine crumbs
15 graham crackers = 1 cup fine crumbs
20 chocolate wafers = 1 cup fine crumbs

Melt margarine and mix thoroughly with crumbs.

Pat into a 9" pie pan. Bake, cool and fill.

Oven: 375°
Time: 6 to 8 minutes

Nutrient Analysis: 1 slice
Exchanges: 1 starch, 1 1/2 fat
Carbohydrate Choices: 1

Calories: 149   Protein: 1g   Carbohydrates: 17g
Fat: 9g   Cholesterol: 2mg   Sodium: 119mg

PIE FILLINGS

Over half the calories and most of the fat in many pies is in the crust. Try "crustless" pies for a delicious low-calorie, low-fat dessert.

APPLE DESSERT OR PIE FILLING

As a pie filling, the APPLE DESSERT goes well in the VANILLA WAFER CRUST, (see preceding page).

Makes 1 (9-inch) pie filling; 8 servings

1	(6-ounce) can frozen apple juice
3/4	teaspoon cinnamon
1/4	teaspoon nutmeg
3	cups fresh apple slices
2	teaspoons cornstarch
1/4	cup cold water

Heat apple juice, cinnamon and nutmeg in a saucepan to simmering. Add apple slices and cook until crisp-tender (15 to 20 minutes). Remove the apple slices and arrange in pie pan or prebaked crust.

Cook until thickened, stirring constantly. Pour thickened apple juice over apple slices in pan or crust. Bake. Serve warm.

Oven: 375°
Time: 7 minutes

Nutrient Analysis: 1 slice
Exchanges: 1 starch
Carbohydrate Choices: 1

Calories: 74   Protein: 0g   Carbohydrates: 19g
Fat: 0g   Cholesterol: 0mg   Sodium: 7mg
Dietary Fiber: 1g

PUMPKIN CUSTARD OR PIE FILLING

Makes 1 (9-inch) pie filling; 8 servings

1/3	cup granulated sugar
1/3	cup brown sugar
3/4	teaspoon cinnamon
1/2	teaspoon ginger
1/2	teaspoon nutmeg
	Pinch of ground cloves
1 1/2	cups canned pumpkin
1	teaspoon vanilla
1 1/2	cups evaporated skim milk
1/2	teaspoon grated orange rind
3	egg whites, slightly beaten
1/4	cup brandy, optional

Combine the sugars, cinnamon, ginger, nutmeg and cloves in a mixing bowl. Stir in the pumpkin.

Add the vanilla, evaporated milk, orange rind and egg whites. Beat with an electric mixer until smooth. Fold in brandy.

Pour into 9" glass pie pan or 1 1/2-quart baking dish and bake.

For pie: Pour into 9" unbaked pie shell and bake.

Oven: 425° for 10 minutes. Reduce heat.
    325° for 45 minutes or until a knife inserted in the filling comes out clean.

Nutrient Analysis: 1 slice
Exchanges: 1 starch, 1/2 skim milk
Carbohydrate Choices: 1 1/2

Calories: 113   Protein: 5g   Carbohydrates: 24g
Fat: 0g   Cholesterol: 0mg   Sodium: 85mg
Dietary Fiber: 2g   Calcium: 133mg

RASPBERRY CHIFFON OR PIE FILLING

Light and airy. Spoon into stemmed glasses or fill NUT CRUST, (page 398) for a refreshing topper to any meal.

Makes 1 (9-inch) pie filling; 8 servings

1 1/4   cups (10-ounce package) sweetened frozen raspberries
1   tablespoon unflavored gelatin
1/2   cup water, room temperature
6   tablespoons sugar, divided
1   tablespoon all-purpose flour
3   tablespoons lemon juice, divided
1/3   cup ice water
1/3   cup nonfat dry milk powder

Thaw raspberries and drain, reserving the juice and saving 8 firm berries for garnish. Soften gelatin in water.

Combine 4 tablespoons of the sugar with the flour in a saucepan. Add reserved raspberry juice and softened gelatin. Stir and heat slowly until sugar is dissolved. Remove from heat and add 2 tablespoons of the lemon juice and the berries. Cool until thick and syrupy, but not set.

Chill the beaters of an electric mixer. In a chilled bowl, combine ice water and nonfat dry milk powder. Beat until soft peaks are formed (about 3 to 4 minutes). Add the remaining tablespoon of lemon juice and beat another 3 or 4 minutes until stiff. Fold in the remaining 2 tablespoons of sugar, blending well on low speed. Fold mixture into raspberry gelatin mixture.

Spoon into stemmed glasses or pour into pie shell and chill until firm. Garnish wih raspberries.

Nutrient Analysis: 1 slice   Calories: 74   Protein: 2g   Carbohydrates: 17g
Exchanges: 1 starch   Fat: 0g   Cholesterol: 1mg   Sodium: 17mg
Carbohydrate Choices: 1   Dietary Fiber: 2g

KEY LIME CHIFFON OR PIE FILLING

VANILLA or GRAHAM CRACKER CRUST, (page 399) is a good choice with KEY LIME.

Makes 1 (9-inch) pie filling; 8 servings

1	tablespoon lime-flavored gelatin
1/4	cup water
1/2	cup warm water
1	cup plus 2 tablespoons nonfat dry milk powder
1/2	cup sugar
1/2	cup fresh lime juice (about 4 large limes)
4	teaspoons powdered egg white*, equivalent to 2 egg whites.

* We suggest using a commercial pasteurized egg product to avoid the possibility of a foodborne illness from eating raw egg products.

Sprinkle the gelatin on the 1/4 cup water to soften.

Mix the milk powder with the 1/2 cup warm water. Heat to steaming (30 to 40 seconds on High in microwave). Stir in gelatin and sugar to dissolve. Cool until thickened.

Add lime juice to milk mixture, stirring.

Beat egg whites until stiff and fold into lime mixture.

Pour into pie pan or cooled baked crust and refrigerate until ready to serve.

Nutrient Analysis: 1 slice   Calories: 94   Protein: 4g   Carbohydrates: 20g
Exchanges: 1 starch   Fat: 0g   Cholesterol: 2mg   Sodium: 69mg
Carbohydrate Choices: 1   Calcium: 120g

PEACH YOGURT DESSERT OR PIE FILLING

Delicious as a "crustless" tart but, if you prefer, this filling goes well with the VANILLA WAFER or GINGERSNAP crumb crusts, (both found on page 399).

Makes 1 (9-inch) pie filling; 8 servings

1	(16-ounce) can sliced peaches, water or juice packed
2/3	cup peach liquid
2	tablespoons sugar
1	envelope unflavored gelatin
1/3	cup frozen orange juice concentrate
1/8	teaspoon almond extract
1/4	teaspoon vanilla
1	cup plain low-fat yogurt

Drain peaches, reserving juice. Combine 2/3 cup peach juice and sugar in a small saucepan. Sprinkle gelatin over top of liquid and allow to soften (about 5 minutes). Heat and stir until gelatin and sugar are thoroughly dissolved. Add orange juice concentrate, drained peaches, almond extract and vanilla.

Cool in refrigerator until slightly jelled, then fold in yogurt.

Pour into pie pan or cooled pie crust. Chill and serve.

Nutrient Analysis: 1 slice
Exchanges: 1 fruit
Carbohydrate Choices: 1

Calories: 65   *Protein: 3 g*   *Carbohydrates: 13 g*
Fat: 0 g   *Cholesterol: 2 mg*   *Sodium: 28 mg*
Dietary Fiber: 1 g

FRUIT PIZZA PIE

When using only one fruit such as strawberries, it is more attractive to mix glaze with fruit and then pour over filling.

Makes 1 (12-inch) pizza pie; 12 servings

Mix granola, margarine, flour and egg white in a food processor or bowl. Spread on 12" pizza pan. Bake. Cool.

Beat together cream cheese, vanilla, banana and sugar. Spread over cooled shell.

Cut the fruit in bite-sized pieces and arrange in an attractive pattern over filling.

Heat fruit juice, cornstarch and lemon juice to boiling. When thickened, remove from heat and cool. Spoon cooled glaze over fruit. Chill and serve.

Oven: 375°
Time: 20 minutes

CRUST:
- 1   cup granola
- 1/4   cup tub margarine
- 1 1/2   cups all-purpose flour
- 1   egg white

FILLING:
- 1   (8-ounce) package fat-free, plain cream cheese
- 1   teaspoon vanilla
- 1/2   very ripe banana
- 1/4   cup confectioners' sugar

FRUIT:
Melon, berries, pineapple. Be creative! Or use one fruit such as strawberries.

GLAZE:
- 1   cup fruit juice (orange, pineapple, apple)
- 2   tablespoons cornstarch
- 1   teaspoon lemon juice

Nutrient Analysis: 1 slice   Calories: 167   Protein: 5g   Carbohydrates: 27g
Exchanges: 1 starch, 1 fruit, 1 fat Fat: 5g   Cholesterol: 3mg   Sodium: 175mg
Carbohydrate Choices: 2   Dietary Fiber: 2g

APPLE CAKE

Warm and crumbly, this delicious cake is the perfect finish for a light meal.

Makes 9 x 9" baking pan ; 16 servings

2/3	cup vegetable oil
1/2	cup sugar
1	egg
1	teaspoon vanilla
1/2	teaspoon baking soda
1	teaspoon baking powder
1/2	teaspoon cinnamon
1 1/2	cups all-purpose flour
1/2	cup raisins
1 1/2	cups diced apples
2	tablespoons chopped pecans

Mix oil, sugar, egg, vanilla, baking soda, baking powder, cinnamon, flour, raisins and apples in a large bowl.

Pour into a nonstick-sprayed 9 x 9" pan. Sprinkle top with chopped pecans. Bake. Serve warm or cold.

Oven: 350°
Time: 30 minutes

Nutrient Analysis: 1 square
Exchanges: 1 1/2 fruit, 2 fat
Carbohydrate Choices: 1 1/2

Calories: 176   Protein: 2g   Carbohydrates: 21g
Fat: 10g   Cholesterol: 13mg   Sodium: 69mg
Dietary Fiber: 1g

SPICY PUMPKIN BARS

Makes 15 x 10" baking pan ; 48 servings

1	cup brown sugar
3	egg whites or 3/4 cup egg substitute
1	cup vegetable oil
1	(16-ounce) can pumpkin (2 cups)
1	cup all-purpose flour
1	cup whole wheat flour
2	teaspoons baking powder
2	teaspoons cinnamon
1	teaspoon baking soda
1/2	cup chopped raisins
1/2	cup chopped nuts

Combine brown sugar, egg whites or substitute, oil and pumpkin in a mixing bowl. Beat until light and fluffy. Combine flours, baking powder, cinnamon and soda. Stir chopped raisins and nuts into dry ingredients and add to pumpkin mixture. Stir thoroughly. Spread batter in an ungreased 15 x 10" jellyroll pan. Bake. When cool, cut into bars.

Oven: 350°
Time: 25 to 30 minutes

Nutrient Analysis: 1 bar
Exchanges: 1 fruit, 1 fat
Carbohydrate Choices: 1

Calories: 93   Protein: 1g   Carbohydrates: 11g
Fat: 6g   Cholesterol: 0mg   Sodium: 49mg
Dietary Fiber: 1g

RHUBARB CAKE

For added attraction, top with a dollop of sweetened MOCK CREAM CHEESE (page 82) or WHIPPED TOPPING (page 410).

Makes 13 x 9" baking pan; 24 servings

1 1/4   cups brown sugar
1/2   cup tub margarine
2   egg whites or 1 egg
1   teaspoon vanilla
1 1/2   cups all-purpose flour
1/2   cup whole wheat flour
1   cup buttermilk or sour skim milk*
1   teaspoon baking soda
2 1/2   cups rhubarb, cut into 1/2" pieces

TOPPING:

1/4   cup granulated sugar
2 1/2   teaspoons cinnamon
1/2   cup chopped walnuts (optional)

* To make sour milk, place 1 tablespoon lemon juice or vinegar in measuring cup and add milk to make 1 cup.

Cream brown sugar and margarine in a mixing bowl.

Add egg whites or egg and beat. Add vanilla, flours, buttermilk or sour milk, and baking soda. Beat until smooth.

Fold in rhubarb. Spread in a nonstick-sprayed 13 x 9" pan.

For Topping: Mix together sugar, cinnamon and walnuts. Sprinkle over the batter. Bake. Serve warm or cold.

Oven: 350°
Time: 35 to 40 minutes

Nutrient Analysis: 1 slice
Exchanges: 1 starch, 1 fat
Carbohydrate Choices: 1

Calories: 114   Protein: 2g   Carbohydrates: 18g
Fat: 4g   Cholesterol: 1mg   Sodium: 104mg
Dietary Fiber: 1g

CARROT CAKE

Deliciously moist and spicy.

Makes 13 x 9" baking pan; 24 servings

1	cup tub margarine
1 1/2	cups sugar
4	egg whites
1	(8-ounce) can crushed pineapple with juice
1	teaspoon vanilla
1 1/2	cups all-purpose flour
1/2	cup whole wheat flour
2	teaspoons cinnamon
2	teaspoons baking soda
3	cups grated carrots
1/2	cup chopped walnuts

Cream margarine and sugar in a mixing bowl. Beat in egg whites. Stir in pineapple and vanilla.

Sift together flours, cinnamon and baking soda. Stir into liquid ingredients and beat well. Fold in carrots and nuts.

Pour into a nonstick-sprayed 13 x 9" baking pan or Bundt pan. Bake.

Oven: 325°
Time: 60 minutes

Nutrient Analysis: 1 slice
Exchanges: 1 1/2 fruit, 2 fat
Carbohydrate Choices: 1 1/2

Calories: 182   Protein: 2g   Carbohydrates: 23g
Fat: 9g   Cholesterol: 0mg   Sodium: 184mg
Dietary Fiber: 1g

APPLE CRISP

Fragrant, bubbling, a fall delight!

Makes 13 x 9" baking pan; 12 servings

8   cups unpeeled, thinly sliced apples
    Juice of 1 lemon
1   teaspoon cinnamon
2   tablespoons whole wheat flour
    Water or apple juice to cover
        bottom of pan, about 1/2 cup

Mix together apples, lemon juice, cinnamon, and flour. Place apple mixture in a nonstick-sprayed 13 x 9" baking pan. Add juice or water to cover bottom only of pan.

TOPPING:

1   cup old-fashioned rolled oats, dry
1/3 cup toasted wheat germ
1/2 cup whole wheat flour
2   teaspoons cinnamon
1/2 cup brown sugar
1/2 cup tub margarine

Mix rolled oats, wheat germ, flour, cinnamon, brown sugar and margarine until crumbly. Sprinkle on top of apple mixture. Bake. Serve warm or cold with a dollop of WHIPPED TOPPING *(page 410)* and a sprinkle of cinnamon.

Oven: 375°
Time: 25 minutes

Nutrient Analysis: 1 serving
Exchanges: 2 fruit, 2 fat
Carbohydrate Choices: 2

Calories: 200   Protein: 3g   Carbohydrates: 30g
Fat: 9g   Cholesterol: 0mg   Sodium: 67mg
Dietary Fiber: 4g

WHIPPED TOPPING

This polyunsaturated substitute has a taste and consistency similar to whipped cream; however, it has no saturated or trans fat. Plan to use immediately as it does break down over time.

Makes 2 cups; 16 servings

2/3 cup evaporated skim milk
3 tablespoons sugar
1/2 teaspoon vanilla
1/4 teaspoon cream of tartar

In an ice cube tray in freezer, chill milk until slushy. Scrape milk into a chilled bowl and with chilled beaters, beat milk on high until fluffy.

Add sugar, vanilla and cream of tartar and beat until stiff. Serve as a topping for desserts or fruit.

Nutrient Analysis: 2 tablespoons
Exchanges: free
Carbohydrate Choices: 0

Calories: 18   Protein: 1g   Carbohydrates: 4g
Fat: 0g   Cholesterol: 0mg   Sodium: 13mg

MERINGUE TORTE WITH FRUIT

Makes 9" round cake pan; 8 servings

4 egg whites
3/4 cup sugar
1 cup low-sodium soda cracker
    crumbs (30 crackers)
1 teaspoon baking powder
1/2 cup chopped nuts (walnuts,
    pecans or almonds)
1/2 teaspoon almond extract

Beat egg whites with electric mixer until they hold stiff peaks. Add sugar gradually while continuing to beat.

Fold in cracker crumbs, baking powder, nuts, and almond extract. Spread in nonstick-sprayed 9" round cake pan (may double recipe and use 13 x 9" pan). Bake. Cool and top with fresh or frozen berries and WHIPPED TOPPING, *(see above).*

Oven: 325°
Time: 30 minutes

Nutrient Analysis: 1 slice
Exchanges: 1 starch, 1 fruit, 1 fat
Carbohydrate Choices: 2

Calories: 179   Protein: 4g   Carbohydrates: 28g
Fat: 6g   Cholesterol: 0mg   Sodium: 149mg
Dietary Fiber: 1g

NEW ZEALAND PAVLOVA

Melt-in-your mouth shell topped with your favorite fruit.

Makes 9" round cake pan; 8 servings

3   egg whites
1   cup sugar
1   teaspoon cornstarch
1   teaspoon vinegar
1   teaspoon vanilla

Beat egg whites in a large bowl until very stiff.

Mix together sugar and cornstarch and fold into egg whites. Fold in vinegar and vanilla.

Spoon onto a baking sheet covered with brown paper to form a mounded 9" circle about 2" high. Bake. Turn off oven and allow to cool in oven.

Invert on plate and remove paper. Top with fresh or frozen fruit (kiwi fruit, strawberries, raspberries, peaches, etc.) and WHIPPED TOPPING, *(page 410).*

Oven: 300°
Time: 50 to 60 minutes

Nutrient Analysis: 1 slice
Exchanges: 1 1/2 starch
Carbohydrate Choices: 1 1/2

Calories: 104   *Protein: 1g*   *Carbohydrates: 25g*
Fat: 0g   *Cholesterol: 0mg*   *Sodium: 21mg*

CHEWY OATMEAL COOKIES

A wheat-free recipe!

Makes 3 dozen cookies; 36 servings

2	cups quick-cooking rolled oats, dry
1	cup brown sugar
1/2	cup vegetable oil
2	egg whites
1/2	teaspoon almond extract
1/2	cup chopped dates
1/2	cup chopped walnuts

Stir together oats, sugar, and oil in a mixing bowl.

Beat egg whites until frothy and add to oat mixture. Stir in almond extract. Stir in dates and walnuts.

Drop by teaspoonfuls onto nonstick-sprayed baking sheet. Bake. Cool before removing from baking sheet.

Oven: 300°
Time: 12 minutes

Nutrient Analysis: 1 cookie
Exchanges: 1/2 starch, 1 fat
Carbohydrate Choices: 1/2

Calories: 78   Protein: 1g   Carbohydrates: 9g
Fat: 5g   Cholesterol: 0mg   Sodium: 5mg
Dietary Fiber: 1g

HEARTY HEART OATMEAL COOKIES

Makes 4 dozen cookies; 48 servings

3/4	cup tub margarine
1/2	cup brown sugar
1/2	cup granulated sugar
2	egg whites
1/4	cup water
1	teaspoon vanilla
1/2	cup whole wheat flour
1/2	cup all-purpose flour
1/2	teaspoon baking soda
1	cup raisins
3	cups old-fashioned rolled oats, dry

Cream margarine and sugar.

Add egg whites, water and vanilla and beat mixture until creamy.

Mix flours and baking soda together and beat into liquid mixture. Stir in raisins and rolled oats.

Drop by teaspoonfuls onto ungreased baking sheet. Bake.

Oven: 350°
Time: 12 to 15 minutes

Nutrient Analysis: 1 cookie
Exchanges: 1 starch
Carbohydrate Choices: 1

Calories: 78   Protein: 1g   Carbohydrates: 12g
Fat: 3g   Cholesterol: 0mg   Sodium: 41mg
Dietary Fiber: 1g

APPLESAUCE SPICE COOKIES

Deliciously soft, moist and chewy. Store in refrigerator to keep fresh.

Makes 6 dozen cookies; 72 servings

1	cup tub margarine
2	eggs, unbeaten
2	egg whites, unbeaten
2	cups unsweetened applesauce
1	tablespoon vanilla
1	cup whole wheat flour
1 1/2	cups all-purpose flour
2	teaspoons baking soda
1	teaspoon allspice
2	teaspoons nutmeg
1	teaspoon cloves
4	teaspoons cinnamon
2	cups quick-cooking rolled oats, dry
2	cups raisins

Mix together margarine, eggs and egg whites, applesauce and vanilla in a large mixing bowl.

Mix together flours, soda, allspice, nutmeg, cloves and cinnamon. Beat into applesauce mixture.

Stir in oats and raisins. Drop by teaspoonfuls onto nonstick-sprayed baking sheet. Bake.

Oven: 350°
Time: 12 to 15 minutes

Nutrient Analysis: 1 cookie
Exchanges: 1/2 starch, 1/2 fat
Carbohydrate Choices: 1/2

Calories: 65   Protein: 1g   Carbohydrates: 9g
Fat: 3g   Cholesterol: 6mg   Sodium: 60mg
Dietary Fiber: 1g

PECAN MERINGUES

A delicate, melt-in-your-mouth cookie.

Makes 3 dozen cookies; 36 servings

1	egg white
1	cup sugar
1	teaspoon vanilla
1	teaspoon flour
1	cup finely chopped pecans

Beat egg white in a medium mixing bowl until it forms soft peaks. Continue beating while gradually adding sugar. Add the vanilla.

Sprinkle the teaspoon flour over mixture, folding in both the flour and pecans.

Drop by small teaspoonfuls onto a baking sheet covered with brown paper. Bake and cool on sheet.

Oven: 275°
Time: 30 to 35 minutes

Nutrient Analysis: 1 cookie
Exchanges: 1/2 starch
Carbohydrate Choices: 1/2

Calories: 45   Protein: 0g   Carbohydrates: 6g
Fat: 2g   Cholesterol: 0mg   Sodium: 2mg

DATE-APPLE-NUT BARS

Makes 13 x 9" baking pan; 24 bars

1	(8-ounce) package pitted dates, chopped (1 1/4 cups)
3/4	cup water
1/2	cup unsweetened applesauce
1	cup sugar, divided
1/2	teaspoon cinnamon
1/2	cup chopped, unsalted nuts
1 1/2	cups all-purpose flour
1	cup quick-cooking rolled oats, dry
3/4	cup tub margarine

Combine dates, water, applesauce, 1/4 cup of the sugar, and cinnamon in a saucepan. Cook over medium heat, stirring occasionally, until thickened. Cool. Stir in nuts and set aside.

Combine flour, oats, and remaining sugar in a large mixing bowl. Cut in margarine until mixture resembles coarse crumbs.

Press half the crumb mixture firmly into a nonstick-sprayed 13 x 9" pan. Cover with date mixture, spreading evenly. Sprinkle remaining crumb mixture over date filling and press down firmly. Bake. Cool and cut into bars.

Oven: 350°
Time: 30 to 35 minutes

Nutrient Analysis: 1 bar
Exchanges: 1 1/2 starch, 1 fat
Carbohydrate Choices: 1 1/2

Calories: 164   Protein: 2g   Carbohydrates: 24g
Fat: 8g   Cholesterol: 0mg   Sodium: 48mg
Dietary Fiber: 1g

APRICOT SPICE BARS

Makes 13 x 9" baking pan; 24 bars

1/3   cup tub margarine
1/2   cup honey
  1   egg
  2   egg whites
1/2   teaspoon vanilla
1/2   cup all-purpose flour
1/2   cup whole wheat flour
1/2   teaspoon baking powder
  1   teaspoon cinnamon
1/2   teaspoon cloves
  1   cup chopped, dried apricots
        (about 6 ounces)

LEMON GLAZE:

1/2   cup powdered sugar
  1   tablespoon lemon juice

Cream margarine in a mixing bowl. Mix in honey. Add egg, egg whites, and vanilla; beat well.

Mix together flours, baking powder, cinnamon and cloves and stir into egg mixture. Stir in chopped apricots.

Spread evenly in nonstick-sprayed 13 x 9" baking pan. Bake. Cool slightly, then drizzle with lemon glaze. Cool and cut into bars.

Oven: 350°
Time: 20 to 25 minutes

Nutrient Analysis: 1 bar
Exchanges: 1 starch, 1/2 fat
Carbohydrate Choices: 1

Calories: 94   Protein: 1g   Carbohydrates: 16g
Fat: 3g   Cholesterol: 9mg   Sodium: 37mg
Dietary Fiber: 1g

FRUIT BARS

Makes 13 x 9" baking pan; 24 bars

1/2	cup chopped dates
1/2	cup chopped dried plums
3/4	cup raisins
1	cup water
1/2	cup tub margarine
1	egg
2	egg whites
1	teaspoon vanilla
3/4	cup all-purpose flour
1/4	cup whole wheat flour
1	teaspoon baking soda
1	teaspoon nutmeg
1	teaspoon cinnamon
1/2	cup broken walnuts

Bring dates, dried plums, raisins and water to a boil in a heavy saucepan. Reduce heat and simmer 5 minutes. Add margarine to hot mixture and let mixture cool.

Beat egg, egg whites and vanilla into cooled fruit mixture.

Mix together flours, soda, nutmeg, cinnamon and walnuts and stir into fruit mixture thoroughly.

Spread in nonstick-sprayed 13 x 9" pan. Bake.

Oven: 350°
Time: 30 to 35 minutes

Nutrient Analysis: 1 bar
Exchanges: 1 fruit, 1 fat
Carbohydrate Choices: 1

Calories: 107   Protein: 2g   Carbohydrates: 13g
Fat: 6g   Cholesterol: 9mg   Sodium: 92mg
Dietary Fiber: 1g

DATE BARS

A truly tasty and satisfying bar. Recipe is an old-time favorite used to feed hungry farmers. This bar was the most frequently requested.

Makes 13 x 9" baking pan; 36 bars

1	pound pitted dates, cut up
1	cup water
2	cups all-purpose flour
2 1/2	cups quick-cooking rolled oats, dry
3/4	cup brown sugar
1	cup tub margarine, melted
1	tablespoon hot water
1	teaspoon baking soda

Combine dates and water in a medium saucepan. Bring to a boil and simmer until thick, about 5 minutes. Cool.

Combine flour, rolled oats and brown sugar in a mixing bowl. Add melted margarine and mix until crumbly. Dissolve baking soda in 1 tablespoon water and add to crumb mixture and mix well.

Pat two-thirds of crumb mixture into a nonstick-sprayed 13 x 9" baking pan. Spread date mixture evenly over crust and sprinkle remaining third of crumb mixture on top of the date mixture. Bake. Cool and cut into bars.

Oven: 325°
Time: 45 minutes

Nutrient Analysis: 1 bar
Exchanges: 1 1/2 fruit, 1 fat
Carbohydrate Choices: 1 1/2

Calories: 138   Protein: 2g   Carbohydrates: 22g
Fat: 5g   Cholesterol: 0mg   Sodium: 79mg
Dietary Fiber: 2g

BROWNIES Á LA HEART

A traditional brownie with a moist, fudgey middle and a thin crackled crust on top!

1/3　cup canola oil
2　ounces pre-melted unsweetened
　　baking chocolate
1　cup sugar
1/2　cup egg substitute
　　(or 2 large eggs)
1/4　cup whole wheat flour
1/2　cup all-purpose flour
1/2　teaspoon baking powder
　　Pinch of salt
1/2　cup coarsely chopped walnuts
　　(optional)

Makes 9 x 9" baking pan; 16 brownies

Beat together oil, melted baking chocolate, sugar, and egg substitute in a large bowl using a wooden spoon. Set aside.

Sift together flours, baking powder and pinch of salt. Add flour mixture to the oil-chocolate mixture. Mix until completely blended. Batter may look lumpy. Fold walnuts in gently, if so desired.

Pour and spread the batter evenly in a nonstick-sprayed, 9-inch square baking pan. Bake for 30 minutes only; the crust will look dull (not shiny). Remove from oven, place on a rack and cool slightly in the pan. Cut into bars immediately.

Oven: 350°
Time: 30 minutes

Nutrient Analysis: 1 brownie　　　Calories: 137　　Protein: 2g　　Carbohydrates: 18g
Exchanges: 1 starch, 1 fat　　　Fat: 7g　　Cholesterol: 0mg　　Sodium: 45mg
Carbohydrate Choices: 1　　　Dietary Fiber: 1g　　Omega-3: 0.44g

HONEY MILK BALLS, UNBAKED

Quick, easy and inexpensive. Pre-schoolers enjoy making and eating these highly nutritious snacks. Roll in toasted sesame seeds or chopped nuts for an added taste treat.

Makes 2 dozen balls; 24 servings

1/2	cup honey
1/2	cup peanut butter
1	cup nonfat dry milk powder
1	cup quick-cooking rolled oats, dry or 1 1/2 cups graham cracker crumbs
1	teaspoon vanilla
1/4	cup toasted sesame seeds or chopped nuts

Combine honey, peanut butter, milk powder and oats or graham crumbs in a mixing bowl. Knead by hand until thoroughly blended.

Shape into small balls and roll in sesame seeds or nuts as desired.

Nutrient Analysis: 1 ball (with sesame seeds)   Calories: 86   Protein: 3g   Carbohydrates: 11g
Exchanges: 1 fruit, 1/2 fat   Fat: 4g   Cholesterol: 1mg   Sodium: 41mg
Carbohydrate Choices: 1   Dietary Fiber: 1g

BRAN BITES, UNBAKED

These nutty-flavored treats are a favorite with all kids, big and little! Flavor and texture are enhanced by aging 2 or 3 days in a refrigerated, tightly-covered container.

Makes 2 dozen balls; 24 servings

3	cups 40% bran flakes, crushed
1/2	cup toasted wheat germ
2/3	cup peanut butter
1/4	cup orange juice
2	tablespoons honey
1/2	cup raisins, chopped

Combine bran flakes, wheat germ, peanut butter, orange juice, honey and raisins in a large bowl. Mix well.

Shape and roll dough between palms to form balls. Chill. Store in refrigerator.

Nutrient Analysis: 1 ball   Calories: 88   Protein: 3g   Carbohydrates: 12g
Exchanges: 1 fruit, 1/2 fat   Fat: 4g   Cholesterol: 0mg   Sodium: 91mg
Carbohydrate Choices: 1   Dietary Fiber: 2g

CHOCOLATE MOUSSE

Delicious!

Makes 3 cups; 6 servings

1/4	cup egg substitute (equivalent to 1 egg)
1	envelope unflavored gelatin
1	tablespoon cold water
1	cup boiling water
1	teaspoon instant coffee
1/2	cup part-skim ricotta cheese
1/2	cup cold skim milk
3	tablespoons unsweetened cocoa
	Pinch salt
6	tablespoons sugar

Combine egg, gelatin and cold water in a blender or food processor. Blend until combined (about 10 seconds). Scrape mixture down and blend 10 seconds longer. Let the mixture stand about a minute or until gelatin softens. Add boiling water and blend until gelatin is dissolved (about 10 seconds).

Add coffee, ricotta cheese, milk, cocoa, salt and sugar. Blend until smooth (about 1 minute). Pour into six dessert glasses and chill until set, at least 2 hours.

Nutrient Analysis: 1/2 cup
Exchanges: 1 starch, 1/2 very lean meat
Carbohydrate Choices: 1

Calories: 98   Protein: 5g   Carbohydrates: 17g
Fat: 2g   Cholesterol: 9mg   Sodium: 66mg
Dietary Fiber: 1g

RICE PUDDING

Slow baking of the brown rice and brown sugar adds a fine carmelized quality.

Makes 4 cups; 8 servings

3/4	cup brown rice, uncooked
1	(12-ounce) can evaporated skim milk, plus water to equal 4 cups
3	tablespoons brown sugar
1/2	teaspoon cinnamon
1/4	teaspoon nutmeg.
1	teaspoon vanilla, optional
1/2	cup raisins

In a 2-quart, nonstick-sprayed, oven-proof dish, mix rice, milk, water, sugar, cinnamon, nutmeg, and vanilla, if desired.

Bake in a slow oven, stirring frequently. If skin forms on milk, skim off.

Stir in raisins during last half hour of baking time. Serve warm or cold.

Oven: 275°
Time: 2 1/2 hours

Nutrient Analysis: 1/2 cup
Exchanges: 2 starch
Carbohydrate Choices: 2

Calories: 146   Protein: 5g   Carbohydrates: 31g
Fat: 1g   Cholesterol: 0mg   Sodium: 64mg
Dietary Fiber: 1g   Calcium: 132mg

VANILLA PUDDING

This versatile pudding is tasty served plain, or in parfait glasses layered with fresh strawberries or other fruit, or as a pie filling.

Makes 4 cups; 8 servings

1/2	cup sugar (or equivalent no-calorie sweetener)
6	tablespoons cornstarch
4	cups skim milk
2	tablespoons tub margarine
1 1/2	teaspoons vanilla

Combine sugar and cornstarch in a medium saucepan and mix well. Add 1/2 cup milk and stir until the sugar and cornstarch are dissolved. Stir in remaining milk.

Bring to a boil over medium heat, stirring constantly. Boil one minute. Remove from heat and stir in margarine and vanilla. Chill.

VARIATIONS:

CHOCOLATE PUDDING

Decrease sugar to 1/3 cup and add 1 1/2 tablespoons of cocoa to sugar and cornstarch mixture.

BUTTERSCOTCH PUDDING

Substitute brown sugar for white sugar. Increase margarine to 1/4 cup.

Nutrient Analysis: 1/2 cup	*Vanilla*	*Chocolate*	*Butterscotch*
Exchanges:	1 starch, 1/2 skim milk 1/2 fat	1 starch, 1/2 skim milk, 1/2 fat	1 starch, 1/2 skim milk 1 fat
Carbohydrate Choices: made with sugar	1 1/2	1 1/2	1 1/2
made with no-calorie sweetener	1	1	1
Calories:	147	132	158
Protein:	5 g	5 g	5 g
Carbohydrates:	25 g	21 g	21 g
Fat:	3 g	3 g	6 g
Cholesterol:	3 mg	3 mg	3 mg
Sodium:	95 mg	95 mg	122 mg
Calcium:	125 mg	126 mg	133 mg

CRANBERRY STEAMED PUDDING

Makes 1 Bundt cake pan; 12 servings

2	cups fresh cranberries
1	cup all-purpose flour
3	tablespoons brown sugar
1/2	teaspoon baking powder
1/4	teaspoon baking soda
1/2	teaspoon cinnamon
1/4	teaspoon nutmeg
1/4	teaspoon allspice
1/8	teaspoon ground ginger
	Dash ground cloves
3	tablespoons vegetable oil
1/2	cup skim milk
3	tablespoons molasses
1/2	cup raisins or chopped dates
1/2	cup chopped nuts

Wash, drain and cut cranberries in half.

Mix flour, sugar, baking powder, baking soda, cinnamon, nutmeg, allspice, ginger and cloves in a bowl.

Add oil, milk and molasses and mix until dry ingredients are moistened. Stir in cranberries, raisins or dates, and nuts.

Spoon into well-oiled, 1-quart mold or casserole or 6-cup fluted tube pan. Cover with lid or foil. Place on a rack in a large steamer or kettle on the stovetop. Pour boiling water into steamer to a depth of 2 inches. Cover. Steam on low heat 1 1/2 to 2 hours or until pudding springs back when lightly touched in center.

Oven Method: Place mold in pan of water and bake at 150° for 1 1/2 to 2 hours.

Serve warm with LEMON SAUCE, *(see next page)*.

Nutrient Analysis: 1 slice
Exchanges: 1 1/2 starch, 1 fat
Carbohydrate Choices: 1 1/2

Calories: 151   Protein: 2g   Carbohydrates: 22g
Fat: 7g   Cholesterol: 0mg   Sodium: 53mg
Dietary Fiber: 2g   Omega-3: 0.46 g

LEMON SAUCE

The crowning glory on CRANBERRY STEAMED PUDDING, (page 422).

Makes 1 1/2 cups; 12 servings

1/3 cup sugar, (or equivalent no-calorie sweetener)
2 tablespoons cornstarch
1 cup hot water
2 teaspoons grated lemon rind
2 teaspoons lemon juice
2 tablespoons tub margarine

Combine sugar and cornstarch in a saucepan. Blend in water. Cook over medium heat, stirring constantly until mixture boils. Boil 1 minute until it is clear and slightly thickened. Remove from heat.

Stir in lemon rind, juice and margarine. Serve warm or cool on steamed pudding.

VARIATION:

ORANGE SAUCE

Substitute orange juice for water and orange rind for lemon rind. Omit lemon juice.

Nutrient Analysis: 2 tablespoons
Exchanges: 1/2 starch
Carbohydrate Choices: made with sugar: 1/2
made with no-calorie sweetener: 0

Calories: 43   Protein: 0g   Carbohydrates: 7g
Fat: 2g   Cholesterol: 0mg   Sodium: 16mg

CARAMEL SAUCE

Delicious over fresh sliced apples, angel food cake or ice milk.

Makes 1 1/2 cups; 12 servings

1	cup sugar (or equivalent no-calorie sweetener)
1/3	cup water
3/4	cup evaporated skim milk, heated
1/2	teaspoon vanilla

Bring sugar and water to a boil in a heavy saucepan. Remove from heat and swirl pan by its handle (don't stir) until the sugar is completely dissolved and the liquid is clear. Cover the pan with a tightly fitting cover and boil over moderately high heat for several minutes. When bubbles are thick, remove cover and continue to boil, swirling pan until syrup turns a light caramel brown. Let cool to about the same temperature as the heated evaporated milk.

Pour caramel into milk: the caramel will lump. Simmer, stirring to melt caramel and blend it with the milk. Stir in the vanilla. Serve warm or cold. (If too thick, add a little more milk and simmer. If too thin, boil down, stirring.)

Nutrient Analysis: 2 tablespoons

Exchanges: 1 starch
Carbohydrate Choices: made with sugar: 1
*   made with no-calorie sweetener: 0*

Calories: 77   Protein: 1g   Carbohydrates: 19g
Fat: 0g   Cholesterol: 0mg   Sodium: 20mg

HONEY FUDGE SAUCE

Great on ice milk or as topping for angel food cake.

Makes 1 1/2 cups; 12 servings

4	tablespoons tub margarine
1	tablespoon cornstarch
2	tablespoons cocoa
1/2	cup honey (or equivalent no-calorie sweetener)
1/2	cup water
6	large marshmallows (or 60 mini)
1	teaspoon vanilla

Melt margarine in a saucepan. Add cornstarch and cocoa, blending well.

Add honey and water and cook over low heat until thick. Add marshmallows and stir until melted. Stir in vanilla. Serve warm or cold.

Nutrient Analysis: 2 tablespoons

Exchanges: 1 starch, 1/2 fat
Carbohydrate Choices: made with sugar: 1
*   made with no-calorie sweetener: 0*

Calories: 93   Protein: 0g   Carbohydrates: 16g
Fat: 4g   Cholesterol: 0mg   Sodium: 35mg

INDEX OF TABLES

INDEX OF TABLES

APPENDIX:

Table 28:   Heart Disease Risk Factors

- Age (over 55)	- High blood cholesterol
- Family history of premature CVD	- High LDL cholesterol (low density lipoproteins)
- Smoking cigarettes/tobacco use	- Low HDL cholesterol (high density lipoproteins)
- Physical inactivity	- High TG (blood fats or triglycerides)
- Over-consumption of alcohol	- Obesity (esp., abdominal or metabolic syndrome)
- Diabetes	- Hypertension (high blood pressure)

Source: US Dept of Health and Human Services, NHLBI, NIH Publication No. 06-5801, January, 2006

The American Heart Association's (AHA) Diet & Lifestyle Recommendations follow in the next two tables. Improving diet and lifestyle is a critical component of the AHA's strategy to prevent cardiovascular disease (CVD), the leading cause of morbidity and mortality in Americans. Here are their Diet and Lifestyle Goals and Recommendations for cardiovascular disease risk reduction.

Table 29: AHA 2006 Diet and Lifestyle Goals for Reducing Risk of CVD

- ❤ Consume an overall healthy diet.
- ❤ Aim for a healthy body weight.
- ❤ Aim for recommended levels of low-density (LDL) cholesterol, high-density lipoprotein (HDL) cholesterol and triglycerides.
- ❤ Aim for a normal blood pressure.
- ❤ Aim for a normal blood glucose level.
- ❤ Be physically active.
- ❤ Avoid use of and exposure to tobacco products.

Source: American Heart Association, "Diet and Lifestyle Recommendations Revision 2006: A Scientific Statement from the American Heart Association Nutrition Committee", *Circulation* 114 (2006): 82-96. The online version, along with updated information and services, is located at: http://circ.ahajournals.org/cgi/content/full/114/1/82

Table 30: AHA 2006 Diet and Lifestyle Recommendations for Reducing Risk of CVD

- Balance calorie intake and physical activity to achieve or maintain a healthy body weight. (Please see the BMI chart on page 431 to determine if your weight falls within a "healthy" range.)

- Consume a diet rich in vegetables and fruits. (Deeply colored vegetables such as carrots, broccoli, peaches, and berries are emphasized because they tend to be higher in micronutrient content than other vegetables and fruits. Please note that fruit juice is less equivalent to the whole fruit in fiber content and satiety value; and often comes with more added sugars and calories.)

- Choose whole-grain, high-fiber foods. (Whole grain products provide both soluble and insoluble fibers. Soluble fiber reduces LDL cholesterol levels and reduces our liver's production of cholesterol; insoluble fiber is associated with decreased CVD risk and slower progression of CVD in high-risk individuals.

- Consume fish, especially oily fish, at least twice a week. (Oily fish are rich in omega-3 polyunsaturated fatty acids and 8 ounces of fish per week is associated with a reduced risk of both sudden death and death from CHD in adults.)

- Limit your intake of saturated fat to less than 7% of energy, trans fat to less than 1% of energy, and cholesterol to less than 300 mg per day by (see page 26):
  –choosing lean meats and vegetable alternatives;
  –selecting fat-free (skim), 1%-fat and low-fat dairy products; and
  –minimizing intake of partially hydrogenated fats.

- Minimize your intake of beverages and foods with added sugars. (About 17% of our calories come from added sugars, which increase our total caloric intake and promote nutrient deficiency.)

Continued on next page.

Table 30: AHA 2006 Diet and Lifestyle Recommendations for Reducing Risk of CVD (continued)

- ♥ Choose and prepare foods with little or no salt. (On average, as our salt consumption increases, so does our blood pressure. A recommendation of 2,300 mg of sodium a day is achievable; 1,500 mg a day is better, but difficult in our high-sodium food supply.)

- ♥ If you consume alcohol, do so in moderation. (Although moderate alcohol intake has been associated with reduced cardiovascular events, alcohol can be addictive and have serious adverse health and social consequences. For these reasons, the AHA recommends no more than 2 drinks a day for men and 1 drink a day for women, to ideally be consumed with meals. A "drink equivalent" is 12-ounces of beer, a 5-ounce glass of wine or 1 1/2-ounces of 80-proof hard liquor.)

- ♥ When you eat food that is prepared outside of the home, follow the AHA Diet and Lifestyle Recommendations. (Increasingly, Americans consume food that is prepared outside of the home, which has adverse health consequences. Foods are often served in large portion sizes, and are high in calories, saturated fat, trans fatty acids, cholesterol and sodium, and are low in fiber and micronutrients. This combination shows a positive association between the more frequently meals are eaten out, the higher the energy intake, weight gain and insulin resistance. Wise food choices are necessary when eating out.)

Source: American Heart Association, "Diet and Lifestyle Recommendations Revision 2006: A Scientific Statement from the American Heart Association Nutrition Committee", *Circulation* 114 (2006): 82-96. The online version, along with updated information and services, is located online at: http://circ.ahajournals.org/cgi/content/full/114/1/82

Table 31: Daily Dietary Fat Recommendations to Reduce Risk of CVD

Fat Recommendations	Total Fat	Sat Fat	Trans Fat	Cholesterol
American Heart Association[1]	25 – 35%	<7%	<1%	<300 mg/day
National Cholesterol Education Program[2]	25 – 35%	<7%	Low as possible	<200 mg/day
USDA & HHS[3] and IOM[4] *(2005 Dietary Guidelines for Americans)*	20 – 35%	<10%	Low as possible	<300 mg/day

Sources: 1) Lichtenstein, A.H., Appel, L.J., Brands, M., et al. Diet and lifestylerecommendations revision 2006. A Scientific statement from the American Heart Association Nutrition Committee. *Circulation* 114: 82-96, 2006. 2) National Cholesterol Education Program (NCEP) Expert panel on Detection, Evaluation, and Treatment of High Blood Cholesterol in Adults (Adult Treatment Panel III). *Third Report of the National Cholesterol Education Program* (NCEP) Expert Panel on Detection, Evaluation, and Treatment of High Blood Cholesterol in Adults (Adult Treatment Panel III) final report. *Circulation* 106: 3143-3421, 2002. 3) U.S. Department of Health and Human Services, U.S. Department of Agriculture. Dietary Guidelines for Americans, 2005. Home and Garden Bulletin No. 232. Washington, D.C.: U.S. Government Printing Office, 2005. Also available online at www.healthierus.gov/dietaryguidelines. 4) Institute of Medicine of the National Academies. Dietary Reference Intakes. Energy, Carbohydrate, Fiber, Fat, Fatty Acids, Cholesterol, Protein, and Amino Acids. Washington, D.C.: The National Academies Press, 2002.

Body Mass Index (BMI) is a number calculated from a person's weight and height. BMI provides a reliable indictor of body fatness for most people and is used to screen for weight categories that may lead to health problems.

Table 32: BMI Index Table

Body Mass Index Table

BMI	Normal						Overweight					Obese										Extreme Obesity														
Height (inches)	19	20	21	22	23	24	25	26	27	28	29	30	31	32	33	34	35	36	37	38	39	40	41	42	43	44	45	46	47	48	49	50	51	52	53	54
												Body Weight (pounds)																								
58	91	96	100	105	110	115	119	124	129	134	138	143	148	153	158	162	167	172	177	181	186	191	196	201	205	210	215	220	224	229	234	239	244	248	253	258
59	94	99	104	109	114	119	124	128	133	138	143	148	153	158	163	168	173	178	183	188	193	198	203	208	212	217	222	227	232	237	242	247	252	257	262	267
60	97	102	107	112	118	123	128	133	138	143	148	153	158	163	168	174	179	184	189	194	199	204	209	215	220	225	230	235	240	245	250	255	261	266	271	276
61	100	106	111	116	122	127	132	137	143	148	153	158	164	169	174	180	185	190	195	201	206	211	217	222	227	232	238	243	248	254	259	264	269	275	280	285
62	104	109	115	120	126	131	136	142	147	153	158	164	169	175	180	186	191	196	202	207	213	218	224	229	235	240	246	251	256	262	267	273	278	284	289	295
63	107	113	118	124	130	135	141	146	152	158	163	169	175	180	186	191	197	203	208	214	220	225	231	237	242	248	254	259	265	270	276	282	287	293	299	304
64	110	116	122	128	134	140	145	151	157	163	169	174	180	186	192	197	204	209	215	221	227	232	238	244	250	256	262	267	273	279	285	291	296	302	308	314
65	114	120	126	132	138	144	150	156	162	168	174	180	186	192	198	204	210	216	222	228	234	240	246	252	258	264	270	276	282	288	294	300	306	312	318	324
66	118	124	130	136	142	148	155	161	167	173	179	186	192	198	204	210	216	223	229	235	241	247	253	260	266	272	278	284	291	297	303	309	315	322	328	334
67	121	127	134	140	146	153	159	166	172	178	185	191	198	204	211	217	223	230	236	242	249	255	261	268	274	280	287	293	299	306	312	319	325	331	338	344
68	125	131	138	144	151	158	164	171	177	184	190	197	203	210	216	223	230	236	243	249	256	262	269	276	282	289	295	302	308	315	322	328	335	341	348	354
69	128	135	142	149	155	162	169	176	182	189	196	203	209	216	223	230	236	243	250	257	263	270	277	284	291	297	304	311	318	324	331	338	345	351	358	365
70	132	139	146	153	160	167	174	181	188	195	202	209	216	222	229	236	243	250	257	264	271	278	285	292	299	306	313	320	327	334	341	348	355	362	369	376
71	136	143	150	157	165	172	179	186	193	200	208	215	222	229	236	243	250	257	265	272	279	286	293	301	308	315	322	329	336	343	351	358	365	372	379	386
72	140	147	154	162	169	177	184	191	199	206	213	221	228	235	242	250	258	265	272	279	287	294	302	309	316	324	331	338	346	353	361	368	375	383	390	397
73	144	151	159	166	174	182	189	197	204	212	219	227	235	242	250	257	265	272	280	288	295	302	310	318	325	333	340	348	355	363	371	378	386	393	401	408
74	148	155	163	171	179	186	194	202	210	218	225	233	241	249	256	264	272	280	287	295	303	311	319	326	334	342	350	358	365	373	381	389	396	404	412	420
75	152	160	168	176	184	192	200	208	216	224	232	240	248	256	264	272	279	287	295	303	311	319	327	335	343	351	359	367	375	383	391	399	407	415	423	431
76	156	164	172	180	189	197	205	213	221	230	238	246	254	263	271	279	287	295	304	312	320	328	336	344	353	361	369	377	385	394	402	410	418	426	435	443

Source: Adapted from Clinical Guidelines on the Identification, Evaluation, and Treatment of Overweight and Obesity in Adults: The Evidence Report.

Source: www.nhlbi.nih.gov/guidelines/obesity/bmi_tbl.htm, accessed November 30, 2007.

Table 33: Estimated Calorie Requirements (in Kilocalories) for Each Gender and Age Group at Three Levels of Physical Activity[a]

Gender	Age (years)	Activity Level[b,c,d]		
		Sedentary[b]	Moderately Active[c]	Active[d]
Child	2-3	1,000	1,000-1,400[e]	1,000-1,400[e]
Female	4-8	1,200	1,400-1,600	1,400-1,800
	9-13	1,600	1,600-2,000	1,800-2,200
	14-18	1,800	2,000	2,400
	19-30	2,000	2,000-2,200	2,400
	31-50	1,800	2,000	2,200
	51+	1,600	1,800	2,000-2,200
Male	4-8	1,400	1,400-1,600	1,600-2,000
	9-13	1,800	1,800-2,200	2,000-2,600
	14-18	2,200	2,400-2,800	2,800-3,200
	19-30	2,400	2,600-2,800	3,000
	31-50	2,200	2,400-2,600	2,800-3,000
	51+	2,000	2,200-2,400	2,400-2,800

[a]   These levels are based on Estimated Energy Requirements (EER) from the Institute of Medicine Dietary Reference Intakes macronutrients report, 2002, calculated by gender, age, and activity level for reference-sized individuals. "Reference size," as determined by IOM, is bsed on median height and weight for ages up to age 18 years of age and median height and weight for that height to give a BMI of 21.5 for adult females and 22.5 for adult males.

[b]   Sedentary means a lifestyle that includes only the light physical activity associated with typical day-to-day life.

[c]   Moderately active means a lifestyle that includes physical activity equivalent to walking about 1.5 to 3 miles per day at 3 to 4 miles per hour, in addition to the light physical activity associated with typical day-to-day life.

[d]   Active means a lifestyle that includes physical activity equivalent to walking more than 3 miles per day at 3 to 4 miles per hour, in addition to the light physical activity associated with typical day-to-day life.

[e]   The calorie ranges shown are to accommodate needs of different ages within the group. For children and adolescents, more calories are needed at older ages. For adults, fewer calories are neeeded at older ages.

Source: U.S. Department of Health and Human Services, U.S. Department of Agriculture. Dietary Guidelines for Americans, 2005. Home and Garden Bulletin No. 232. Washington, D.C.: U.S. Government Printing Office, 2005. Also available online at www.healthierus.gov/dietaryguidelines.

INDEX:

COOKING À LA HEART REORDER PAGE &
OTHER APPLETREE PRESS HEART-HEALTHY BOOKS & REFERENCES

♥ **COOKING À LA HEART**
2010 Revisions, Third Edition
Over 400 heart-healthy recipes.
Softcover, Item #125 . . . .$24.95
Two copies $40.00

♥ **GIFTS OF THE HEART**
Over three dozen heart-healthy
recipes for gift giving.
Softcover, Item #150 . . . . $ 8.50
Two copies $12.00

♥ **WHAT'S FOR BREAKFAST?**
Over 100 time-sensitive, low-fat
recipes to either start or end the day!
Softcover, Item #140 . . . .$13.95
Two copies $23.00

♥ **VEGETARIAN HOMESTYLE COOKING**
A collection of 175 easy-to-prepare,
culturally-diverse recipes.
Softcover, Item #130 . . . .$15.95
Two copies $27.00

♥ **HEALTHY MEXICAN COOKING**
In English or Spanish. Over 160 heart-
healthy, authentic Mexican recipes.
Softcover, Item #160 . . . .$15.95
Two copies $27.00

♥ **DIABETIC GOODIE BOOK**
Over 190 low-carbohydrate, heart-
healthy recipes, no artificial sweeteners.
Softcover, Item #180 . . . .$15.95
Two copies $27.00

♥ **VEGETARIAN COOKING FOR HEALTHY LIVING**
Over 130 ultra low-fat recipes that
meet the Dean Ornish guidelines.
Softcover, Item #190 . . . . $17.95
Two copies $30.00

♥ **CARB, FAT & CALORIE GUIDE**
Nutrient analysis for more than
4,000 foods, 17 restaurant chains.
Softcover, Item #405 . . . .$7.95
Two copies $13.00

♥ **SPORTS NUTRITION GUIDE**
Nutrient analysis for 4,000 foods
including sports drinks, bars & gels.
Softcover, Item #110 . . . .$8.95
Two copies $15.00

♥ **A SELF-MONITORING SYSTEM**
A checkbook-style food journal.
Nutrient analysis for 1,500 foods.
Full set w/ 1-month Log $7.95
Full set w/ 3 additional Logs $15.00

✂ *Cut on dotted line*

ORDER FORM

Mail to:

Appletree Press, Inc.
151 Good Counsel Drive
Suite 125
Mankato, MN 56001-3198
eatwell@hickorytech.net

Ship to:
Name _____

Organization _____

Street Address _____

City _____

State _____ Zip _____

Daytime Phone Number ( ) _____
Make checks payable to: **Appletree Press, Inc.**
☐ Check   ☐ Money Order   ☐ VISA   ☐ Mastercard

Card No. _____
Signature _____
Expiration Date (month/year) _____

Qty.	Item #	Title	Unit Price	Total

Shipping Costs		
		Subtotal
up to $20.00 add $5.00		Shipping and Handling
$20.01 to $50 add $7.00		
$50.01 to $80 add $9.00		MN state residents add 6.5% sales tax
$80.01 to $100 add $11.00		
Over $100 add 10%		TOTAL

CALL TOLL FREE 1-800-322-5679   VISIT OUR WEBSITE www.appletree-press.com